Teaching Strategies

TEACHING STRATEGIES

A Guide to Better Instruction

Sixth Edition

Donald C. Orlich
Washington State University

Robert J. Harder
Washington State University

Richard C. Callahan
Callahan Associates

Harry W. Gibson
Saint Martin's College

HOUGHTON MIFFLIN COMPANY   Boston   New York

Senior sponsoring editor: Loretta Wolozin
Development editor: Lisa Mafrici
Project editor: Gabrielle Stone
Production/design coordinator: Jennifer Meyer Dare
Senior manufacturing coordinator: Sally Culler

Cover design: Diana Coe/ko Design.

Cover painting © by Al Held, courtesy of
Crown Point Press and NextMonet.com.

Printed in the U.S.A.

Library of Congress Catalog Card Number: 00-131416

ISBN: 0-618-04287-3

2 3 4 5 6 7 8 9—CRW—04 03 02 01

Brief Contents

v

Contents

Chapter 4   Instructional Design   125

Preface

The 21st century presents all teachers and students with new challenges. Both must master the tools of the information age and prepare for the new opportunities it offers. Teachers must respond to demands for greater professionalism and reform, and they must help an increasingly diverse mix of students prepare for life in an ever more global and competitive world. This edition of *Teaching Strategies: A Guide to Better Instruction* focuses on improvement of educational experiences for all and on teachers as leaders and pivotal decision makers in this context. Each chapter in this extensively revised and new edition has been condensed and more tightly rewoven with an emphasis on the classroom teacher's instructional needs. Driving the book throughout is the core belief that teachers have the power to make a profound difference in their students' lives. Using this book, teachers can improve their skills and strategies and learn to blend technical competence with artistic sensitivity as they change and grow as professionals.

Purpose and Intended Audience

This book has multiple uses. Novices and experienced teachers alike have found it a valuable source of sound, tested, and humane educational strategies. It is a reliable guide for making logical, systematic instructional choices. In-service teachers have reported that the book is a valuable and easy-to-use resource.

The authors illustrate a broad spectrum of instructional methodologies and techniques that are workable in today's complex classrooms. *Teaching Strategies* is designed primarily for use in courses in instruction for those preparing to become elementary or secondary school teachers. Topics are treated in-depth to help prospective teachers master the broad range of competencies required for state and national certification. Our goal is to make a genuine contribution to the profession by providing the most current theories and showing how best to apply them in today's schools.

What's Covered in the Sixth Edition

The revised text is organized into three distinct parts. Part I, titled "Frameworks for Instructional Decisions," examines the culture of the schools and presents the fundamental frameworks and community goals within which teachers set personal goals and make daily instructional decisions. Chapter 1, "The School Milieu," maintains its important role in presenting an overview of the school milieu, describing the legal structure of the public schools, and providing an updated view of school reform. In addition, we discuss the diverse students you will teach in grades K–12 and the various socioeconomic factors that affect teaching. The related concept of educational equity—a theme we treat throughout the new edition with even stronger emphasis—is introduced here. New to the chapter is the introduction of the all-important concept of teacher as decision maker.

Chapter 2, "A Vision of Effective Teaching," is essentially a new chapter. It begins with a brand new discussion and graphic organizer of holistic instruction, a contextualizing section that picks up on Chapter 1's decision-making theme and that sets the stage for most of the major topics in the remainder of the book. The next section presents three major perspectives that can guide systematic decision making—developmental, behavioral, and cognitive. Finally, there are two new major sections—one on diversity and equity and one on professional lifelong learning. Each of these sections integrates key material that had previously been treated in separate chapters toward the end of the book.

In Part II, "Fundamental Tools for Instructional Planning," we vividly illustrate the basic tools and knowledge base for effective instructional planning. Chapter 3, "Goals, Standards, and Outcomes for Instruction," continues to focus on the goals and objectives of instruction; however, the discussion of the writing of instructional objectives is now reorganized and more comprehensive. In addition, the related discussion of cognitive taxonomies are more tightly focused on instruction. We discuss how national, state and local standards are used for planning, highlighting in current terms the changing role of national standards.

Chapters 4 and 5 continue to define and demonstrate the process of instructional design with a variety of useful planning methods, planning resources, and instructional models. Chapter 4, "Instructional Design," now contains a strong research-based section that illustrates subsequent topics on planning. It also includes a new section on the construction of individualized education programs (IEPs). Including this coverage reflects this edition's emphasis on integrating coverage of special needs educational issues within related text discussions. Chapter 4 concludes with a section on how expert teachers plan that directly applies the field experiences of award-winning teachers to the knowledge base. Chapter 5 is retitled "Sequencing and Organizing Instruction" to reflect its emphasis on the two critical planning angles of sequencing *and* organizing. In a newly structured, updated, and refocused concluding section, we show how teachers can adapt their plans using a multimethodology approach, thus meeting the needs of students with diverse learning styles.

Part III—"Instruction as a Dynamic Process in Classrooms"—presents the dynamic and interactive aspects of teaching and provides the core knowledge base for creating a lively and productive learning environment. Chapter 6, "Managing the Classroom Environment," introduces classroom management as a technique for establishing a positive and supportive environment. Within a newly organized format, we maintain our presentation of a broad continuum of management systems, illustrated with practical applications. Throughout, we stress the concept of equity and the need to create classroom routines that foster smooth classroom operations.

Chapter 7, "The Process of Questioning," continues to provide the most thorough treatment of the questioning process that you will find in any methods textbook. In addition to illustrating the process of classroom questioning, this edition highlights the essential issue of how teachers can better attend to and develop higher-level questioning. We have also included a new questioning strategy—that of reflective questioning.

In a substantially reorganized format, Chapter 8—"Small-Group Discussions and Cooperative Learning"—explores and highlights how to use six basic types of small-group discussion to create exciting lessons and to encourage active student participation. A newly synthesized section describes in practical terms how to establish and maintain small groups. We also include new material on collecting feedback from small groups.

Chapter 9, "Inquiry Teaching and Higher-Level Thinking," opens with a stronger, more tightly woven discussion of the nature of thinking and how it can be taught. We present in practical detail the primary two avenues for teaching thinking; inquiry-based methods and specific techniques that emphasize problem solving and critical thinking skills.

Chapter 10, "Monitoring Student Successes," focuses on monitoring student progress. This chapter has been extensively revised to provide in its very first section all-important contexts for classroom assessment. This includes purposes for and areas of assessment, simple core definitions, and emphasis on the relationship of assessment to planning and instruction. The entire chapter has been refocused to emphasize the classroom teacher's needs. Both test item writing and grading, and topics of importance to teachers, receive full treatment.

The entire book is deliberately reduced in scope and is very tightly focused on instructional strategy and teaching techniques. We provide the prerequisite technical skills needed to be successful in the classroom. Overarching themes, such as the use of technology within the classroom, or the instructional needs of diverse students, receive attention in discussions throughout the book. You will find a wide array of ideas from which to select the strategies that best meet your instructional goals and the learning goals of your students.

Special Features

A brand new two-color text format highlights several acclaimed pedagogical features designed to organize and illustrate the content and make the text easier to use:

- *Instructional Strategies,* a brand new feature, provides up-to-date strategic ideas and techniques for direct application in the classroom.
- *Concept maps* introduce each chapter. The maps identify the key chapter topics and serve as handy visual organizational aids.
- *Margin notes* throughout the text highlight key concepts.
- *Key terms* are highlighted in bold print to draw the reader's attention to these important building blocks of a professional vocabulary and listed at the end of each chapter. The Glossary contains all the key terms, with operational definitions.
- *"Reflect" questions,* interspersed throughout the text, ask the reader to stop and reflect on the previously learned content and place it into an experiential context, thereby enhancing its personal and professional relevance.
- A *"Closing Reflection"* concludes each chapter and provides formative questions for thought on the contents of the chapter.
- *Summaries* at the end of each chapter aid the reader in pinpointing major concepts.
- *Graphic overview lists* are inserted in logical places to give a quick reference to ideas, concepts and main points. These boxed lists aid the reader by reducing redundancy and providing explicit summary statements.

■ *Helpful resources* listed at the end of each chapter will help readers follow up on specific topics and thus enlarge their professional competence.

■ *Internet resources* include specific sites where more information and interactive activities can be found.

User-friendly is the term that best describes the format and presentation of the sixth edition. This book encourages readers to engage with the information presented, to make it their own, and to expand their professional horizons.

To accompany the text, an Instructor's Resource Manual is offered (in both print and on-line formats) to provide the instructor with additional teaching and assessment support materials. The Houghton Mifflin Company Teacher Education Station Web site also provides resources for beginning and experienced education professionals. It includes information about new books, key learning themes, and links to other Houghton Mifflin Teacher Education Web sites developed especially to support new and practicing teachers.

Professional Acknowledgments

The authors express their appreciation to the colleagues who contributed to the earlier editions of this text. These include Dr. Anne Remaley of the Renton, Washington Public Schools; Dr. Constance H. Kravas of the University of California, Riverside; Dr. Andrew J. Keogh of Ohio Dominican College; Dr. R. A. Pendergrass, retired superintendent of the Bakersfield, Missouri, public schools; Dr. Donald P. Kauchak of the University of Utah; Dr. Eileen M. Starr of Valley City State University; and Dr. Foster M. Walsh of the Spokane, Washington, public schools. Each helped make the previous editions of the book relevant and useful, and their insight continues to be reflected in the sixth edition.

A number of reviewers critiqued this edition and we thank them and the many students for their suggestions: Dr. Raymond Griffin of Virginia State University; George M. McLain of Alvernia College; Dr. Bobbette M. Morgan of the University of Texas at Arlington; Dr. Barbara R. Munson of the University of Portland; Dr. Frederick A. Staley of Arizona State University; Dr. Jane B. Swiderski of LeMoyne College; and Dr. Shirley F. Yamashita of the University of Hawaii at Manoa.

General Acknowledgments

The authors wish to thank Sandra Tyacke for her outstanding job of preparing the many manuscripts necessary for this project. The authors express their appreciation to the staff of Houghton Mifflin—Loretta Wolozin, Lisa Mafrici, Jean Zielinski DeMayo, Merryl Maleska Wilbur, Gabrielle Stone, and Sarah A. Rodriguez. Their help is more than observable in the final product.

Donald C. Orlich

Frameworks for Instructional Decisions

Part 1 introduces the school milieu and selected factors that affect what is taught and how. We also provide a vision of the many interacting components of instruction and their cyclical nature. In Chapter 1, we discuss various social, cultural, and educational factors that have an impact on the ways that you teach. We make a strong plea for multimethodology. This chapter sets the stage for the key role of teacher as decision maker. Chapter 2 establishes the big picture of instruction by illustrating how sociopsychological perspectives shape our techniques of presentation. We show how meaningful instruction is also cyclical and how all elements of the cycle inform teacher decisions. We make a strong plea for instructional equity, and we close with an overview of why educators at all levels must be lifelong learners. Part 1 is an overview of the foundations of effective instruction, which we systematically expand throughout the remainder of the book.

Each chapter begins with the concept map or advance organizer that highlights the topics to be presented. Read each map beginning with the upper left cell and progress clockwise around that cell and clockwise around the entire map. These maps show how the topics covered in each chapter are interrelated. The maps not only are useful study tools but also provide a model that you can adapt in your own instructional planning.

1

The School Milieu

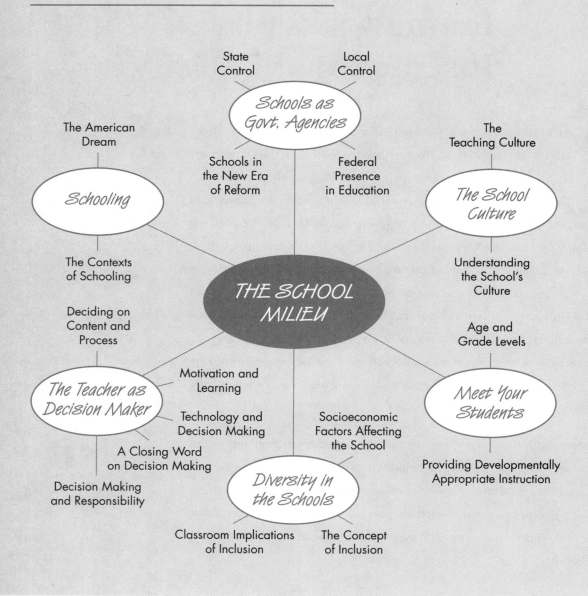

State Control

Local Control

Schools as Govt. Agencies

The American Dream

The Teaching Culture

Schools in the New Era of Reform

Federal Presence in Education

Schooling

The School Culture

The Contexts of Schooling

THE SCHOOL MILIEU

Understanding the School's Culture

Deciding on Content and Process

Age and Grade Levels

Motivation and Learning

The Teacher as Decision Maker

Technology and Decision Making

Socioeconomic Factors Affecting the School

Meet Your Students

A Closing Word on Decision Making

Decision Making and Responsibility

Diversity in the Schools

Providing Developmentally Appropriate Instruction

Classroom Implications of Inclusion

The Concept of Inclusion

Like many prospective teachers, Virginia Lynch has been part of the educational system for many years. Now she is preparing for her first full-time job, and she has begun to think about the nation's public schools as a system. Who runs the schools? What segments of society have a stake in their quality and success? What are their functions? Who will be Virginia's boss when she becomes a public school teacher?

Most new teachers have questions like these about the school system and their place within it. This chapter will help you answer questions like Virginia's and help you find your place within the school system. As you read, think about how you would answer the following questions:

- What are the functions of schooling?
- How are the public schools organized and run?
- What kind of organizational culture is most prominent in the schools?
- How do educators attempt to meet the needs of a diverse student body?
- What are the "kids" like?
- What decisions do teachers make?
- What role can technology play in today's schools?

Section 1: Schooling

As we move into the third millennium, the nation's public schools are its largest industry. Projected expenditures for all K–12 schooling approaches $393 billion a year in 2002. Add to that an estimated $226 billion for higher education, and the educational enterprise accounts for a tidy 7 percent of the U.S. gross domestic product. Teachers recognize that as members of this "industry," they must have a broad understanding of instruction. Teachers and administrators acknowledge the need to analyze teaching in terms of what and whom are taught, and this book views this approach as an important ideal. This chapter provides a theoretical and practical structure to guide action in the classroom. Our intent is to provide a series of general instructional models for all teachers. But first, let's set the stage by exploring some expectations members of our society have for schooling.

The American Dream

Education helps fulfill ambitions.

By and large, the American public believes that the nation's schools provide students with the knowledge, skills, and competencies they need to be successful. For millions of individuals, the public schools have provided the opportunities that have allowed them to realize their own "American dream." Thus many believe that success comes with education—and from an economic standpoint, there is little doubt that this is often true.

The dream is not uniformly achieved, however. Not all individuals in our society profit equally from public education. The reasons vary, from socioeconomic factors to language diversity. Perhaps the best that we can expect from schools is that they assure every student an equal access to opportunity. The chance to achieve one's dream is a great self-motivator. Thus every educator has a moral obligation to enhance the potential for all students.

The Contexts of Schooling

Schooling is very interpersonal.

The Social Context   Schooling has a group orientation. The entire process is social—that is, it is highly dependent on personal interactions. One of the first things a child learns in school is that the individual must make accommodations to the group. Within this social milieu, behaviors are changed, learning takes place, and the individuals involved all change. Schools provide a social resource that individuals learning on their own might lack. The interactions of the individuals in a school provide a **recursive,** or indefinitely repeating, set of experiences that create **synergistic,** or greater than the sum of their parts, relationships among them. Although the schools exist for their students, it is the presence of the students and others within them that make the schools what they are as institutions. Both the students and the institution evolve as a consequence of social interactions. (See Giddens 1984 for a thought-provoking treatment of the issues of agent and agency.)

Pluralism is obvious in any school.

Now add to these interactions the phenomenon we call **pluralism,** and you can appreciate the social interactions and conflicts that can be predicted to take place in the schools. The term *pluralism* refers to the fact that our society and our schools are composed of many different types of people, creating a mixture of nationalities, races, classes, religions, occupational groupings, philosophies, value systems, and economic theories. Given this broad social spectrum, it is inevitable that you will observe contradictory points of view as a teacher (see *Social Context of Education* 1997).

You will observe **intrapersonal** conflicts, in which an individual tries to reconcile conflicts within his or her own value structure. You will also observe **interpersonal** conflicts, in which the values of different individuals or groups openly clash. These kinds of conflicts generate considerable energy. Sometimes the energy is positive and leads to common problem-solving and beneficial activities. In other cases, the energy leads to disharmony. As a teacher, one of your major roles will be to foster positive social interactions and relationships.

Effective schools are caring institutions.

The Emotional Context   Education is a helping profession: people who enter it tend to do so for altruistic reasons. This dimension of the profession, caring for others, adds a human element to the impersonal buildings and institutionalized delivery systems of the public schools. The close interactions between teachers and students forge bonds of trust and mutual support (see Katz, Noddings, and Strike 1999).

When caring is part of the **organizational ethos,** the fundamental character and values of an organization, then it is a bit easier to help students of all ages develop moral and ethical values. Do not be alarmed by the last sentence. Yes, the schools have an obligation to teach such values, and virtually all parents or guardians strongly endorse them, since they fall under the umbrella of being a good citizen (see Beck 1998). Reemerging on the educational scene is

---

Contextual Aspects of Schooling

- Equal access to opportunity
- Socializing processes
- Pluralistic
- Helping profession
- Values developed
- Basics extended

---

the old notion that the schools should be involved in "character education," that they should have a genuine commitment to teaching values, ethics, and integrity (see Kelly 1999a, Rosemond 1999). Character building is recognized as a way of making the school a neighborhood community and ensuring that all students can enjoy it without fear (Etzioni 1997, Ryan and Bohlin 1999).

The same rationale might be applied to teaching healthy personal development and to promoting a host of other psychological characteristics that fall under the rubric of the *whole child.* That is, schooling is not just to impart cognitive knowledge; the schools have a responsibility and an interest in helping all children develop into well-adjusted individuals with positive attitudes and positive self-esteem (see Weiner 1992). If you adopt a caring attitude, then you will perceive children or adolescents or early adults in a different light than if you view them only as objects to be taught or manipulated (see Buber 1970).

The Educational Context   Just what composes the educational context of our schools? This is a tough question to answer, for it depends on your own educational philosophy. Over the years, the schools have either inherited or subtly adopted a social philosophy aimed at accommodating many social, emotional, and familial needs in addition to educational ones. Yes, the schools still teach the basics. But "the basics" now extend to many topics that were once considered extras. To be sure, reading, communicating, mathematics, science, history, and geography still form the core academic competencies, but the schools now also teach health and life skills, HIV/AIDS prevention, driving, and a host of other skills, both social and behavioral. This is the

---

Reflect Reflect Reflect

- Visit different schools. Observe the symbols that are displayed in cases and on the walls or that are evident in the lunchroom and locker rooms. What conclusions do you reach about what is valued in those schools?
- Search the Internet, using the topic of "school expectations." What is your reaction?

complicated montage we call the curriculum today. We will return to the topic of the curriculum in Chapters 3, 4, and 5, when we discuss lesson designs.

Section 2: Schools as Government Agencies

Each state controls its own public education.

In the United States, public education is the responsibility of the states. Since the U.S. Constitution is silent on education, each state, through interpretations of the Tenth Amendment, has assumed **plenary,** or complete, jurisdiction over the schools. Each state addresses education in its constitution. It is important for teachers to know this point. State control of education will have a direct impact on your teaching, since you will be acting as an agent of the state. For example, class sizes are indirectly determined through state laws and legislative appropriations. All states have laws regarding what types of discipline may be administered in classrooms. The states delegate educational authority and responsibility to boards and agencies and through various legal provisions.

How can state legislatures conduct the everyday business of schools? This problem is resolved by delegating authority to the state board of education. Each state board has a chief state school officer, usually called the state superintendent of public instruction. The actual work of the state board is done through the state department of education, headed by the superintendent of public instruction, which is the basic **regulatory agency** for education in each state. Authority is then further delegated to local school boards. We'll discuss these in more detail, but first let us focus on the state.

State Control

State boards of education are either elected or appointed. They are given specific powers and duties by the state legislature or state constitution. Table 1.1 illustrates the subdivision of power by level. In most cases, state boards establish graduation requirements for high schools, set the basic curriculum for grades K–12, and prescribe teacher licensing provisions.

The chief state school officer (CSSO) is elected to office in fifteen states and appointed in thirty-five. The CSSO is the primary **liaison** with the legislature and directs the state department of education. It is the CSSO who carries out the directives and policies of the state board.

All states have a state department of education that handles all the details of state control. These duties include supervising transportation, vocational programs, special education, testing, and many more school functions.

Obviously not every possible duty or responsibility is listed in Table 1.1, but it gives you a general idea of the basic roles that each agency or agent plays.

TABLE 1.1

State-Level Responsibilities for Public Education

State Legislature	State Board of Education	Chief State School Officer	State Department of Education
Serves as plenary authority on education	Educates teachers	Functions as liaison between state board and legislature	Enforces all laws, rules, and regulations
Appropriates funds	Sets curriculum	Acts as executive officer for state board	Supervises schools
Makes laws affecting education	Determines high school graduation requirements	Administers state department of education	Implements state laws and policies
Approves appointees to state board	Prescribes teacher licensing provisions	Recommends actions to the state board	Provides support services to school districts

Local Control

All state legislatures except Hawaii's further delegate some of the responsibility for public education to local school districts, through either elected or appointed boards of school trustees. (Board of school trustees, board of education, school board, local board, board, and school directors are synonymous.)

Local authority is delegated by the state.

School districts are arbitrary political divisions over which a specific local school board has limited jurisdiction. They receive all their authority from the state legislature. State legislatures can alter or abolish existing school districts through the passage of appropriate measures. This nation's 14,883 (Gray 1999) school districts are not sovereign entities; they exist for specific purposes, just as do other special local districts. The number of school districts varies from 1 in Hawaii to 17 in Nevada, 1,101 in Texas, 445 in Iowa, and 14 in Tennessee.

The School Board   The local district comes under the jurisdiction of the local school board, whose members are either elected or appointed. The number of people on local boards varies greatly throughout the United States, but boards most frequently have five, seven, or nine members. State statutes generally specify the board's duties, which typically include setting attendance areas, levying taxes, constructing facilities, hiring all personnel, authorizing all payments, and approving all actions of the district superintendent of schools. Rules and regulations issued by the state board of education and the state superintendent must also be obeyed by local boards of education.

School boards have vast powers.

Experts in school administration agree that local boards should establish local school policy, or the general objectives or direction of their schools. This includes performing such tasks as those listed in the box on page 8. The

---

Tasks in Establishing Local School Policy

- Organize the board's operations.
- Establish educational vision for the community.
- Identify instructional areas to be supported.
- Create administrative structure for district.
- Establish business and operations procedures.
- Issue contracts for personnel and businesses.
- Identify student services and activities.
- Approve instructional programs.
- Manage school and community relations.

---

district superintendent of schools implements local policy. The areas of control are very broad: don't be surprised to be handed a three-hundred-page policy manual on your first day on the job.

Local school boards serve as arms of the state legislatures that create them. School board members act as local agents of the state, performing certain specified functions (see Essex 1999). The courts have consistently held that school board members and teachers are in fact state officials, not local officials. This also means that while you may be "true to your school," you are, in fact, considered an employee of the state. You are subject to all laws, rules, and regulations made by state agencies that affect the schools. In some states, such as Washington, your basic salary schedule is designed and approved by the state legislature. Even your fringe benefits, such as retirement, health, and dental insurance plans, are under state supervision.

The Superintendent of Schools   The powers and duties of the school board usually vary from state to state and, within a state, from district to district. The appointment of a district superintendent of schools may well be one of the most important actions a school board can take. Typically, the local superintendent acts as the executive officer of the board, carrying out the board's policies and acting as its chief administrative officer. Most school board members in the United States serve without pay.

The Principal and the Teachers   Just as it is impossible for the state legislature to direct all the educational enterprises within a state, it is often impossible for the superintendent to personally supervise all the schools within a district. For that reason, each school has a principal, who is responsible for the school's total operations. The principal acts as liaison with the district superintendent of schools, ensures that educational standards are enforced, supervises all personnel in the building, and coordinates the work of neighborhood school advocacy groups.

Last, but certainly not least, comes the teacher, who stands on the educational front line, where teaching and learning really take place. While you are subject to the authorities described above, in reality it is you who will control the instructional and learning environments of your classroom. You have a responsibility to provide the best educational services to all who show in your classes—every day. You make the difference on the person-to-person level.

Schools in the New Era of Reform

School reform has been a *project in works* for what is now the United States of America since the founding of the Massachusetts Bay Colony in 1619. While we must acknowledge a great deal of difference between public schools of the seventeenth century and those of the twenty-first century, one fact rings true: the citizens of the country have great expectations for their schools, and the schools have never quite met those expectations. Thus we find scholars such as Larry Cuban (1990) describing the scenario as "Reforming Again, Again and Again"; and David B. Tyack and Cuban describing educational reform

TABLE 1.2

Major Reports on School Reform	
Report	**General Findings**
Federal Programs Supporting Educational Change. Vol. V: *A Summary of the Findings in Review* (Berman et al. 1975)	A report that states that the quality of the reform is the critical element. Most educational innovations are fads.
"Effective Schools for the Urban Poor" (Edmonds 1979)	A report that presents the foundation for the effective schools movement.
A Nation at Risk: The Imperative for Educational Reform (U.S. Department of Education 1983)	A report that shocked the nation and initiated a flurry of new state laws, reports, and increased high school graduation requirements.
A Place Called School (Goodlad 1984)	A major study showing a flatness of instructional methods in schools.
A Nation Prepared: Teachers for the 21st Century (Carnegie Foundation 1986)	A report calling for higher standards and benefits for America's teaching corps.
. . . the best of educations (Chance 1986)	A detailed study of reform in seven states showing many changes but few that were substantive.
Learning a Living: A Blueprint for High Performance (U.S. Department of Labor 1992)	A report focusing on skills young people need to succeed in the world of work.
What Teachers Have to Say About Teacher Education (Council for Basic Education 1996)	A scathing examination of teacher education, which states principles for needed improvement.
Goals 2000: Reforming Education to Improve Student Achievement (U.S. Department of Education 1998)	A report noting that Congress wants to reform education and raise standards.

efforts as *Tinkering Toward Utopia* (1995). Of course, reformers want to improve the schools, but just what passes for improvement is not at all clear, as is shown by the nearly 14,000 published journal articles on the topic in the ERIC database. (See also Bracey 1997.)

Reform ideas are plentiful.

Even as early as 1986, Bill Chance (1986) reported that there were 275 educational task forces organized for school reform or improvement in the United States alone, all publishing reports. Table 1.2 on page 9 lists a few of the major reports on school reform and a brief synopsis of their findings.

Federal Presence in Education

The secretary of education heads the U.S. Department of Education in Washington, D.C., and is a member of the Cabinet. The box below illustrates the department's basic functions. Congress passes legislation and appropriates funds for **categorical school aid,** which is provided for very specific educational purposes and programs. For example, one of the early federal programs to be supported was vocational education. In 1975, Congress broke new ground by passing Public Law 94-142, the Education for All Handicapped Children Act. For the first time, a federal law determined how schools and teachers were to interact with children with disabilities. The act is enforced by the U.S. Department of Education. Each state department of education had

---

Basic Functions of the U.S. Department of Education

- Fact finding—Collecting and disseminating educational information and statistics
- Research—Studying problems that are of interest to Congress, the states, school boards, administrators, teachers, and scholars
- Service—Providing consultants to state and local education agencies and helping to direct education surveys
- Administration—Administering federal funds in educational programs not specifically under the jurisdiction of any other federal agency

---

Reflect Reflect Reflect

- How are your state board of education and state superintendent selected? How do these processes compare nationwide?
- Ask an international student at your university how the schools are administered in his or her country.
- Interview five non-education majors. Ask them what "school reform" means to them.

to organize a unit to administer provisions of the act. We'll return to this law in Section 5 of this chapter.

The U.S. Department of Education is the link between the legislative and executive branches of the federal government and between the federal government and states and territories. It administers most of the federal programs that focus on the schools. For a very interesting discussion of this federal unit, read *The Thirteenth Man,* by Terrell H. Bell (1988), a former secretary of education.

Just exactly what constitutes reform or improvement is yet unclear, but the list in the box on page 12 shows some of the elements or concepts associated with contemporary school reform.

One characteristic overrides the current school reform era: the desire to help all children achieve at a greater level of academic proficiency. The curriculum and school-related content are the focal points in all state and national reform efforts. We will discuss this aspect again in Chapter 3.

Obviously, we cannot present every element of the school reform movements, but we encourage you to examine at least your own state's reform package to have a better understanding of how it will affect your specific teaching field. Our main point in this brief introduction is to alert you that

The school is a daily destination for millions of youngsters. © Alan Carey/The Image Works.

> ### Elements of School Reform
>
> - Class size
> - Curriculum modification
> - High technology/computers
> - Instructional methodologies
> - Prerequisite standards for all
> - Reinvention, per se
> - School choice
> - Student accountability
> - School safety
> - Teacher preparation
> - Testing and assessing

what you teach and to some extent how you teach it will be impacted by school reform efforts.

Section 3: The School Culture

Understanding the School's Culture

In all schools—elementary, middle, or secondary—there is a unique quality that has been labeled the **school culture.** This emergent theoretical concept has taken on importance in recent years as educators have determined that the massive attempts begun during the 1970s and 1980s to implement meaningful change in the schools have been unsuccessful. We know that reforms are needed to improve public education, but to date few reforms or reformers ever considered the culture of the schools. Two notable exceptions are John I. Goodlad (1984) and Ann Lieberman and Lynne Miller (1999).

What is a school culture? To respond properly to this question would require the remainder of this book, but we'll define it simply as the total environment in which schooling takes place. A school's culture includes all the people in the school and the way the school operates. The box at the top of page 13 lists only a few of the elements that determine a school's culture.

School culture is all inclusive.

Let us summarize several points about school culture (see Lieberman and Miller 1999 for a detailed discussion). First, a school's culture is characterized by great uncertainty. The explicit values of the schools are not easily identified or agreed upon. A student's education is not a product; nevertheless, schools are continually compared to an industrial, product-oriented model. That is, the metaphor most often used to describe student outcomes is the school's "product." But schools do not produce a physical product. They shape the minds of millions of children. They create a love of learning. They strive to

---

Elements of School Culture

■ Vision	■ Attitudes	■ Evaluation
■ Values	■ Expectations	■ Feedback
■ Roles	■ Caring	■ Openness
■ Power relationships	■ Cooperation	■ Cliques
■ Motivators	■ Competition	■ Unions
■ Clubs	■ Student activities	■ Hallways

---

expand students' horizons. We feel that it is very unfair to compare the intellectual pursuits of students to products that roll off an assembly line, such as television sets or computers.

Second, the **school ethos,** that is, the interactions within the environment, differs greatly among schools within any one district and across districts; hence there is no simple prescription that will improve all the schools. The more state legislatures draft specific laws to fix conceived ills in education, the more problems arise—frequently as a direct effect of those very laws, which are rarely well thought out. Local values have more to do with whether school improvement efforts succeed than do those imposed from outside (Kelly 1999b).

Third, norms of teaching practices differ from school to school. Although norms and values differ significantly between elementary and secondary school teachers, teaching is an isolated activity for all of them. Teachers interact intensively with children or adolescents all day, with little professional contact with colleagues. Teachers learn their roles through experience, regardless of the amount and content of their formal education. This is not to negate teacher preparation programs. They are very important (see Grossman 1990). But to meet the specific needs of their students, practicing teachers must "fine-tune" the methods and strategies that are part of their professional knowledge base. The classroom provides the real test of whether or not a technique is effective and of which students will benefit from it.

Fourth, instructional methods and practices are complex and often lack a strong research base. There is a rather extensive list of **empirically** supported teaching techniques and strategies that improve classroom learning, however. But the dissemination of educational research is very slow; and that alone is a reason to be committed to lifelong learning. (For a summary of successful and some less-than-successful instructional techniques, see Cuban 1984; Ellis and Fouts 1997; Gage 1985; Orlich 1985; Waxman and Walberg 1991).

The School as a System   The primary concept associated with the school culture movement is that of the system. A system is an entity composed of many elements or components that interact in a positive manner to reach a specific goal. A school district is an example of a system. It is a human creation—a collection of people, buildings, machinery, materials, rules, and conventions. Systems have subsystems: a school district has attendance areas,

> Many practices are simply "best intuitive practices."

different types of schools, bus routes, and so on. And these subsystems have several smaller subsystems of their own: a high school, for example, has athletic teams, specific academic programs, vocational units, service groups, union and nonunion employees, student groups, faculty groups, and clubs.

Systems and subsystems are important because they function as a whole, and they interact in a manner that either stimulates or retards more interaction. The *effective schools movement* and *school site education* advocates understand that systems and subsystems must function at a very high rate of efficiency; otherwise, their elements begin to deteriorate.

The interactions within a system are critical for the system's **organizational health.** If the business office ignores a teacher's request for instructional materials, then that office may have a negative impact on student learning outcomes. If a principal is a poor leader, then his or her school will probably display poor morale and poor student achievement. If the central office forces teachers to teach to some *party line* (ordering them to use some technique or other selected arbitrarily by an administrator), then the teachers will tend to do so halfheartedly and will subvert the policy, no matter how good the office's intent.

Profiling gives focus to reform efforts.

School cultures do not just happen—they develop over time. To determine some of the elements of any school's culture, we can complete a profiling process (Blum and Butler 1985). Profiling is done to identify what exactly in a school needs improving. This is a somewhat scientific way of determining priorities. A call to conduct a profile can come from any group that wants to enhance a school's effectiveness. The process entails collecting and analyzing several data sets, including (1) scores on student achievement tests, (2) measures of student progress in selected areas over a given time period, (3) student promotion and retention rates, (4) graduate competency measures, (5) measures of student attitudes toward school, and (6) student social behavioral indicators. A set of profiles addressing the above six areas would illustrate schoolwide strengths and weaknesses, and from these relevant changes could be made. In his book *A Place Called School*, John I. Goodlad (1984) outlines processes that can be used to identify critical elements of a school's culture.

External Influences   Public schools confront many ambiguities that affect how teachers and children perform (Sarason 1996). As noted previously, a school's specific objectives are often unclear, and they vary from school to school and from district to district. Take sex education, for example. Teaching practice in this area is not at all clearly defined. One state tried to forbid the mention of sexually transmitted diseases, while another mandates instruction in HIV/AIDS prevention in grades 5 through 12. So local standards will always be one element of school culture.

Internal Influences   Educators are vulnerable to the internal environment. Teachers enter the profession after having spent seventeen years in an "apprenticeship of observation" (Lortie, cited in Shulman 1987). Entering teachers have already been in school for sixteen or seventeen years and have received a tremendous amount of instruction. One cliché often heard in education is that "you teach the way you were taught," university courses in education notwithstanding. The implication of that remark is that you have to take cues from the experienced teachers in your school. This implies that experience and personal intuition are superior sources of teaching technique than teachers' professional knowledge base. Yes, experience is important—but stressing it to this extent is a classic example of supporting the status quo. As you complete each chapter of this book, your personal and professional knowledge base will greatly expand. When you complete your teacher education program, you will be intellectually prepared to enter the profession.

Teachers often work in seclusion, not sharing their work with other professionals or with the outside world. As a result, teachers tend to develop personal teaching styles that may not be beneficial to student learning. Over the academic year, principals or supervisors might spend a total of one or two hours observing and evaluating a teacher, with greater time for a novice and less for a veteran; but the vast amount of service that any teacher performs goes uncritiqued or unnoticed by fellow professionals.

Working in isolation is one aspect of many school cultures that tends to perpetuate the "batch processing" of students, that is, using large classes and large-class techniques. This is especially noticeable in self-contained elementary school classrooms and subject-centered high schools. The physical isolation keeps new ideas from spreading. If you do not have opportunities to observe your colleagues, you may miss out on some great ideas (see Hargreaves and Fullan 1998).

School cultures tend to be independent of one another.

Schools tend to develop their own independent culture, apart from other schools in the same district. Their norms and values may be generated from the inside. As a result, subtle or even intentional pressures may be placed on teachers to conform. This unfortunate tendency undermines the profession, since education, like all professions, is rooted in the development of its practitioners' individual expertise. And, indeed, novice teachers have at their disposal a broad range of teaching strategies. This book is designed to help develop the best teachers possible. Study this and the remaining chapters so that you will influence your environment instead of becoming its victim. In that way, the ethos of your school can evolve; you can establish new norms that stress problem solving, active teaching, and positive student expectations. We advocate entering into professional discussions with other teachers in your school. Share books and journals with one another. This is one way of helping to shape the intellectual and instructional dimensions of your school's culture.

Metaphors carry powerful connotations.

The Influence of Metaphors   The **metaphors** we use to describe a school reflect how we personally view its culture. The way we communicate about schooling affects our motives and personal convinctions (see Irwin-DeVitis and DeVitis 1998). Industrial imagery is evident in talk about the "products" of education, the "bottom line," and "delivery systems." If a school's culture is impersonal, then just listen to how its students and programs are described; that is, listen for the metaphors the teachers and administrators use. They may use images of buildings, war, flower gardens, targets, containers, railways, or even schools, among others. Our speech helps shape our school's culture, which shapes our actions.

Time and School Culture   The use of time is determined by a school's culture. Although state law may govern how the school day is divvied up, it is a truism that there is never enough time to meet all the demands placed on educators. Experienced teachers acknowledge that not having enough time to prepare for classes is a barrier to effective teaching (see Elmore, Peterson, and McCarthy 1996). You and your colleagues need to discuss how to use planning

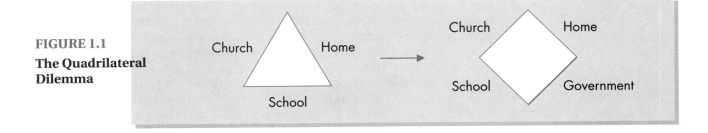

FIGURE 1.1

The Quadrilateral Dilemma

and instructional time more efficiently. This may require some classroom observations to identify possible short-cuts or time-saving techniques.

The Quadrilateral Dilemma   The last aspect of school culture that we will cover is really a societal issue. The schools face the *quadrilateral dilemma* (see Figure 1.1). The schools are one component of that grand system that links the home, religious institutions, and the government. The classic triangle—home, church, school—began in the New World in 1647 in the Massachusetts Bay Colony, with passage of the "Olde Deluder Satan Act." From that time until the latter half of the twentieth century, these three institutions worked together to acculturate youth. The church provided morals, religion, ethics, values, and philosophy. The home provided a human support group, nurturing, self-esteem, confidence, and care. While protecting all those cultural ideals, the school provided the skills young people would need to become productive members of society. Each institution was an extension of the others.

Then great changes came. The home evolved into a two-worker or single-parent household. The influence of the church lessened. The federal government shifted social, child-rearing, and nurturing tasks to the schools. Suddenly the school had a whole host of responsibilities that were not its function within the classic triangle. The dilemma appears because of the entrance of the federal government and the import of its laws, rules, and regulations on the classic three institutions. Federal intervention in local public schools is creating "adjustment" problems for all four institutions.

The school must perform many social functions.

All this means that some of the time in school is now devoted to its social functions, not really its educational ones, which were once rather narrowly defined. These added responsibilities were imposed on the schools by the larger environment, and you'll be expected to help meet them. But you are entering teaching. Let us now discuss that topic in detail to see how it all fits into the concept of culture.

The Teaching Culture

Teachers bask in the success of their students, and students' success reflects on their teachers' **efficacy.** It is great to be with winners. That statement is true whether you are a second-grade teacher whose pupils have mastered addition or a high school French teacher whose students have grasped the concept of the subjunctive.

Strive to be intentionally inviting.

Teachers may be placed into one of four levels of functioning, listed in the box below, based on the extent to which they attain this kind of success (Purkey and Novak 1996). The highest-level teacher, the one who is intentionally inviting, strives for student success. These teachers reinforce their own most powerful incentive.

> ## Teachers' Levels of Functioning
>
> - Intentionally disinviting
> - Unintentionally disinviting
> - Unintentionally inviting
> - Intentionally inviting

One job incentive is recognition as an excellent teacher (Ulriksen 1996). This incentive is reflected in your students' warmth, enthusiasm, and appreciation of your efforts. Again, this is a strong **intrinsic motivator.** Remember how you felt when your teacher helped you complete a tough assignment, or when you accomplished something and shared that feat with the responsible teacher? Yes, those are the real glows in a teacher's eyes!

The respect of colleagues is another incentive. Phi Delta Kappa, the educational honors society, once had the motto "the esteem of our colleagues is the foundation of power." Such esteem helps make teachers feel a sense of efficacy, a feeling that they can get the job done. Effective teachers demonstrate a sense of efficacy. They believe that they control their own classroom destinies, and they show behaviors related to self-actualization, which is Abraham Maslow's (1970) highest need (see Weasmer and Woods 1998 for an excellent discussion of efficacy).

Teachers are intrinsically motivated.

You gain respect from your colleagues when your students achieve better than expected, when they are successful in your classes, and when the tough cases are not tough for you. These accomplishments will result if you use the broad spectrum of teaching strategies we illustrate in the ensuing chapters. Efficacy, in the last analysis, is being able to see yourself doing the job, no matter how difficult or demanding it is. See Thomas R. Guskey's (1998) treatment of the concept of efficacy, in which he elaborates on personal competence and self-determination.

Another incentive is working with other professionals. As we pointed out earlier, most teachers are isolated from other professionals for most of a typical working day. Part of being a teaching professional is working on school problems, curriculum projects, or instructional designs with your colleagues. These activities allow you to participate in the decision-making processes of the school. Working in a collegial manner with your fellow professionals to improve the environment for learning is one aspect of teacher empowerment, in which the concept of efficacy is moved up one level to collective action rather than referring only to individual excellence.

Our very brief treatment of school culture is intended to provide you with a simple glimpse of a most complex institution. The school culture has a

School cultures are malleable.

profound impact on your teaching. We know of a high school where a large sign in the teachers' lounge proclaims, "School Business Is Not Discussed Here." Do you want to predict what kind of teacher culture has evolved there? (Maybe you'd rather not.) But you immediately become a part of any school's culture, and you can have an impact on it. Being efficacious is the quickest way to influence that culture. The essence of this book is to help you develop a variety of instructional skills so that you can develop into the best teacher that you can be; can't ask for much more.

Let us now examine the clientele of the schools, the students.

Reflect Reflect Reflect

- In which subsystems of the school's culture did you participate?
- Listen to the metaphors being used to describe your institution: Any generalizations?
- Form a discussion group and analyze the concept of the quadrilateral dilemma.

Section 4: Meet Your Students

Age and Grade Levels

The schools of this nation and nearly all others on the planet are designed to acculturate youth into society. The organization of any country's schools illustrates a long history of change and compromise. In the United States, and in many other countries that have modeled their system after ours, there are four different classes of schools. The school for young children might be called *preschool, nursery school,* or *kindergarten.* Regardless of the label, the primary mission of this school is to prepare children for entry into elementary school. In these preschools, children are taught entry-level competencies that help ensure school success. In our experience, children who come from broken or dysfunctional homes find this institution to be a safe haven. It is warm and caring, and the children learn something too. And because about 50 percent of an individual's intellectual development occurs in the period from conception to age four, 30 percent between the ages of four to eight, and only 20 percent after that, early education is important (Bloom 1964).

The elementary grades are usually divided into primary grades (1, 2, and 3) and intermediate grades (4, 5, and 6). If you examine any set of longitudinal achievement data, you will see that the children in the primary grades tend to do nicely. However, something happens at grade 4. This is a departure point for the curriculum. First, children no longer read simply for the enjoyment of reading. Now they must read and demonstrate an understanding of the content or apply it in some way. Second, the classroom's print materials and textbooks change rather abruptly from a narrative style to an expository style. Children who are good readers by grade 3 tend to do better than their poorer-reading peers.

Language arts are a critical educational foundation.

Learning verbal language and expressing oneself orally and in writing play a large part in the curriculum for the primary grades (and well they should, we might add). The schools strongly emphasize literacy skills—including reading, writing, speaking, and even spelling—at this stage. These skills form a prerequisite foundation for future expansion into literature, creative writing, expository writing, and critical thinking. Literacy is so important that it is national goal number 6 in the Goals 2000 program (see Chapter 3). To be successful in school, one must be proficient in the language arts. School success begets school success, because schooling takes place primarily through verbal and literary interactions.

The intermediate grades tend to stress various subjects or disciplines. In some schools the content areas are distinct; in others content lines are blurred by interdisciplinary instruction and curricula (see Jacobs 1997). The middle grades vary administratively across districts. In some cases they include grades 5–8; in others it is grades 6–8; in yet others it is grades 7 and 8. Some school districts use a junior high school configuration, grades 7–9. Why is there so much variation? In some cases, separation of preadolescents and adolescents from younger children reflects a recognition of the emerging developmental needs of this group. The configuration may be based on adolescents' cognitive, social, or physical developmental needs. Or it may be based on chance: perhaps a building is about to become available and some suggests, "Let's have a middle school."

Middle school youth are psychologically full of change.

Middle school is perhaps the most exciting place to teach. Every day, adolescents experience rapid change in all domains. They tend to be quick to follow anybody—gangs, teachers, coaches, art instructors, band leaders, shop teachers. Their hormones are pumping. First, young girls become transformed into young women; the boys lag behind in maturation for a year or so. You'll observe human physical changes immediately upon walking into a middle school. There are also great intellectual changes taking place. Around grade 6 or 7, adolescents experience a brain growth spurt. They are intellectually hungry. By grade 8 there tends to be a lax period; this year tends to be one of transition before entering high school (see Lounsbury and Clark 1990).

The curriculum and instruction in middle schools should provide for content and process explorations. The student should be challenged to do good work and to achieve at the highest possible level. By the way, this is the last level where illiterate students and students lacking mathematical ability can be helped. If they are simply passed on to high school, their academic failure is ensured.

Next, in the United States, comes high school. Because it is a comprehensive institution, it must accommodate at least three types of instruction: college preparatory, vocational, and general. This system is unique to the United States, for in most other countries students are tracked into either college preparatory or vocational programs, and these placements are almost irreversible.

It is the high school that receives the most praise and the most blame in the popular press (see Angus and Mirel 1999; Berliner and Biddle 1995; Bracey 1995). The job of high school teachers obviously includes teaching the content area disciplines—history, English, foreign languages, mathematics, science—but it also includes advising students about higher education and career options, counseling, mentoring, and much, much more.

High school teachers have the same societal and moral obligation to provide their students with the best possible educational experiences as do all other teachers. Of course, we know that the extra, or **cocurricular activities**—sports, clubs, interest groups—are disproportionately emphasized in some high schools. But let us not lose sight of the purpose of acculturation. These activities simulate the clubs, philanthropic groups, and other organizations that provide a sense of community in the adult world. We would like to offer just one statement for anyone who wants to make a generalization about the American high school. In a profound conclusion, one of America's premier educational critics, James B. Conant, observed that you can judge high schools or improve them, but only "school by school" (1959, p. 96).

Providing Developmentally Appropriate Instruction

Developmentally appropriate materials enhance learning.

Elementary School   The instructional methods employed by teachers at various grade levels tend to reflect their students' age and developmental level. In the preschool arena, the focus is on motor development; manipulating perceptions; self-reflection, or understanding meanings; problem solving; realizing expectations; and understanding emotions (Gemelli 1996). This is only one way to organize instruction for young children. For a useful overview, see the National Association for the Education of Young Children (NAEYC) guidelines for developmentally appropriate practices (Bredekamp 1997; Ball and Pence 1999). There is much more, but for our purpose these suffice.

In general, children in the elementary grades tend to exhibit the traits listed in the box below (adapted from Gemelli 1996).

Children in elementary school can understand events and take another's perspective. They can observe phenomena and begin to construct cause-and-effect relationships. Their numeracy skills expand rapidly, and they feel good about achieving tasks that they might not have realized they can do. Again, there is much more than what the professional literature addresses. You can

---

Traits of Elementary School Students

- Strong need for peer identification
- Functioning at the concrete operations stage (see Chapter 2)
- Ability to think logically
- Rational process development
- Understanding of processes
- Understanding of symbols
- Quantitative skills development
- Ability to memorize
- Development of self-esteem

now appreciate all the nonacademic skills and processes that take place in elementary schools. The schools do much more than teach the "three R's."

Nevertheless, reading is the key to future academic success. As we mentioned earlier, expanded literacy is a national goal. And literacy demands are changing: with the advent of the technological age, for example, all children must be able to read and comprehend technical manuals. Helping all children to become literate and mastering key basic skills is the primary mission of the elementary school.

All students bring their social, emotional, psychological, and physical baggage with them as they pass through the schoolhouse doors. When a traumatic episode happens to one member of the group—an automobile accident, a death in the family, a teenage suicide—an immediate impact is felt in the school. As a sensitive teacher, you need to be aware of these external factors, because they have a negative impact on education.

Middle School   One distinguishing characteristic of middle school youngsters is their perception of their own visibility (Muth and Alvermann 1999). Middle school students think they are on center stage and that the whole world is watching them. In adolescence, peer group identity is of utmost importance. This trait is the reason for the much-used phrase "everybody is doing it." "Everybody" might just be the one most popular boy or girl in school. Fads spring up on Monday and disappear by Friday.

The emotional energy of middle school students is unsurpassed. Discovery, excitement, and exploration all mark these students. Earlier we mentioned the hormone explosions that occur at this age. Adolescents are preoccupied with their new bodies. Facial pimples are of intergalactic significance. Interpersonal problems erupt in the classroom like Mt. St. Helens—only they occur about once every hour. A best friend at noon is a worst enemy at dismissal (see Steinberg 1993, especially "Hallways, Lunchrooms, and Football Games"). The box below lists a few traits of this age group (adapted from George, Lawrence, and Bushnell 1998).

You like excitement? Then, hey, the middle school is for you. And oh, yes, we do teach academic subjects there also. There tends to be some integration of the disciplines at these grades. The typical middle school schedule usually

---

Traits of Middle School Students

- Beginning of puberty
- Peer group identification
- Realistic ambitions
- Reasonable ideals
- Socialization
- Some belligerence
- Formation of personal opinions
- Abundant emotional energy

combines some single-subject classes, such as science and math, with some integrated ones, such as social science and language arts.

High school students begin to show maturity.

High School   At last, students reach high school. Developmental levels in grades 9–12 range from early adolescence to adulthood, and you'll find a commensurate age span of about thirteen to nineteen years of age. The box below lists some significant traits to consider as you make instructional decisions for high school students (adapted from Gemelli 1996). Any experienced high school teacher could add another page or more of traits, but these will give you an idea of the differences between grade levels.

Let us close with a quick review of the much-ballyhooed *generation gap*. We reviewed the psychiatric literature and found reference to a worldwide survey of twenty thousand urban, middle-class teenagers. The authors of the study (Offer and Offer 1975) concluded that the vast majority of teenagers enjoyed a positive relationship with their parents, accepted the basic values of their society, and were not in a state of turmoil. Further, they were neither rebellious nor felt that any generation gap existed. If each generation were to reject completely the values and standards of its parents or elders, social chaos would be the result (Esman 1990).

Traits of High School Students

- Development of early formal thinking
- Ability to understand conflicts
- Some challenging of authority
- Development of self-reliance
- Control of emotions
- Understanding of values
- Ability to set goals
- Interest in sexual attributes

Reflect Reflect Reflect

- Examine the curricula for early elementary and intermediate grades in your area. How do they compare to the middle school curriculum?
- Interview a middle school principal and a few teachers. Ask for their perceptions of the students they work with.
- Set up an Internet chat room and discuss the appropriate roles for the twenty-first-century high school.

Socioeconomic Factors Affecting the School

So far we have focused on the institution of the school and the players within it. Now we need to examine some socioeconomic factors—factors that are not controlled by schools, teachers, or students. A society's schools mirror its values and injects them into curricula and instructional practices. But schools are also deeply affected by negative social factors, and in many cases these factors negate one of education's most important premises: that students show up at the schoolhouse door ready to learn. Examine the box below for a list of some socioeconomic factors that tend to work against acculturation (also see Orlich 1994). We present these data with a strong cautionary note: *do not use such information as an excuse not to teach these children.*

Now, add to the boxed list one more fact: nearly 20 percent of all children of age three to seventeen have one or more developmental, learning, or behavioral disorders (Fuchs and Reklis 1992). In other words, on a random draw, one out of five of your students will have a social or learning problem that requires special attention! In this section, we will survey some of the

You must take the students who walk in your door.

Socioeconomic Factors that Impact Schooling

- Nationally 63 percent of children live in two-parent families.
- In 1996 the number of babies born to unmarried women was more than 1.2 million.
- Twenty percent of children live in poverty, with 14 percent living with "high-risk" families, that is, those with six poverty-related characteristics.
- In low-income families, 34 percent of children were highly engaged in school compared to 45 percent of children in higher-income families (Items 1–4, Annie E. Casey Foundation, 1999).
- Sixty-five percent of K–12 students are white, and 35 percent are non-white (U.S. Department of Education, 1997).
- On an average, 6 percent of students are absent on a typical school day.
- In central city high schools with high poverty levels, the average daily absentee rate is 12 percent.
- At least half the children in poverty live in a female-headed household.
- Eighty-two percent of black children in poverty live in a female-headed household, compared to 46 percent of white and Hispanic children (last four items from U.S. Department of Education, 1996, Indicators 42 and 44).
- Hispanic youth have the highest high school dropout rates. In 1997 the rates were 25.3 percent for Hispanic youths, 13.4 percent for black, and 7.6 percent for white (Kaufman, Klein, & Frase, 1999, iii).

accommodations you will have to make in order to meet the needs of students with learning and behavioral disabilities (see also Chapter 4).

From this quick socioeconomic perspective, you can see that the American dream approaches a nightmare for many children who attend our public schools. The groups described in the box on page 23 will need an extra boost from the schools, which were established to be helping and caring institutions. (It is really the professionals and others within the schools that make them so.) While you may not be able to eliminate these socioeconomic conditions, you can provide the positive expectation that all youth will succeed in school.

The Concept of Inclusion

Let us now focus on a method to ensure that all children have equal educational opportunities. The method is **inclusion.** It means placing children with mild, moderate, or even severe disabilities in regular classrooms. The method explicitly assumes that regular classes provide an appropriate educational environment for these children (Smith and Dowdy 1998). The stimulus for inclusion is a series of federal laws that guarantee all children, regardless of disability, a free and appropriate education. Does it work? One major study shows that inclusion helps all students achieve five affective or attitudinal benefits: (1) the nondisabled learn to be more responsive to others, (2) new and valued relationships develop, (3) nondisabled students learn something about their own lives and situations, (4) children learn about values and principles, and (5) children gain an appreciation of diversity in general (Helmstetter and Peck 1996). In short, students taught in inclusive classrooms take on an attitude of caring and tolerance.

Let us now quickly review the legislative events that gave the legal impetus for inclusion.

Public Law 94-142   In 1975 Congress passed PL 94-142, the Education for All Handicapped Children Act. How important is this law? Dean C. Corrigan, a college professor, wrote in 1978 that "this act is the most important piece of educational legislation in the history of this country." The act is based on the assumption that all children with handicaps can benefit from public education and have a right to it. Although the law and its accompanying regulations tend to be technical, *every* teacher in the United States must understand its implications, for no teacher, school, or class is exempt from it. There are several key concepts that, at this stage in your career, you must understand about PL 94-142, today amended and called *IDEA,* or the *Individuals with Disabilities Education Act.*

IDEA must be carefully understood.

This law initially established that all handicapped children between the ages of three and twenty-one are entitled to free public education. Today the operative term is *disability.* The law defines individuals with disabilities to include those who are mentally retarded, hard of hearing, deaf, speech impaired, visually handicapped, seriously emotionally disturbed, or orthopedically impaired; have multiple handicaps; or have other health impairments or learning disabilities and therefore need special educational services.

It is estimated that 12.4 percent of the students enrolled in grades K–12 receive special services as a consequence of meeting the legal definition of an individual with disabilities. Nationally, the number of disabled children and youth is reported to be 5.6 million (U.S. Department of Education 1998, p. 138).

A fundamental principle behind IDEA is that all students with disabilities have the right to be served in the **least restrictive environment** possible. This has led to the general practice of **mainstreaming,** or inclusion—that is, placing disabled children in regular classrooms. Following the principle of the least restrictive environment means that children who are disabled must be educated and treated in a manner similar to their nondisabled peers. Youngsters placed in inclusion programs are typically supported in the classroom and on the playground by specialists. If the child is able to participate in school activities—academic lessons, lunchroom activities, recess, games—he or she must be included. This shifts the professional emphasis away from the separation of special education and regular education classes and requires new models of collaboration. Regardless of how the law is interpreted in your district, you will undoubtedly teach students whose needs require accommodation in instruction, materials, or setting, and it will become increasingly clear that all students can benefit from some individualized instruction.

However, providing the least restrictive environment can also mean placing a child with disabilities in a special room, not in a regular classroom. It may even mean institutionalizing the child in a special school or in a private school. The deciding factor is where the child will receive the most beneficial services.

The IEP   Another requirement that will affect you as a teacher is the need to prepare a written **individual education plan** (IEP) for every student with a disability in your class. The IEP must specify the goals or objectives of the educational services you plan to provide, the methods of achieving those goals, and the exact number and quality of the exceptional services to be rendered to the child. The box below identifies the IEP elements specified in the *Federal Register* (1977).

Federal law requires that the IEP be formulated by a team consisting of a parent, the child, the child's teacher, a professional who has recently

---

Legally Prescribed Elements of an IEP

1. Documentation of the current level of the student's educational performance
2. Statement of the expected goals or educational attainments to be achieved by the end of the year
3. List of short-term instructional objectives leading to the mastery of the annual goals
4. Specification of precise special services to be offered
5. Documentation of any related required services
6. Specification of the amount of time the student will participate in regular educational programs
7. List of projected dates and duration of service
8. Identification of methods to determine mastery

evaluated the child, and others as designated by the local education agency. The last category usually includes the school principal or a special education resource person.

The IEP must list all special activities and regular class activities in which the child will participate. Dates and duration of services must be stated. Objectives and evaluation procedures must be given. A minimum of one IEP meeting must be held each year, and the law requires that the child's parents receive written notice of the IEP meeting.

The IEP is mandatory.

The evaluation process is also legally specified and is somewhat unique. It requires that an interdisciplinary team of professionals assess the student's achievements based on the objectives and services stated in the IEP. The team formally notes the child's progress on each objective or service prescribed for the child. (We discuss this technique, also known as instructional alignment, in Chapter 3.)

If you wonder whether you will have the skills to draft an IEP, this book (Chapters 3, 4, and 5) will provide many of the technical skills that all teachers need to devise any educational objective or plan. (Also see Bateman 1998 for detailed examples of IEPs.)

PL 94-142 also requires that the records of students with disabilities be kept secure. Even a federal investigator cannot examine a child's records without first getting parental permission. Parents, however, have unlimited access to all educational records. Furthermore, a parent may amend (in writing) any statement in his or her child's file. Finally, the school must keep a record of all persons who have access to the child's record and why they have it.

If there is disagreement (for example, between a child's parents and a teacher) over an IEP or what is in a child's file, the child's parents have the right to an impartial hearing. Such hearings can be lengthy and time consuming for all concerned, however. Sometimes parents (or a school district) will sue in a court of law to have an unsatisfactory IEP changed. The judgment of the court will then take precedence over the IEP. It is even possible for such cases to go all the way to the Supreme Court.

What happens to the student while the courts are determining the appropriate IEP? The student will remain in the school setting to which he or she was originally assigned. This is done so that the child has the benefit of some formal schooling while the case is being decided.

Equal educational opportunity is a civil right.

The Americans with Disabilities Act   Another significant law, the Americans with Disabilities ACT (PL 101-336), became effective on January 26, 1992. This act is not directly about education, but it has implications for it since it defines services to persons with disabilities as a civil right (indeed, civil rights were the basis of PL 94-142 as well, since it was based on the Civil Rights Act of 1964). The act requires that persons with disabilities be ensured access to the same types of buildings, services, and programs that are accessible to people without disabilities. Obviously, buildings will not be your immediate concern or responsibility as a teacher. But you could be sued for a civil rights violation if you withhold services or programs from a child with disabilities. Keep in mind, in civil rights cases, you are generally assumed to be guilty until proven innocent. So it is critical to learn the elements of IEPs and to plan effectively for all students with disabilities in your classes.

Classroom Implications of Inclusion

If we were to discuss all the classroom implications of inclusion, it would fill this book. We must, however, mention three powerful legal implications here. The first addresses the issue of individual versus group rights, the second concerns the rights of teachers, and the third is related to the concept of *due process*. These are complex issues whose applications are situation specific. We encourage you to refer, for starters, to introductory-level literature on school law (such as the chapter on legal issues in Ornstein and Levine 1997; see also Ellis and Geller 1993).

Reflect Reflect Reflect

- Make a list of conditions you might anticipate to cause interpersonal conflicts in a mainstreamed class or fully inclusionary one.
- Examine the Internet to locate sites about IDEA. What topics are emphasized?

Section 6: The Teacher as Decision Maker

In this book we stress the concept of teaching artistry (see Harris 1998). Like an artist, a teacher makes decisions from both a technical and a creative perspective. Great artists display not only a mastery of technical skills—painting, glass blowing, sculpting—but also artistic judgment. They also know when and in what way to apply those technical skills. In teaching as in art, we call this ability *creativity.*

Artistry is developed with experience.

Teacher artistry doesn't just happen. Teachers develop their art by using carefully planned, fine-tuned lessons that reflect an understanding of many different teaching techniques. Each technique is skillfully applied to gain the desired intellectual, social, affective, or kinesthetic skills. The best teachers know the tools of their craft and when and how to use them. They develop artistry by being aware of both what they are doing and how what they do affects their learners. They are constantly aware that the decisions they make affect the intellectual, attitudinal, and psychomotor skills of their students. But above all, they make decisions.

Decision Making and Responsibility

Implicit within the concept of decision making is the notion of *responsibility.* Teachers cannot pass the buck. If you make a decision, you must be willing to take responsibility for both the implementation and the outcome. As we mentioned previously, some decisions are made for you—class sizes, time

Teachers are responsible for instructional decisions.

schedules, curriculum guides, lunch schedules. But you make the instructional decisions (see U.S. Department of Education 1998, Chart 2).

In our opinion, many teachers do not recognize their responsibility for making decisions. They tend to blame the administration or the school board. To be sure, administrative regulations and school board policies do govern some instructional procedures and content. But most classroom instructional decisions are, in fact, the teacher's. It is you who will answer such questions as "Should I spend one period on the map-making activity or two?" "Shall I have the students prepare poster sessions for small group presentations?" "How many periods can I allot for a class activity?" On the surface these are not monumental decisions, but they do have an impact on your students. Our plea is that you take responsibility for making such decisions and that you make them logically and deliberately—not according to impulse.

One way to begin acting more deliberately is to use "if-then" logic in your thinking. For example, *if* you desire to encourage students to learn through inquiry techniques, *then* you must provide them with the initial learning skills they need to make inquiries. This technique helps raise your level of cognitive awareness; it provides a cognitive map for you to use in generating rules and principles. Using this mental map allows you to consider the causes and effects of your actions and statements and to think about relationships between classroom activities and students. Teachers who take responsibility for decision making obtain as much information as possible about both students and subject matter and then develop an instructional plan geared for success. This plan is based on their conclusions about the interaction between the subject matter, the students, and the teacher. See Figure 1.2 for the If-Then Cognitive Map.

FIGURE 1.2

The If-Then Procedure Cognitive Map

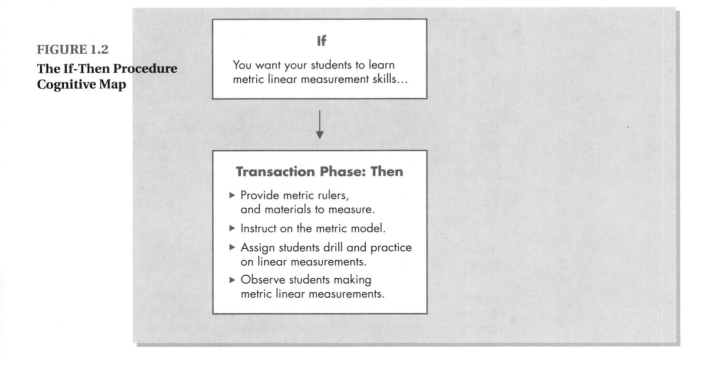

If

You want your students to learn metric linear measurement skills…

Transaction Phase: Then

► Provide metric rulers, and materials to measure.

► Instruct on the metric model.

► Assign students drill and practice on linear measurements.

► Observe students making metric linear measurements.

A team of teachers making a decision on appropriate student materials. © Michael Zide.

There is no one "right" way to teach anyone or anything.

If there is one indisputable statement about teaching, it is that there is no one "right" way to teach anything or anyone. With alarming frequency, educational authorities and critics announce that they have discovered the answer to the nation's teaching problems. The literature is full of advocates for behavioral objectives, outcome-based education, instructional theory into practice (ITIP), individually guided instruction, whole language reading techniques, math manipulatives, activity-oriented science, learning styles, and assertive discipline. Many of these approaches are based on sound analyses and investigations of teaching and learning. Most are related to a specific kind of teaching activity, a specific philosophy of education, or the specific perspective of the discipline for which they were developed. We will discuss many of these approaches in this book, of course, and you can use any or all of them without believing in them as panaceas.

Unfortunately, however, many advocates, in their eagerness to "spread the word" about their particular approach, attempt to convince other educators that their method is, at long last, the *right* one. Such pronouncements, no matter how well intentioned, tend to be naive. The truth is that most teachers will never use the method, and teachers who have never heard of it will achieve success using an eclectic mix of methods combined with wisdom, logic, a sound knowledge of educational psychology, and seasoned artistry.

We thus caution you from the beginning: we will never say that we have discovered "the" teaching method to use in a given situation. Instead we will present a series of options, all of them practical and all able to provide results. In other words, we will follow our own theory. If teaching is a decision-making activity based on individual teachers' skills, knowledge, and artistry, then there ought to be a variety of means for accomplishing any instructional objective. The goal of this book is to help you learn to choose from these options. The context in which any method is used predicates its success; this is the notion of relevance.

Deciding on Content and Process

As you plan to teach a subject, you must remember that the processes that students use to master the content of a lesson are just as important as the content itself. Cunard Steamship Lines once advertised that "getting there is half the fun!" The same idea applies to teaching. Students must know how to accomplish what you want them to learn. And once they know how to get there, they'll enjoy the journey.

For example, a middle school math teacher wants to teach her students how to use ratios. Before they can use ratios, however, the students must master various skills and processes. They must be able to understand the meaning of division, to comprehend the concept of whole numbers, to conceptualize the notion of proportions, and to perform basic arithmetic operations. These different kinds of knowledge are typically divided into two categories—knowing *what* (***declarative knowledge***) and knowing *how* (*procedural knowledge*). Table 1.3 shows the distinction.

Instruction involves teaching both content and process.

Table 1.3 illustrates the teaching of ratios to middle school students. There are at least four specific concepts to master, listed on the left. Mastering these concepts involves both declarative knowledge or content (rules, facts, information), and procedural knowledge, or processes. (Division, for example, entails both cognitive and procedural knowledge.) We use this example because many of the academic concepts taught in school are a mix of some content base (poetry, art, history, geography, science) and processes (writing, drawing, analyzing, experimenting). The table illustrates how learning one concept—ratios—calls for a carefully integrated approach that requires students to know and understand both content and processes, when applicable.

TABLE 1.3

Declarative Versus Procedural Knowledge

Specific Concept	Declarative Knowledge (Content/Information)	Procedural Knowledge (Thinking Skills and Processes)
Division	Yes	Yes
Whole numbers	Yes	No
Dividing whole numbers	Yes	Yes
Stating ratio (interpretation)	Yes	Yes

You can make your instructional decision-making process more deliberate by being aware of content and process implications.

Grade-Level Considerations When prospective teachers are asked what concerns them most as they anticipate beginning their career, many secondary education majors identify knowledge of subject matter as their chief concern. Thus, prospective secondary school teachers tend to be "subject oriented." In contrast, prospective elementary school teachers tend to be "child oriented." Their primary objective is to help children grow and mature mentally and physically, not just to teach mathematics, science, or writing. This means that the activities of elementary school teachers will be oriented toward processes, such as helping children adjust from their home environment to the institutional dimensions of school. However, the elementary school teacher's approach, in which process comes first and content second, may create some conflict within any school system.

An often-heard complaint from high school teachers is that in the elementary and middle grades, processes are stressed to the detriment of content. There may be substance to this argument, but the situation is not caused by any individual teacher. Rather, the problem is the result of instructional decisions made by school district curriculum committees. This is one of the realities of school politics.

In the middle schools, the emphasis begins to shift from a human-growth orientation to a content orientation. It is critically important for middle school educators to understand that young adolescents are just beginning to emerge cognitively from Jean Piaget's concrete operational stage and are entering the initial formal stage (refer to Seifert and Hoffnung 1997). To teach this group effectively, teachers must combine hands-on activities with thinking activities for all major concepts. Techniques such as preparing time lines, conducting experiments, designing charts and graphs, classifying, and sequencing are useful to learners at this age. By high school, however, teachers tend to focus on content. The subject matter is first, last, and always the focus, although not to the exclusion of all other considerations.

Who decided on these emphases? Teachers determined these priorities in response to the subtle pressures placed on them by institutions of higher education and perhaps even by society at large. More than half a century ago, anthropologist Clyde Kluckhohn (1949) concluded that the schools of any society mirror that society. The wishes and beliefs of a society are subtly translated into the values, curricula, and instructions of its schools. This was demonstrated in the late 1960s and early 1970s when many secondary school educators wanted to "humanize" secondary schools by making them more process oriented (see Read and Simon 1975). But when newspaper writers, school board members, legislators, and parents began to pressure high school teachers to improve test scores, raise academic standards, and add content, those same teachers refocused their efforts on content.

It is hard for all of us in education to realize that processes must be taught along with content. It is even more difficult to understand the motives of any teacher who says, "Well, if they didn't have the knowledge or techniques before they got into my class, that's too bad!" If students do not have the so-called **prerequisite skills,** then you as a teacher must provide them. If you do

School emphasis on growth can cause interschool conflicts.

not, then your students will fail. If you provide the basics, then your students will be successful. The decision is yours.

Equity Considerations   Thus far our discussion has focused on decision making based on students' cognitive level, but your decisions should also be affected by equity considerations. What do we mean by *equity?* In our view the term means that *every* student in your class has an equal opportunity to learn. Equity means that you consciously decide to include all members of the class in all activities. This means fairness in asking questions, in delegating student work assignments, and in providing access to resources, such as computer time. In short, it means that you give every student an equal opportunity to excel.

We are, quite frankly, bothered by curriculum frameworks designed around minimum competencies. Instead, curriculum frameworks should stress individual excellence. And this is where you come into the process: if you decide to hold every student responsible for doing his or her very best, your students will rise to the occasion. In this book we provide you with a multitude of different ways to reach every student. The aim of the public schools should be to help every child reach the highest level of human potential of which he or she is capable. That is what we mean by *equity*.

> Equity means an equal opportunity to excel for all students.

Motivation and Learning

It has been amply demonstrated that the vast majority of school-age children can master most topics, assuming the content is appropriate and learning is paced appropriately (see Bloom 1984). You, as the teacher, will be responsible for making decisions that will help every student in your class. A particularly important one is to encourage each child to take responsibility for learning. This is an important attitude. Teachers can teach only if the learner has some desire to learn. We call that desire **motivation.**

Motivation is the inner drive to do something—to finish a book, complete a tough assignment, make the cross-country track team. Motivation is an abstract concept, but it will become very much a part of your vocabulary. Winning coaches have more going for them than good players—they are also great motivators. They can get their players to perform better than they think they are capable of performing. The same principle applies to great teachers.

In the classroom, you try to motivate students to do their best work. You may appeal to their inner self, hoping that they are intrinsically motivated (that is, that they will do an assignment to please themselves, because they enjoy it, or to meet a challenge). We appeal to students' intrinsic motivation when we say, "You can do it!" Doing good school work for its own sake is a powerful incentive as is persistence.

However, not all students are intrinsically motivated, so we must resort to **extrinsic motivators.** These include stars on a paper, letter grades, special treatment (a party or time off to do something a student wants to do on his or her own), and even prizes. Part of the artistry of teaching is in knowing when to use intrinsic motivators and when to use extrinsic motivators. Part of the science of teaching is in determining which ones to use on specific students

> Motivating students to learn is a joint responsibility of teacher and learner.

(See Raffini 1996 for an interesting treatment on the topic; also refer to Purkey and Novak 1996 and Schunk 1998.)

The processes of teaching, learning, and motivating all take place in a specific social and organizational setting. How this setting is structured, in terms of the number of students and the amount of instructional time, will influence the instructional decisions you make. It makes a difference whether your school day consists of seven 50-minute periods or four 90-minute periods and whether your class has sixteen or thirty-two students (see Mosteller 1995). School culture is another aspect of the setting that will affect your instructional decisions. If your school honors learning, then you will be supported by everyone in your environment. If learning is not honored explicitly, then your work will be made much more difficult.

Technology and Decision Making

The American culture is permeated by the influence of technology, as is the world's. It is not our intent to provide an in-depth treatment of the topic, for there are excellent resources such as Mark and Cindy Grabe's *Integrating Technology for Meaningful Learning* (1998). Our intent is to provide a brief awareness of the role that *your decisions* will play in using technology to enhance student learning and excitement in the classroom.

Some Traditional Technologies   It may surprise you, but many classroom technologies or instructional tools have been long used. These include the "software" of asking questions, using evaluation rubrics, mastery learning, specifying instructional objectives, and cooperative learning. And don't forget those "hardware" items of the overhead projector, chalkboard, textbooks, microscopes, and skill saws; they were all one-time major innovations. Granted, the above are all "low tech" in characteristic. So let us list some of the contemporary technologies in the box below that you will find in the twenty-first-century classroom.

Obviously, you will not be using every item listed, but as your career

---

Current High-Tech Classroom Technologies

■ Audiocassette recorders	■ Satellite television links
■ CD-ROMs	■ Simulations
■ Distance learning links	■ Talking books
■ E-mail	■ Television
■ Internet	■ Tutorials
■ Laser discs	■ Two-way interactive TV
■ Optical scanners	■ Videocassette recorders
■ Personal computers	■ Videodiscs
■ Public radio	

continues, you will undoubtedly use these and other yet-to-be-introduced technological innovations. Our main concern is that you analyze each technology for its potential to help your students achieve their maximum potential. You will make decisions for your students and perhaps others as you plan for the appropriate integration of any technology as an *instructional tool*. We deliberately used the term *tool* because all the modern and not-so-modern technologies are simply tools that make the process of learning a bit more efficient. Let's just "wink" at two useful tools—personal computers and the Internet.

Personal Computers   The personal computer has found its way into the schools at every level from preschool to graduate school. There is one personal computer in U.S. public schools for every ten students. This technology is used for a wide variety of instructional uses—see the box below.

The schools are becoming increasingly technologically oriented.

These uses are very commonplace now, so we will expand on just the last one—data collection. Students in science laboratories often perform activities that require observing phenomena and tabulating data. Through the use of peripheral equipment that attaches to a personal computer, students can determine the acceleration of objects released on inclined planes, chart temperature changes over long periods of time, and determine pH values for acid and base solutions. There are many other uses that relieve students of the drudgery associated with collecting data. The time they save gives them greater opportunity to analyze their data. Further, students learn to graph, chart, or display data so that they can communicate their findings to others.

Oh, yes—personal computers are also used for games. The schools should encourage the use of educational games, since they reinforce a love of learning. Quite obviously, you, the teacher, must plan to integrate technology into your classroom lessons in such a way that the experiences are meaningful.

Telecommunications—Cyberspace   As you know, the Internet is a montage of thousands of computer networks that cover the planet. The uses of the "Net" and the World Wide Web are numerous, but for our purposes, we want to see how this system of systems enhances instruction. One of the most basic uses of the Net is to send e-mail. It allows teachers, students, and anyone else who has an e-mail address to communicate directly and almost instantaneously. This is a great way to stimulate perfection of the language arts and

---

School Uses of the Personal Computer

- Word processing
- Drill and practice exercises
- Tutorials
- Simulations
- Interactive multimedia lessons
- Databases
- Spreadsheets
- Data collection

communication. E-mail is a one-way method of communication. To communicate effectively, your students must be very explicit, clear, and lucid. Using e-mail, students can learn about different cultures, communicate directly with other schools in other parts of the country or world, and markedly increase their appreciation of other cultures.

A second instructional use of the Internet is to search for information. The Net is loaded with data and information. Your students can search for this information either from their classroom or from the school's library or computer resources room. (A few Web sites for your use are listed at the end of each chapter.) Again, through the Net, students can interact over great distances. One of the authors of this book has been working with a network of middle and senior high school teachers to monitor water quality of selected streams, rivers, and lakes. The students involved in the project collect relevant data sets and enter them into one central Web site. Anyone on the globe can obtain the data and compare them to those collected locally. This is certainly taking the classroom to the field.

For example, one of your authors was associated with nine school districts in a novel application of technology, literacy, and science. The program was dubbed The ESP Project. Children in grades 3–8 were provided laptop computers to take home and use with their families. The science was field oriented: tracking bird movements, observing where native plant and animal species were located, determining local water quality, charting star movements, predicting weather. Students would gather their data, write individual and team reports on the computer, and present findings to their classmates. Then each class compiled the reports and, using the Internet and self-constructed Web pages, shared the findings with the other schools. Needless to say, these children improved not only in science but also in literacy. This is but one case study of successfully integrating technology with curriculum.

Obviously, the full potential of the available technological resources has yet to be reached in the schools. We predict that school reform in the twenty-first century will focus on expanding learning opportunities through electronic media. And just think, you are on stage as the excitement commences.

A Closing Word on Decision Making

As a classroom teacher, you'll be exceeding air traffic controllers in the number of decisions made per day. As we stress in Chapter 6, a large number of decisions will be made as a consequence of your personal observations of the class—who is doing what, what is being done, what you can anticipate. You are the primary decision maker on how your classroom is organized and managed for instruction.

As you develop the artistry and science of teaching, you will become more aware of how your decisions affect the intellectual and attitudinal development of your students. You alone make the decision to be organized and well prepared. Effective teaching is deliberate and planned. And as national and state standards become more broadly incorporated into curriculum designs, you will find that some of your control over content will be modified. This point is expanded in Chapter 3. But those are policy issues that will affect all teachers. We are primarily concerned about classroom decisions.

Effective teaching is dynamic.

We remind you that effective teaching involves dynamic interactions between and among teachers and administrators, teachers and teachers, teachers and learners, and learners and learners in which all participants are continuously making decisions—including that all-important student decision to embrace learning.

A Closing Reflection Reflection Reflection

- Organize an Internet chat room and discuss the issue of equity as you apply the concept to "inclusionary classrooms."
- Observe and shadow a teacher for one hour. How many decisions could you infer were made? Discuss your tabulations with the teacher and compare notes. Any surprises?
- Examine the educational literature for discussions relating to process vs. content. How do they compare to our presentation on the topic?
- Interview a classroom teacher to determine how technology is impacting the classroom.

Summary

1. The schools play a vital role in the acculturation of youth in our society.
2. The public schools are state-controlled institutions.
3. The culture of a school affects all those within it.
4. There is a wide range of cultures, individuals, and values to be accommodated in the public schools.
5. Each school level—elementary, middle, and high—has an accompanying set of human characteristics that tend to be unique to the attending age group.
6. The public schools have a legal commitment to provide an equal educational opportunity to all youth, regardless of ability or disability, race, or socioeconomic circumstances.
7. Technological advances will impact the delivery of instruction at all levels of schooling.
8. Decision making is a key element for effective instruction.

Key Terms

categorical school aid (p. 10)

cocurricular activities (p. 20)

declarative knowledge (p. 30)

efficacy (p. 16)

empirically (p. 13)

extrinsic motivator (p. 32)

inclusion (p. 24)

individual education plan (p. 25)

interpersonal (p. 4)

intrapersonal (p. 4)

intrinsic motivator (p. 17)

least restrictive environment (p. 25)

liaison (p. 6)

mainstreaming (p. 25)

metaphors (p. 15)

motivation (p. 32)

organizational ethos (p. 4)

organizational health (p. 14)

plenary (p. 6)

pluralism (p. 4)

prerequisite skills (p. 31)

recursive (p. 4)

regulatory agency (p. 6)

school culture (p. 12)

school ethos (p. 13)

synergistic (p. 4)

Helpful Resources

Gilbert, R. N., and M. Robins. *Welcome to Our World: Realities of High School Students.* Thousand Oaks, CA: Corwin Press, 1998, 180 pp.

This qualitative description of high school life provides a sobering reality check for any prospective teacher.

Grabe, M., and C. Grabe. *Integrating Technology for Meaningful Learning* (2nd edition). Boston: Houghton Mifflin, 1998, 440 pp.

The authors provide a truly understandable work with clear illustrations on how classroom teachers can use the full spectrum of modern technology to enhance student learning.

Purkey, W. W., and J. M. Novak. *Inviting School Success: A Self-Concept Approach to Teaching, Learning, and Democratic Practice* (3rd edition). Belmont, CA: Wadsworth, 1996, 222 pp.

This little book might be the most important statement about positive school interactions that you will ever read. We invite every middle school and high school teacher to read it.

Rose, L. C., and A. M. Gallup. *Annual Phi Delta Kappa/Gallup Poll of the Public's Attitudes Toward the Public Schools.*

In each September issue of the *Phi Delta Kappan,* a major national poll is reported. We encourage you to examine the current issue for up-to-date information.

Rubinstein, R. E. *Hints for Teaching Success in Middle School.* Englewood, CO: Teacher Ideas Press, 1994, 169 pp.

Here is a practical book on the issues facing middle school students and how you can effectively address them. High school teachers are often first hired in middle schools. There is advice here you won't get elsewhere.

Internet Resources

❖ Apple Computer's Web site provides resources for multimedia and education, including information about building a low-cost multimedia system at home or in school.

http://www.apple.com/support/

❖ The U.S. Department of Education provides an enormous listing of education-related Internet resources.

http://www.ed.gov/

❖ Two sites provide important information on developmental and age-level characteristics: the ERIC Clearinghouse on Elementary and Early Childhood Education

http://ericeece.org/

❖ and *the Adolescence Directory On-Line*

http://education.indiana.edu/cas/adol/adol.html

❖ The National Center for Research on Cultural Diversity and Second Language Learning maintains the following site:

http://lmrinet.gse.vcsb.edu/ncrcdsll/others.html

❖ The following site offers a wealth of information about the Americans with Disabilities Act and IDEA:

http://janweb.icdi.wvu.edu/kinder/

❖ The University of Kansas Special Education Department offers resources for teaching students with mental retardation or learning disabilities:

http://www.sped.ukans.edu/

❖ The National Association for the Education of Young Children (NAEYC) provides a wide range of materials and resources for educating youngsters:

http://www.naeyc.org/

References

Angus, D. L., and J. E. Mirel. *The Failed Promises of the American High School, 1890–1995.* New York: Teachers College Press, 1999.

Ball, J., and A. R. Pence. "Beyond Developmentally Appropriate Practice: Developing Community and Culturally Appropriate Practice." *Young Children* 54(2) (1999): 46–50.

Bateman, B. D. *Better IEPs: How to Develop Legally Correct and Educationally Useful Programs* (3rd edition). Longmont, CO: Sopris West, 1998.

Beck, J. *Morality and Citizenship in Education.* London: Cassell, 1998.

Bell, T. H. *The Thirteenth Man: A Reagan Cabinet Memoir.* New York: Free Press, 1988.

Berliner, D. C., and B. J. Biddle. *The Manufactured Crisis: Myth, Fraud and the Attack on America's Public Schools.* New York: Addison-Wesley, 1995.

Berman, P., P. W. Greenwood, M. W. McLaughlin, and J. Pincus. *Federal Programs Supporting Educational Change,* Vol. V: *A Summary of Findings in Review.* Santa Monica, CA: Rand Corporation, R-1589/4HEW (ABR.), 1975.

Bloom, B. S. *Stability and Change in Human Characteristics.* New York: John Wiley & Sons, 1964.

Bloom, B. S. "The 2 Sigma Problem: The Search for Methods of Group Instruction as Effective as One-to-One Tutoring." *Educational Researcher* 13(6) (1984): 4–16.

Blum, R. E., and J. A. Butler. "Managing Improvement by Profiling." *Educational Leadership* 42(6) (1985): 54–58.

Bracey, G. W. "The Fifth Bracey Report on the Condition of Public Education." *Phi Delta Kappan* 77(2) (1995): 149–160.

Bracey, G. W. "A Nation of Learners: Nostalgia and Amnesia." *Educational Leadership* 54(5) (1997): 53–57.

Bredekamp, S., editors. *Developmentally Appropriate Practice in Early Childhood Programs Serving Children from Birth Through Age 8* (revised edition).

Washington, DC: National Association for the Education of Young Children, 1997.

Buber, M. *I AND THOU*. W. Kaufman, translator. New York: Charles Scribner's Sons, 1970.

Carnegie Forum on Education and the Economy, Task Force on Teaching as a Profession. *A Nation Prepared: Teachers for the 21st Century*. New York: Carnegie Corporation, 1986.

Annie E. Casey Foundation. *National Survey of America's Families*. Baltimore, MD: Annie E. Casey Foundation, 1999.

Chance, W. *. . . the best of educations*. Chicago: The John D. and Catherine T. MacArthur Foundation, 1986. (Released in 1988 by The Education Commission of the States, Denver.)

Conant, J. B. *The American High School Today: A First Report to Interested Citizens*. New York: McGraw-Hill, 1959.

Corrigan, D. C. "Public Law 94-142: A Matter of Human Rights, A Call for Changes in Schools and Colleges of Education." In *Teacher Education: Renegotiating Roles for Mainstreaming*. J. K. Grosenich and M. C. Reynolds, editors. Reston, VA: Council for Exceptional Children, 1978.

Council for Basic Education. *What Teachers Have to Say About Teacher Education*. New York: Council for Basic Education, 1996.

Cuban, L. "Reforming Again, Again, and Again." *Educational Researcher* 19(1) (1990): 3–13.

Cuban, L. *How Teachers Taught: Constancy and Change in American Classrooms 1890–1980*. New York: Longman, 1984.

Edmonds, R. "Effective Schools for the Urban Poor." *Educational Leadership* 37 (1979): 15–27.

Ellis, J., and D. Geller. "Disciplining Handicapped Students: An Administrator's Dilemma." *NASSP Bulletin* 77(550) (1993): 22–39.

Ellis, A. K., and J. T. Fouts. *Research on Educational Innovations* (2nd edition). Larchmont, NY: Eye on Education, 1997.

Elmore, R. F., P. L. Peterson, and S. J. McCarthey. *Restructuring in the Classroom: Teaching, Learning and School Organization*. San Francisco: Jossey-Bass, 1996.

Esman, A. *Adolescence and Culture*. New York: Columbia University Press, 1990.

Essex, N. L. *School Law and the Public Schools: A Practical Guide for Educational Leaders*. Boston: Allyn and Bacon, 1999.

Etzioni, A. *The New Golden Rule*. New York: Basic Books, 1997.

Federal Register, Vol. 42. Washington, DC: U.S. Government Printing Office, August 23, 1977, pp. 42474–42515.

Fuchs, V. R., and D. M. Reklis. "America's Children: Economic Perspectives and Policy Options." *Science* 255 (3 January 1992): 41–46.

Gage, N. L. *Hard Gains in Soft Sciences: The Case of Pedagogy*. Bloomington, IN: Phi Delta Kappa, 1985.

Gemelli, R. *Normal Child and Adolescent Development*. Washington, DC: American Psychiatric Press, 1996.

George, P. S., G. Lawrence, and D. Bushnell. *Handbook for Middle School Teaching*. New York: Longman, 1998.

Giddens, A. *The Constitution of Society*. Cambridge: Polity Press, 1984.

Goodlad, J. I. *A Place Called School*. New York: McGraw-Hill, 1984.

Grabe, M., and C. Grabe. *Integrating Technology for Meaningful Learning* (2nd edition). Boston: Houghton Mifflin, 1998.

Gray, D. National School Boards Association, 1999.

Grossman, P. L. *The Making of a Teacher: Teacher Knowledge and Teacher Education*. New York: Teachers College Press, 1990.

Guskey, T. R. "Teacher Efficacy Measurement and Change." Paper presented at the American Educational Research Association, San Diego, April 13–17, 1998.

Hargreaves, A., and M. Fullan. *What's Worth Fighting for Out There?* New York: Teachers College Press, 1998.

Harris, A. "Effective Teaching: A Review of Literature." *School Leadership & Management* 18(2) (1998): 169–183.

Helmstetter, E., and C. A. Peck. "An Ethic of Caring." *Universe* 9(1) (1996): 14–15, 26.

Irwin-DeVitis, L., and J. L. DeVitis. "What Is This Work Called Teaching?" *Educational Theory* 48(2) (1998): 267–278.

Jacobs, H. H. *Mapping the Big Picture: Integrating Curriculum and Assessment K–12*. Alexandria, VA: Association for Supervision and Curriculum Development, 1997.

Katz, M. S., N. Noddings, and K. A. Strike. *Justice and Caring: The Search for Common Ground in Education*. New York: Teachers College Press, 1999.

Kaufman, P., S. Klein, and M. Frase. *Dropout Rates in the United States*. U.S. Department of Education, National Center for Educational Statistics, NCES 1999-082, March 1999.

Kelly, T. F. *Character Education: Natural Law, Human Happiness and Success*. http://www.drtomkelly.com/index.shtml 1999(a).

Kelly, T. F. "Why State Mandates Don't Work." *Phi Delta Kappan* 80(7) (1999): 543–546.(b)

Kluckhohn, C. *Mirror for Man: The Relation of Anthropology to Modern Life.* New York: Whittlesey House, 1949.

Lieberman, A., and L. Miller. *Teachers—Transforming Their World and Their Work.* New York: Teachers College Press, 1999.

Lounsbury, J. H., and D. C. Clark. *Inside Grade Eight: From Apathy to Excitement.* Reston, VA: National Association of Secondary School Principals, 1990.

Maslow, A. *Motivation and Personality* (2nd edition). New York: Harper & Row, 1970.

Mosteller, F. "The Tennessee Study of Class Size in the Early School Grades." *The Future of Children* 5(2) (1995): 113–127.

Muth, D. K., and D. E. Alvermann. *Teaching and Learning in the Middle Grades.* Boston: Allyn and Bacon, 1999.

National Commission on Excellence in Education. U.S. Department of Education. *A Nation at Risk: The Imperative for Educational Reform.* Washington, DC: National Commission on Excellence in Education, 1983.

Offer, D., and Offer, J. B. *From Teenage to Young Manhood: A Psychological Study.* New York: Basic Books, 1975.

Orlich, D. C. "The Dilemma of Strong Traditions and Weak Empiricism." *Teacher Education Quarterly* 12(1985): 23–32.

Orlich, D. C. "Social Challenges to America 2000." *The Education Digest* 59(7) (1994): 4–6.

Ornstein, A. C., and D. U. Levine. *Foundations of Education* (6th edition). Boston: Houghton Mifflin, 1997.

Purkey, W. W., and J. M. Novak. *Inviting School Success: A Self-Concept Approach to Teaching, Learning and Democratic Practice* (3rd edition). Belmont, CA: Wadsworth, 1996.

Raffini, J. P. *150 Ways to Increase Intrinsic Motivation in the Classroom.* Needham, MA: Allyn and Bacon, 1996.

Read, D. A., and S. B. Simon, editors. *Humanistic Education Sourcebook.* Englewood Cliffs, NJ: Prentice Hall, 1975.

Rosemond, J. "Above All, Teach Kids Honesty." *Spokesman-Review,* 13 September 1999, p. B3. http://www.rosemond.com/parenting.

Ryan, K., and K. E. Bohlin. *Building Character in Schools: Practical Ways to Bring Moral Instruction to Life.* San Francisco: Jossey-Bass, 1999.

Sarason, S. B. *Revisiting "The Culture of the School and the Problem of Change."* New York: Teachers College Press, 1996.

Schunk, D. H. "Goal and Self-Evaluative Influences During Children's Cognitive Skill Learning." *American Educational Research Journal* 33(2) (1998): 359–382.

Seifert, K. L., and R. J. Hoffnung. *Child and Adolescent Development* (4th edition). Boston: Houghton Mifflin, 1997.

Shulman, L. S. "Knowledge and Teaching: Foundations of the Reform." *Harvard Educational Review* 57(1) (1987): 1–22.

Smith, T. E. C., and C. A. Dowdy. "Educating Young Children with Disabilities Using Responsible Inclusion." *Childhood Education* 74(5) (1998): 317–320.

Social Context of Education. Washington, DC: Office of Educational Research and Improvement, National Center for Education Statistics, 1997 (released 1998).

Steinberg, A. *Adolescents and Schools: Improving the Fit.* Cambridge, MA: The Harvard Educational Letter, HEL No. 1, 1993.

Tyack, D. B., and L. Cuban. *Tinkering Toward Utopia: A Century of Public School Reform.* Cambridge, MA: Harvard University Press, 1995.

Ulriksen, J. J. "Perceptions of the Secondary School Teachers and Principals Concerning Factors Related to Job Satisfaction and Job Dissatisfaction." Doctoral Dissertation, Los Angeles, University of Southern California, 1996.

U.S. Department of Education. *America 2000: An Education Strategy.* Washington, DC: U.S. Government Printing Office, 1991.

U.S. Department of Education. National Center for Education Statistics. *The Condition of Education 1996.* NCES 96-304. Washington, DC: U.S. Government Printing Office, 1996.

U.S. Department of Education. National Center for Education Statistics. *The Condition of Education 1997.* NCES 97-388. Washington, DC: U.S. Government Printing Office, 1997.

U.S. Department of Education. National Center for Education Statistics. *The Condition of Education 1998.* NCES 98-013. Washington, DC: U.S. Government Printing Office, 1999.

U.S. Department of Education. Office of Educational Research and Improvement. *Goals 2000: Reforming Education to Improve Student Achievement.* Washington, DC: U.S. Government Printing Office, 1998.

U.S. Department of Education. *Mini Digest of Education Statistics 1997.* http://nces.gov. See Table 6.

U.S. Department of Education. *Mini Digest of Education Statistics 1999.* http://nces.gov. See Figure 3.

U.S. Department of Education. *Projections of Education Statistics to 2008.* http://nces.ed.gov/pubs98/. See Tables 1, B8, 34, 37, and chap. 6.

U.S. Department of Labor. *Learning a Living: A Blueprint for High Performance.* A SCANS Report for America 2000. Washington, DC: U.S. Government Printing Office, April 1992.

Waxman, H. C., and H. J. Walberg. *Effective Teaching: Current Research.* Berkeley, CA: McCutchan, 1991.

Weasmer, J., and A. M. Woods. "I Think I Can: The Role of Personal Teaching Efficacy in Bringing About Change." *Clearing House* 71(4) (1998): 245–247.

Weiner, B. *Human Motivation: Metaphors, Theories, Research.* Newbury Park, CA: Sage, 1992.

A Vision of Effective Teaching

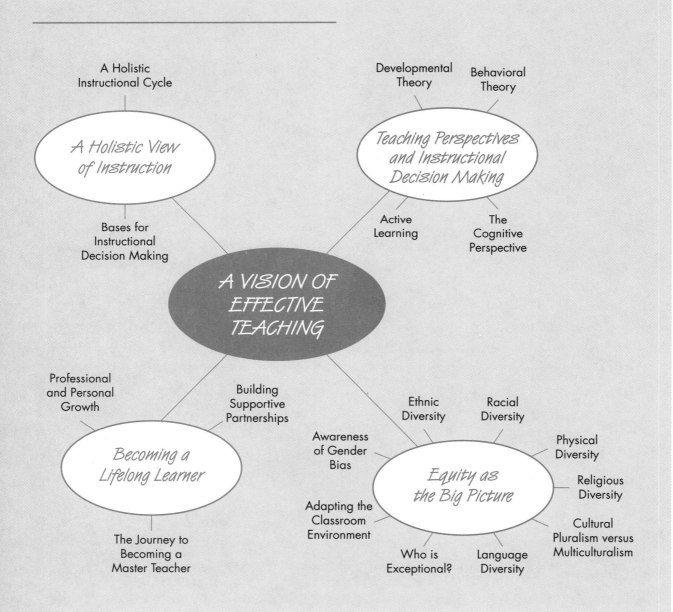

A Holistic
Instructional Cycle

*A Holistic View
of Instruction*

Bases for
Instructional
Decision Making

Developmental
Theory

Behavioral
Theory

*Teaching Perspectives
and Instructional
Decision Making*

Active
Learning

The
Cognitive
Perspective

*A VISION OF
EFFECTIVE
TEACHING*

Professional
and Personal
Growth

Building
Supportive
Partnerships

*Becoming a
Lifelong Learner*

The Journey to
Becoming a
Master Teacher

Awareness
of Gender
Bias

Adapting the
Classroom
Environment

Ethnic
Diversity

Racial
Diversity

Physical
Diversity

Religious
Diversity

*Equity as
the Big Picture*

Who is
Exceptional?

Language
Diversity

Cultural
Pluralism versus
Multiculturalism

A s Robert sat in his education class, he wondered why he was being exposed to so many different instructional and learning perspectives. Then while observing a classroom, prior to student teaching, a *gestalt-type* event took place. It became very clear to him why teachers needed to know several different learning models. Multiple instructional models and psychological theories seemingly were being applied by the master teacher that he was observing.

When Robert assumed his initial teaching position and was assigned to his own class, he had some experience, professional knowledge, and educational theory on which to base his instructional decisions. More important, as Robert planned for various lessons, he considered the "big picture" in the planning, with details unfolding in the process. As he gained more professional skills and confidence, his teaching subtly changed to incorporate newly learned ideas and practices.

In Chapter 1, you got a snapshot of the process of schooling. Now let's explore the learning frameworks and other considerations that directly impact your own instructional decision making.

As you read, think about how you would respond to the following questions:

- How do I envision a dynamic instructional cycle?
- How might learning perspectives affect my instructional decisions?
- How do I ensure instructional equity for every student?
- Will I ever learn all the "tricks of the trade"?

Section 1: A Holistic View of Instruction

A Holistic Instructional Cycle

As Robert realized in this chapter's opener, dynamic instruction is viewed as a *grand picture,* not simply a linear sketch. Thus, we begin with the notion that several elements of instruction are envisioned and then the discrete parts are identified. This is the notion of a **holistic instructional view.** Our view implies that as a teacher, you simultaneously shift back and forth from the big picture that you have for your students to the specific parts that you want mastered.

For example, this textbook emphasizes the procedural, or technical, aspects of instruction. Taken collectively, all ten chapters interact with the attitudinal and psychological components of teaching plus that all-important learner. Figure 2.1 attempts to illustrate this phenomenon.

Bases for Instructional Decision Making

Observe the dynamic interaction that takes place between the four elements in Figure 2.1. Each element informs the others.

Even though you are systematic in your approaches to instruction, you must still respond flexibly and effectively to the numerous on-the-spot decisions that you make during every instructional activity. For example, when

FIGURE 2.1

A Holistic Model of Instruction

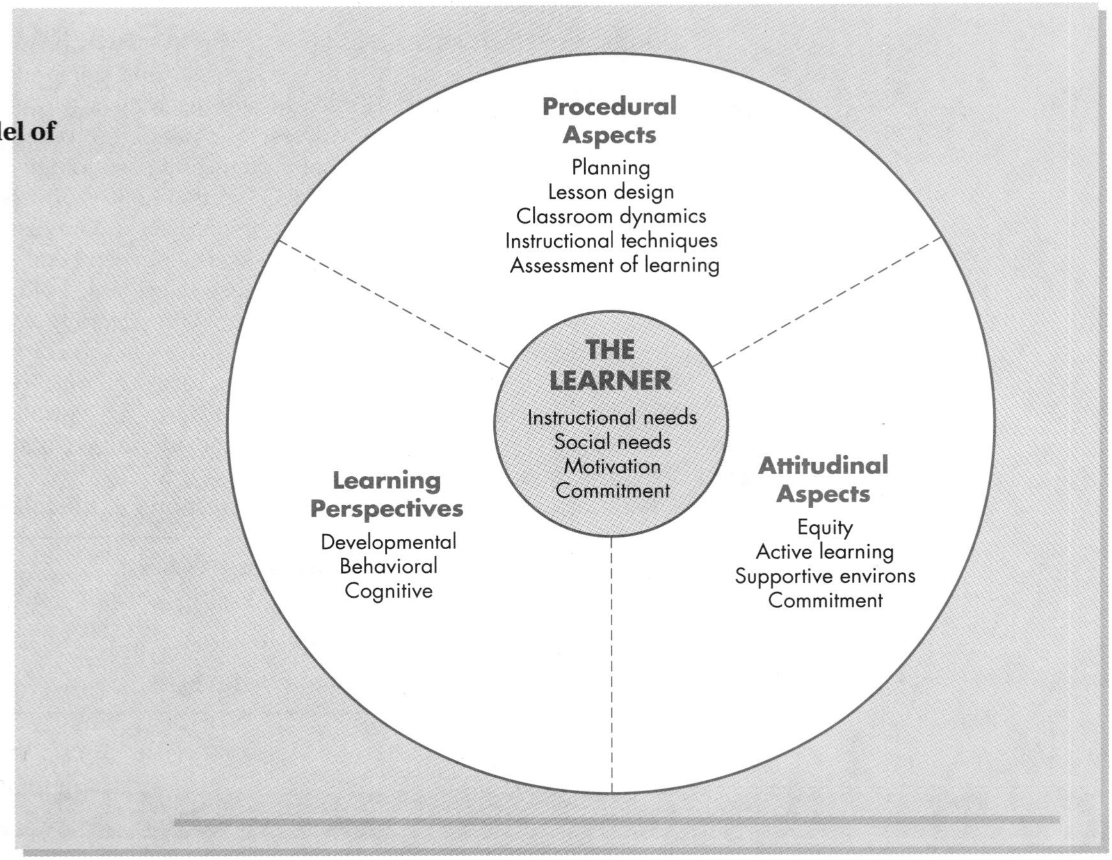

Procedural Aspects

Planning
Lesson design
Classroom dynamics
Instructional techniques
Assessment of learning

THE LEARNER

Instructional needs
Social needs
Motivation
Commitment

Learning Perspectives

Developmental
Behavioral
Cognitive

Attitudinal Aspects

Equity
Active learning
Supportive environs
Commitment

you begin a new unit of instruction, you want to establish some common experience for the entire class.

You might decide to show a video or take the class to the computer center to "surf the net." Then after making this decision, you ask yourself, "What purpose does this introductory activity have to do with the lesson as a whole?" You also ask yourself what big ideas you are trying to stress in this unit. You actually conduct a "self-brainstorming episode." Or you might be working with a team of teachers and as a group you'll brainstorm ideas. The main point is that you try to envision the entire teaching scenario before you ever begin teaching it.

In addition, you need to consider the learning perspective from which you might approach either the entire class or subgroups within the class. You also need to consider the content to be learned. The easy part of teaching is to cover content. The hard part is deciding what is to be covered (or deleted), how fast, by whom, and to what degree of depth. Additionally, you'll have to decide what assignments are to be made and how many different informational sources will be assigned, including the Internet. If the latter, then you need to reserve the computer center or make a schedule for sharing those three computers assigned to your classroom. Granted, these are not decisions

---

Holistic Instructional Considerations

- What is the instructional purpose or goal?
- Who are the learners?
- How will content be covered?
- What management decisions are required?
- What techniques or processes do I use?
- How will responsibilities be shared?
- What instructional resources do we have?
- What special student considerations must be made?
- How is instructional equity ensured?
- How is the learning assessed?

---

of great pith and moment, but they need to be considered within a holistic vision before you begin the unit. In the box above, we list some of the big picture considerations that you must make to be an effective instructor.

By thinking about several instructional aspects at once, you actually complete a holistic picture. That is, you are considering variables that can affect both your teaching and the students' learning. Further, such vision planning helps you to be more organized and systematic. As this chapter unfolds, you'll realize how the interaction of theory and practice are complementary to all teaching acts.

In Figure 2.1, you can visualize the continual interaction between and among the four key elements and all of the subelements. Obviously, the learner and the learner's needs are always at the center of this model. It is for the learner that you use different instructional techniques. The learners' successes help to create the conditions by which all the elements coalesce. As you progress through this textbook, you will be provided with in-depth coverage on the principal procedural components of Figure 2.1. Although we briefly address the psychological and attitudinal elements, other courses will provide you with in-depth coverage of these topics. And the reason you chose to be a teacher is to work with learners—of all ages.

Now let us examine three major theoretical perspectives as they apply to teaching.

Reflect Reflect Reflect

- Sketch out an application of a holistic idea for an area in which you anticipate teaching.
- Gather a few peers and discuss the various interactions that appear to take place in classrooms.

From your study of educational psychology, you know that there are several learning theories or perspectives that can guide teaching and learning. We will briefly introduce here three perspectives that tend to have a great impact on what is taught and how it is presented: the *developmental, behavioral,* and *cognitive* perspectives. The specific teaching strategies that you decide to use will probably be based on one of these three or on an **eclectic** model—one that borrows or mixes approaches. Our treatment here will be very general, focusing on how learning theories apply to instructional strategies. You can refer to a standard educational psychology text for more detailed information about each theory.

Developmental Theory

Piaget's Developmental Stages   A very popular teaching and learning model is the *developmental* approach, most often associated with Jean Piaget (1896–1980). This model assumes that humans evolve intellectually in various overlapping stages. In Piaget's model (1969), there are four stages or periods of development—the **sensorimotor stage,** from birth to two years; the **preoperational stage,** from two to eight years; the **concrete operational stage,** from eight to eleven years; and the **formal stage,** from eleven to fifteen years and up. The last stage is what schools attempt to reach, what we loosely call the thinking and analyzing stage. However, the bulk of students in middle and high school are still at the concrete operational stage, and thus they require many illustrations, models, pictures, and activities. Again, we deliberately simplify this model for purposes of introduction; we assume that you have studied or will study this theory in depth in other teacher education classes.

Piaget's stages are not fixed but overlap.

The developmental stages in Piaget's model are not fixed for any one individual or group; instead, they tend to overlap. In the middle school grades, for example, you will find a wide range of developmental levels, from students who are not yet in the early concrete operational stage to students who have already reached the formal stage. High school students also show a range of mental development. Additionally, the developmental stages are not uniformly attained for different academic disciplines: an individual might be at the formal stage in the social sciences but only at the concrete stage in mathematics.

For intellectual growth to occur, teachers must provide students with key experiences or activities. We will return to this point under Implications of Developmental Theory for Instructional Decision Making, below.

Vygotsky's Socially Mediated Learning   A popular learning theory that has emerged in the domain of the language arts is one proposed by Lev Vygotsky (1896–1934). (You'll see his name spelled Vygotskii sometimes.) His **schema,** or model, of intellectual growth centers not on developmental stages but on what he terms the **zone of proximal development** and on patterns of social interaction (Vygotsky 1962).

The zone of proximal development is the difference between the intellectual level a child can reach on his or her own and the level he or she can potentially reach if aided by an expert peer or adult. How do you know where a given child's zone falls? You find out somewhat by trial and error. When your instruction is appropriate for the child's zone, learning occurs rather rapidly. Instruction outside the zone is not effective.

There are no maturation levels such as those implied by Piaget's stages of growth. If a child does not learn some concept, according to Piaget's theory, the child was not developmentally ready. For a Vygotskian, the instruction was outside the child's zone of proximal development.

The second aspect of Vygotsky's theory is that learning has a social quality. As a child listens to a discussion, the child can think along. Eventually, the child **internalizes** the ideas and can then work individually. Social interaction is a key to learning.

The role of social interaction is important to Vygotsky's model.

Implications of Developmental Theory for Instructional Decision Making

In Piaget's theory, two concepts for instructional effectiveness are critical: age and individual appropriateness (see Adey and Shayer 1994; Bredekamp 1997). If you subscribe to Piaget's stages of growth, then you will attempt to find age-appropriate materials. That means for grade 3 you need materials that can be mastered by nine- or ten-year-olds. The same ideal would apply to instructing sixteen-year-old high school sophomores.

As a Piagetian, you would first introduce some activity that has learning value. After the children had experienced the activity, you would label the concept being taught so that your students could understand the experience and the formal term together. For example, if you were teaching the concept of time zones, you might show students a map of the USA and tell them what time it is in various cities. Then you would have the children come to some conclusion about what happens to times as you move from east to west or vice versa. Once students had gained some more experience with this exercise, you would label the zones Eastern, Central, Rocky Mountain, and Pacific. The learning experience must be age appropriate. One of your authors taught time zones to seventh graders in this way and they did not quite master it, but by the eighth grade they could compute the time in Boston given the time in San Francisco.

How would you approach the time zone lesson using Vygotsky's model? First, you would assess your students' zone of proximal development to determine whether introducing the concept would be worthwhile or futile. In the early primary grades, for example, you can teach children how to tell time, but the concept of time zones is simply beyond their zone of proximal development. No matter how hard you might try to teach the concept, the children would not understand it.

But if the children were ready, say by the sixth or seventh grade, you would probably divide the class into small discussion groups and provide each team with maps, markers, and time information for various cities. The groups would be actively and socially involved in trying to visualize some pattern related to times. Finally, with your help, one group would come to the conclusion that there are four distinct time zones in the continental USA.

Theories can guide
instructional practice.

Each group would share this finding. Finally, each learner would understand the concept on an individual basis.

But suppose two students still could not solve time zone problems alone. What would you do then? You would continue the social interaction aspect by assigning peer tutors to the students who had not mastered the time zone concept and hope that further social interaction would complete the learning cycle.

There is much more detail to these theories, especially for Vygotsky's as it pertains to the psychosocial development of adolescents. This group tends to enter a traumatic period between twelve and sixteen years of age. We refer you to the seminal work by Erik Erikson, *The Life Cycle Completed* (1982), in which he discusses the various interpersonal and intrapersonal crises that emerge for adolescents.

Reflect Reflect Reflect

- Prepare a chart that illustrates the key elements of Piaget's and Vygotsky's theories. Where are they different? Where are they similar?
- Examine a school district curriculum guide for some selected grade level. Do you find terms such as *developmental* or *age appropriate* in the guide?

Behavioral Theory

A Brief Description   According to the **behavioral perspective,** learning can be defined as an observable change in behavior. The modern behavioral movement was initiated by B. F. Skinner (1938), who coined the term **operant conditioning.** This term is an adaptation of the stimulus-response concept long known in psychology. However, if you use operant conditioning, you control the stimulus that follows a given response. For example, if a student answers a difficult question correctly, then you immediately give the student some praise or even a new pencil. You are then positively reinforcing the student for appropriate behavior.

Using operant conditioning, or **behavior modification,** usually requires some kind of reward system. Rewards can be extrinsic, such as passes for free time, small gifts, or tokens that can be collected and converted into a prize. They can also be intrinsic—the pleasure received from meeting a challenge or learning something new.

Behaviorism is a very complex model, with many ramifications and applications to life outside of education. So we will focus on just one more element of the theory—**transfer of learning.** This term refers to the act of applying something learned in some specific situation to a novel or new setting. For example, you have just completed instruction on ratios. One of your students comes up to you and says, "Do you realize it is cheaper per ounce to buy a twenty-ounce bottle of soda pop than a ten-ounce bottle?" You ask the student to tell you more. The student then shows how by setting up ratios to determine per-ounce costs, the relative unit values can be computed. You smile! (We will discuss this technique in detail, as it relates to behavioral management, in Chapter 6.)

Direct Instruction When you apply behavioral theory to instruction, you will find yourself establishing specific learning objectives and building a sequence of learning activities that proceed from simple to more complex. More than likely you will adopt a teaching model that is called **direct instruction** (see Carnine 1993). This model has its foundations embedded in behavioral principles. It is a popular technique, and we illustrate it here as an application of the behavioral perspective.

Direct instruction relies on the application of behavioral principles.

Direct instruction is often called "whole group" or "teacher-led" instruction. Basically, the technique involves academic focus, provides few optional choices for student-initiated activities, tends to be large-group oriented, and tends to emphasize factual knowledge. In response to those who have criticized direction instruction as being oriented toward rote learning, one study showed that elementary school pupils taught via direct instruction showed progress in the higher-order intellectual areas associated with problem solving (Elliot and Shapiro 1990). A review of the research indicates that direct instruction does transfer skills across a broad range of learners and subject

Direct instruction is not a rigid, low-level instructional model.

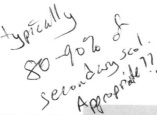 *typically 80-90% of secondary scl. Appropriate??*

focus of course, use as base to emply other models

Instructional Strategies

Direct Instruction

Strengths of Direct Instruction

- Content delivered to entire class
- Teacher controls focus of attention
- Process maximizes available time
- Feedback assesses class understanding of learning
- Teacher focuses on class objectives
- Teacher provides clarity through explanations
- Less teacher preparation required
- All students work on some task

Steps of Direct Instruction

1. Review and check previous work.
2. Present new material in small units.
3. Provide for guided practice.
4. Provide for feedback and correctives.
5. Supervise independent seat work.
6. Review concepts every week and every month.

areas (Adams and Engelmann 1996). The technique is used to increase on-task learning time, thinking skills, problem solving, computer literacy, writing skills, and science learning.

Barak Rosenshine summarized steps for using the technique effectively (Rosenshine and Meister 1995). These steps and the strengths of the system are listed in the box on page 49.

Programmed Instruction   When you use computer-assisted instruction, the basic learning theory supporting the technique is grounded in the behaviorist concept of **programmed instruction.** That technique provides for small, discrete increments of instruction plus immediate reinforcement for correct responses. When you use lessons that are subdivided into achievable components or modules, you use behavioral principles. We will expand on these topics in Chapters 3 and 4.

Reflect Reflect Reflect

- Examine your own educational experiences. What types of instruction were closely associated with behavioral principles?
- Seek information on behaviorally constructed programs, such as the popular DISTAR.

The Cognitive Perspective

Cognitive science is applied in various learning and teaching strategies.

Cognitive Psychology   We have briefly explored selected aspects of the developmental and behavioral theoretical perspectives that will affect your instructional decision making. We want to provide you with a framework for analyzing any instructional model or curriculum to discover its theoretical basis. You can then align your teaching methods with the content, thereby helping your students be more successful learners.

Over the past several years, a school of thought has emerged that we label **cognitive psychology.** The goal of this model is to develop student academic and thinking skills from a novice level to a more expert level. Obviously, it takes maturity and time for this transition to occur. One way to help it along is to teach students how to think about thinking and how to make plans to learn new information more efficiently.

A second major goal of cognitive psychology advocates is to provide adequate experiences in which students structure the learning and teaching themselves. Obviously, students will need to have access to knowledge, know how to organize it, and be self-motivated to learn. The box on page 51 gives a quick overview of the cognitive model (from Ashman and Conway 1993).

Cognitive Teaching Tips   As you examine the list in the box on page 51, you will undoubtedly note that some of these principles overlap with those of other learning theories. Further, you might even infer that school environments play a major role in motivating students to become active learners. Yes,

Instructional	Selected Principles of the Cognitive Model of Instruction
Strategies	■ Students engage in active learning and problem solving.
	■ Students use a wide range of learning strategies.
	■ Time is allocated for students to apply new skills.
	■ Responsibility for learning and problem solving is transferred from teacher to student.
	■ Strategies to be learned by students are clearly specified.
	■ Rate of student learning is determined by the teacher.
	■ Teacher is responsible for instructional decisions.

they do, and there are some interactive elements in all learning theories. But what strategies should you use to incorporate cognitive ideas into your teaching? Let's just list a few that are used in **processing information.**

The first process is one called **mnemonics**—the use of some memory-aiding device. A mnemonic device commonly used in mathematics is "Please Excuse My Dear Aunt Sally," which reminds students that in algebraic operations the correct order is Parentheses, Exponents, Multiply, Divide, Add, Subtract. Surely you have used mnemonic devices to remember a series or chain of events.

A second strategy is to create charts or time lines. Enter a middle school history class, and you will probably see a time line skirting the entire perimeter of the classroom. This helps students visually place historical events into order.

Observe the beginning of each chapter in this book, where we provide a concept map. This tool is an information-processing device to help you learn and remember what each chapter covers.

Visualizing is a method often used in physical education. Participants try to understand just how they will dance, run a course, take a turn on a ski hill, or complete some game strategy. Visualization techniques are also very helpful when a student is setting up laboratory equipment or in solving a multi-step problem. Remember, it is your responsibility to teach your students how to use these cognitive devices. Kids do not come preprogrammed.

We will expand on the concept of planning in Chapters 4 and 5, where we provide a series of models that fit our theme of multiple methodologies. Then, in Chapter 9, we will illustrate several methods by which to stimulate and apply problem-solving skills. But this is a good point to introduce student-initiated learning.

Student-initiated learning assumes social responsibility on the part of each learner.

Learner-Activated Instruction   One of the more difficult tasks you will face as a teacher is to structure your classroom in a way that will let your students initiate learning on their own. A major set of decisions that you will continuously make during your teaching career concerns instructional control. At one end of the instructional spectrum (see the box on p. 52) is

---

The Spectrum of Instructional Control

Student-Initiated Learning ◄--------► Direct Instruction (Teacher Initiated)

---

student-initiated learning, where students determine how to reach the desired learning outcomes. A classroom that uses student-initiated learning will be a maze of activity: small groups, working groups, and individuals working on projects or activities simultaneously. There is little sequencing of instruction, and the teacher can be observed moving about the room acting as a prompter, question asker, clarifier—in short, a facilitator of learning.

At the other end is teacher-initiated instruction, or direct instruction, which we have already introduced. In this mode you will find an academic focus, little choice of activity for individual students, large-group instruction, and teacher domination over most curricular and instructional decisions. Table 2.1 contrasts these two approaches. The table is included for comparison purposes only; actual practice may be quite different.

Obviously, there are many more facets to these two models of instructional control. That is where you come in. You make the decisions, for the most part, concerning how to structure the content and the processes by which it is delivered. Clearly, you need to examine several models of instruction. You need to identify the key features and relative strength of each model. We have already played our hand—we strongly support using as many different instructional techniques or methods as possible. Why? Because it helps you make decisions deliberately about the best instructional practice for any given content or student need, it helps you involve students actively, and it helps you choose the best level of instructional control for the situation at hand (see Silberman 1996; Stover, Neubert, and Lawlor 1993).

Constructivist Theory and Practice   Constructivist philosophy, which has evolved over the last half of the twentieth century, is a subset of the cognitive

TABLE 2.1

Student-Initiated Instruction Versus Direct Instruction	
Student-Initiated Instruction	**Direct Instruction**
Flexibly arranged furniture	Somewhat fixed arrangements
Emphasis on individual or small group work	Delivery to entire class
Teacher as facilitator	Teacher as controller
Little concern about time	Time used efficiently
Varied assessments	Prompt delivery of feedback
Emphasis on exploration	Emphasis on fundamentals
Flexible classroom structure	Tight classroom structure
Simultaneous activities	All students on same task
Time-consuming preparation	Preparation time minimal

SOURCE: Adapted from Kohn 1996.

Instructional Strategies

Tenets of Modern Social Constructivism

- Learning is dependent on the prior conceptions the learner brings to the experience.
- The learner must construct his or her own meaning.
- Learning is contextual.
- Learning is dependent on the shared understandings learners negotiate with others.
- Effective teaching involves understanding students' existing cognitive structures and providing appropriate learning activities to assist them.
- Teachers can utilize one or more key strategies to facilitate conceptual change, depending on the congruence of the concepts with student understanding and conceptualization.
- The key elements of conceptual change can be addressed by specific teaching methods.
- Greater emphasis should be placed on "learning how to learn" than on accumulating facts. In terms of content, less is more.

[handwritten marginalia: students responsible for own learning; active learning; "physically building; knowledge; "symbolically; "socially; "theoretically; "don't forget objective/outcome"]

perspective. As educators and others begin to seek a more student-centered instructional model, they tend to be drawn toward what might be called the social-constructivist camp. Current thinking is summarized in the box above (Anderson et al. 1994).

Let us very briefly amplify the above assumptions. Now, keep in mind that our discussion here is of pure or theoretical constructivism; what you find in actual practice will cover an entire spectrum, including limited use, selected use, mixed use, and even inappropriate use of the concept. Constructivism is not a monolithic philosophy or methodology—it encompasses a range of beliefs and pedagogical approaches (Davis, Masher, and Noddings 1990).

Prior Experience　The foundation of the constructivist model is the idea that learners bring with them prior knowledge and beliefs. Learning builds on what learners have already constructed in other contexts.

Personal Construction of Meaning　Another hallmark of the model is that learners must construct what they learn. For example, just giving students vocabulary exercises in science and social studies may not result in their assimilating those concepts. The model calls for learners to be active. Rote memorization is antagonistic to the constructivist. However, learners can construct and use memorization strategies on their own. For example, constructivists hold that children can understand multiplication tables at once if they see them as arrays.

Contextual and Shared Learning　The constructivist model requires concrete experiences rather than abstract presentations. In addition, learners

Social constructivists stress active learning in a socially interactive environment.

deepen their knowledge by shared experiences. Cooperative learning and discussions are key strategies (see Chapter 8).

Changing Roles for Teachers and Learners   In the constructivist model, learners and teachers learn from each other. Teachers look for signals from learners so that they may facilitate understanding. The teacher is not perceived as the sole authority; rather, the teacher facilitates learning, guiding and supporting learners' own construction of knowledge.

Active Learning

At this point you probably have many questions about the three theoretical perspectives and their approaches to instruction. For example, how should you structure your classroom? Will there be active learning? What roles will you play? Let's address each of those points.

Regardless of your theoretical orientation, you will probably structure your classroom to enhance interaction between you and your students. You will likely set up a cheerful, inviting classroom, covering the walls with student work and posters appropriate for your class. Think of your classroom as a place for work. Yes, we strongly believe that school is the work of youth. And if you stress pride in work, you will get it. In Chapters 6 and 8, we amplify this discussion about structuring the classroom.

Active learning requires the use of many different teaching techniques.

Along the same lines, you must master many different teaching strategies. If you are to encourage active learning, then you need to know how to organize, plan, and conduct lessons according to different methods. By doing so you will help every student achieve success, since the use of multiple methods will help you address a variety of learning styles. There is much to consider when making instructional decisions. Our goal has been to elevate your initial thoughts on the topic to a higher level.

Snapshots of Reality   Up to now we have considered the teacher's role as decision maker in the context of the classroom setting and several theories of learning. Most significantly, we have proposed a hybrid model of instruction that views the teacher as an artist. We have shown that regardless of the setting or the philosophical orientation of the lesson, the teacher's role in using multimethodology is key to active learning. We turn now to a brief survey of several

Reflect Reflect Reflect

- What resources and skills would you need to implement student-initiated learning?
- What conclusions can you draw from empirical studies about the cognitive achievements of students schooled in student-initiated, direct-instruction, and constructivist classes?
- How can you make your teaching style active yet maintain academic rigor?

contemporary descriptions of schooling. Our purpose here is to show you the important impact your decisions will have on your students' behavior.

In *A Place Called School*, John I. Goodlad (1984) and his research team reported on a series of feeder schools. (A feeder school is a school, such as an elementary or middle school, that "feeds" students into another school, such as a high school.) The study provides a snapshot of a twelve-year progression of schooling, addressing a series of issues that impinge on the schools: teacher preparation, instruction, curricula, leadership, research, and the entry age of students. In 1970, C. E. Silberman said the schools of America exhibited a "mindlessness"; Goodlad said American classrooms displayed a "flatness." Goodlad found that most teachers spent the bulk of their time handling routine matters and that whole-group instruction was the predominant form of teaching. Of importance to us is Goodlad's description of the instructional techniques used. At any given time, a teacher has a wide array of methods by which to approach an instructional objective or activity. But Goodlad and his associates found that only elementary school teachers tended to use many of the available techniques, whereas the high school teachers they observed primarily used only lectures, written work assignments, testing, and quizzing. Teacher domination of the class was strikingly evident in the fact that teachers out talked the entire class by a ratio of three to one! Such teachers surely are not using interactive or discussion techniques.

In the box below, we summarize the top four instructional activities that Goodlad and his associates observed.

Goodlad's Top Reported Activities (1984)

- Written work
- Listening to explanations/lectures
- Preparing for assignments
- Practice/performance

To compare the Goodlad's findings directly is not empirically possible; however, in 1999 the U.S. Department of Education released the findings of a national survey of teachers in K–12 schools providing us with some *rough* comparative data. Table 2.2 lists the findings in four general areas: grouping, instructional practices, instructional materials, and instructional technologies used.

There appear to be similarities in that teachers still tend to use whole-group instructional practices and tend to use lectures and teacher-led recitations most frequently.

In yet one other report released in 1999 by the Third International Mathematics and Science Study (TIMSS), there tended to be a flatness of instructional methods in American schools. The most depressing finding was that "in the judgment of independent mathematics and mathematics education experts, none of the U.S. lessons evaluated in the TIMSS videotape study was considered to contain a high-quality sequence of mathematical ideas,

TABLE 2.2

Nationally Reported Activities

Grouping
- Whole group instruction
- Small-group work
- Individual projects

Instructional Practices
- Teacher lectures
- Teacher whole-group presentations
- Teacher-led recitations
- Student-led recitations

Instructional Materials
- Textbooks
- Supplemental exercises

Instructional Technologies
- Chalkboard and overhead projector
- Instructional manipulatives
- Computers, videos, electronic media

SOURCE: U.S. Department of Education 1999a, Tables 2, 3, 4, and 5, pp. 13–19.

compared to 39 percent of the Japanese lessons and 28 percent of German lessons" (U.S. Department of Education 1999a, p. 6).

Your vision for teaching is important.

The Alternative: Interactive Strategies   These data are not provided to dishearten you but as a reality check against which you can compare your teaching culture and environment. Obviously, many teachers have not yet embraced active learning or the learning perspectives discussed previously. Schooling doesn't have to be "flat." Teachers make the classroom exciting. Teachers set the stage for active, productive scholarship; whether it is fourth-grade social studies or the senior honors English class. We restate our topic in question form: Where were the holistic visions of educators in the studies we noted? Obviously, the visions were apparently of passive learning by passive learners.

By contrast, in this book, you will be provided with many of the interactive teaching strategies that are recommended by national groups such as the National Board for Professional Teaching Standards and the Educational Testing Service (see Danielson 1996). In the box on page 57, we illustrate just a few techniques that create an active learning classroom environment. These will be developed in depth in the remaining chapters of our book.

The national standards, which we will introduce in Chapter 3, require interactive classrooms where high educational expectations are the norm. (We could wax eloquently on this, but it is a topic for another book.) So we leave perspectives of learning and move to a critically important socioeducational issue: equity.

A Baker's Dozen Examples of Active
Learning Strategies

- Cooperative learning groups
- Inquiry-oriented activities
- Teacher demonstrations
- Teacher–student joint planning
- Use of hands-on, minds-on activities
- Use of internet resources
- Use of instructional manipulatives
- Small-group discussions
- Student-conducted demonstrations
- Student-initiated projects
- Student portfolios
- Student presentations of work
- Student self-evaluations

Reflect Reflect Reflect

- Reexamine Table 2.2. Do you observe any distinct instructional trends?
- To what extent are your own schooling experiences reflected in Table 2.2 or in the "Baker's Dozen" box?

Section 3: Equity as the Big Picture

The past two decades have seen a rise in the volume and rhetoric of arguments, pro and con, concerning diversity, multiculturalism, and other emerging social issues. No one is arguing that the racial and ethnic makeup of the United States and its schools is not diverse. However, the proper educational approach to take in light of this diversity is an issue that is subject to debate, and a heated debate it is. As a future teacher, you will need to weigh in on this debate and consider various viewpoints. Awareness of student diversity is an important element of responsive instructional decision making. As Arthur M. Schlesinger, Jr., so ably stated, "Our public schools in particular have been the great instruments of assimilation and the great means of forming an American identity. What students are taught in schools affects the way they will thereafter see and treat other Americans, the way they will thereafter conceive the purposes of the republic. The debate about the curriculum is a debate about what it means to be an American" (Schlesinger 1993, p. 17).

Our nation's diversity is its most compelling strength and also its greatest challenge.

The diversity of our students is our most compelling strength and also our greatest challenge. Until our educational institutions evolve a strategy for maximizing the potential of all our youth, regardless of gender, race, ethnicity, or disabilities, we will have a country of "haves and have-nots." This is an institutional challenge; in the meantime, teachers can make a difference on a personal level.

It is essential that you first understand clearly the many factors that will contribute to diversity in your classroom. During the 1995–96 school year, for example, 33 percent of the students in U.S. central-city schools (grades K–12) were African American, and 25 percent were Hispanic. Of all children aged eight to fifteen in U.S. schools, almost 8 percent speak a language other than English at home. And of the children who speak a language other than English at home, approximately one-third test below their normal grade level on standardized tests (National Center for Education Statistics 1998, Indicator 43).

Should school curricula promote unity or exalt differences?

The United States is an amalgam of many diverse ethnic, language, racial, and religious groups. Further diversity results from the broad spectrum of

Inclusive classrooms welcome all learners.
© Evan/Johnson/Jeroboam.

physical characteristics in the population (physical characteristics include gender, disabilities, physical dimensions, and traits). This diversity makes it difficult to define "an American culture." While the people of the United States may have a common root language and many shared values, we are truly a culturally plural society. As a society, we have both commonalities and differences; we are similar in some ways and different in many others. The question you will have to face as a teacher is this: should the selection of instructional objectives and teaching strategies promote unity or exalt differences? Or should it do both?

Lest you conclude that diversity is a concern only for central-city schools, let's examine a bit of data from a small rural community in Washington State with a K–12 student enrollment of 529. There are ninety-two Russian-Ukranian students, eighty-nine Hispanic students, twelve Native American students, and four Asian students, accounting for 37 percent of the district's students. With the exception of the Native American students, English is not the language any of these students speak at home.

One of our goals in this section is to broaden the scope of discussion on diversity. Accordingly, we address not just ethnicity and race but also language diversity, physical diversity, regional diversity, and religious diversity. Although we address these different facets of diversity as distinct topics, it is important to recognize their overlapping nature. *Caveat emptor,* we focus on the concept of **equity** as being all encompassing. We realize that each topic in Section 3 has several books devoted to it, full courses taught in schools of education, and even areas of graduate specialization. However, we present the topics only to establish an overview of them. Our rationale is explained in Section 4.

Ethnic Diversity

An ethnic population is a group of people classed according to common traits, customs, or social views (Gollnick and Chinn 1990). Common ethnic traits include heritage, values, and rituals. *Heritage* refers to inherited cultural

---

Instructional **Strategies**

Incorporating Students' Ethnic Heritage into Instruction

- Discuss diverse ethnic groups' heritage, values, and rituals.
- Use local representatives of ethnic groups as resources and role models for achievement, demonstration, and explanation.
- Incorporate activities and materials that reflect local traditions and appropriately augment the more traditional curriculum.
- Acknowledge and affirm each student's unique ethnic background and show how it adds to our national character and unity.
- Discuss different ethnic groups' participation in historical events and provide literature that illustrates different ethnic groups' heritage, values, and rituals.

models for housing, foods, clothing, music, family structure, and education. Values include group behavioral norms, ethics, religious beliefs, and commonly held attitudes. An ethnic group's rituals frequently include aspects of festivals, dance, sports, medicine, and religion.

Within an ethnic group, values, rituals, and heritage are intertwined and interdependent.

The challenge you face is to join a concern for ethnic diversity on the one hand with an equal concern for academic and social norms on the other. The educator's task is to provide a developmentally appropriate instructional program that values diversity while fostering achievement. The box on page 59 provides a few ideas for incorporating students' ethnic heritage into your instructional plans.

The essence of ethnic inclusion is to stress that America is built on a foundation of diverse participation and contributions. Examinations of the roles of diverse ethnic groups in American history and culture should provide a critical review of both positive and negative impacts.

Racial Diversity

There is great diversity within each racial group in the United States, just as there is great diversity within the larger society.

Although race is the most recognizable element of diversity, it is frequently the most misunderstood. "In the United States, a race is frequently defined as a group of individuals who share certain physical or biological traits, particularly phenotype (skin color), body structure and facial features" (Marable 1991, p. 179). Race is too often defined narrowly, in terms of skin pigmentation and hair and eye coloring. Scientific research has shown that a broad spectrum of physical characteristics are found within all so-called racial groupings; thus certain physical characteristics do not necessarily define a race or racial membership (see Levine and Havighurst 1989, for an elaboration). Likewise, the ethnic and cultural diversity within each racial group is as broad as the ethnic and cultural diversity within the broader society. Diversity in physical traits, ethnic background, and culture crosses all racial boundaries (Seligman 1992).

However, members of specific racial groups *do* have distinct experiences in society and common perceptions of it, and this is where racial difference has an impact on the schools. Much of this difference can be accounted for by

Instructional Strategies

Working Toward Racial Unity in the Schools

- Encourage parental participation and responsibility within the institutional framework of the schools.
- Open channels of communication among schools, communities, and parents that encourage the use of programs aimed at improving family stability and achievement for all racial groups.
- Help all students to participate in class activities.
- Discuss with students the economic risks of dropping out of school.
- Provide short- and long-term instructional plans that stress academic success for all students.

Educational achievement is influenced by economic and social factors.

history, economics, and environment. Research has demonstrated that educational achievement is influenced by economic and social factors: a stable family; educated parents; and a higher household income are clear predictors of educational success (Erhlich and Feldman 1977, p. 123). In the United States, racial minorities have often been denied these advantages.

While the definition of race may face continued debate, the implications of race for our classrooms is clear; our schools have the obligation to find the best methods and materials to achieve the best result for *all* students. You can suggest adaptations to the school curriculum that reflect the racial identity of all your students and the historical and literary contributions that have been made by members of all races. To create a positive educational environment that promotes racial unity, consider the points in the box on page 60. (See also James A. Banks, 1997b.)

Physical Diversity

While great attention has been paid to gender and racial discrimination in recent years, relatively little attention has been given to the **physical diversity** of the population and to discrimination based on physical characteristics. People do lose jobs, find career and social opportunities limited, and feel a general lack of societal acceptance due to various physical attributes (Portman and Carlson 1991). The elements of physical diversity include age, sex, physical condition, physical attributes, and physical impairments and disabilities.

Our society is extremely conscious of physical diversity and clearly labels some characteristics desirable and others undesirable.

Our society is extremely conscious of people's physical attributes. Newspapers and magazines offer advertisements for hair transplants, body sculpting, weight reduction, contact lenses, shoe lifts, and skin toners and lighteners. All these offers are aimed at helping the individual cope with societal expectations and prejudices (see Russell, Wilson, and Hall 1992). These prejudices are very real. In the schools they may be directed at students who

- Are physically disabled or have physical symptoms of a mental disability
- Are obese or have acne
- Are more physically mature or immature than their peers
- Possess uncommon physical attributes such as premature balding, unusual hair color, extremely small or large stature, or an unusual voice

In Chapter 1 we discussed federal laws that seek to protect the rights of the physically diverse and disabled. Your job is to ensure that all students have equal access to instruction and essential services and that discrimination based on physical attributes and other characteristics is not tolerated.

Religious Diversity

The students who attend public schools do not park their religious beliefs and practices outside the schoolhouse door. While the practice of religion is a protected right in private schools, for the public schools religion is a walk on a tightrope. The place of religion in the schools is regulated by the Constitution and the Supreme Court's interpretation of it (Bates 1993). As a public school teacher, you must respect the separation of church and state. You may not proselytize for your denomination or ridicule other religions. The religious diversity of your community provides an excellent opportunity for you to teach respect and tolerance of personal beliefs.

The observance of religious holidays is commonplace in our society and in our schools. The winter break for some is the Christmas holiday season for others. We see no problem in discussing, as is appropriate, the various Christian, Jewish, Islamic, and other major religious holidays as they occur. This is diversity.

Reflect Reflect Reflect

■ Our calendar is the product of a Roman emperor and a Roman Catholic pope. It may surprise many that other calendars designed around religious observances and events exist. This might be one way of showing that religious celebrations are defined through different calendar systems. Contact the Smithsonian Institution or the Library of Congress to obtain information about other calendars. Respect and tolerance are two values that could emerge from this exercise.

Cultural Pluralism versus Multiculturalism

As an educator, the challenges of **cultural pluralism** are broad yet very personal. The challenge is well summed up by Arthur M. Schlesinger, Jr.: "What happens when people of different ethnic origins, speaking different languages and professing different religions, settle in the same geographical locality and live under the same political sovereignty? Unless a common purpose binds them together, tribal hostilities will drive them apart" (Schlesinger 1993, p. 10). As an educator in the United States today, part of your job is to suppress those hostilities. To do so, you will need to address such questions as these: How do I address the needs of students from diverse cultures? How can I promote knowledge of and value for cultural pluralism through my curriculum, while achieving academic goals? How can I ensure that my own cultural perspective does not inhibit the opportunities and perspectives of others? Such questions are meant to challenge your thinking and to prepare you for the decisions required of any teacher entering a classroom today. (This entire section is really a reflection of the affective domain; see Chapter 3.)

Pluralism is a long-established concept that denotes a mixture of nationalities, races, classes, religions, ethnic groups, and value systems. However, **multiculturalism** is a relatively new concept and has many different operational definitions. Multiculturalism deemphasizes the focus on Western cultural and historical canons and instead gives equal credence to all cultural groups and their value systems.

A quote from James A. Banks is a good starting point for our discussion of multiculturalism. Banks asserts that multiculturalism will promote the sharing of power by encouraging students to "participate in social change so that victimized and excluded ethnic and racial groups can become full participants in society" (1997a, p. 198).

Your own cultural perspective must not inhibit the opportunities and perspectives of others.

It is self-defeating to exclude Western culture from the curriculum.

It is within this context of prior exclusion and future participation that educators like you must seek to balance multiculturalism with academic goals. William Sierichs, Jr., underscores the balance educators must achieve when he states: "There is much the world can learn from the West. Rejecting Western culture is a form of intellectual self-mutilation as severe as rejecting multiculturalism" (Sierichs 1994, p. 114). In other words, it is self-defeating to exclude Western culture and literature in favor of another brand of ethnocentrism. Our educational policy should be inclusion, not exclusion. Clearly, we can all agree that minority groups have contributed mightily to the country we have become, and thus schools at all levels can and should be doing more about teaching minority group history and culture. Most educators will grant that having pride in one's people plays a vital role in building self-respect, and this can translate into academic achievement. *Include all, exclude none!*

Having pride in one's people plays a vital role in building self-respect, and this can translate into academic achievement.

It is not difficult to include multicultural education in your classroom. It takes nothing away from Shakespeare or Emily Dickinson to include the dramas of August Wilson and the poetry of Langston Hughes in the school curriculum.

While the above examples offer several of the more obvious suggestions for including diverse cultural perspectives in the curriculum, others require significant rewriting of the Western flavor of today's public school curriculum. It is not the purpose of this text to propose a multicultural or **Afrocentric curriculum** but rather to initiate a discussion and build interest in personal exploration. With this in mind, we recommend that you read and evaluate the philosophical and psychological underpinnings of multicultural and Afrocentric education. A beginning point might be with the writings of Molefi Kete Asante (1987) and James A. Banks (1993, 1997(a)(c)). They provide a context for understanding the basic viewpoints associated with multicultural and Afrocentric education and diversity.

Reflect Reflect Reflect

■ A culturally pluralistic curriculum is a necessity in an ethnically diverse society. But the motives behind curricular reform sometimes go beyond the desire for a more honest representation of the past. Is multiculturalism a reaction against Anglo culture or Eurocentrism? At what point does it pass over into an ethnocentrism of its own?

Language Diversity

Language barriers are the greatest impediments to social and economic advancement in our country.

Language is the vehicle for most learning and communication in a classroom. Therefore, if the educator fails to understand and respond appropriately to the language of the student (and vice versa), academic achievement will suffer. Language barriers are the greatest impediment to social and economic advancement in our country. If obtaining an advanced education in the United States depends on the individual's success with standard English, then failure to master standard English dooms the individual to the economic underclass (Ogbu 1990), since personal income tends to rise with education (see

TABLE 2.3

Projected 2002 Median Income of Year-Round, Full-Time Workers, 25 Years or Older, by Years of School

Years of Education	Median Income ($) Male	Female
Less than 9th grade	20,290	14,820
9 through 12, with no diploma	25,389	17,519
High school graduate	23,109	22,793
Some college, but no degree	37,541	26,114
Associate degree	38,823	30,486
Bachelor's degree	49,418	35,726
Bachelor's degree and more	55,753	38,743
Master's degree	60,104	44,768
Doctoral degree	71,572	48,627
Professional degree	87,328	55,809

SOURCE: U.S. Bureau of the Census 1996, Table P-9. Projections by authors based on 1996 data.

Table 2.3). Mastery of a country's common or standard language is thus essential for its inhabitants' economic and social progress.

Approximately 2.1 million children in our schools are classified as having limited English proficiency (National Center for Education Statistics 1997, NCES 97-472). These individuals need to become proficient in English to break down the barriers to economic achievement and mobility. Better paying jobs require high technical and verbal skills. Therefore, the schools can play an important role in contributing to our nation's economic success. As a global economic power, the United States and its businesses require employees who are language-endowed (Postman 1995, p. 149). Bilingual speakers are in great demand. Encouraging such capabilities is of the utmost importance for our citizens and our country. However, all students must achieve competence in the remainder of their school curriculum, including proficiency in the language of business here—English. Thus, as educators, we must prepare students to be skilled in several languages and competent in standard English if they are to prosper economically and feel whole personally. We must learn to value language diversity and teach our students to do the same (see the box below).

Instructional
Strategies

Valuing Language Diversity

- Incorporate language skill components into all courses and units.
- Recognize the importance of language diversity and informal student language usage.
- Encourage mastery of English as soon as possible.
- Encourage mastery of a student's native or second language.

Instructional

Strategies

Integrating ELL Students into Your Classroom

1. Provide a warm, encouraging environment by using techniques such as the buddy system and group work, which allow students to practice language skills and receive assistance from peers.

2. If possible, use satisfactory/unsatisfactory grading until students can successfully complete assignments.

3. Avoid forcing students to speak up immediately. Students may need a long wait time, especially when being introduced to new concepts.

4. Have meaningful, relevant print material available in your classroom. Many ELL students read better than they speak.

5. Record important lessons or lectures on tape for use by students.

6. Start classroom interaction with questions that can be answered with a simple yes or no.

7. Try to talk individually with students.

8. Encourage students to use their bilingual dictionaries.

9. Become informed about students' culture.

10. Incorporate and recognize students' culture whenever appropriate.

Reflect Reflect Reflect

- What might be an ideal time to introduce students to a second language? What factors are relevant to this decision?

- How can various cultures and languages be incorporated into some of your lessons? What specific problems might your students have with the subject matter due to cultural factors? What will you do to help them overcome their difficulties?

However, as the twenty-first century progresses, a critical set of decisions is being made, primarily at the state level, to shift from a bilingual education model, in which students are taught their first and second languages simultaneously, to immersion. The immersion approach is to prepare non-English-speaking students in a "crash course" of English and integrate the students into the English-speaking classrooms as quickly as possible. The decision on which model will be followed will be made state by state.

As a new teacher, you may not be familiar with the first languages or cultures of many of your students. We suggest that you consult with your principal and district English-Language Learner (ELL) specialist for helpful learning techniques for your charges. The Instructional Strategies box above lists several suggestions of our own.

Who Is Exceptional?

In Chapter 1 we introduced the topic of providing instruction to children with disabilities. There we discussed the Individuals with Disabilities in Education Act (IDEA) as well as the major points of Public Law 94-142 and subsequent amendments to it. Now we would like to expand that treatment to include gifted students and students with learning disabilities. Our focus is on how you can adapt your instruction to meet the learning needs of a diverse school population.

A wide variety of students can be described as exceptional.

There are many definitions of **exceptionality**—up to twenty-seven different categories of it (Ysseldyke and Algozzine 1995). Here, for the sake of clarity, we explain six generally agreed upon categories that can be used to describe the range of students that may be present in your classroom (Kirk and Gallagher 1996). (See the box below.) You can teach to all these groups by adapting your basic instructional strategies.

You are not alone when helping any child with disabilities or giftedness. The inclusion principle has caused a shift in the deployment of school

---

Categories of Exceptionality

- *Intellectual.* Includes both students who have superior intelligence as well as those who are slow to learn
- *Communicative.* Students with specific learning disabilities or speech or language impairments
- *Sensory.* Students with auditory or visual disabilities
- *Behavioral.* Students who are emotionally disturbed or socially maladjusted
- *Physical.* Students with orthopedic or mobility disabilities
- *Multiple.* Students with a combination of conditions, such as cerebral palsy and dyslexia

---

Specialists Who Can Help You Plan for Exceptional Students

- Speech therapist
- Social worker
- School nurse
- Resource room specialist
- Reading specialist
- School psychologist
- Home teacher

- Caseworker
- Tutors
- Physical therapist
- Signer (for hearing-impaired students)
- Instructional technologist
- Readers (for visually impaired students)

personnel from individual teachers to collaborative efforts. The box on page 66 lists specialists who can help you with exceptional children in your classes. Your collaborating team members will help you adapt your curriculum for selected students. A large number of options are available to you for adapting your instruction. Today's teaching professionals recognize the need to build on students' strengths and learning preferences as a way of remedying their weaknesses. Happily, there are many approaches and curricula available to support your goals for all learners. The box below lists a few sample tools and strategies.

Tools and Strategies for Adapting Instruction to Meet Special Needs

- Mastery learning
- Study/strategy skills training
- Tutoring
- Cooperative learning
- Computer-assisted programs
- Listening labs
- High-interest books
- Large print or braille materials
- Task groups
- Buddy systems
- Special teachers

Adapting the Classroom Environment

In Chapter 6 we describe classroom management as an environmental concern. The classroom environment consists of and is affected by everything and everyone within it, human and nonhuman. To create an **inclusionary classroom,** you must strive to create an inclusive, interactive classroom environment (see also Slavin 1996).

Before proceeding, we offer two caveats: first, an inclusionary classroom is a volatile social milieu. One emotionally disturbed child can, in one explosive outburst, ruin the entire day for you and all the other students. We acknowledge that potential problem. But by continuously observing students and paying attention to their behavioral clues, you can avoid, perhaps even predict, unwanted interruptions (refer to Chapter 6). Our plea to you is to sharpen your observation skills.

The second caveat is that you must set the tone for the classroom. Under your direction, teamwork, cooperation, independence, autonomy, and competition are all brought into action. You make the decision to adapt instruction to help every child. What are some ways you can install and maintain a diverse and inclusionary classroom? The box on page 68 lists several specific

Instructional

Strategies

Adapting Instruction to Promote Success for All

- Promote autonomy.
- Promote student-initiated learning.
- Organize support groups.
- Use multimethodology.
- Illustrate a caring attitude.
- Celebrate learning.
- Instill pride in workmanship.
- Rearrange the room for positive interactions.
- Stress student responsibility.
- Accommodate students with special needs.
- Vary the pace of instruction.
- Collaborate with colleagues.

ways. Note that we will cover these in detail in various chapters. This implies that adapting instruction to individual needs is something that you will be doing every day, all day long.

Adapting your classes to encourage learning for all students is a full-time job. Discuss your plans with the principal, the school counselor, the school nurse, the social worker, and other support personnel. You are not alone. There is a wide range of specialists who can provide that extra effort—just when the load seems too heavy to lift. Master teachers develop a collaborative network of assistants who can make the environment positive, caring, productive, and equitable (see Chapter 12 and Berman and Berreth 1996).

Reflect Reflect Reflect

- If you had a hearing-impaired student in your class, how would you adapt the classroom environment to meet his or her needs? How about a student who is highly gifted in science and math? A student who is socially underdeveloped?

Awareness of Gender Bias

In October 1992, a new talking Barbie doll was introduced. One of the phrases Barbie could say was, "Math class is tough!" The public outcry, especially from women's groups, was too much for Mattel, Barbie's maker. Mattel quickly recalled the line of dolls and dropped the phrase from Barbie's repertoire.

By contrast, in September 1992 an ad for Microsoft Corporation showed two very young girls (three or four years old) taking apart a complicated-looking apparatus. The photo caption encouraged youthful curiosity. These two examples show that bias against women, and a few hopeful signs of change, are both a part of our culture.

Gender bias is ubiquitous in our society.

Bias against women needs to be openly discussed in a book such as this, because such bias affects one-half of the student population. Myra Sadker, David Sadker, and Susan Klein (1991) summarized findings from dozens of studies of subtle and not-so-subtle ways women and girls are shortchanged by educational materials.

SIGNS OF GENDER BIAS IN EDUCATIONAL MATERIALS

- Women and girls tend to be vastly underrepresented in textbooks, and that tendency grows worse at higher grade levels.
- Males outnumber females by as much as six to one in stories and folk tales commonly used in schools.
- In history texts, traditionally male activities (hunting, for example) are discussed in depth, while women's activities receive a scant sentence or two.
- Newbery and Caldecott medals are awarded far more frequently to boy-oriented books than to girl-oriented books.
- Boys or men are usually portrayed as heroes, while women or girls are shown as selfish or dependent.

The list of bias in learning materials could be expanded (see Sadker and Sadker 1994), but what of classroom instruction? The authors cited study after study showing that in elementary schools, boys received more praise, criticism, and rewards from teachers than girls. Young girls tended to receive "neutral" teacher reactions. In general, teachers expect less from girls, and therefore girls develop a **learned helplessness.** That condition is notably described by Peggy Orenstein (1994).

Gender bias is perhaps most serious in mathematics and the sciences, fields in which women are vastly underrepresented (Linn and Hyde 1989). The National Science Foundation is currently making an all-out effort to recruit women and minorities into math, science, and engineering programs, so perhaps this will change. Girls need to be encouraged to complete science and mathematics courses in high school in order to assume leadership roles in the nation's best jobs. Between 1982 and 1992, there was an increase in the number of girls enrolled in all high school science classes. In 1982 only 9 percent of high school girls completed physics. By 1992 the figure had risen to 21 percent (compared to 28 percent for boys).

In mathematics, a higher percentage of girls than boys completed algebra I and II, geometry, and trigonometry between 1982 and 1992; however, boys still outnumber girls in high school calculus classes. But between 1982 and 1992, the percentage of girls completing high school calculus increased by 245 percent!

The evidence tends not to support any sexual superiority.

From these historical trends it appears that girls are increasingly being encouraged to enroll in physical science and mathematics classes (see Rop 1998). Thus, the trend is toward equity in these critically important intellectual arenas (all data from Suter 1996, Figure 3.3 and Appendix Tables 3.4 and 3.5).

Nevertheless, the test scores of girls in the fourth, eighth, and twelfth grades lag behind those of boys in both science and mathematics. A higher percentage of boys than girls score at or above critical anchor points on the science and mathematics achievement tests administered by the National Assessment of Educational Progress (NAEP).

In mathematics proficiency, girls in grade 4 (age nine) tended to score slightly lower than boys did on the 1996 NAEP assessment. However, in grade 8 (age thirteen), there was no gender difference in scale scores. At age seventeen (grade 12), boys again had only a slight lead over girls in mathematics achievement. In earlier NAEP studies, the achievement differences between girls and boys also occurred in grade 12 (Reese 1997). However, all age and gender groups showed improved scores in 1996 when compared to the 1990 and 1992 assessments.

The mathematics test results from NAEP show a decline in male dominance.

In science, the 1996 NAEP assessment showed boys just slightly ahead of girls at grades 4, 8, and 12 (O'Sullivan et al. 1997). Educationally, except at grade 12, there is virtually no difference in the scores. One may conclude that gender differences are subsiding.

But rather than concentrating on which gender is "ahead" at what grade level or in what year, the important question, the one that will affect your teaching career, is how to ensure that every boy and every girl in your classes receives **instructional equity.** The answer to that question touches upon one of the central premises of this book: that you must make your classes intentionally inviting, for everyone.

Encourage all children to enroll in "tougher" high school classes.

Misinformation and Low Expectations   Socialization and cultural mores have a powerful effect on girls in school, and gender stereotypes and the media tend to perpetuate misinformation regarding girls' abilities (Jacklin 1989). People assume that girls will suffer from math anxiety, so the girls oblige. Thus it is extremely important for teachers to communicate high expectations to girls and to be intentionally inviting to improve girls' motivation and success in mathematics and science classes.

Classroom social interactions can contribute to the development of dependent behaviors and a lack of confidence in young girls. By grade 6, young girls report less confidence in their mathematical ability than boys, even when the girls achieve at the same level as boys (Fennema 1987). This should be a red flag for any teacher who works with girls, minority students, or non-English-speaking children. If you show preference or lowered expectations for any group or individual, you are reinforcing learned helplessness. **Sex-role stereotyping** can be reduced or eliminated in classrooms by talking about it openly, stressing the value of learning, and communicating high expectations for everyone. All students must be given an equal opportunity to succeed, because *interest in a subject is a by-product of success* (Bloom 1968). For too long educators have operated on the erroneous belief that success is a by-product of interest.

Success in a subject creates interest in it.

Instructional Implications of Gender Equity   As a teacher, you must provide leadership opportunities for both girls and boys. If boys are always asked to lead or to set up apparatus in science classes, then girls will simply assume

Instructional	Promoting Gender Equity in Your Classroom
Strategies	■ Call on girls as often as you call on boys. ■ Rotate classroom responsibilities and leadership roles between girls and boys. ■ Use wait time in your questioning (see Chapter 7). ■ Make no distinctions between boys and girls in assigning problems. (Some teachers assign easy problems to girls and difficult ones to boys.) ■ Add to reading lists stories or books about women prominent in the subject area being studied. ■ Assign research reports on women's contributions to the topics being studied. ■ Place equal numbers of girls and boys in small discussion and cooperative learning groups (see Chapter 8). ■ Organize a brainstorming session to answer the question "How are girls treated in our school compared to boys?"

Design gender-neutral classroom interactions.

dependent roles. Obviously, complex social and emotional processes take place in classrooms. The manner in which a teacher engages every student has potential learning overtones. This means that you must be consciously aware of your verbal and nonverbal actions and reactions to every class member, every day!

Teacher educators have expressed little attention to promoting gender equity (Sanders 1997). This is unfortunate, and omission of this topic at the preservice level has at least one major implication: new teachers may enter the classroom unaware of subtle behaviors and biases that are unintentionally disinviting to girls (Campbell and Sanders 1997).

What can you do to make a difference to promote gender equity in your classroom? In the box above are some suggestions that we have observed in classrooms or learned through experience. Providing gender equity is part of creating an inclusionary classroom.

While we have been addressing the unique gender biases that appear in many classrooms, let us not lose sight of the importance of helping every student feel the thrill of success. This is what teaching is all about. We are all in a "helping profession." It is our moral obligation to help every student—girls, boys, minorities, children with disabilities, non-English-speakers, and those with limited English-speaking proficiencies—succeed to the maximum of that individual's capacity in whatever we teach.

Technology is rapidly changing the ways we teach. Yet with the advent of new teaching technologies, we must not forget that teaching and learning are very human dimensions. The humanness of schooling is one of the messages we have woven into this chapter. The more humanely we treat those who walk or wheel into the classroom, the more positive our impact will be on those individuals with whom we come into contact.

When addressing any diversity issue, values and value systems come into play. The messages in this chapter are all affectively oriented; that is, they challenge our basic value structure and the attitudes we express through our words, actions, and deeds. Our job is to instill a love of learning in every student. If our teaching is biased, we may unintentionally alienate some of our students from the disciplines we teach. This, in turn, may adversely affect their desire to learn. Perhaps the observation made by Robert F. Mager (1968), the person who popularized behavioral objectives, is appropriate to end this section. He wrote, "If I do little else, I want to send my students away with at least as much interest in the subjects I teach as they had when they arrived" (p. i).

Reflect Reflect Reflect

- Interview a teacher and principal in your hometown. Ask them how many different ethnic groups are represented in their school.
- List the elements of instruction that you can control that will ensure instructional equity among the races represented in your classes.
- Examine a middle school curriculum guide for American literature. What evidence do you find that an attempt is being made to provide a multicultural perspective?
- Interview an ELL teacher and ask for suggestions on integrating ELL students into your classroom activities.
- List at least four observations that can signal that one of your students has a specific learning disability.
- What steps can you take to avoid subjecting your students to gender bias?

Section 4: Becoming a Lifelong Learner

You may be surprised to see a topic about your future being introduced so early in the book. Yes, we gave that great thought and concluded that if you are made aware of future educational options, then you might have a broader vision of your own higher education experiences. Please refer to Figure 2.1 and observe how the technical procedural elements interact with the others. Many of the technical aspects of teaching simply take time to achieve. Time and experience add the dimension of relevance. Actually, teaching brings relevance to your technical competence.

Professional and Personal Growth

As stated earlier, education is a helping profession. You have specific reasons for becoming a teacher: you may want to impart knowledge and skills to young people; or you may want to help create a better-educated society; or you may want to have a satisfying, rewarding, and challenging career. In any case, teaching is an enormous job, and no teacher education program can thoroughly prepare you for it. It is safe to assume that you will need continuing education in order to become a master teacher.

Master teachers are outstanding in their classrooms and the profession.

What is a **master teacher?** Generally, a master teacher is skilled in the technical aspects of teaching and is one from whom other teachers seek professional advice. The title is earned through reputation. Master teachers are outstanding in their classrooms and in their field. They have the esteem of their colleagues. Students remark that "you're the best teacher I ever had." School patrons and parents speak of master teachers in glowing terms. Throughout this book we emphasize the dual nature of teaching as both a science and an art. Master teachers know the science of instruction and apply the art of teaching.

How much formal education do you need to be an effective classroom teacher? The answers to this question vary. Teaching expertise in all areas requires a combination of experience and continuing (formal) professional development. In some domains, such as the arts and business, ongoing learning is primarily carried out in practice, often with mentors or experienced practitioners. In other domains, such as special education, ongoing learning requires continuing formal education. But to become master teachers, all teachers must continue their education.

However, teachers become *master teachers* through *experience*, not just through education. They demonstrate basic academic proficiencies, *plus* they learn from rich experiences in their schools and communities. Thus, you need to develop a vision that guides you toward that honored status of becoming a *master*.

You now have a foundational knowledge of instruction.

After you assimilate the content of this book, you will have a head start on most practicing teachers. You will develop a firm foundation on which to build additional professional knowledge and to practice in an artful and thoughtful manner.

There is no question about the knowledge explosion in education. It would be impossible for you to read all of the books published this year alone about teaching, teachers, or the schools. Add to that paper stack the virtual university—the Internet—and you could spend all of your waking hours studying and never read all there is to know about the field of education. But don't feel overloaded and helpless. There is a way to expand your knowledge base in a systematic manner.

Traits of Adult Learners

- Enjoy planning for learning
- Conduct their own learning experiences
- Learn best when needs and training coincide
- Need opportunities to apply new learning
- Seek independent study options
- Seek the practical
- Are self-directed
- Enjoy being facilitative
- Establish clearly defined objectives

Begin by asking yourself, "Where do I want to be six months from now? Three years from now? Ten years from now?" Write down those goals. Then ask yourself, "What do I have to do to achieve my immediate goal? My longer-term goals?" Perhaps your first goal is to gain work experience and to be mentored by a master teacher. Your long-term goal may be to attain an advanced degree and additional subject-matter expertise and to become a master teacher yourself. Eventually, you may want to achieve more expertise in carrying out research and to publish your work in the professional literature.

As you gain teaching experience, you will begin to accumulate a reserve of valuable practice skills and teaching insight. There is a high probability that you will become more self-directed and will initiate continuing education for yourself, which will give you more background knowledge and a wider repertoire of instructional techniques. You will find yourself enjoying problem-centered learning. You will appreciate hands-on learning. You will seek job-related skills. In short, you will be demonstrating the behaviors of teachers who have matured to the **adult model of learning.** (See box page 73).

Adult learners incorporate theory and experience into practice.

Building Supportive Partnerships

Up until now we have implied that continuing education is something you do on your own. However, networks and supportive partnerships are great ways to aim toward mastery. Possible helpers range from an assigned mentor to an international professional association. Once you begin work in a school, you'll be offered some assistance by almost every employee. Let us begin with the bigger picture and work down.

Formal Organizations   One of the first organizations that you will voluntarily join or be required to join is the local bargaining unit. It will be affiliated with the National Education Association (NEA) or the American Federation of Teachers (AFT). These groups, commonly known as teachers' unions, offer several professional development programs for new teachers. These are staffed by master teachers who have proven their effectiveness. Seminars or short courses are designed with you in mind. Select the ones that meet your most immediate needs.

Professional organizations sponsor a wide variety of professional development programs for their members.

Beginning-Teacher Assistance Programs   Then there are the beginning-teacher assistance programs (B-TAPs). California was an early innovator in establishing a state-funded program with the goal of helping new or beginning teachers make the transition from student to teacher. This program has been widely copied, and about one-half of the states now have some formal induction program. You will be assigned to an experienced teacher, or **mentor,** who is recognized for instructional excellence. Your mentor will help you identify and resolve problems. Your mentor will observe you as you teach and provide a few tips. With your mentor "in your corner," troublesome problems can be identified and quickly resolved. A mentor can help make your first year of teaching a positive experience.

Professional Associations   There are scores of professional associations directly involved in teacher-related activities. All these groups sponsor work-

Being active professionally opens doors for personal contacts.

shops, seminars, clinics, short courses, and institutes on a wide spectrum of topics and interests. All hold state, regional, or national conferences.

Professionals attend conferences for a variety of reasons; one is to establish a network of personal contacts. Through such networks you can benefit from others' expertise and build your own human potential. You are just an e-mail address away from someone who shares your passion for art, biology, history, or reading. Personal contacts become powerful sources of knowledge about practical classroom matters. Through such networks you become part of a dissemination loop. They allow you to communicate with other professionals who are also just beginning their careers in education.

Local Resource Persons   Here we list some of the individuals who can help you do a better job of teaching during your first year (see the box below).

Become acquainted with all the employees in your school.

For example, you are sure to request help from the teacher across the hall during your first year of teaching, if only because you don't know who's supposed to replace your light bulbs. You might need to consult the bus driver to find out if a problem student causes trouble during the ride to school as well as during classes. The school guidance counselor can tell you what assessment options are available to help you decide whether a student has a learning disability or needs some behavioral intervention. The school secretary can help you interpret the many forms you'll have to complete on a regular basis. The bookkeeper will help you order needed teaching supplies. Coaches develop a special relationship with students, so call on them if you have a question about one of your students. All the persons on the list can help you—if you ask them.

Handy List of Local Helpers

School People

- School custodian
- Mentor
- Library director
- Playground supervisor
- Teacher across the hall
- Counselor
- Head coach—male sports
- Bus driver
- Principal
- School secretary
- Assistant principal
- Bookkeeper
- Computer technician
- Peer coach
- Vocational rehabilitation counselor
- Head coach—female sports
- Lunch aide
- Superintendent of schools

Community People

- A jogging partner
- Public health nurse
- City recreation director
- Chamber of commerce director
- State welfare agency head
- Planned Parenthood executive
- Goodwill director
- Community chest executive

The Journey to Becoming a Master Teacher

We end as we began: the journey to becoming a master teacher is one of continuous reflection, study, preparation, work, and execution. The ranks of master teachers are filled with individuals like you. Each one started teaching with apprehension, doubt, and some confidence. Your sense of efficacy will begin to grow with your first successful planned teaching episode. Each further success will add to that sense. Sure, there will be problems, even disasters. But you can learn from your mistakes. Reflect. Review your plans. Seek solutions. That is how beginning teachers become master teachers.

Earlier in this chapter, we mentioned that you would be provided with an "overview" of several important educational topics and issues. Well, the jig is up. We know that in most basic methods textbooks, the authors try to provide information on just about every conceivable topic. We do not! At this juncture in your career, you do not have the experiential basis for judging the effectiveness or ineffectiveness of the many instructional methods or teaching strategies that are published, espoused, or championed. Our book is structured to provide you with basic instructional methods that you need to begin teaching. It is your professional responsibility to expand your frame of reference and knowledge base. Thus, we delimit the number of topics being covered.

But to illustrate the vast array of topics that you may want to cover when you have teaching experience and can then better evaluate their efficacy, we present Table 2.4. Peruse the topics. Ask yourself, At what point in my career will I need to study them and incorporate them into my repertoire of instructional methods? In our opinion, the listed topics form a basis for continued

TABLE 2.4	**Forty-Eight Topics for Future/Lifelong Learning**

Administrative Topics
- Collaborative action research
- Conflict management
- Effective schools
- Leadership skill training
- Organization development
- Paideia schools
- School support teams
- Stress-reduction programs
- Team teaching

Curriculum Design
- Content analysis
- Curriculum mapping
- Economic education
- Integrating curriculum
- International curriculum

TABLE 2.4   **Forty-Eight Topics for Future/Lifelong Learning (continued)**

- Instructional theory into practice
- Mastery learning
- Multicultural education

Evaluation and Assessment

- Conducting formative evaluation
- Effect size
- Evaluation rubics
- Performance assessment
- Program evaluation
- Student portfolios

Learning Styles

- Brain research-based learning styles and brain hemisphericity
- Dimensions of learning
- Emotional intelligence
- Field dependence and independence
- Modalities of learning
- McCarthy 4MAT system
- Multiple intelligences

Special Education Considerations

- At-risk youth
- Bilingual learners
- Diagnostic-prescriptive teaching
- Differentiated instruction
- Direct instruction
- English-language learners
- Independent learning
- Gifted and talented models
- Multiage classrooms
- Teacher effectiveness training
- Teaching study skills

Teaching Methodologies

- Asynchronous learning
- Circles of learning
- Cooperative learning models
- Constructivist classrooms
- Internet enhanced classrooms
- Socratic teaching
- Technology and distance learning

lifelong learning. However, as you enter teaching, only a select number of teaching techniques can be mastered or even understood, let alone practiced. Newer techniques or models can be examined and evaluated as part of your professional growth plans, although at this time many concepts are not relevant to you.

A Closing Reflection Reflection Reflection

- Gather a few peers and discuss the background one would need to utilize holistic planning.
- To what extent can an active learning model reflect the developmental, behavioral, or cognitive perspectives?
- What attitudinal attributes would a teacher and the class need to embrace the concept of instructional equity?
- Why should you be concerned about professional growth a few years hence when at this point in time you might not yet be teaching?

Summary

1. Instructional decisions have two components: the holistic vision and detailed implementation.
2. Instructional decisions are predicated on the learner's needs.
3. Piagetian theory assumes that learners develop in stages and that instruction should be developmentally appropriate.
4. Vygotskian theory asserts that for any concept there is a right time to teach it and that learning requires social interaction.
5. Behavioral techniques require the application of appropriate reinforcement.
6. The cognitive model of instruction assumes that students are always active learners and that students should assume more responsibility to learn.
7. Social constructivism posits that prior experience and shared learning are part of the instructional context.
8. For a significant number of students, educational success appears to be related to their school's sensitivity to and respect for equity, whether it is defined in terms of diversity, ethnicity, race, language, disability, or gender.
9. The skillful and deliberate inclusion of multicultural activities in the classroom promotes appreciation of the value of all cultures, as well as pride, self-respect, and dignity for all students.
10. In the United States, proficiency in English is a prerequisite for success in school and beyond, and proficiency in a second language is a valuable asset. Therefore, the schools have a dual responsibility to increase students' proficiency in English and to provide programs that allow *all* students the opportunity to become multilanguage proficient.

11. Gender biases have been found in textbooks, educational activities, and classroom interactions. Gender equity is an important goal of the inclusionary classroom. Teachers must be aware of the danger of placing low expectations on girls.

12. Lifelong learning is a holistic vision for professional educators.

Key Terms

adult model of learning (p. 74)	**learned helplessness** (p. 69)
Afrocentric curriculum (p.63)	**master teacher** (p. 72)
behavioral perspective (p. 48)	**mentor** (p. 74)
behavior modification (p. 48)	**mnemonics** (p. 51)
cognitive psychology (p. 50)	**multiculturalism** (p. 62)
concrete operational stage (p. 46)	**operant conditioning** (p. 48)
cultural pluralism (p. 62)	**physical diversity** (p. 61)
direct instruction (p. 49)	**preoperational stage** (p. 46)
eclectic (p. 46)	**processing information** (p. 51)
equity (p. 59)	**programmed instruction** (p. 50)
exceptionality (p. 66)	**schema** (p. 46)
formal stage (p. 46)	**sensorimotor stage** (p. 46)
holistic instructional view (p. 43)	**sex-role stereotyping** (p. 70)
inclusionary classroom (p. 67)	**student-initiated learning** (p. 52)
instructional equity (p. 70)	**transfer of learning** (p. 48)
internalize (p. 47)	**zone of proximal development** (p. 47)

Helpful Resources

Thousands of papers and books have been written on the topics discussed in this chapter. The following sources are of particular value.

American Association of University Women. *Shortchanging Girls, Shortchanging America.* Washington, DC: American Association of University Women Foundation, 1994, 19 pp.

The AAUW report is a synthesis and executive summary of research studies that present evidence that girls are not receiving the same quality of education as boys. The report points out the absence of topics about girls in the current educational debate, presents a variety of achievement data for females in the schools, examines sex and gender bias in testing, and provides several recommendations to improve schooling for both girls and boys.

Banks, J. A. "The Canon Debate, Knowledge Construction and Multicultural Education." *Educational Researcher* 22(5) (1993): 4–14.

A national debate is raging over the role of diversity and multicultural education in the school curriculum. In our opinion, Banks presents the single best analysis of the entire conflict. He skillfully shows the interrelationships of four types of knowledge—personal, popular, mainstream academic, and transformative academic. A case example using The Westward Movement is used to show how multicultural concepts can be incorporated into the curriculum.

Good, T. L., and J. E. Brophy. *Looking in Classrooms* (8th ed.). New York: Longman, 2000, 500 pp.

Two prominent educational researchers provide firsthand observations of what transpires in classrooms.

Howard, G. R. *We Can't Teach What We Don't Know: White Teachers, Multiracial Schools.* New York: Teachers College Press, 1999, 141 pp.

Howard presents a journal of his several years of teaching in racially diverse schools. His work stresses the need to create caring and humane schools—a major thesis of this book.

Jackson, P. W. *The Moral Life of Schools.* San Francisco: Jossey-Bass, 1998, 323 pp.

Here is a book that will extend your perspective on the aims of education and make you think about how the structure and organization of schools affect instruction.

Landers, M. F., and H. R. Weaver. *Inclusive Education: A Process, Not a Placement.* Swampscott, MA: Watersun Publishing Company, Inc., 1997, 268 pp.

An easy-to-use guide to aid teachers with inclusive classes. Especially useful are the many resources and ideas on how to structure an inclusive classroom.

Internet Resources

✤ The University of Washington sponsors *Project DO-IT* (disabilities, opportunities, Internetworking, and technology). The goal is to increase representation of individuals with disabilities in science, mathematics, and technology academic programs and careers. Dr. Sheryl Burgstahler is the project director.

> **http://weber.u.washington.edu/~doit/**
> **(e-mail: doit@u.washington.edu)**

✤ *The Clearinghouse on Computer Accommodation* provides information on all types of adaptive and assistive technology to promote inclusions.

> **http://www.gsa.gov/coca/cocamain.html**

✤ Columbia University's Institute for Learning Technologies maintains a Web site that features documents and projects on increasing student motivation.

> **http://www.ilt.columbia.edu/ilt/**

✤ The Jean Piaget Society database is an on-line source of information and publications on Piagetian developmental ideas.

> **http://www.piaget.org/**

❖ The American Indian Science and Engineering Society of Boulder, Colorado, features a Web site that provides cultural connections in science areas for underrepresented minority students.

http://spot.colorado.edu/~aises/aises.html

❖ The Multicultural Pavilion, sponsored by the University of Virginia, provides a vast array of multicultural materials, including an online discussion site.

http://curry.edschool.virginia.edu/go/multicultural/

❖ The National Clearinghouse for Bilingual Education provides assistance for issues dealing with linguistically and culturally diverse students.

http://www.ncbe.gwu.edu

❖ Melissa's "Myriad Art Education Page" provides educational ideas, lesson plans, and skills to incorporate art with all cultures.

http://www.geocities.com/Athens/8020/arted.html

❖ The American Psychological Association maintains a site containing databases, information, abstracts, news, and other related information.

http://www.apa.org

References

Adams, G. L., and S. Engelmann. *Research on Direct Instruction: 25 Years Beyond DISTAR.* Seattle: Educational Achievement Systems, 1996.

Adey, P., and M. Shayer. *Really Raising Standards: Cognitive Intervention and Academic Achievement.* New York: Routledge, 1994.

American Association of University Women. *Shortchanging Girls, Shortchanging America.* Washington, DC: American Association of University Women Foundation, 1994.

Anderson, R. D., et al. *Issues of Curriculum Reform in Science, Mathematics and Higher Order Thinking Across the Disciplines,* OR 94-3408. Washington, DC: U.S. Department of Education, Office of Research, 1994.

Asante, M. K. *The Afrocentric Idea.* Philadelphia: Temple University Press, 1987.

Ashman, A. F., and R. M. F. Conway. *Using Cognitive Methods in the Classroom.* New York: Routledge, 1993.

Banks, J. A. "The Canon Debate, Knowledge Construction and Multicultural Education." *Educational Researcher* 22(5) (1993): 4–14.

Banks, J. A. "Multicultural Education: Characteristics and Goals." In *Multicultural Education: Issues and Perspectives* (3rd Edition). J. A. Banks and C. M. Banks, editors. Boston: Allyn & Bacon, 1997a.

Banks, J. A. *Educating Citizens in a Multicultural Society.* New York: Teachers College Press, 1997b.

Banks, J. A. *Teaching Strategies for Ethnic Studies* (6th Edition). Allyn & Bacon, 1997c.

Bates, S. *Battleground: One Mother's Crusade, The Religious Right and the Struggle for Control of Our Classrooms.* New York: Poseidon Press, 1993.

Berman, S., and D. Berreth. "Schools as Moral Communities: Methods for Building Empathy and Self-Discipline." Task Force Paper. Washington, DC: The Communitarian Network, 8 May 1996.

Bloom, B. S. "Learning for Mastery." *Evaluation Comment* 1(2) (1968): 2.

Bredekamp, S., editor. *Developmentally Appropriate Practice in Early Childhood Programs Serving Children from Birth through Age 8* (revised edition). Washington, DC: National Association for the Education of Young Children, 1997.

Campbell, P. B., and J. Sanders. "Uninformed But Interested: Findings of a National Survey on Gender Equity in Preservice Teacher Education." *Journal of Teacher Education* 48(1) (1997): 69–75.

Carnine, D. W. "Effective Teaching for Higher Cognitive Functioning." *Educational Technology* 33(1) (1993): 29–33.

Danielson, C. *Enhancing Professional Practice: A Framework for Teaching.* Alexandria, VA: Association for Supervision and Curriculum Development, 1996.

Davis, R. B., C. A. Masher, and N. Noddings, editors. *Constructivist Views on the Teaching and Learning of Mathematics.* Reston, VA: National Council of Teachers of Mathematics, 1990.

Elliott, S. M., and E. S. Shapiro. "Intervention Techniques and Programs for Academic Performance Problems." In *The Handbook of School Psychology* (2nd Edition). T. B. Guthin and C. R. Reynolds, editors. New York: John Wiley & Sons, 1990.

Erhlich, P. R., and S. S. Feldman. *The Race Bomb: Skin Color, Prejudice and Intelligence.* New York: Quadrangle Press, 1977.

Erikson, E. H. *The Life Cycle Completed.* New York: Norton, 1982.

Fennema, E. "Sex-Related Differences in Education: Myths, Realities and Interventions." In *Educator's Handbook.* V. Richardson-Koehler, editor. New York: Longman, 1987.

Gollnick, D., and P. Chinn. *Multicultural Education in a Pluralistic Society.* Columbus, OH: Merrill, 1990.

Good, T. L., and J. E. Brophy. *Looking in Classrooms* (8th edition). New York: Longman, 2000.

Goodlad, J. I. *A Place Called School.* New York: McGraw-Hill, 1984.

Howard, G. R. *We Can't Teach What We Don't Know: White Teachers, Multiracial Schools.* New York: Teachers College Press, 1999.

Jackson, P. W. *The Moral Life of Schools.* San Francisco: Jossey-Bass, 1998.

Jacklin, C. M. "Female and Male: Issues of Gender." *American Psychologist* 44(2) (1989): 127–133.

Kirk, S. A., and J. J. Gallagher. *Educating Exceptional Children* (8th edition). Boston: Houghton Mifflin, 1996.

Kohn, A. "What to Look for in a Classroom." *Educational Leadership* 54(1) (1996): 54–55.

Landers, M. F., and H. R. Weaver. *Inclusive Education: A Process, Not a Placement.* Swampscott, MA: Watersun Publishing Company, Inc., 1997.

Levine, D., and R. Havighurst. *Society and Education* (7th edition). Boston: Allyn & Bacon, 1989.

Linn, M. S., and J. S. Hyde. "Gender, Mathematics and Science." *Educational Researcher* 18(8) (1989): 17–27.

Mager, R. F. *Developing Attitude Toward Learning.* Palo Alto, CA: Fearon, 1968.

Marable, M. "Blacks Should Emphasize Their Ethnicity." In *Racism in America: Opposing Viewpoints.* W. Dudley and C. Cozic, editors. San Diego, CA: Greenhaven, 1991.

National Center for Educational Statistics. *The Condition of Education, 1992.* Washington, DC: U.S. Department of Education, 1992.

National Center for Educational Statistics. *The Condition of Education, 1995.* Washington, DC: U.S. Department of Education, 1995.

National Center for Educational Statistics. *The Condition of Education, 1998.* Washington, DC: U.S. Department of Education, 1998.

Ogbu, J. "Understanding Diversity: Summary Comments." *Education and Urban Society* 22(4) (1990): 425–429.

Orenstein, P. *Schoolgirls: Young Women, Self-Esteem and the Confidence Gap.* New York: Doubleday (and American Association of University Women), 1994.

O'Sullivan, C. F., C. M. Reese, and J. Mazzeo. *NAEP 1996 Science Report Card for the Nation and the States.* Washington, DC: National Center for Education Statistics, 1997.

Piaget, J. *Psychologie et Pedogogie.* Paris: Denoel/Garnier, 1969.

Portman, P., and T. Carlson. "Speaking Out Against the Silence." *Teaching Education* 4(1) (1991): 183–187.

Postman, N. *The End of Education.* New York: Alfred A. Knopf, 1995.

Reese, C. M., K. E. Miller, and J. A. Dosse. *NAEP 1996 Mathematics Report Card for the Nation and States.* Washington, DC: National Center for Education Statistics, 1997.

Rop, C. "Breaking the Gender Barrier in the Physical Sciences." *Educational Leadership* 55(4) (1998): 58–60.

Rosenshine, B., and C. Meister. "Direct Instruction." In *International Encyclopedia of Teaching and Teacher Education* (2nd edition). L. W. Anderson, editor. Tarrytown, NY: Elsevier Science, Inc., 1995, pp. 143–149.

Russell, K., M. Wilson, and R. Hall. *The Color Complex.* New York: Harcourt, Brace, Jovanovich, 1992.

Sadker, M., and D. Sadker. *Failing at Fairness: How America's Schools Cheat Girls.* New York: Charles Scribner's Sons, 1994.

Sadker, M., D. Sadker, and S. Klein. "The Issue of Gender in Elementary and Secondary Education." In *Review of Research in Education,* Vol. 17. C. Grant, editor. Washington, DC: American Educational Research Association, 1991.

Sanders, J. "Teacher Education and Gender Equity. *ERIC Digest.* Washington, DC: ERIC Clearinghouse on Teaching and Teacher Education, ED 408 277, May 1977.

Schlesinger, A. M. *The Disuniting of America: Reflections on a Multicultural Society.* New York: Norton, 1993.

Seligman, D. A. *Question of Intelligence.* New York: Birch Lane Press, Carol Publishing Group, 1992.

Shayer, M., and P. Adey. *Towards a Science of Science Teaching: Cognitive Development and Curriculum*

Demand. London: Hinemann Educational Books, 1981.

Sierichs, W., Jr. "Multicultural Education Is Helpful." In *Culture Wars: Opposing Viewpoints.* F. Whitehead, editor. San Diego, CA: Greenhaven Press, Inc., 1994.

Silberman, C. E. *Crisis in the Classroom: The Remaking of American Education.* New York: Random House, 1970.

Silberman, M. L. *Active Learning: 101 Strategies to Teach Any Subject.* Needham, MA: Allyn and Bacon, 1996.

Skinner, B. F. *The Behavior of Organisms.* New York: Appleton-Century-Crofts, 1938.

Slavin, R. E. "Neverstreaming: Preventing Learning Disabilities." *Educational Leadership* 53(5) (1996): 4–7.

Stover, L. T., G. A. Neubert, and J. C. Lawlor. *Creating Interactive Environments in the Secondary School.* Washington, DC: National Education Association, 1993.

Suter, L. E., editor. *Indicators of Science and Mathematics Education 1992.* Washington, DC: National Science Foundation, 1993 (NSF 93-95).

Suter, L. E., editor. *Indicators of Science and Mathematics Education 1995.* Arlington, VA: National Science Foundation, Directorate for Education and Human Resources, 1996 (NSF 96-52).

Titus, J. J. "Gender Messages in Education Foundations' Textbooks." *Journal of Teacher Education* 44(1) (1993): 38–43.

U.S. Bureau of the Census. "Historical Income Tables of Persons in the United States." *Current Population Reports.* Series P-60. Washington, DC: U.S. Government Printing Office, 9 December 1996.

U.S. Department of Education. Office of Educational Research and Improvement, National Center for Education Statistics. *1993–94 Schools and Staffing Survey: A Profile for Limited English Proficient Students: Screening Methods, Program Support and Teacher Training.* NCES 97-427. Washington, DC: 1997.

U.S. Department of Education, National Center for Education Statistics. *Projections of Education Statistics to 2008.* Consumer Price Index. Table B8. *http://nces.ed.gov* 1999.

U.S. Department of Education. Office of Educational Research and Improvement. *Highlights from TIMSS: Overview of Key Findings across Grade Levels.* Washington, DC: National Center for Education Statistics, 1999a. NCES 1999-081.

U.S. Department of Education. National Center for Education Statistics. *What Happens in Classrooms? Instructional Practices in Elementary Schools, 1994–95.* NCES 1999-348, by R. R. Henke, X. Chen, and G. Goldman. Washington, DC: 1999b.

Vygotsky, L. S. *Thought and Language.* Cambridge, MA: M.I.T. Press, 1962.

Ysseldyke, J. E., and B. Algozzine. *Special Education: A Practical Approach for Teachers* (3rd edition). Boston: Houghton Mifflin, 1995.

Fundamental Tools for Instructional Planning

Part 2 presents you with the basic tools for instructional planning. Goals, outcomes, objectives, taxonomies, lesson and unit planning, and sequencing are the most static elements of teaching. But as Michelangelo's *David* illustrates as he stands poised to throw a rock at Goliath, thought and contemplation precede action, and they may have a brilliance in their own right. Planning provides the basis for the dynamic, interactive phases of teaching.

In Part 2 you will also consider using an instructional planning model with lesson design. Tips from outstanding teachers are featured. This section gives you the entry-level skills you will need to plan effective lessons and to discuss instructional planning with any experienced teacher or would-be educational reformer.

3

Goals, Standards, and Outcomes for Instruction

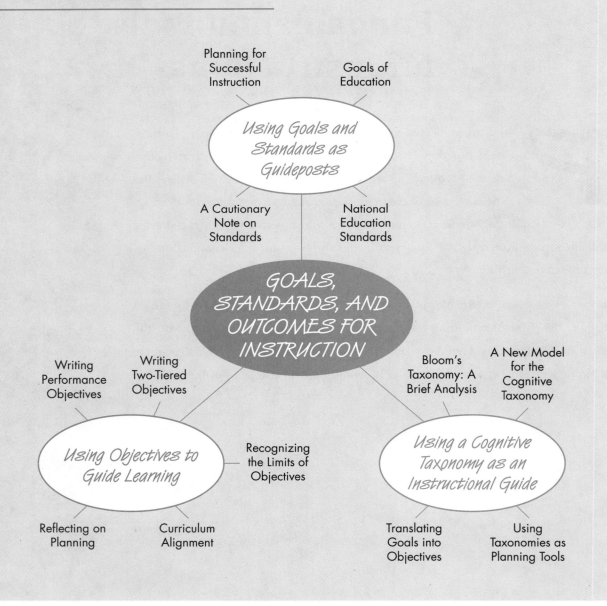

Planning for Successful Instruction

Goals of Education

Using Goals and Standards as Guideposts

A Cautionary Note on Standards

National Education Standards

GOALS, STANDARDS, AND OUTCOMES FOR INSTRUCTION

Writing Performance Objectives

Writing Two-Tiered Objectives

Bloom's Taxonomy: A Brief Analysis

A New Model for the Cognitive Taxonomy

Using Objectives to Guide Learning

Recognizing the Limits of Objectives

Using a Cognitive Taxonomy as an Instructional Guide

Reflecting on Planning

Curriculum Alignment

Translating Goals into Objectives

Using Taxonomies as Planning Tools

As a high school and college student, Alfredo had been critical of teachers who did not clearly communicate their instructional goals to their students. He remembers thinking, "Why don't teachers tell us what they expect from us and present material in a systematic manner?"

Now, as a new high school history teacher with an assignment of two basic courses, an advanced course, and an elective course, Alfredo is overwhelmed with the task of organizing the first week's lessons. Here are just a few of his questions: "How much material can I cover in one period? How is what is taught in my courses related to other courses? How do I use the curriculum guides, textbooks, and all the information I learned in college? How do I plan for survival?"

This chapter, together with Chapter 4, will help you find out how to solve problems similar to Alfredo's. In this chapter we will provide basic information that will help you put instructional planning in perspective. In Chapter 4 we will go into the specifics of setting goals and objectives for instruction. As you read this chapter, think about how you would address the following questions:

- What processes do teachers use to plan successful instruction?
- What are my goals for my students?
- How can I use a cognitive taxonomy of objectives as an instructional guide?
- How can I write clear objectives for my learners that will guide them to success?

Section 1: Using Goals and Standards as Guideposts

Planning for Successful Instruction

One hallmark of teaching as an organized activity is the process called **planning.** If you wish to instruct in a systematic manner, then you will need to devote a substantial proportion of your time and activity to planning—deciding what and how you want your students to learn. Master teachers exhibit three common traits: they are well organized in their planning, they communicate their instructional objectives effectively to their students, and they have high expectations for their students. The box below summarizes these traits.

The more systematic your instructional planning, the greater the probability that you will succeed. Planning instruction or lessons means establishing

Master Teachers

- Create well-organized plans
- Communicate objectives to students
- Hold high expectations for all students

Lesson plans are priority lists.

priorities, establishing goals and objectives, and establishing learning priorities for students. **Goals** are stated in broad and general terms. They are really statements of intent. For example, one commonly stated goal of education is "to produce a literate citizenry." This is a noble goal, and it shows intent. To achieve a goal, a series of action steps is needed, which we'll call **objectives.** One such objective, to meet the goal of producing a literate citizenry, would be that "formal reading instruction will be delivered in grades 1 through 6." Goals are general, while objectives are more specific. Written lesson plans set out in advance your priorities concerning time, learning materials, objectives, and types of instruction. They are tools for success, both for you and for your students. Let's expand on these points.

Time—we have only so much of it. Even master teachers cannot create a single extra second in the day, but master teachers do *control* time by systematically and carefully planning its productive use for instruction. The lesson plans teachers prepare help them organize and deliver their daily lessons efficiently. Numerous studies have shown that for teachers, being well organized correlates highly with effectiveness (see Yinder and Hendricks-Lee 1995).

The types of lesson plans used by teachers vary widely due to the teacher's experience, the grade level, and the subjects being taught. Writing lesson plans is similar to learning to ride a bicycle. Beginners concentrate on balance, feet on the pedals, and hands on the bars. Only short trips are completed. With experience, pedaling and balance become automatic, and the focus is on safety, comfort, and fun. New teachers tend to overplan, that is, prepare very elaborate plans, being careful not to omit any point; more experienced teachers prepare brief plans. Of importance is that all teachers need to make wise decisions in helping their students reach the intended outcomes.

Effective teachers plan carefully.

To be effective and systematic in your planning, you must become aware of the decision areas and techniques of lesson preparation. The goal of this chapter is to provide you with the basic information you need to make instructional plans. In Chapter 4 we will build on this foundation with more specific information and present an instructional planning model that will help you format actual written lesson plans.

As a new classroom teacher, you will probably begin making detailed plans by imitating a favorite teacher. Later, after further study and experience, you will expand or adapt the basic planning skills you have acquired to your students' specific needs. Classroom innovations are usually developed once you are in your own classroom with your own set of learners, have developed your own instructional resources, and have experimented with various strategies. Although the fundamental steps in lesson planning remain the same, the basic formula is always modified to suit individual teachers' objectives and style.

Planning is nothing more than thinking about what you want accomplished. You think about the details, such as who does what, when, for what length of time, and what opportunities will be created for effective student learning. This is a good spot to introduce you to Louis E. Raths's classic dictum (1967, pp. ix–xi). As a teacher, you are responsible for providing opportunities for changing behavior. Students may or may not change. If they don't, that's not the teacher's responsibility. Teachers do not manipulate children to change. Teachers model, demonstrate, and encourage. Any changes are up to the student!

The main objective of lesson planning is to ensure that all activities and processes provide a supportive educational environment for the learner. Teachers sometimes forget about the learner and concentrate instead on the teaching process or on what is being taught. If lesson planning is to be a useful task, it must always focus on the interaction between what is to be learned and the learner.

Teachers who develop highly structured and detailed plans rarely adhere to them in lock-step fashion. Indeed, such rigidity would probably hinder rather than help the teaching and learning process. For example, you may plan for a twenty-minute student activity, only to discover it requires sixty minutes to complete. You would then make the appropriate adjustment in your plan to ensure student success. The planning tools described in this chapter should be thought of as guiding principles, as aids rather than blueprints to systematic instruction. Although you have prepared carefully (perhaps precisely) to teach a lesson effectively, you must allow for flexible delivery. During the actual classroom interaction, you need to make adaptations and add artistry to each day's plan.

Goals of Education

Webster's New World Dictionary defines a goal as "an object or end that one strives to attain." In the education profession, goals are general statements describing the desired outcomes of schooling. For example, literacy is a goal of all schools in the United States and a goal shared with schools throughout the world.

In the United States the states are responsible for education. State laws and local regulations govern all U.S. schools. State legislatures, state boards of education, and local boards of education all have the legal right to require that the schools teach certain subjects, skills, or ideals. Arizona, for example, requires a course on the free enterprise system. Virginia and several other states require a state history course in high school. Nearly every state has a legislated physical education curriculum. As goals are converted into laws mandating specific content, there is a tendency for the states to also control the curriculum—the books, tapes, videos, teacher guides, and such—and processes used to teach the content.

Goals provide an instructional direction.

However, teachers make the final decisions about how and what to teach. Teachers must sift through the goals, establish priorities, and select those goals that they think are important. The most valuable goals will then take precedence in the classroom.

But remember, it is not the goal itself that is taught. The goal is simply the framework within which content, skills, processes, and attitudes are taught. Goals are abstractions that inspire action. They are almost never completely attained. Objectives, by contrast, are stated as action elements stemming from goals. Objectives are the means by which we seek to achieve our goals.

In many countries, educational goals are established by professionals in a national ministry of education. Since education in the United States is the responsibility of the states, the U.S. Department of Education has limited influence on educational goals. Instead, local citizens and local and state agencies tend to have the greatest influence on establishing and implementing goals.

> ### National Education Goals for the Year 2000: Approved 1994
>
> - First, all children in America will start school ready to learn.
> - Second, the high school graduation rate will increase to at least 90 percent.
> - Third, American students will leave grades 4, 8, and 12 having demonstrated competency in challenging subject matter, including English, mathematics, science, foreign language, civics and government, economics, arts, history, and geography; and every school in America will ensure that all students learn to use their minds well, so that they may be prepared for responsible citizenship, further learning, and productive employment in our modern economy.
> - Fourth, the nation's teaching force will have access to programs for professional development.
> - Fifth, U.S. students will be first in the world in science and mathematics achievement.
> - Sixth, every adult American will be literate and will possess the knowledge and skills necessary to compete in a global economy and to exercise the rights and responsibilities of citizenship.
> - Seventh, every school in America will be free of drugs and violence and will offer a safe, disciplined environment conducive to learning.
> - Eighth, every school will promote parental involvement and participation to promote the social, emotional, and academic growth of children.

There are a number of prescribed national goals for education.

There have been noteworthy attempts by national groups to influence the goals of education in the United States. One recent attempt to set national goals for education was the National Education Goals for the Year 2000, the product of an education summit called by President George Bush in October 1989. All of the nation's governors attended this historic meeting (including Bill Clinton, who was then governor of Arkansas). The box above lists in brief form the eight main educational goals prescribed by the summit and approved by Congress in 1994.

A key impetus for developing these goals was to help U.S. students meet the challenges of the new world economy. The complete text and accompanying strategies can be obtained on the Web at **http://www.ed.gov/legislation/ GOALS2000/TheAct/.** The issue of improving education finds its way into all social, professional, and business forums today.

National Education Standards

National standards are guiding education reform.

Recently, professional groups and associations have become involved in establishing educational goals (see Table 3.1). The **National Science Education Standards,** by the National Research Council (1996), and *Benchmarks for*

TABLE 3.1

A Sampling of National Education Standards	
Report Title and Author	**Brief Description**
Achieving World Class Standards: The Challenge for Educating Teachers (Lieb 1993)	The proceedings of a study group on educating teachers to meet world-class performance standards.
Assessment Standards for School Mathematics (National Council of Teachers of Mathematics 1995)	Standards for assessing the efficacy of math teaching.
Benchmarks for Science Literacy (American Association for the Advancement of Sciences 1993)	The *Benchmarks* set the framework for science reform under "Project 2061."
Curriculum and Evaluation Standards for School Mathematics (National Council of Teachers of Mathematics 1993)	Curriculum standards for Grades K–12 are presented.
National Science Education Standards (National Research Council 1996)	The National Academy of Sciences presents its version for K–12 science.
Standards for the English Language Arts (National Council of Teachers of English (1996)	The NCTE presents its standards for language arts instruction.
Foreign Language Standards: Linking Research, Theories, and Practices (Phillips 1999)	The American Council on the Teaching of Foreign Languages makes a detailed statement.

Science Literacy, by the American Association for the Advancement of Science (1993), are two attempts by science education professional groups to provide guidance through educational standards—that is, to provide criteria against which performance may be judged. The goals of these national education standards are to produce students who are able to

- Use scientific principles and processes appropriately in making personal decisions
- Experience the richness and excitement of knowing about and understanding the natural world
- Increase their economic productivity
- Engage intelligently in public discourse and debate about matters of scientific and technological concern

The push for standards is inspired by many factors, but most importantly by increased global competition in an increasingly technological world. (See also J. F. Jennings's discussion about the politics involved, 1998.)

The term standards has multiple meanings and applications. Science education **standards**, for example, are criteria by which to judge the quality of what students know and are able to do, the quality of the science programs available to them, the quality of the science teaching they receive, the quality of the system that supports their science teachers and programs, and the quality of their school's assessment practices and policies. Science education standards also refer to a vision of learning and teaching science. In both capacities, as performance criteria and as an educational vision, science

TABLE 3.2

National Research Council Standards Content Requirements, Grades 9–12			
Unifying Concepts and Processes	**Science as Inquiry**	**Physical Science**	**Life Science**
Systems, order, and organization	Skills necessary to engage in scientific inquiry	Structure of atoms	The cell
Evidence, models, and explanation	Understanding about scientific inquiry	Structure and properties of matter	Molecular basis of heredity
Change, constancy, and measurement		Chemical reactions	Biological evolution
Evolution and equilibrium		Motion and forces	Interdependence of organisms
Form and function		Conservation of energy and increase in disorder	Matter, energy, and organization in living systems
		Interactions of energy and matter	Behavior of organisms
Earth and Space Science	**Science and Technology**	**Science in Personal and Social Perspectives**	**History and Nature of Science**
Energy in the earth system	Abilities of technological design	Personal and community health	Science as a human endeavor
Geochemical cycles	Understandings about science and technology	Population growth	Nature of scientific knowledge
Origin and evolution of the earth system		Natural resources	Historical perspectives
Origin and evolution of the universe		Environmental quality	
		Natural and human-induced hazards	
		Science and technology in local, national, and global challenges	

SOURCE: Reprinted by permission from *National Science Education Standards.* Copyright © 1995 by the National Academy of Sciences, p. 111. Courtesy of the National Academy Press, Washington, DC.

education standards provide a concrete expression of national goals and a banner around which reformers can rally. Table 3.2 on page 92 lists the content requirements as defined by the National Research Council's standards for grades 9–12.

It must also be noted that standards are to be applied to *all* children. *All* children are expected to meet the standards, and in most states they are all tested at various grade levels to determine their proficiency. (See Bracey 1999 for a thought-provoking critique.)

Reflect Reflect Reflect

- How does the *National Science Education Standards* seek to address the increasingly competitive nature of the world economy?
- Are there common elements or themes in the collective set of goals that have been recently published?
- What issues do your state's education goals or standards address? How are they related to national standards?

A Cautionary Note on Standards

As we noted in Chapter 1, educational reforms have many components. The dominant factor seems to be the creation and implementation of standards. But before we continue the discussion of standards, we want to include an intriguing "aside" about reform: that educational reform is a *hot issue button* is a gross understatement. The popularity of the topic is shown by more than 16,000 published reports, papers, and documents cited in the ERIC database. (Reform is good topic for your term papers.)

Now we return to our principal discussion. Mike Schmoker and Robert J. Marzano (1999) discuss the phenomenon of national standards and caution about "excessive tendencies" (p. 17) in standards documents. One key point they make is that school success is not contingent on national standards as much as on teachers knowing what students are to learn and how to stay focused on instruction.

Too few citizens or even reformers fail to realize that the Goals 2000 legislation makes the following point in the enabling section: "to promote the development and adoption of a *voluntary national system of skill standards and certifications*." (*H.R. 1804,* dated 1994, italics by authors.) The U.S. Congress had the idea of encouraging voluntary systems of standards. The rash of professional and state pronouncements makes this educational enthusiasm appear to take on a mandatory onus.

Several states are implementing their own adaptations of various national standards via state learning requirements. And as we have pointed out, the U.S. Congress promotes *voluntary* standards, the bulk of states has made learning standards, or whatever they are labeled, *mandatory.* This is fully

National educational standards are voluntary.

within their legal jurisdiction because the interpretation of the Tenth Amend-ment of the U.S. Constitution gives the respective states control over public education. Accompanying the standards, many states now have "high-stakes student tests" where state tests are used to penalize schools not performing to some arbitrary standard.

State guidelines prescribe student learnings.

For example, the state of Washington, through its Commission on Student Learning, is defining what all students in the state will be expected to know and be able to do. The program is called Essential Academic Learning Requirements. An example of an "essential learning," or standard, in social studies and history and what the student needs to do to meet this standard are described in Table 3.3. (Note that while the wording of the standard shown in Table 3.3 is a bit ambiguous, it *is* typical of the way in which many state ed-ucational standards are presented at the current time.)

TABLE 3.3

Essential Academic Learning Requirements, Social Studies and History

Essential Learning 1: The student understands and examines major ideas, eras, themes, devel-opments, turning points, chronologies, and the cause-and-effect relationships among them in Washington State, U.S., and world history.

To meet this standard, the student must be able to accomplish the following:

Benchmark 1	Benchmark 2	Benchmark 3
Place events from his or her life and the lives of others in chronological order.	Construct a chronology from timelines, biographies, or narratives of people, ideas, and events.	Analyze and critique the connections and causalities of historical events.
Construct timelines, biog-raphies, or narratives of people and events from the local community.	Identify and explain turn-ing points and key ideas in the following eras in North American history: cultural encounters through 1620; European coloni-zation and settlement (1585–1763); revolution, independence, Articles of Confederation, Constitution (1754–1815); Expansion and Reform (1801–1861); Civil War and Reconstruc-tion (1861–1877).	Identify and explain turning points and key ideas in the following eras in U.S. his-tory: development of the industrial United States emergence (1870–1900); of modern America (1890–1930); Great Depression and World War II (1929–1945); postwar United States (1945–1970); contem-porary era (1968–present).
Explore cultural heritage of self and others.	Examine historical contri-butions of various individuals and groups (e.g., indigenous people, immigrants, political and social leaders).	Examine how diverse peoples have expressed themselves in art, science, religion, government, business, and technology.

SOURCE: Commission on Student Learning 1996, p. 46.

Susan H. Fuhrman (1999) cautions that state standards-based reform efforts and their accountability (testing) approaches may not improve student achievement if the systems' capacity-building is not enhanced. That means providing the resources necessary for all students to learn. And the authors of the joint position statement of the International Reading Association and the National Association for the Education of Young Children state: "IRA and NAEYC believe that goals and expectations for young children's achievement in reading and writing should be developmentally appropriate, that is, *challenging but achievable,* with sufficient adult support" ("Learning to Read and Write," 1998, p. 8, italics in original).

Being more critical, Thomas W. Shiland (1998) argues that the *National Science Education Standards* is an atheoretical document because it fails to prescribe scientific theories worth knowing. In a similar vein, Peter London (1997) labeled national standards for arts education as being antithetical to both democracy and the cultivation of art. Susan Ohanian (1999) sums the entire national standards movement very succinctly in the title of her scathing critique—*One Size Fits Few: The Folly of Educational Standards.*

Reflect Reflect Reflect

- Surf the net at the URL below for Australia's national goals. Compare them to Goals 2000.

    http://www.curriculum.edu.au/mceetya/publicat/pub341.htm

- Using the Internet, research the topic of national standards to locate advocates and adversaries. What themes emerge?

- Examine the Internet for your own state's standards. How do they compare with the national statements?

Section 2: Using a Cognitive Taxonomy as an Instructional Guide

Translating Goals into Objectives

Identifying and defining instructional objectives takes planning. One way to begin is with broad goals and then work toward specific objectives. This is a deductive process: you proceed from general statements to specific ones.

In Chapter 4 we detail the process of defining objectives that fit coherently into a specific unit or lesson plan. Here we will concentrate on defining objectives that fit into three broad instructional domains: the cognitive, affective, and psychomotor domains. In this book we will emphasize the cognitive domain, since most of what teachers explicitly do fits into this category. And the state and national standards are cognitively driven.

There are three major domains of instruction.

The **cognitive domain** encompasses objectives that deal with the recall or recognition of knowledge and the development of intellectual abilities and skills. Most curriculum development focuses on the cognitive domain. Objectives within this domain are most clearly defined using descriptions of student behavior (Bloom et al. 1956).

The **affective domain** is the area that concerns attitudes, beliefs, and the entire spectrum of values and value systems. For example, committing to follow ethical behavior is an affective value. This is an exciting area that curriculum developers are now exploring (Krathwohl, Bloom, and Masia, 1964).

The **psychomotor domain** involves aspects of physical movement and coordination. It integrates cognitive and affective events with bodily actions (Moore and Quinn 1994). For example, developmental physical education programs have objectives drawn from the psychomotor domain of instruction.

Tables 3.4, 3.5, and 3.6 outline the general categories and levels of the three domains. We turn now to a detailed discussion of the cognitive domain.

TABLE 3.4

General Categories of the Cognitive Domain

Category	Cognitive Implication
Knowledge	Knows facts, concepts, symbols, principles
Comprehension	Understands meanings
Application	Transfers knowledge to new settings
Analysis	Reduces complex issues to components
Synthesis	Blends older ideas into novel or creative uses
Evaluation	Generates criteria for judging

SOURCE: *Taxonomy of Educational Objectives: The Classification of Educational Goals, Handbook I: The Cognitive Domain*, edited by Benjamin S. Bloom, et al.. Copyright © 1956 by the Longman Publishing Group. Reprinted by permission of Addison-Wesley Educational Publishers, Inc.

TABLE 3.5

General Levels of the Affective Domain

Level	Characteristics
Receiving (attending)	Willing to listen to some message and point
Responding	Willing to make choices about issues
Valuing	Willing to exhibit a behavior that shows a commitment to a principle
Organization	Willing to defend values
Characterization by a value or value complex	Willing to allow values to drive behavior

SOURCE: *Taxonomy of Educational Objectives: Handbook II: Affective Domain*, edited by David R. Karthwohl, et al. Copyright © 1964 by the Longman Publishing Group. Reprinted by permission of Addison-Wesley Educational Publishers, Inc.

TABLE 3.6

Levels of the Psychomotor Domain

Level	Performance
Imitation	Models skill development
Manipulation	Performs skill independently
Precision	Exhibits skills effortlessly and automatically

SOURCE: Moore and Quinn, *Classroom Teaching Skills*, McGraw-Hill Companies, © 1998.

A **taxonomy** is a cumulative, hierarchical system for describing, classifying, and sequencing learning activities. Although a taxonomy is basically a classification system—a way of categorizing selected items into naturally related groups, such as plants, animals, performance objectives, or questions—it is more than just that. What differentiates a taxonomy from a simple classification system is that a taxonomy is *hierarchical;* that is, the items in a taxonomy are grouped by level or rank. The method by which the items in a taxonomy are ranked depends on the organizing principle and on the type of taxonomy.

The cognitive taxonomy has multiple levels.

Bloom's taxonomy classifies cognitive behaviors into six categories, ranging from fairly simple to more complex. These categories are briefly described in Table 3.7. Like other taxonomies, Bloom's is hierarchical, in that learning at higher levels is dependent on having attained prerequisite knowledge and skills at lower levels. We begin our discussion of the taxonomy with a description of the first level—knowledge.

TABLE 3.7

Characteristic Behaviors of the Cognitive Domain

Level	Characteristic Student Behaviors
Evaluation	Making value decisions about issues, resolving controversies or differences of opinion
Synthesis	Creating a unique, original product that may be in verbal form or may be a physical object
Analysis	Subdividing something to show how it is put together, finding the underlying structure of a communication, identifying motives
Application	Problem solving, applying information to produce some result
Comprehension	Interpreting, translating from one medium to another, describing in one's own words
Knowledge	Remembering, memorizing, recognizing, recalling

SOURCE: *Taxonomy of Educational Objectives: The Classification of Educational Goals. Handbook I: The Cognitive Domain,* edited by Benjamin S. Bloom et al. Copyright © 1956 by the Longman Publishing Group. Reprinted by permission of Addison-Wesley Educational Publishers, Inc.

Knowledge   This is the category that emphasizes remembering—either by recall or recognition. An example of a recall operation is a fill-in-the-blank exercise; an example of a recognition operation is a multiple-choice exercise requiring the recognition of information previously encountered. Both processes involve the retrieval of information stored in the mind. The information is retrieved in basically the same form as it was stored. For example, if an elementary school social studies teacher teaches his or her students on one day that Washington, D.C., is the capital of the United States, then an appropriate knowledge-level question to ask on the next day would be "Name the capital city of the United States." In answering this question, the student would be retrieving the knowledge in the same form as it was received.

The primary focus of knowledge-level objectives is the storage and retrieval of information. In answering a knowledge-level question, the student must find the appropriate signals in the problem, those that most effectively match the relevant knowledge stores. The student is not expected to transform or manipulate knowledge but merely to remember it in the same form as it was presented. Knowledge-level activities may consist of

1. Recalling specific *facts* or *bits of information* (for example, Who was the first president of the United States?)
2. Recalling *terminology* or *definitions* (for example, What is a noun?)

Knowledge forms the foundations for thought.

Although the knowledge level forms the factual foundation for the rest of the categories, its overuse in the classroom causes a number of problems:

1. Simply recalling information does not actively involve the learner. Students are often poorly motivated when much of their work consists of memorizing facts.
2. Because knowledge-level questions usually have only one right answer, they do not lend themselves to classroom sessions in which students work together to discuss and solve a problem. Consequently, students' interpersonal and problem-solving skills are not adequately developed.

Knowledge-level objectives do have their place, however. Effective-schooling studies provide evidence that attention to lower-level skills helps students learn higher-order skills more effectively (Rosenshine and Stevens 1986). A general rule of thumb to use in judging which knowledge-level objectives should be included in the curriculum is to ask yourself, "Will this knowledge be useful to the student at a later time in one of the higher categories?" If the answer is no, you should possibly redesign the lesson.

Reflect Reflect Reflect

- Why would you include a knowledge-level objective in a lesson plan?

Comprehension   The basic idea behind the comprehension category is for students to understand the material, not just memorize it. For example, memorizing the Pledge of Allegiance falls into the knowledge category, but understanding what the words mean would fall under comprehension. However, unlike some of the higher categories, the comprehension level does not ask students to extend information, merely to integrate it into their own frame of reference. That is, if students rephrase material into their own words, or if they organize it to "make sense" to themselves personally, they will probably learn the material more quickly and retain it longer (Slavin 1991; Woolfolk 1995).

Comprehension is the key to higher intellectual levels.

The comprehension category is an essential gateway to higher levels; if students don't understand something, they can't use it to engage in the higher-level processes of analyzing and solving problems (Good and Grouws 1987). It is worth your time and effort to ensure that all students understand an idea before you ask them to use it in more complex activities.

The comprehension category is divided into four components: interpretation, translation, examples, and definitions. In this section we describe each component and provide examples of questions for each one.

Interpretation   **Interpretation** involves the student's ability to identify and comprehend the major ideas in a communication and to understand the relationship between them. For example, a student who is asked to relate one idea in an essay to another must go through the process of interpretation: giving meaning to a response by showing its relationship to other facts. This relationship may be shown by comparing and contrasting or by demonstrating similarity. "How" and "why" questions often call for some type of interpretation. In answering these questions, the student relates major points and, by so doing, shows an understanding of them. Following are some examples of interpretation questions. Note that the italicized key words may be used in a variety of disciplines to frame comprehension objectives or questions.

- *What* are *some similarities* between French and German sentence structure?
- *What differences* exist between the high school curricula of today and those of the 1950s?

Translation   **Translation** involves changing ideas from one form of communication into a parallel form, retaining the meaning. Reading a graph or describing the main point of a pictorial cartoon are examples of translation. Another example of translation is summarization. In summarization, the student translates a large passage into a shorter, more personal, form. Translation questions require the student to construct or change the material into a different form:

- Describe in your own words the first paragraph of the Declaration of Independence.
- Record the results of your laboratory findings in tabular form and summarize your findings.

Examples   One of the best ways a person can demonstrate comprehension of an idea is to give an **example** of it:

- Give an example of a quadratic equation.
- Name two countries that are constitutional monarchies.

In asking students to provide examples of an abstraction, the teacher should require that those examples be new or previously undiscussed. Otherwise, the student will be operating only at the knowledge level, remembering examples from previous classes.

Definitions   A **definition** requires students to describe a term or concept in their own words. This involves more than just repeating verbatim a textbook or dictionary definition. The teacher expects students to formulate the definition with words that are familiar and meaningful to them, for example:

- Define, in your own words, the knowledge category.
- Explain in your own words the meaning of the term *photosynthesis*.

Note that these examples call on the student to do more than just open the dictionary and copy meaningless words or synonyms.

> ## Reflect Reflect Reflect
>
> - When should you use comprehension-type questions?
> - Generate at least three comprehension-type questions appropriate to your students' grade level.

Application   The **application** category involves using information to arrive at a solution to a problem. In operating at the application level, the student typically is given an unfamiliar problem and must apply the appropriate principle or method to it without being told to do so. The student must therefore choose the correct method and use that method correctly. When evaluating an answer to an application problem, you should check both the solution and the process, because how a student solves a problem may be more important than the answer he or she obtains. To be sure that a question reaches the application level, you must make the problem *unique* or *novel*. (If the class went over the same problem the day before, the task for the student would involve mere recall, not application.)

The two-step application process can be visualized as shown in Figure 3.1. In the first step of the process, the student encounters a new problem and

FIGURE 3.1

Application Problems as a Two-Step Process

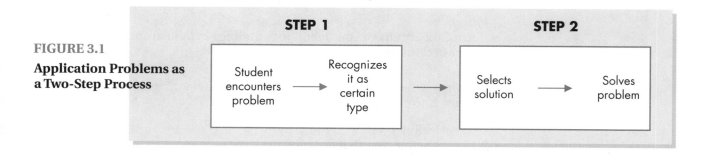

Students can work in harmony toward achieving meaningful goals. © Suzie Fitzhugh

The application level requires understanding.

recognizes it as a type of problem solved before. During the second step of solving an application-level problem, the student selects an appropriate solution and applies it to the data at hand. This solution can consist of an algorithm, a formula, an equation, a recipe, or a standardized set of procedures for handling a specific type of problem.

If you view application problems as a two-step process, you can analyze students' responses and dignose problems on the basis of error patterns (Tatsuoka and Tatsuoka 1987). If students are having difficulty recognizing certain equations, then you need to give them a wide variety of these types of problems to recognize and prescribe solutions for. However, if students can recognize equations but cannot plug the values in the problem into the correct formula or equation, give them practice in the computational aspects of the problem. This is another example of how the taxonomy keeps teachers adapting instruction to meet diverse student needs.

An example will help differentiate the application category from other categories. Typically, an application problem has one solution, but there may be alternative ways to solve the problem. These usually involve the use of formulas or principles that have been learned previously with the student selecting the appropriate application to solve the problem.

For example, students encounter a problem in which the formula $a^2 + b^2 = c^2$ should be used. To evaluate performance at the application level optimally, wait a few weeks after the original presentation of the content and then introduce a new problem dealing with right triangles. This will ensure that students can demonstrate the knowledge in a unique and novel situation. They are doing more than using a formula on a math test because it was the only topic covered for the previous three weeks.

> ## Reflect Reflect Reflect
>
> - Give an example of an application problem from your own field of study.
> - What must students do in each of two steps to solve an application problem appropriately?

Analysis   Application involves bringing together separate components to arrive at a solution. **Analysis** is the reverse of that process; it involves taking apart complex items—such as speeches, written communications, organizations, or machines—and explaining their underlying organization. The emphasis in analysis-level operations is on explaining how the various parts of a complex process or object are arranged or work together to achieve a certain effect.

Analysis can be differentiated from comprehension by means of the depth of processing involved. Comprehension involves finding similarities and differences in making comparisons. Basically, the task at that level is to show relationships that can be discovered by understanding the communication itself. Analysis, however, involves looking beneath the surface and discovering how different parts interact. In this sense analysis involves working backward, taking a situation or event and explaining how all the parts fit together to produce a total effect. Comprehension, on the other hand, primarily involves describing what that effect is.

We can subdivide the analysis category into two subcategories: identifying issues and identifying implications.

Identifying Issues   In this type of analysis operation, students subdivide a broad communication into its constituent parts. This entails discovering the "skeleton" of a communication, since the issues involved are sometimes not explicitly stated in the communication. In this sense, identifying the issues means going beyond the information in the message to show the relationship between assumptions and key points, stated or otherwise.

Following are examples of questions that ask students to identify issues:

- Using the six campaign speeches of the presidential candidates, point out the major differences between the candidates, relating the differences to specific sections of the speeches.
- Explain the main points of the Bill of Rights in terms of current injustices.

Analytic thought goes beyond knowledge

Stating Implications   Stating implications requires students to identify the relationship between two propositions. The relationship may be expressed in terms of influence, association, or necessary consequences, and it need not be stated directly. Following are examples of questions that ask students to state implications:

- What were some of the motives behind the NATO interventions in Bosnia?
- Why do many organizations keep lobbyists in Washington, D.C.?

Reflect Reflect Reflect

- Under what circumstances would you use analysis questions that ask students to identify examples? To state implications? Give examples of both.

Synthesis   **Synthesis** entails the creative meshing of elements to form a new and unique entity. Because its key is creativity, the synthesis category may be the most distinctive and one of the easiest to recognize—but it may also be the most difficult to teach. Synthesis is the process of combining parts in such a way as to constitute a pattern or structure that did not exist before. A research paper can belong to either the application or synthesis category, depending on the level of originality it displays. If the paper is comprehensive and thorough but does not add new knowledge to the topic, we would consider the writer to be operating at the application level. If, however, the writer puts ideas together in new or unique patterns or creates new idea configurations, then we would consider the writer to be engaging in a synthesis-level activity.

Because of the stress on creativity, operations at the synthesis level are usually difficult to grade objectively. You need to use more subjective judgment in evaluating synthesis operations than in evaluating operations at other levels. However, be sure your judgments are based on appropriate criteria; otherwise your commends may stifle creativity. To encourage creativity, give your students ample leeway in their creative expression.

Like the other levels, synthesis can be subdivided in terms of the type of processing involved and the products of those operations—unique or original communication, plans for operations, and creating abstractions.

Synthesis approaches the realm of creativity

Unique or Original Communication   In one type of synthesis, the product or performance is a unique type of communication, such as an essay, speech, or original art form, such as a poem, a painting, or a musical composition. Students' originality and creativeness are among the criteria used in evaluating these products (see also McAlpine et al. 1987; Ennis 1985b; Paul 1985).

Plans for Operations   The second subcategory of the synthesis level involves developing a plan or proposed set of operations to be performed. These operations result in the creation of a tangible product. This tangible product and the creativity displayed in creating it are the two distinguishing characteristics of the synthesis level.

Creating Abstractions   The third type of synthesis involves creating a set of abstract relations. This typically involves working with observed phenomena or data and forming patterns that did not exist before. For example, you might ask students to experiment with liquids of different densities and then formulate hypotheses about what they observed. In social studies, after students have studied the constitutions of a number of different nations, you might ask them to formulate principles for drawing up a workable constitution.

Reflect Reflect Reflect

- Design a synthesis task for students in your content area or grade level. In which subcategory does your task belong?

Evaluation   **Evaluation** requires making decisions on controversial topics and substantiating these decisions with sound reasons. Judgment is to evaluation what creativity is to synthesis. Evaluation questions ask students to state their judgments and to give the criteria upon which they are based. To function at the evaluation level, the student must (1) set up appropriate standards or values and (2) determine how closely the idea or object meets the standards or values.

The evaluation category projects the analysis category into another dimension. An evaluation question requires the student, besides analyzing, to make a judgment. The criteria for judgment must be clearly identified, and the quality of the evaluation response should be graded according to how well the student has met the criteria.

An evaluation response should consist of two parts:

1. The student should establish criteria on which to base his or her judgment.
2. Using the prescribed criteria, the student should state his or her own judgment.

For example, if you ask the question, "To what extent should the federal government regulate health care?" you are asking the student first to decide what regulatory role the federal government should play and then to determine to what extent that role should apply to health care. There will be some difference of opinion about the role of the federal government. This brings out the subjective and creative component of evaluation. The student must exercise judgment in matching these criteria with the subject being evaluated.

Criteria are formed usually from one of three sources:

1. Cultural or social values
2. Religious or historical absolutes
3. Individual justifications

Examples of each follow:

1. "The expectations for the twenty-first-century public schools are excessive." This statement could be answered in several ways, depending on which social or cultural values the person answering it believes to be important.
2. "Should abortion be legalized?" To some people this is a religious question and is couched in absolute values; to others it is a personal moral decision; and to still others, it is a medical decision.
3. "To what extent are educational standards useful or useless?" Different people would probably arrive at different answers based on their different value systems.

Did you notice how the evaluation category of the cognitive domain tends to overlap with the lower levels of the affective domain? Yes, there is a **correlation** between feelings, attitudes, values, and the way we select criteria by which to judge or evaluate.

Evaluation is not just opinion.

Because different students have different values, you will receive different responses to the same evaluation question. You can use evaluation questions to help students learn to live with and accept the different views of others, thus preparing them for a life in a pluralistic society. You can also prepare students for taking a stand on issues with evaluation questions such as "What do you think is best/worst or more/most important?" But caution: always require a *rationale*. Opinions, for the most part, are irrational.

Reflect Reflect Reflect

- The last three items in the cognitive taxonomy—analysis, synthesis, and evaluation—are often called higher-order skills. What makes them of a "higher order"?

- How could you encourage your students to use these skills when you teach controversial subjects?

- Examine Table 3.3 and categorize the various benchmarks via Bloom's taxonomy.

Bloom's Taxonomy: A Brief Analysis

In the almost fifty years that Bloom's taxonomy has existed, it has been widely used and accepted by educators at all levels. Research on the taxonomy, as well as research in cognitive psychology, has generally supported the ideas behind the taxonomy but has also raised some questions about its internal structure. This section focuses on that research.

Questions and Concerns About the Taxonomy   Despite its widespread acceptance and use, Bloom's taxonomy has raised some persistent questions. One question is about its comprehensiveness. Some critics state that the taxonomy is too narrow and does not include all the important outcomes taught in our schools (Furst 1994). When you think about the broad range of goals existing in such diverse areas as home economics, art, music, and physical education, you can see that this concern is probably valid. As this chapter points out, teachers in these diverse areas can still use the taxonomy, but they will have to adapt it to their own classrooms. In fact, all teachers seem to do this—they personalize any educational idea to make it their own (see Lieberman and McLaughlin 1992).

A second concern centers on whether the levels in the hierarchy are discrete or overlapping. You may have encountered this problem yourself as you tried to keep the levels separate. For example, is application of a formula knowledge, comprehension or application? Though a problem for researchers, this concern is not as great for individual teachers using the taxonomy to guide their teaching.

Orlich (1991) raised some questions about the sequence of the levels. Though he supports the general idea of increasing cognitive complexity, he questions whether progress through the taxonomy occurs in six uniform steps. Again, this is more of a research problem than an instructional one.

Uses of the Taxonomy   The taxonomy has been much used in curriculum and test construction. It has been used in general curriculum design (Pratt 1994), to provide stimulating experiences for preschoolers through technology (Morgan 1996), and in test construction (McLaughlin and Phillips 1991). Researchers have found Bloom's taxonomy to be a useful analytic tool as well. For example, the six conceptual levels in the taxonomy were used to relate data obtained from a satellite remote sensing exercise. Concepts and principles associated with the statellite images were arranged in hierarchical order that ranged from simple data (knowledge) to interpretations and evaluations of data (Marks, Vitek, and Allen, 1996). Other researchers have made use of the taxonomy for analyzing verbal interactions in a classroom (Fisher and Hiebert 1990).

> The cognitive taxonomy is widely applied in education.

Perhaps the taxonomy's greatest contribution has been in the development of a professional language. Teachers and administrators who describe and analyze instruction know that terms such as *knowledge level* and *higher levels of learning* will be understood by educators everywhere. This universal vocabulary, reflecting a specialized body of knowledge, was an essential step in the professionalization of teaching (Metzger 1987).

> Comprehension is a gateway to all of the cognitive levels.

The importance of the comprehension category as a gateway to the other levels is also becoming clear. In a retrospective review of this area of cognitive psychology, Raymond Nickerson (1985) argued convincingly that comprehending an idea or concept is an essential prerequisite to applying it, analyzing it, or using it creatively or evaluatively. Thus, teachers need to make a special effort to determine that students understand an idea before asking them to use it.

The overriding message is clear. If your students are to learn effectively, you need to plan and implement strategies that require internal processing of information. Establish goals, lay a knowledge base, and teach actively toward higher cognitive levels.

Reflect Reflect Reflect

- Have you ever been in a class where it was evident that a taxonomy was used as an instructional technology?
- How helpful do you find the taxonomy?
- What drawbacks to it do you see?

A New Model for the Cognitive Taxonomy

Since 1956, Bloom's taxonomy has provided a number of useful insights about teaching and learning in the classroom. Then came Raymond Nickerson's monumental "Understanding Understanding" (1985). That paper triggered a serious reexamination of the nature of understanding and its role in Bloom's taxonomy. When Arnold B. Arons (1988) examined concepts similar to Nickerson's, his studies created more speculation about the role comprehension plays in learning. Many other researchers contributed pieces to our dilemma and puzzle (Wittrock 1986; Jones 1986; Ennis 1985a; Beyer 1988; Whimbey 1984; Haller, Child, and Walberg 1988; McPeck 1981). Based on these works, we constructed a novel interpretation of how the cognitive taxonomy may operate. It breaks away from the traditional way of depicting the six major categories of the taxonomy (see Figure 3.2), which imply that students must climb the steps one at a time. That analogue (model) has generally persisted since 1956.

The cognitive taxonomy may resemble the Bohr atom.

In Figure 3.3 we offer here a novel way to illustrate the interactive nature of the cognitive taxonomy's categories. This model should actually be viewed as a three-dimensional form, like the solar system or the Bohr atom. Our model shows that as learning occurs, knowledge and all other categories

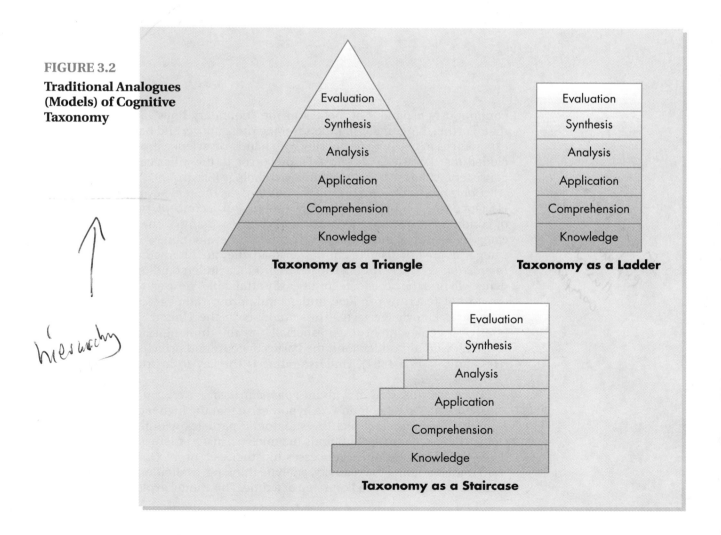

FIGURE 3.2

Traditional Analogues (Models) of Cognitive Taxonomy

Evaluation
Synthesis
Analysis
Application
Comprehension
Knowledge

Taxonomy as a Triangle

Evaluation
Synthesis
Analysis
Application
Comprehension
Knowledge

Taxonomy as a Ladder

Evaluation
Synthesis
Analysis
Application
Comprehension
Knowledge

Taxonomy as a Staircase

FIGURE 3.3

Interactive Model of Cognitive Taxonomy

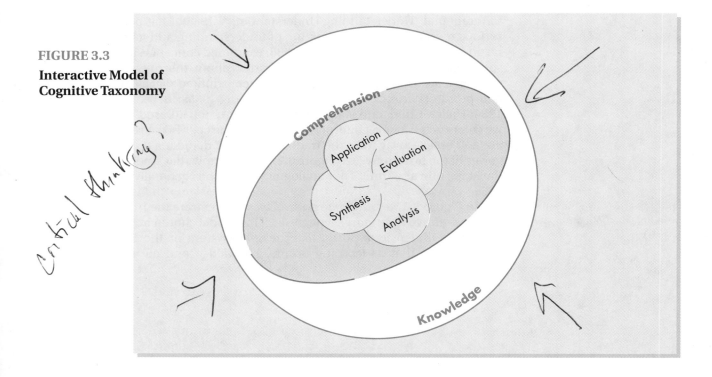

[handwritten note: Critical thinking?]

[handwritten note: "In own words" explain" illustrate compare]

continuously expand. The breaks in the "boundary lines" attempt to show that. Further, after analyzing the several writers above, and based on our own experiences in teaching (especially with hands-on science programs), we concluded that knowledge is simply a precursor to the other categories. This is consistent with research in cognitive psychology (Slavin 1991; Wakefield 1996).

Comprehension—that is, *understanding*—is the real key to the other levels. Once you comprehend, or truly understand, a concept, principle, law, set of conditions, or skills, then you can branch into any of the remaining four categories—application, analysis, synthesis, or evaluation. We submit that the categories are not discrete entities; instead, they are interactive. *Critical to the interaction is understanding.* Teach to produce understanding, and your students will find the other categories easily attainable. We assert that U.S. teachers do not teach to produce understanding but rather teach to produce a superficial knowledge level. Thus students in the United States do rather poorly on achievement tests, especially on the thinking skills sections, because they do not understand the basic concepts and principles being tested (Hess and Azuma 1991). Understanding is the key to instructional success (Wittrock 1992.)

We close this section with an *emergent theory.* We want you to send us your thoughts on this model. We hypothesize that the higher categories of the cognitive taxonomy act like the subatomic particles within an atomic nucleus. There is a "force" that binds the nucleus, just as there is a "quality" that holds the higher cognitive processes together as a unity. One moves rapidly from understanding to creativity, analytic thinking, evaluation, or application without having to proceed one step at a time. This model explains the interactions of all elements of the cognitive domain. As John I. Goodlad says in *A Place Called School* (1984, p. 236),

> Only *rarely* did we find evidence to suggest instruction (in reading and math) likely to go much beyond merely possession of information to a level of understanding its implications and either applying it or exploring its possible applications. Nor did we see activities likely to arouse students' curiosity or to involve them in seeking a solution to some problem not already laid bare by teacher or textbook.
>
> And it appears that this preoccupation with the lower intellectual processes pervades social studies and science as well. An analysis of topics studied and materials used gives not an impression of students studying human adaptations and explorations, but of facts to be learned.

Schooling tends to stress lower cognitive levels.

Reflect Reflect Reflect

- As you examined our model, did it make sense to you?
- Did it seem to be applicable to your classroom?
- If you have some question or comment about our model, please write the authors care of the publisher, or e-mail us at dorlich@wsu.edu.

Using Taxonomies as Planning Tools

Teaching can be envisioned as a triad of strategies, outcomes, and evaluations, as illustrated in Figure 3.4. In this model the formulated outcomes, or objectives, determine both the teaching strategies and the evaluation procedures—all the elements affect all the others. A taxonomy can be used in each of these activities: in formulating outcomes or objectives at an appropriate level, in developing classroom questions and learning exercises, and in constructing evaluation instruments congruent with the outcomes and strategies to be employed. In other words, you can use taxonomies to decide what to teach, how to teach, and how to evaluate the effectiveness of your teaching (see Daggett 1996).

Taxonomies are planning tools.

We acknowledge the broad array of adaptations that you can make with the taxonomy. However, for our immediate purpose, we will focus only on planning uses, since other topics are amplified in subsequent chapters. Effective teaching requires that teachers think strategically about the taxonomic level of objectives, questions, and test items when they plan. Five different ways that a taxonomy can help in the planning process are listed below. (You may want to add your own after reading ours.)

1. *Provide a Range of Objectives.* A taxonomy provides a range of possible outcomes or objectives for any subject. Closely examining the categories may prevent you from overemphasizing one dimension of learning, such as knowledge, in your teaching. In this respect a taxonomy not only adds variety to your repertoire but also gives greater breadth to your objectives.

FIGURE 3.4

A Model of Teaching Alignment

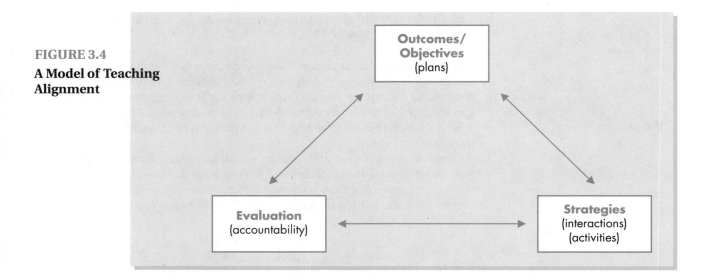

2. *Sequence Objectives.* An analysis of learning tasks suggests the learning experiences necessary for the student to obtain the intended outcomes. A taxonomy provides one means of sequencing learning from simple to complex outcomes.

3. *Provide a Cognitive Structure.* Research has shown that students learn and retain information better if it is organized into some type of cognitive structure rather than presented as isolated items (Hohn 1995). Taxonomies can provide cognitive structure to students by showing them how facts can be used in the application, analysis, synthesis, and evaluation of other ideas.

4. *Provide a Learning Model.* By experiencing a series of learning activities sequenced based on a taxonomy, students are able to perceive that learning is logical and sequential, thus obtaining a model of learning that they can use even after they leave the classroom.

5. *Reinforce Learning.* Because each lower category of the taxonomy is subsumed by the next-higher category, reinforcement of previous learning occurs if learning experiences are sequenced in terms of a taxonomy. Further, activities can be focused on a specific level.

Instructional

Strategies

Using the Taxonomy as a Planning Tool

- Provide a range of objectives.
- Sequence objectives from simple to complex.
- Show the relationship of objectives.
- Plan for logical and sequential activities.
- Build on previous learnings.
- Plan for appropriate levels of instruction and assessment.

Section 3: Using Objectives to Guide Learners

So far in this chapter we have considered two sources teachers can draw upon in writing objectives and planning instruction: (1) goals and standards and (2) cognitive taxonomies. We turn now to a third major resource teachers need in planning: knowledge of how to write good educational objectives. The value of creating objectives, both long and short term, is to provide intent and direction to your instruction. Students need to know where they are going and why. In this section we provide guidelines for writing and evaluating objectives.

You can use several techniques to state objectives. We demonstrate first the most specific formats because they add the greatest clarity and structure. This type of objective, called performance objectives, was developed by Robert F. Mager. Next we will present a different format, a two-tiered model elaborated by Norman E. Gronlund (1995). Throughout our entire objectives discussion, it is important to keep in mind that there is no right way or wrong way to state outcomes or objectives. The key point is that you must alert the students to what they are to learn. Don't say "study this poem" if you want students to memorize it. Instructional fairness is the essential prerequisite in specifying learning outcomes, objectives, or whatever.

We will close the chapter with some final words on curriculum alignment, by which we mean congruence among objectives, teaching strategies, and assessment or evaluation.

Writing Performance Objectives

Performance objectives are very precise statements of what you expect the student to do (Mager 1962). Although performance objectives are written in a wide variety of styles, three elements are generally included:

1. The statement of an observable behavior, or performance, on the part of the learner

2. A description of the conditions under which learner behavior or performance is to occur

3. The prescription of a minimally acceptable level of performance on the part of the learner

The Performance Statement   The first element of a performance objective is an **outcome,** generally a verb that indicates what the learner is to perform, do, or produce. Verbs such as *match, name, compute, list, assemble, write,* *circle,* and *classify* describe observable learner behaviors or outcomes, which will help you evaluate student achievement of performance objectives. For example, if you state that the student must name the capital cities of ten states listed, the student's behavior is manifested when this performance takes place; everyone will know that the student has attained the stated objective or outcome.

The specifications of the performance come from the general goals, of course. If you teach social studies in the United States, one goal always will be to provide instruction about the U.S. system of government and Constitution. An intermediate goal surely will be to study the Bill of Rights. Specific performance objectives may be as follows. The learner will

1. Paraphrase the first ten amendments to the U.S. Constitution
2. Distinguish between statements that are from the Bill of Rights and those that are not
3. Conduct a survey to determine how many students in the high school can identify the Fifth Amendment

Performance statements are precise.

Words such as *know, understand, analyze, evaluate, appreciate, comprehend,* and *realize* are not action verbs. While such terms are important in describing the processes of learning and behaving, they are not observable actions and thus cannot be used when writing performance objectives. However, these terms are used plentifully in state and national standards documents. Such terms may be used when you specify goals, as noted in our discussion of taxonomies. Remember that you make the decisions about the kind of performance you think is most appropriate or relevant. Thus, the first and most important element of any performance objective is selecting the action verb and its direct object.

Elaboration of Conditions   The second element in prescribing a performance objective is elaboration, or description, of the conditions under which the learner is to perform the behavior. The conditions refer to the circumstances under which the learner must perform. Generally, conditional elements refer to

1. What materials may be used to perform the tasks
2. How the performance may be accomplished—for example, from memory, from the textbook, or using a computer program
3. Time elements (although time may also be used in evaluation)
4. Location of the performance (in the classroom, in a gymnasium, or in the library)

Conditional elements are the "givens."

For example: "With the aid of the periodic table, the student will list the atomic weights of the first ten elements." Note that the conditional statement is "with the aid of the periodic table." This tells students that they need not memorize the atomic weights; they should simply identify them from the periodic table. We often refer to the conditional component of a performance objective as a "statement of givens": "given this" or "given that," the learner will accomplish something.

The conditional element of a performance objective is the "fair play" part of the instruction. How many times have you walked into a class to find that when the teacher said to "study" a poem, the actual or implied meaning, at least according to the teacher, was to "memorize" the poem? The imprecision of such conditions is confusing, if not demoralizing. We recommend that you always present this element of instruction to students explicitly, whether you use performance objectives or not.

The box below contains a list of a few conditional statements that could be included in the appropriate performance objectives.

Sample Conditional Statements

- "From memory . . ."
- "Using a map, a compass, a ruler, and a protractor . . ."
- "On a computer disk, which describes . . ."
- "Given six different material samples with labels . . ."
- "From the notes taken while viewing . . ."
- "Within a ten-minute time span and from memory . . ."
- "Using IRS Form 1040A . . ."

These are some examples of the conditions under which a student can achieve a desired performance objective. The teacher sets the conditional statement in advance and gives it to the student. We recommend that the condition be the first component of the performance objective. We believe it has a significant impact on instructional planning and teacher behavior, so it should never be omitted.

Conditions must be realistic. Even though feasible, "reciting the Declaration of Independence from memory in five minutes" would be an inappropriate condition. One must always ask, "What is my main priority for the objective?" If memorizing is the priority, then that condition will define the attainment of the objective. If identifying the key ideas in the Declaration of Independence is the priority, then a condition less rigorous than memorization would be more compatible with the objective.

An integrated social studies and language arts outcome might be written as follows:

> Students will read the two essays [specify essays] found on the Internet. Orally, they will analyze the main points, showing how figures of speech and metaphors enrich the meanings. Each student must prepare a one-page, written summary of the historical and social events that affected each author, using the reference books reserved for this unit. Students will prepare their reports during the class time on the computers scheduled exclusively for class use. Before final drafts are prepared, each paper must be critiqued by two members of the working group for grammar, spelling, and punctuation.

The Criterion Measure The third element of a performance objective—the definition of an acceptable standard of performance—is perhaps the most difficult to write. This standard may be referred to as the criterion measure, level of performance, minimum criterion, or minimum acceptable performance. Whatever term is used, the designated level is the minimum or lowest level of acceptable performance. When this is specified, students know in advance exactly what the standards are by which their work will be judged.

Following is a list of clearly written criterion measures (the condition and the performance verb are missing from the statements):

1. ". . . 70 percent of a given list of problems."
2. ". . . within 2 mm. . . ."
3. ". . . nine out of ten of the elements. . . ."
4. ". . . within five minutes, with no more than two errors of any kind."
5. ". . . the project will be compared to the two models completed by the instructor."
6. ". . . without any grammatical or spelling errors."
7. ". . . containing one dependent and one independent clause."

Criterion measures alert students to expectations for success.

Each of these criterion elements states a well-defined standard the student can strive for. These standards are always devised so that students have a high probability of achieving them and will thus be encouraged to continue to strive toward meeting the established criterion. A word of caution: many teachers expect far too much from their students and set standards that are too high or impossible to reach. You must know at what level your students are working so that you can establish reasonable minimum standards—a skill that is part of the artistry of teaching.

Frequently an instructor will require 100 percent of the class to attain 100 percent of the objective—that is, for everyone to demonstrate complete mastery. This is called a 100/100 criterion measure. There are many areas in which an instructor will require mastery, such as basic reading skills, math facts, using equipment, or learning safety procedures. In these cases, mastery is the minimum acceptable level of performance. Again, you the professional must make that decision. The mastery criterion is most appropriate when completing prerequisite or entry-level tasks, since later skills are contingent on successfully performing the initial ones.

While carefully defined standards of student performance are essential to a well-written performance objective, we recognize that much of what is taught in the classroom focuses on activities or experiences. Providing meaningful criterion measures for instruction of this type will be easier if you keep two things in mind. First, remember that activity, experience, or competency learning experiences are made up of previous learning that can be given clear standards of student performance. For example, the activity of playing volleyball is made up of a number of specific behaviors that can be isolated and given clear criterion measures. Competence in building a multimedia presentation is preceded by many skills that more easily provide clear standards of student performance. Performance objectives that focus on activities, experiences, or competencies are often more global in scope, and criterion measures for them can be difficult to write. However, they are always preceded by smaller increments of learning, for which clear standards of performance can be written. In effect, the totality of all the objectives that precede an activity, experience, or competency objective make up the criterion measure for that objective.

Second, to write only narrow, skill-based performance objectives would destroy much of the richness that should be a part of every classroom. Many times it is the activity or experientially focused instruction that gives a classroom spice and interest. Do not avoid writing objectives in which the criterion measure is not as precise and tight as you might like. Broadly stated objectives in which the criterion measure is less well defined are to be desired as long as they flow from a sequence of clearly articulated objectives. For example: "Describe at least four conditions of the Great Depression of the 1930s that were missing in the recessions of the 1980s and 1990s." As you will learn, much of the most exciting, high-level learning comes from mastering the lower-level material and skills that precede it (see Rohwer and Sloane 1994). The box below summarizes the approach to use for complex tasks.

Objectives for Complex Tasks

- Focus on prerequisite knowledge and skills.
- Use broadly focused objectives for complex tasks.

Criterion Grading   A word of caution must be expressed about criterion levels. Far too frequently the teacher prescribes a percentage or a time as the evaluation element of the performance objective. For example, if time is a critical factor in the real world—as in CPR, braking actions (that is, in a car), or manipulating machinery—then a timed criterion is appropriate. But to set a time for student learning experiences that is identical to that of professionals in the field is inappropriate. Skills can be built or improved by using variable criterion measures, just as they can with any systematic method. Thus, a criterion measure of thirty seconds for a skill in the first experience may be reduced systematically as learners improve. Typing teachers have observed this principle in action many times. As time goes by, students are allowed fewer mistakes per time period. In short, the standards for an A or even a C grade are shifted to higher levels of achievement as the course progresses.

Assignment of grades can be based on objective criteria.

Some educators have criticized performance objectives for seemingly forcing them into giving A grades for minimal student performance. This need not be the case. As a teacher, you may write performance objectives with clear criterion measures and make the meeting of those objectives worth any letter grade you choose. For example, you may state that meeting the criterion measures in your objectives will earn your students a C grade. Not meeting the criterion measures in your objectives will earn students a grade of less than C, and performing beyond your objectives will earn a grade higher than C. We provide a detailed discussion about grading in Chapter 10.

Several alternative methods are available for using performance objectives and grades. You may choose to write several performance objectives for a single sequence of instruction. Each objective can be progressively more difficult, with each worth a higher letter grade. Thus, meeting performance objective 1 earns a grade of D, while meeting objective 2 earns a grade of C, and so on. Rather than pressuring the teacher into giving a high grade for mediocre performance, carefully phrased performance objectives enable the teacher to prescribe a precise value and meaning to grades in terms of overt learner performance.

Writing Two-Tiered Objectives

The second kind of objective you should know about is Gronlund's (1995) two-tiered model, which lists a general objective first, followed by specific learning outcomes or performance objectives. For example, if you were teaching a social studies lesson on map skills, you might use the model shown in the box below.

The Gronlund format is a useful and practical way to state objectives.

(The following discussion is adapted from Linn and Gronlund 1995, pp. 27–46.) Gronlund argues persuasively that although advocates of *behavioral* or *performance objectives* (the terms are virtually synonymous) won't accept verbs such as *know* and *understand* in objectives, these are precisely the outcomes we want. We work hard so our students will know the meaning of mass in physics or understand the similarities between America's Revolutionary War and our involvement in Vietnam. Thus, it is counterproductive not to state objectives in terms of knowing and understanding.

Gronlund resolves the issue by using two levels of specificity in stating intended learning outcomes. The first level, termed **general instructional objectives,** states the most general level desired, which requires teacher judgment. The objective must be specific enough to guide instruction but not

---

Gronlund's Two-Tiered Format

1. List general objective or statement.
   - Learn basic map-reading skills, or
   - Learn basic topographic map skills.

2. State specific performance goals or outcomes.
   - Identify north as always at the top of the map (convention).
   - Calculate map scales.
   - Determine elevations on topographic map for designated sites.

Samples of General Instructional Objectives

- *Knows* basic terminology
- *Understands* concepts and principles
- *Demonstrates* critical thinking skills
- *Writes* a well-organized essay
- *Critically* evaluates a poem
- *Appreciates* poetry

so specific as to require separate objectives for each act the student makes. The box on the bottom of page 116 (adapted from Linn and Gronlund 1995, pp. 39–40) contains examples.

The verbs are quite general, leaving you a wide range of specific behaviors that could be used to indicate achievement. This range is a great help in planning instruction. As an objective, "Understands concepts," for instance, helps you select the appropriate concepts and design instruction to lead your students toward understanding them.

General instructional objectives are also, for the most part, content free. Most of the above objectives could apply to almost any subject. That is intentional. Using such generic objectives, if you select carefully, means you don't have to write entirely new objectives for each class or topic. The box below provides further examples of useful verbs to use with general instructional objectives.

Following each instructional objective are several **specific learning outcomes,** which indicate what specific student behaviors will be accepted as evidence that the instructional objective has been satisfactorily attained. For instance, there are many ways to satisfy each objective in the list below, and none of the objectives can be mastered beyond any possible further

---

Sample Verbs to Use With General Instructional Objectives

- Knows
- Demonstrates
- Relates
- Writes
- Appreciates

- Understands
- Applies
- Interprets
- Evaluates
- Comprehends

Examples of Instructional Objectives with Specific Learning Outcomes

Understands the meaning of concepts

- Explains the concept in own words
- Identifies examples of the concept
- Creates examples of the concept
- Distinguishes between similar concepts

Demonstrates skill in critical thinking

- Identified logical fallacies
- Withholds judgment until adequate evidence is acquired
- Recognizes fallacious reasoning in written and spoken communications

improvement. Thus the teacher must include only enough specific learning outcomes (at an appropriate level) as is reasonable. Again, the examples in the box on bottom of page 117 will clarify the differences.

The specific outcomes are expressed with verbs that actively identify what the student will do. They are the same verbs used to state performance objectives already discussed, and they serve the same purpose—stating an observable behavior. Although specific learning outcomes are similar to the performance objectives, they do not necessarily indicate a condition, performance, and criterion.

Notice again how these objectives can help you plan and organize your instruction. The final objective in the box, dealing with fallacious reasoning, tells you to include both oral and written explanations and examples in your instruction and evaluations.

Sometimes a third level of specificity is useful, to clarify how students will demonstrate achievement of the general instructional objective and as a guide for constructing test items. Note the three levels in the example in the box below.

Example of Instructional Objective with Three Levels of Specificity

- Demonstrates skill in critical thinking
- Identifies logical fallacies
- Recognizes use of red herrings in oral debate

Recognizing the Limits of Objectives

Even well-written objectives are not an educational panacea that will resolve all learning problems. Objectives have limited purposes; they are only a means to an end, not an end per se. The purpose of the objective is to communicate the exact intent of the lesson. The objective is one component of the lesson plan. The teacher can construct technically correct objectives but can fail completely in the classroom because of a lack of teaching skills and interpersonal competencies or strategies.

When developing lessons that use objectives, the teacher must accept the following four assumptions.

1. Learning is defined as a change in the learner's observable performance.
2. Behavioral changes are observable in some form and may be measured by *appropriate* measuring devices over a specified period of time.
3. Observed learner outcome is directly linked to the teaching strategies, the content, or the media used.
4. The majority of children at all ages can master appropriate subjects at some acceptable developmental level if they are given enough time and adequate, appropriate learning experiences.

Reflect Reflect Reflect

- Have you ever been provided with a list of three-part performance objectives in your own classes? If so, describe your reaction.
- Have you ever had to specify learning objectives in a very precise manner? What was the effect on the results?
- As you think about writing objectives for your own lessons, which of the two kinds of objectives presented in this discussion do you believe will prove more useful to you as a teacher? Would your response change if you focus instead on which would prove more helpful to your students? Why or why not?

Curriculum Alignment

Another rationale for performance objectives centers around the concept of curriculum alignment (Cohen 1987 and 1995; Steinbrink and Jones 1991). In its simplest form, a curriculum is composed of objectives, instruction, and assessment, which we show diagrammatically in Figure 3.4. When all three elements match—that is, when instruction and assessment focus on stated objectives—alignment exists. Curriculum alignment is much more difficult to attain than it seems. Teachers emphasize different learning experiences based on their skills and interests. Students have different talents and have mastered different skills at different levels. Teachers have a variety of materials to use for instruction. Performance objectives do, however, provide a key teachers can use to align the instruction in their own classrooms. For that matter, performance objectives are essential for alignment at the district and building level as well.

The basis for successful curriculum alignment is in the process of carefully analyzing the skills, competencies, and other measures of student learning that you want to result from instruction. You test what you teach and you teach what is in your objectives—this is an idea that is simple to state but difficult to carry out without carefully planned and written performance objectives. Curriculum can be aligned from either end of the process—the objective end or the assessment end. Too often, what teachers teach is influenced by what they know or anticipate will be on the tests. To make instructional decisions based on what is to be tested is to pervert the process. Done correctly, assessment flows from the decisions you made about what is best for your students to learn. Start from the objectives, and make the rest of the process fit. If your objectives are clear and sharp, instruction and assessment will be aligned. The box on page 120 summarizes curriculum alignment.

Curriculum alignment ensures fairness.

When all parts of the curriculum—performance objectives, activities, instruction, and assessment—are congruent (in alignment), student learning improves dramatically. Curriculum alignment has been identified as a principal sign of effective schools (see Kelly 1991). Curriculum alignment has been proven as a major tool in changing less successful schools into successful ones.

Curriculum Alignment

- Start from your objectives, not from assessment.
- If your objectives are clear, instruction and assessment will be aligned.
- Curriculum alignment is a recurring cycle.

All in all, curriculum alignment is a powerful concept—one that begins with identifying your objectives.

Reflecting on Planning

Planning is a time-consuming process for the beginning teacher. Although you have spent many hours in the classroom as a student, you have probably never been responsible for student learning. As you gain experience, you will begin to know which activities take detailed planning and which do not.

Plans are dynamic, not set in stone.

Knowing when to abandon plans so as to take advantage of that unintended learning opportunity is a master teacher's skill. A good plan provides you with the context for this decision. Does this new opportunity (teachable moment) contribute more positively to the objectives of the lesson? Are you meeting a student's important need with a lesson detour? A teacher must exhibit a balance between preparation and flexibility in executing the plan. That, of course, is the artistry of teaching.

Addressing individual differences is extremely difficult. Even experienced teachers struggle to meet the learning needs of all their students. Initially, students in your class will need to adapt to your teaching style. As you gain experience and confidence in the teaching and learning processes, you will begin planning for and addressing individual student needs.

Planning is a dynamic process. It often seems downright chaotic. The United States is unique in that responsibility for planning and teaching at the classroom level rests with you, the teacher. In most countries teachers are told what to teach and often even how to teach. With this in mind, you should be even more aware that—if state standards shift from general statements to specific learner objectives—you might be responsible only for the "how" part.

In this chapter we have described the basic planning tools of goals, taxonomies, and objectives and provided examples of how to use these tools to develop instructional plans. Don't be afraid to refine, modify, or experiment with these tools. You are the technicians: the tools are there to serve you and those all-important students.

Summary

1. Instructional planning requires a careful consideration of student needs, content goals, and instructional techniques.

A Closing Reflection Reflection Reflection

- Why is planning essential for successful instruction?
- How does planning allow you to become more or less spontaneous?
- How can outcomes be used to aid in your planning?
- List the pitfalls and advantages of using a planning device such as a cognitive taxonomy.
- Reflect on your teacher education classes. How many instructors use one of the two kinds of objectives described in this chapter?
- Answer this question: "How can I be sure that my planning reflects what my students should really learn?"

2. Goals are broadly stated intentions; objectives or outcomes are specific expectations.

3. Instructional planning follows a cycle ranging from prelesson planning to postlesson reflection.

4. National standards are in vogue and guide state and local efforts to plan instruction.

5. Instruction can be planned around the cognitive, affective, and psychomotor domains.

6. The cognitive domain tends to be the focus of school curricula.

7. Performance objectives show learners what is expected, how the work will be done, and what the minimum standards are.

8. Curriculum or instructional alignment ensures that objectives, content, activities, teaching techniques, and assessment are congruent.

Key Terms

affective domain (p. 96)

analysis (p. 102)

application (p. 100)

cognitive domain (p. 95)

correlation (p. 105)

definition (p. 100)

evaluation (p. 104)

example (p. 99)

general instructional objectives (p. 116)

goals (p. 88)

interpretation (p. 99)

objectives (p. 88)

outcome (p. 111)

performance objectives (p. 111)

planning (p. 87)

psychomotor domain (p. 96)

specific learning outcomes (p. 117)

standards (p. 91)

synthesis (p. 103)

taxonomy (p. 97)

translation (p. 99)

Helpful Resources

Anderson, L. W., and L. A. Sosniak, editors. *Bloom's Taxonomy: A Forty-Year Retrospective.* Ninety-Third Yearbook of the National Society for the Study of Education, Part II. Chicago: University of Chicago Press, 1994, 214 pp.

This volume presents a historical sketch of Bloom's taxonomy and of the impact it has had for nearly half a century.

Mager, Robert F. *Preparing Instructional Objectives.* Belmont, CA: Fearon Publishers, 1962, 60 pp.

This is the little book that started it all. Mager popularized the work of Ralph W. Tyler, and the outcomes movement was born with educators embracing the concepts as Gospel. You'll be entertained as you read.

Wiggins, G., and J. McTighe. *Understanding by Design.* Alexandria, VA: Association for Supervision and Curriculum Development, 1999, 201 pp.

This is a consciousness-raising book on unit and curriculum development. The authors provide a design template and application standards. They model instructional alignment.

Internet Resources

❖ The URL below will provide information and a list of several other Internet sites all relating to Bloom's Taxonomy.

http://www.uct.ac.za.projects/cbe/mcqman/mcqappc.html

❖ The current status of Goals 2000 and related educational issues are provided via an on-line database managed by the U.S. Department of Education.

http://www.ed.gov/

❖ Information about state standards and related educational research can be obtained from the University of Minnesota National Center for Applied Research and Educational Improvement.

http://carei.coled.umn.edu/Default.html

References

American Association for the Advancement of Sciences. *Benchmarks for Science Literacy: Project 2061.* New York: Oxford University Press, 1993.

Anderson, K. W. "Research on Teaching and Teacher Education." In *Bloom's Taxonomy: A Forty-Year Retrospective,* L. W. Anderson and L.A. Sosniak, editors. Ninety-Third Yearbook of the National Society for the Study of Education, Part II. Chicago: University of Chicago Press, 1994, pp. 126–145.

Anderson, L. W., and L. A. Sosniak, editors. *Bloom's Taxonomy: A Forty-Year Retrospective. Ninety-Third Yearbook of the National Society for the Study of Education, Part II.* Chicago: University of Chicago Press, 1994.

Arons, A. B. "What Current Research in Teaching and Learning Says to the Practicing Teacher." Robert Karplus Lecture. National Science Teacher Association, National Convention, St. Louis, April 9, 1988.

Beyer, B. "Developing a Scope and Sequence for Thinking Skills Instruction." *Educational Leadership* 45(7) (1988): 26–30.

Bloom, B. S., M. D. Engelhart, E. J. Furst, W. H. Hill, and D. R. Krathwohl. *Taxonomy of Educational Objectives: The Classification of Educational Goals. Handbook I: Cognitive Domain.* New York: David McKay, 1956.

Bracey, G. W. "The Ninth Bracey Report on the Condition of Public Education." *Phi Delta Kappan* 81(2) (1999): 147–168.

Cohen, S. A. "Instructional Alignment: Searching for a Magic Bullet." *Educational Researcher* 16(8) (1987): 16–19.

Cohen, S. A. "Instructional Alignment." In *International Encyclopedia of Teaching and Teacher Education* (2nd edition) L. W. Anderson, editor. Tarrytown, NY: Elsevier Science Ltd., 1995, pp. 200–204.

Commission on Student Learning. *Raising Standards: A Guide to Essential Learnings for Washington Students.* Olympia, WA: The Commission, 1996.

Daggett, W. R. "The Challenge to American Schools: Preparing Students for the 21st Century." *School Business Affairs* 62(4) (1996): 4–13.

Ennis, R. H. "Critical Thinking and the Curriculum." *National Forum* 65(1) (1985a): 23–31.

Ennis, R. H. "A Logical Basis for Measuring Critical Thinking Skills." *Educational Leadership* 43(2) (1985b): 44–48.

Fisher, C. W., and E. W. Hiebert. "Characteristics of Tasks in Two Approaches to Literacy Instruction." *Elementary School Journal* 91(1) (1990): 3–18.

Fuhrman, S. H. "The New Accountability." *CPRE Policy Briefs.* Philadelphia: Graduate School of Education, University of Pennsylvania, RB-27-January 1999.

Furst, E. J. "Bloom's Taxonomy: Philosophical and Educational Issues." In *Bloom's Taxonomy: A Forty-Year Retrospective.* L. W. Anderson and L. A. Sosniak, editors. Chicago: University of Chicago Press, 1994, pp. 28–40.

Good, T. L., and D. A. Grouws. "Increasing Teachers' Understanding of Mathematical Ideas Through Inservice Training." *Phi Delta Kappan* 68 (1987): 778–783.

Goodlad, J. L. *A Place Called School.* New York: McGraw-Hill, 1984.

Gronlund, N. E. *How to Write and Use Instructional Objectives* (5th edition) New York: Macmillan, 1995.

Haller, E. P., D. A. Child, and H. J. Walberg. "Can Comprehension Be Taught? A Quantitative Synthesis of 'Metacognitive' Studies." *Educational Researcher* 17(9) (1988): 5–8.

Hess, R. D., and H. Azuma. "Cultural Support for Schooling: Contrasts Between Japan and the United States." *Educational Researcher* 20(9) (1991): 2–8.

Hohn, R. L. *Classroom Learning and Teaching.* White Plains, NY: Longman, 1995.

H. R. 1804, "Goals 2000: Educate America Act." Washington, DC: 103rd Congress, January 25, 1994.

Jennings, J. F. *Why National Standards and Tests? Politics and the Quest for Better Schools.* Thousand Oaks, CA: Sage Publications, 1998.

Jones, B. G. "Quality and Equality Through Cognitive Instruction." *Educational Leadership* 43(7) (1986): 4–11.

Kelly, T. F. *Practical Strategies for School Improvement.* Wheeling, IL: National School Services, 1991.

Krathwohl, D. R., B. S. Bloom, and B. B. Masia. *Taxonomy of Educational Objectives. The Classification of Educational Goals. Handbook II: Affective Domain.* New York: David McKay, 1964.

"Learning to Read and Write: Developmentally Appropriate Practices for Young Children." Joint Position Statement of the International Reading Association and the National Association for the Education of Young Children. *Young Children* 53(4) (1998): 30–46.

Lieb, B., compiler. *Achieving World Class Standards: The Challenge for Education Teachers.* Washington, DC: U.S. Department of Education, Office of Educational Research and Improvement. Proceedings of the OERI Study Group on Educating Teachers for World Class Standards, 1993.

Lieberman, A., and M. W. McLaughlin. "Networks for Education Change: Powerful and Problematic." *Phi Delta Kappan* 73(9) (1992): 673–678.

Linn, R. L., and N. E. Gronlund. *Measurement and Assessment in Teaching* (7th edition). Englewood Cliffs, NJ: Merrill, 1995.

London, P. "National Standards for Arts Education, No: Local Standards, Yes." *Educational Horizons* 76(1) (1997): 28–32.

McAlpine, J., S. Jeweler, B. Weincek, and M. Findbiner. "Creative Problem Solving and Bloom: The Thinking Connection." *Gifted Child Today* 10 (1987): 11–14.

McLaughlin, M. W., and D. C. Phillips, editors. *Evaluation and Education at Quarter Century.* Ninetieth Yearbook of the National Society for the Study of Education, Part II. Chicago: University of Chicago Press, 1991.

McPeck, J. E. *Critical Thinking and Education.* New York: St. Martin's Press, 1981.

Mager, R. F. *Preparing Instructional Objectives.* Belmont, CA: Fearon, 1962.

Marks, S. K., J. D. Vitek, and K. P. Allen. "Remote Sensing: Analyzing Satellite Images to Create Higher

Order Thinking Skills." *The Science Teacher* 63(3) (1996): 28–31.

Metzger, W. "A Spectre Haunts American Scholars: The Spectre of Professionalism." *Educational Researcher* 16(6) (1987): 10–18.

Moore, K. D., and C. Quinn. *Secondary Instructional Methods.* Madison, WI: WCB Brown & Benchmark, 1994.

Morgan, T. "Using Technology to Enhance Learning: Changing the Chunks." *Learning and Leading with Technology* 23(5) (1996): 49–51.

National Council of Teachers of English. *Standards for the English Language Arts.* Urbana, IL: The Council and International Reading Association, 1996.

National Council of Teachers of Mathematics. *Assessment Standards for School Mathematics.* Reston, VA: The Council, 1995.

National Council of Teachers of Mathematics. *Curriculum and Evaluation Standards for School Mathematics.* Reston, VA: Commission on Standards for School Mathematics, 1993.

National Research Council. *National Science Education Standards 1995.* Washington, DC: National Academy Press, 1996.

Nickerson, R. "Understanding Understanding." *American Journal of Education* 93 (1985): 201–239.

Ohanian, S. *One Size Fits Few: The Folly of Educational Standards.* Portsmouth, NH: Heinemann, 1999.

Orlich, D. C. "A New Analogue for the Cognitive Taxonomy." *The Clearing House* 64(3) (1991): 159–161.

Paul, R. "Bloom's Taxonomy and Critical Thinking Instruction." *Educational Leadership* 42(8) (1985): 36–39.

Phillips, J. K., editor. *Foreign Language Standards: Linking Research, Theories and Practices.* Lincolnwood, IL: National Textbook Company and American Council on the Teaching of Foreign Languages, 1999.

Pratt, D. *Curriculum Planning: A Handbook for Professionals.* New York: Harcourt Brace College Publishers, 1994.

Raths, L. E. *Teaching for Thinking: Theory and Application.* Columbus, OH: C. E. Merrill Books, 1967.

Rohwer, W. D., Jr., and K. Sloane. "Psychological Perspectives." In *Bloom's Taxonomy: A Forty-Year Perspective*, L. W. Anderson and L. A. Sosniak, editors. Ninety-Third Yearbook of the National Society for the Study of Education, Part II. Chicago: University of Chicago Press, 1994, pp. 41–63.

Rosenshine, B., and R. Stevens. "Teaching Functions." In *Handbook on Research on Teaching* (3rd edition). M. Wittrock, editor. New York: Macmillan, 1986.

Schmoker, M., and R. J. Marzano. "Realizing the Promise of Standards-Based Education." *Educational Leadership* 56(6) (1999): 17–21.

Shiland, T. W. "The Atheoretical Nature of the National Science Education Standards." *Science Education* 82(5) (1998): 615–617.

Slavin, R. *Educational Psychology* (3rd edition). Englewood Cliffs, NJ: Prentice-Hall, 1991.

Steinbrink, J. E., and R. M. Jones. "Focused Test Review Items: Improving Textbook-Test Alignment in Social Studies." *The Social Studies* 82(2) (1991): 72–76.

Tatsuoka, K. K., and M. M. Tatsuoka. "Bug Distribution and Statistical Pattern Classification." *Psychometrika* 52 (1987): 193–206.

U.S. Department of Education. *America 2000: An Education Strategy.* Washington, DC: U.S. Government Printing Office, 1991.

Wakefield, J. F. *Educational Psychology: Learning to Be a Problem Solver.* Boston: Houghton Mifflin, 1996.

Whimbey, A. "The Key to Higher Order Thinking Is Precise Processing." *Educational Leadership* 42(1) (1984): 66–70.

Wiggins, G., and J. McTighe. *Understanding by Design.* Alexandria, VA: Association for Supervision and Curriculum Development, 1999.

Wittrock, M. "Students Thought Processes." In *Handbook of Research on Teaching* (3rd edition). M. Wittrock, editor. New York: Macmillan, 1986.

Wittrock, M. C. "Knowledge Acquisition and Comprehension." In *Encyclopedia of Educational Research* (6th edition). M. C. Alkin, editor. New York: Macmillan, 1992, pp. 699–705.

Woolfolk, A. E. *Educational Psychology* (6th edition). Boston: Allyn and Bacon, 1995.

Yinger, R. J., and M. S. Hendricks-Lee. "Teacher Planning." In *International Encyclopedia of Teaching and Teacher Education* (2nd edition). L. W. Anderson, editor. Tarrytown, NY: Elsevier Science Ltd., 1995, pp. 188–192.

Instructional Design

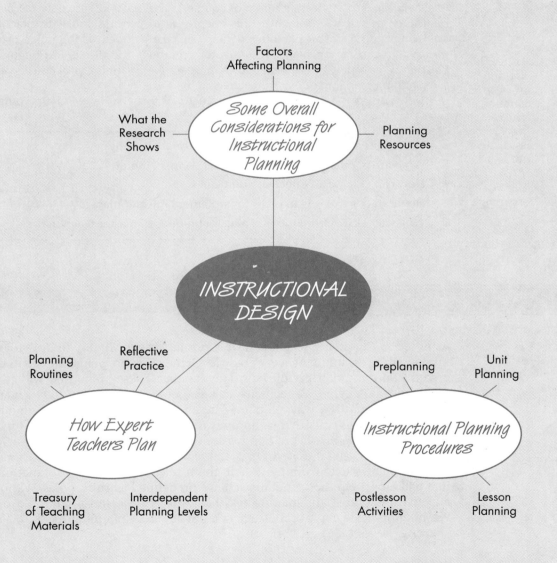

Reflecting on her experiences as a student and her new knowledge about long-term goals, instructional and performance objectives, and the several domains of learning and their taxonomies, Chaka feels more comfortable about planning instruction for her students. She's confident in her understanding of these concepts, at least at a basic level, and she recognizes their importance in planning and implementing instruction.

Now, though, Chaka begins to consider some implications of her new knowledge. She wonders, for instance, about how to specifically arrange instructional time; how to be sure to include all that's important; how to arrange facts, concepts, and generalizations into manageable pieces for teaching and learning—in short, how to plan as master teachers do.

What Chaka is reflecting upon, of course, is the reality of instructional planning. Our principal objective in this chapter is to provide you with practical guidelines for systematic planning, to help you create effective long-range plans, unit plans, and lesson plans. The chapter continues the discussion begun in Chapter 3, covering three main topics: preparation, planning procedures, and the planning practices of expert teachers.

New concepts and techniques introduced in this chapter will help you answer the following questions:

- What factors must I consider for instructional planning?
- What are planning levels and how do I connect them?
- How can I create an effective unit plan?
- How can I devise lesson plans to implement my unit plans?
- What can I learn from the planning techniques of master teachers?

Section 1: Some Overall Considerations for Instructional Planning

Teachers have a basic responsibility to plan and deliver effective instruction.

As noted in Chapter 3, teachers have a primary responsibility to design and implement instruction. At every grade level, they prepare plans that aid in the organization and delivery of their daily lessons. These plans vary widely in their style and degree of specificity. Just as there are many ways to teach and learn, there are many ways to plan—there is no single "best" way. Some instructors prefer to construct elaborately detailed, impeccably typed outlines; others rely on the briefest of handwritten notes. Probably most teachers fall somewhere between these extremes. But regardless of the format they choose, master teachers use planning to help them select the content and methods that will most help their students achieve predefined learning goals. Without effective planning, students are less likely to achieve those goals. As one Washington State high school teacher put it, "Less planning leads to less learning" (Walsh 1992, p. 114).

What the Research Shows

Studies of the actual processes that teachers use in planning were conducted primarily in the early 1970s through the 1980s. Christopher M. Clark and Penelope L. Peterson (1986) prepared the high water mark for the genre. Although it is now dated, their work and that of others led to a set of research-based findings described below. These findings will be useful to you as you begin instructional planning.

1. *Researchers have neither identified nor validated any widely accepted or consistently practical planning model* (see Sardo-Brown 1988; Walsh 1992, p. 21). Plans, planning efforts, and planning methods vary widely among teachers. Planning seems to be influenced most by the selection of learning activities, instructional objectives, content, students' age, available time, and teaching strategies. Of these, *time* and *proven activities* appear to have the greatest influence on the way that teachers plan.

2. *Teachers use a variety of lesson plan formats.* Time is a critical teaching constraint, and all teachers organize blocks of instructional time in lessons for years, semesters, months, weeks, and a day. Content is also a major consideration, and teachers generally organize content into coherent segments called *unit plans* and subsequently into manageable parts called *lesson plans.* (See Clark and Peterson 1986; Sadro-Brown 1988; Kagan and Tippins 1992; Wiggins and McTighe 1998; and Price and Nelson 1999.)

The calendar is a key planning tool.

3. *Planning serves as a guide to action.* Plans are written to act as a guide during the instructional interactions. In this regard, plans provide and maintain a sense of direction and instill confidence in your teaching. Of course, weekly or daily lesson plans are typically an administrative requirement in most schools (Clark and Peterson 1986).

4. *Teachers tend to carry much of their planning in their mind rather than on paper.* Particularly as they gain experience, teachers may make notes about main ideas, yet they base much of their daily teaching on mental images of how the instruction should best proceed. Thus, in your observations of teachers, you may note large differences in the amount of planning that appears on paper. Until you have several years' experience, we will urge you to make written plans; the more you work out your plans on paper, the more effective you will become (Sardo-Brown 1988; Wolcott 1994).

5. *Teachers rarely plan in the linear model often encouraged in textbooks.* Many years ago, Ralph W. Tyler (1949) suggested a sequential planning process of several steps: (1) specify an objective, (2) select appropriate learning activities, (3) organize the activities, and (4) specify an assessment process. The method has been frequently taught in teacher education programs, but practicing teachers seem to use it infrequently. Instead, teachers mostly use a recursive process that focuses on previous successful activities, perceived student needs, and ongoing curriculum programs (Wolcott 1994).

6. In their review of "Excellence in Teaching," Maribeth Gettinger and Karen Callan Stoiber (1999) illustrate the point that planning for instruction is the key to excellence. In every model they present, a teacher must first plan,

but that plan must be flexible so that it can be adapted to fit the actual "teaching moment." We, too, make a plea for flexibility in the delivery of instruction.

Summary of Teacher Planning

- Planning is based on a plethora of models.
- Planning serves a wide array of purposes.
- Planning often goes on in the "head."
- Planning is seldom linear.
- Planning must be flexible.

Factors Affecting Planning

Instructional planning is a complex process.

As you can well imagine, you have much to consider when you plan instruction. We have summarized below some of the initial areas you need to think about. These are not in any order of importance, but each is important. You will find it useful, especially at the beginning, to write your thoughts for each area. This will help you focus your thinking and confirm that you've considered each area. An excellent source to help with these steps is Allan C. Ornstein (1997).

Student Considerations   Students are the reason for and focus of your instruction. What do you know about them, individually and as a group? Are they easy or difficult to motivate? What do you already know about the subject you're planning? How might they best learn? What accommodations will be needed for special students?

Content and Process Considerations   What main ideas and concepts are involved? Will you need to teach skills as well? In what order should the instruction be arranged? Can you devise a variety of learning activities and instructional methods to teach the material?

Time Considerations   How much time is available for this part of the instruction? Are other school functions—assemblies, plays, extracurricular activities—or holidays and vacations likely to interfere? Do you need more than a day or a period?

School Considerations   Are there district or state learning outcomes or standards to be considered? Graduation requirements? Legal requirements for special students?

Resources   In addition to school textbooks and supplementary materials, are other resources available in the community, such as historical sites, museums, art galleries, or other special places? Are there people within the community who might provide a perspective?

Teacher Considerations   How knowledgeable are you about the material you're planning? Can you arrange what you know in terms that students will understand?

Planning Considerations

- Students
- Content and processes
- Time
- School
- Resources
- You—the teacher

Planning Resources

Numerous resources are available to help you with instructional planning, and we discuss several of the major ones after the Reflect box. Remember, however, that effective teachers do not limit themselves to resources specifically designed for planning or for the education professional—they fill file drawers and cabinets with materials they have found useful in a lesson or unit or that simply look as if they might be useful. As a secondary school history teacher, one of your authors of this book had a large collection of pictures of wooden sailing ships showing the masts and rigging in detail and describing how the ships were operated. Together with other materials, these helped students visualize and understand the reality of Columbus's journey and other "voyages of discovery."

Reflect Reflect Reflect

- Interview a few different teachers from a range of grade levels—at elementary, middle, and secondary schools. Ask what techniques they use to construct lesson plans.
- How do their responses compare with what has been discussed thus far in this chapter?
- List a few materials that you think might help students more clearly understand concepts in your teaching area.

Curriculum guides and state standards are excellent planning sources.

Curriculum Guides   Most schools have **curriculum guides**—statements detailing what should be taught in each grade and in each content area. These guides are created by the state as "standards" or "essential student learnings," and sometimes by the district, but they are almost always written by teams of teachers after careful consideration of the aims and goals of local schools. The example goal statements below were written by several groups of teachers in Washington State to meet local needs. Curriculum guides are often phrased in broad terms such as these, thus giving individual teachers freedom to develop appropriate units and lessons. (See criticism of "Curriculum Guides" in English 1987.)

Essential Academic Learnings in Reading, #3

The student reads different materials for a variety of purposes. To meet this standard, the student will:

- Read to learn new information, such as reading in science, mathematics, technical documents and for personal need.
- Locate and use information to perform tasks such as using schedules, following directions, filling out job applications and solving problems.
- Read for literary experience in a variety of forms such as novels, short stories, poems, plays and essays to understand self and others [Washington State Commission on Student Learning, 1996, pp. 2–3].

Notice in the above example that "reads different materials for a variety of purposes" is a goal statement, as explained in Chapter 3. Each bulleted statement shows what students can do to reach the goal. This very desirable goal applies to all levels and subjects in the curriculum; it is as relevant to first graders as it is to high school physics students, and it can be approached at a variety of levels, from simple to complex, in all grades. The goal statements provide an excellent example of how to state a two-part objective. Each goal statement could be an instructional objective. The bulleted statements could then state specific or performance objectives of how students will demonstrate evidence of mastery.

Curriculum guides are the first place to look when you are considering what to teach and how to plan instruction. They provide a framework—in terms of both time and subject matter—for organizing instruction. Guides spell out, often in great detail, the specific knowledge and skills students are expected to attain and the attitudes they should exhibit. They tend to be arranged by grade level for elementary schools and by content area for middle and secondary schools. Of particular benefit to new teachers, they identify what instruction your students have already had as well as what will be expected of them after your grade or course. Start here! (See also Tyler 1949 for a rationale that has stood the test of more than one-half century.)

Textbooks   A second major indicator of what to plan, as well as a significant source of planning aids, is the text or texts adopted by the school. Especially for elementary teachers, these can offer useful insights into the curriculum, and how to plan for and how to teach it. School districts often buy a series of elementary school texts from a single publisher—a set of materials to teach math, for instance, from kindergarten through grade 6. Teachers often say, "We're using Scott-Foresman Science," or "We've had much success with Houghton Mifflin's literacy program."

These textbook series generally provide a structured sequence of lessons. They specify instructional objectives, provide a variety of teaching suggestions, offer supplementary readings and practice aids, and include an evaluation program. Many also provide lessons designed specifically to help with cooperative learning, thinking processes, decision-making skills, and a variety of problem-solving techniques. Assuming that the materials meet your objectives, they can be an extremely useful resource, helping you make the best use of your planning time. Publishers' aids deserve much study and consideration.

The following illustrates the variety of individual resources provided by one fourth-grade text—*Heath's Math Connections* (published by Houghton Mifflin Company as of 1996):

Textbook publishers' supplementary materials provide much planning help.

- *Student text* featuring four lesson types with formats varied to match students' level of understanding, from concrete to abstract.
- *Teacher's edition,* an annotated version of student text with chapter planning guides, chapter themes and objectives, and suggestions for additional teaching activities, discussions, and evaluation tools beyond those provided in the text.
- *Writing activities* for each lesson.
- *Thinking skills activities* with challenging problems that frequently have multiple solutions or may be solved by a variety of methods.
- *Regular activities* such as "Every Day Counts," a guide to ten minutes of daily classroom conversation about mathematics.
- *Testing program* with several different assessments for each chapter, from informal through standardized format. Answers and evaluation suggestions are provided, as are hints for organizing portfolios and assessing difficult areas such as problem solving and estimation.
- *Emphasis on thinking processes* rather than simply computation and recall. Students are required to support an opinion, classify items into lists, interpret diagrams, and determine cause and effect. A "Why Should We Learn This?" feature makes it clear to students that concepts learned in the lessons are useful outside of school.

Much valuable assistance is available from publishers; just be sure that the materials match your objectives, and don't be overwhelmed by the quantity—nobody uses all of the materials for a particular subject. Decide which items are most appropriate for your objectives, your students, and the time available.

Other Resources   Beyond formal school curriculum guides and the supplementary materials associated with textbooks, there are myriad sources of materials that successful teachers use to bring life to their lessons. The following list is suggestive, not comprehensive. Your imagination and the experience of one year of teaching and thoughtful planning should double its length:

- *Colleagues.* In general, other teachers will be more than willing to help you find resources and to discuss what works well for them. School librarians can be especially helpful, not only in suggesting resources but also in helping you determine how to include them into instruction (see especially Wolcott 1994).
- *Retail Stores.* Shops such as School Daze and Academic Aids specialize in "after-market" materials for teachers. They carry much excellent

supplementary material for elementary and middle school teachers, and some for secondary school teachers. Many teachers spend much time and money in such stores.

- *The Internet.* There is a tremendous amount of educational material on the Internet and the World Wide Web. There are unit and lesson ideas for all subjects and grades. If you are selective and can adapt the materials you find to fit your students and objectives, then cyberspace can be a positive force in your planning. We provide suggested sites at the end of each chapter.

- *Local Libraries, Museums, and Historical Sites.* Each of these can offer considerable aid in structuring a lesson.

- *Government Agencies.* From local police departments to county agencies to the Library of Congress—the thoughtful teacher uses all of these and more to make learning a hands-on and stimulating activity.

Reflect Reflect Reflect

- Add a few more resources to those discussed in the chapter.
- Which resources seem most useful to your teaching area?
- Name some of the resources used by teachers you know or teachers you had in elementary or secondary school.
- How might you incorporate the goal "reads different materials for a variety of purposes" into your subject?

Section 2: Instructional Planning Procedures

From a consideration of planning materials, we now turn to a detailed description of useful planning steps. Experienced, successful teachers do not follow a standard planning procedure. All teachers, however, wrestle with common factors that determine the success of their instruction. Refer to Figure 4.1, which illustrates planning steps in the form of a cycle. We will discuss these steps in the order they appear on the chart, but remember that teachers do not necessarily consider each factor in that order. Planning is more a recursive than a linear process: the teacher considers instructional objectives in terms of learning activities and then reconsiders each in terms of time and student abilities. All parts are interdependent; a change here will likely mean a correction there.

As stated earlier, much instructional planning is done mentally and may never appear on paper. Effective teachers, especially after several years of experience, rehearse much of their instruction in their heads or by talking to themselves. Plans are never far from their minds, and more than one unit or lesson plan has been worked out in the shower or at the shopping mall

(Sardo-Brown 1988; Kagan and Tippins 1992). One outstanding high school teacher noted, "Planning is not just when I am sitting at my desk and writing. Planning includes plenty of think time when I am considering possibilities" (Walsh 1992, p. 198). We noted earlier that as a beginning teacher you are well advised to write out your plans in some detail. The writing process itself helps you focus your thinking and detect confusion or inconsistency that would otherwise inevitably come out during instruction.

Preplanning

As Figure 4.1 shows, it is useful to consider several general concerns before focusing on unit and lesson planning:

- *Goals.* Of your various instructional goals, which are the most relevant for the present purpose?
- *Long-Range Plans.* In this grading period, semester, or year, what days are available for instruction and which are taken for other purposes?
- *Content.* What is the content to be taught?
- *Processes.* What processes will most effectively reinforce the content?

FIGURE 4.1

The Instructional-Planning Cycle

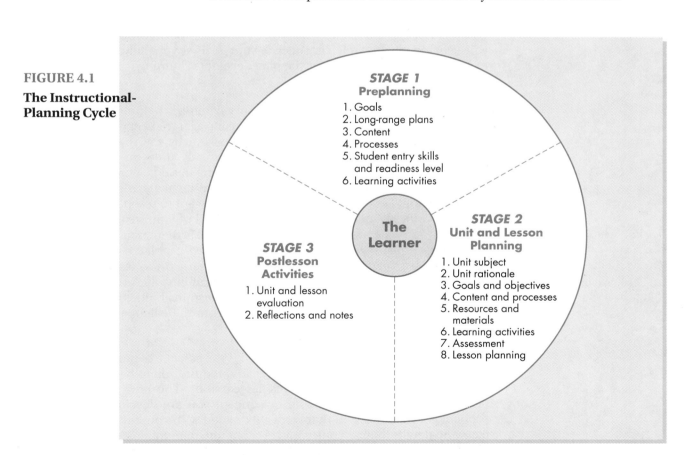

Several planning concerns are addressed at the preplanning stage.

- *Student Entry Skills and Readiness Level.* What must your students know to be successful in the planned course of instruction? Do they need prerequisite instruction?

- *Learning Activities.* What learning activities seem most relevant to the content and your instructional goals?

Reviewing Goals and Standards   We have stressed that instructional goals are one of your most important concerns. If you don't know where your instruction is going, you are irresponsible as a teacher. As noted previously, middle and high school teachers will find that national standards, available for most subjects, are an excellent source of goals. For example, in 1995 the National Center for History in the schools specified this standard: "Students should be able to demonstrate understanding of the Spanish conquest of the Americas by describing the social composition of the early settlers and comparing their motives for exploration and colonization" (p. 48). In 1989 the National Council of Teachers of Mathematics published this standard: "In grades K–4, the study of mathematics should include opportunities to make connections so that students can use mathematics in their daily lives" (p. 32).

District and national standards and goal statements can be a significant help in organizing your instruction. So can the goals from publishers' materials, already mentioned. Even though you find yourself implementing society's goals, don't be reluctant to include goals that seem relevant to your students, your district or school, and what you believe is important in the subject. You will also find yourself referring back to your goals as you plan, perhaps adding to or subtracting from them as the plan develops. Planning is, indeed, a recursive process.

Developing Long-Range Plans   A useful beginning, before school starts, is to create a long-range planning calendar, using a large sheet of paper for each month. (This is a planning technique borne out by the research of Sadro-Brown [1988], for example.) Mark what you already know on your calendar—holidays, in-service days, dates for each grading period, semester end dates, and any other pertinent data. The remaining days make up the time available for instruction. How can you fit everything you want to teach or must accomplish into those remaining squares? Try to fit all of your instructional major topics into the calendar. Do you have too many? Is there not enough time for all? You have just faced one of teaching's biggest problems—there just isn't time for all we need to do. You now begin assigning priorities, deciding what topics to include, which to deemphasize or combine with others, and which to omit. This is one of your most important responsibilities as a teacher, so consider the choices carefully. We will return to the calendar idea when we consider unit and lesson planning.

Deciding on Content   Providing content is the essence of most lessons. Textbooks are content rich, maybe too rich, and require you to be selective about what you will actually stress. Consider carefully. The only content that is needed is relevant to the theme or concept you are developing. You have probably endured classes that were overloaded with content; they had more facts and details than anyone could ever want to remember. Don't let yours be one of those classes; prune out any content that is irrelevant to your major idea. But work hard to find and include activities and examples that make clear to your students the main ideas of your focus topic.

Deciding on Processes   As we noted in Chapter 1, processes are as important to teach as content. Thinking processes—imagining, problem solving, comparing and contrasting, analyzing, organizing, classifying, and numerous others (can you think of some?)—are critical to almost any subject or topic you are teaching. As you identify content for your units and lessons, note also what thinking processes your students might reasonably need to understand the material. Then make it a point to identify these processes during instruction, helping students to become more aware of deliberate uses of their own thought processes. Consider the following example.

In planning a social studies unit on America's Civil War, you want to include material on the several causes. One way to approach this material is to ask students to consider the question "What reasons would *you* need to justify killing an acquaintance or even a family member (as happened in the Civil War)?" In discussing the question, students can respond by analyzing reasons, classifying and categorizing ideas and arguments, determining importance, and justifying decisions. By planning ahead for this attention to processes, you can be sure to include it.

Students' entry skills and readiness level should be considered in planning.

Identifying Students' Entry Skills and Readiness Levels   Another important task, at the early planning stage as well as at all subsequent ones, is to identify your students' **entry skills** and **readiness levels.** What do students already know? Do they have sufficient knowledge to understand what you will be teaching? Are their basic skills adequate for the planned activities, or must you also teach these? As much as 50 percent of the variability in achievement among students can be attributed to insufficient knowledge or skills (Bloom 1976, p. 167; House, Hurst, and Keely 1996).

The sixth principle of the Coalition of Essential Schools requires all students entering high school to have sufficient skills or to receive remediation to gain the necessary skills to be successful (Sizer 1996, p. 154). It is possible that the widespread adoption of constructivist learning theory, with its emphasis on prior knowledge and teaching for understanding, has the potential to reduce the problems related to insufficient entry skills and knowledge. (See Wiggins and McTighe 1998.)

There are various ways of determining students' readiness level. In general, elementary and middle school teachers and schools accept a student's promotion as confirmation that he or she is ready for the next grade, although emergent literacy is often assessed each year at the primary levels. For high school students, whose instruction is arranged by subjects rather than grade level, placement testing is sometimes done, especially in math and English. In most cases, however, placement within a grade or class is assumed to indicate readiness until evidence to the contrary accumulates.

Nevertheless, teachers need to be as certain as possible about student readiness. One critical factor is each student's reading achievement level. Students who are several years below their grade level in reading (their cumulative folders will show such data) will likely need special materials. You may even have to prepare taped cassettes of readings or arrange for peer tutoring to help some students. Reading level is perhaps the teacher's best guide to

> **Reflect** Reflect Reflect
>
> - Identify several entry skills needed by students at a particular grade level for classes in your instructional area.
> - Think of activities that would help a student link each of the following to his or her experience: discrimination, friendship, and democratic processes.

readiness, lacking a subject-specific assessment. If cumulative data are unavailable (often the case for new and transfer students), there are several reliable standardized measures of reading levels designed for classroom use.

An effective way to identify entry levels is to give a pretest—either from one of the major test publishers or, more likely, one you've written. Ask yourself what knowledge and skills a student would need, beyond reading level, to understand the proposed instruction. If you can identify several skills or pieces of information, write a short quiz and administer it to see if most students are ready. Remember, you are determining the skills students need to *begin* the new unit—not the skills they should learn from it!

Experience will soon show you which entry skills should be assessed. In the meantime, you will find that most current standard instructional materials provide a range of grade-appropriate options, although you will need to make some changes for some students.

Creating Learning Activities   **Learning activities** are hands-on, interactive experiences that help students connect lectures and texts to their own experience. Laboratory experiments in science represent one example; debates and mock trials in social studies are another. These should be considered in your long-term planning, although they will play a larger part in your unit planning.

As a beginning teacher, you have to find or create such activities; after a few years experience, you should have several file drawers full of activities that have worked with past students. As you construct your long-term calendar and consider the goals you need to work toward, try to block out time for those activities that were (or are expected to be) particularly useful in helping students succeed (see Brophy and Alleman 1991; Pressman and Dublin 1995; Price and Nelson, 1999).

Unit Planning

Unit plans help make instruction manageable.

As teachers, we divide instructional time and topics into pieces to make learning manageable. Since we can't teach everything all at once, we sort out content into blocks called **units,** and we arrange these across time using our long-range planning calendar. However, having subdivided our instruction into pieces to make it **manageable**, we must also be careful to allow time to pull the pieces together again to make the content **understandable.** Again, the planning calendar and unit plan are our best tools. "Unit planning is the most important as well as the most time-consuming level of planning for each teacher" (Walsh 1992, p. 178).

An eighth-grade social studies teacher planning a year's course in U.S. history serves as a convenient example. To make learning the subject manageable, the teacher divides it chronologically: the pre-Columbian era, colonial times, the revolutionary period, and the present. (Note that chronology is neither the only nor necessarily the preferred way to organize history classes; it is simply used as a familiar example to illustrate a point about instructional planning.)

Teachers of other grades and subjects might use **topics** as an organizer. In science, topics such as matter, sound, electricity, leaves, and waste disposal could well serve as organizers. Language arts teachers might organize their ideas around topics such as love, friendship, or heroes to integrate literature and composition. Primary and lower elementary grades do much the same with seasons, holidays, or special events.

To continue the unit planning, the teacher then makes a subjective judgment—based on his or her content knowledge, student readiness levels, and the desired outcomes—about the relative importance of each topic. Those deemed more important will need relatively more class time. Working with the planning calendar and topic list, the teacher then arranges the topics in the desired order (sequences them), leaving time within each unit to analyze the topic and combine it with other material as needed.

The method of planning just described seems reasonable and logical, yet in practice it becomes both messy and frustrating. The basic problem, as we noted previously, is that you will inevitably want to cover more material than you can fit into the available time. The big questions then become "What must be included?" and "What must I omit to make enough room?" All teachers, at all levels, face this dilemma—and no one answers it easily. The penalty for not answering these questions at the planning stage, though, is that they may inadvertently omit some important material or dwell too long on less important matters.

Having identified major topics and worked them into your planning calendar, you are now in a position to make detailed plans to provide instruction for each topic. Most teachers call these unit plans.

Reflect Reflect Reflect

- Within each of the following content areas, identify several topics around which you could build a unit: Euclidean geometry, America's Vietnam experience, Columbus's impact on the Western Hemisphere, and presidential elections.

Unit planning is the mainstay, the "bread and butter," of teachers at all levels—both teachers of self-contained elementary school classes and teachers of content-specific middle and secondary school classes such as science and history. And though teachers plan in a variety of ways, the unit plans

---

Parts of a Unit Plan

- Subject or topic
- Rationale
- Instructional objectives
- Content
- Processes
- Resources
- Learning activities
- Evaluation

---

they develop contain a number of common elements, as listed in the box above.

Although we will discuss these elements separately, in practice you are more likely to move back and forth among them recursively rather than to proceed in a straight line through them.

Defining the Unit Subject   Unit subjects or topics vary across both grade levels and content areas. Often, as in the example of history, the subject seems apparent—the Civil War, the Great Depression. Mathematics also seems self-explanatory—fractions, division, polynomials. These are reasonable topics, and effective units can certainly be built around them You can create many similar examples within your own subject field.

Concepts can organize instruction around students' interests.

Concepts   Teachers at all levels find they can often tie content to student interests by building units around concepts. We will explore this term more deeply in Chapter 5, but for now think of **concepts** as "category" words, enabling us to group many individual objects or ideas under a common label. For example, *desk* is a word (concept) that stands for all the objects we see that have "desky" characteristics. (Can you name some characteristics?) Since a desk is a concrete object, it's easy to get agreement on most of its characteristics. As concepts become more abstract, however (love, anger, friendship), people often have vague and different ideas about their characteristics. These abstract concepts are ones that students often are confused by and/or simply find interesting. Thus, concepts almost automatically become useful unit topics.

For instance, a language arts teacher might select "Friendship" as a unit concept or topic. Students could then read and write short stories, plays, poems, biographies, and other works that would help them better understand the topic, themselves, and others. Alternatively, teachers might have students suggest concepts that interest them, perhaps with different small groups or individuals making explorations and reporting to the class. Notice, by the way, that this approach works on students' interests and builds knowledge from their present level—which is one basis of constructivist learning theory (see Roskos 1996).

The accompanying box on page 139 lists some possible themes or concepts for U.S. history units. Note that they focus on people, ideas, and trends rather than chronology.

Examples of Historical Concepts

- Elections
- Economic depressions
- Immigration and emigration
- Changing laws for changing times

Elementary school teachers, particularly those in self-contained classrooms, often include ideas from several content areas in their thematic units, thus developing an **interdisciplinary unit.** For instance, in the "Friendship" unit, in addition to the language arts activities, the teacher might include social studies by helping the children develop questionnaires and make a survey of what other students in the school consider to be characteristics of friends. During art time students might create pictures illustrating types of friendship—people with animals or animals with animals, for instance, as well as the varieties of friendship among people. Math might be included by making charts and graphs of the results from the questionnaires. The concept could even be integrated into lunch time. Only the teacher's and students' imagination limit the possibilities (see Martin 1995; Martinello and Cook 2000; McDonald and Czerniak 1994; Castanos 1997).

Students can be involved at all levels—selecting the concept and determining what content areas might be involved, what activities are appropriate, and even what instruction (or instructional methods) might be most useful (Lang, McBeath, and Hébert 1995).

Student participation in preplanning, as noted above, requires teachers to account for these activities in their long-range plans. Having the students help preplan instruction is not a spontaneous act.

Questions and generalizations work well as unit topics and content organizers.

Questions and Generalizations   Although concepts make excellent unit organizers and planning tools, they are not your only choices. A well-worded question can effectively focus your unit (or lesson) and aid in deciding what to include or leave out. Consider the following question: "In what ways were America's War of 1812 and the Vietnam War similar?" What information would be useful in a response? A detailed description of each war is not necessarily relevant, nor is a lengthy discussion of causes and results—unless such information is relevant to the question. Notice how focus and content of the unit are almost dictated by the wording of the question.

Here's another example that could organize biology or ecology by examining evolution and extinction. "Who will survive?" Again, notice how usefully the question focuses and organizes content. Such a unit allows plenty of room for investigation of both historical evolution and current threats to species.

In addition to questions, generalizations (a full discussion is presented in Chapter 5) can be useful for organizing unit content. **Generalizations** are

Instructional

Strategies

Generalizations Used as Unit Topics

- The development of the personal automobile revolutionized social and family behavior.
- Waterways, as paths of transportation, determined much of the course of colonization.

inferential statements that express a relationship between two or more concepts, can be verified, and have a predictive value. Two examples follow. "As you shorten or lengthen a vibrating string, the sound increases or decreases, respectively." "Cold fronts cause a temperature drop in the affected geographic areas." Notice how instruction is almost automatically selected and organized by making clear the concepts involved and exploring the relationships. Notice also that both questions and generalizations provide built-in **motivation** because both present students with a question to be answered or a problem to be solved rather than just a statement of "learn this."

As you consider organizing units, try to consider what you hope the students will remember long after they leave your class. Certainly, much information will be soon forgotten, but if you have helped them organize knowledge in ways that clarify concepts, answer questions, and explain relationships in terms they understand, they will have truly learned.

Reflect Reflect Reflect

- What are some useful focusing questions in your subject area?

Defining the Rationale   A **rationale** answers the question "Why is it important to your students to learn this material?" The response should be a reasoned one, not just "It's good for them," "It's required at this grade," or "They have to have it to get into another class." These reasons might be true, but you need to identify a more substantial one, and you need to be intellectually honest with yourself, your students, and your profession. If a parent asks why you are teaching certain material, he or she deserves a thoughtful response based on the importance of the content to the student. So do your students. (And they, at least in high school, are apt to be more blunt in their request: "Hey! How come we gotta learn this stuff?") In the box on page 141, we provide two example rationales.

Defining Goals and Objectives   In planning units and lessons, teachers need to develop learning outcomes in the three areas of content understanding (as opposed to simply memorizing facts), skills/processes, and attitudes. These three areas drive instruction at all levels, although the emphasis among them may shift across the grade levels and for content areas. The focus in elemen-

Instructional

Strategies

Example Rationales for Units

Primary Science Unit

I believe that understanding scientific principles and processes is important for every student. Helping students become interested in science at an early age will increase their motivation to want more science as they get older. Additionally, doing science at an early age is an excellent introduction to such higher thinking processes as observing, classifying, making inferences, and withholding judgment until sufficient data have been gathered. Thus, this unit on water, besides having many informative, interesting activities, will help prepare students mentally for enjoying the observation of the world around them.

Ninth-Grade Literature Unit

Through a study of Greek mythology, this unit helps students build a foundation for understanding imagery and symbolism in literature. Additionally, students should gain appreciation for differing worldviews and human diversity as they examine ancient peoples' perspectives on life and nature. Mythology lies at the source of many themes, images, and symbols in both classical and modern literature. Learning to understand and enjoy these ancient tales will help students understand and interpret all literature.

tary school may be on skills/processes with content being stressed more in middle school, and by high school, most of the focus is in the content realm. At all levels, however, instruction must integrate skills and processes with content understanding.

Attitudes—such as willingness to share or cooperate, to enjoy reading or music or dance, to suspend judgment until sufficient facts are known, and to tolerate ambiguity in decision making—are not specified as objectives as often as content and process. Nonetheless, they are important for students to recognize and deserve more teacher attention than they seem to receive.

At the risk of repetition, we emphasize that these three areas of content understanding, skills/processes (especially thinking processes), and attitudes are interrelated—we probably don't teach or learn purely in any one of them without involving at least one of the others. "Thinking" obviously requires something to think about (content) as well as a willingness to do so (attitude). It is simply convenient for planning and instruction to separate these and emphasize one part or another. Students (and teachers) need to be reminded frequently, however, that learning and understanding are integrated, holistic acts.

What should unit outcomes be? They are best stated as general instructional objectives. (You might want to check back through our full discussion of objectives writing in Chapter 3.) Try to include objectives from each of these areas: content, skills/processes, and attitudes. These objectives should be attainable (not necessarily mastered) in perhaps as little as a week or as

Instructional

Strategies

Example Unit Outcomes

Examples of Subject Matter/Content Outcomes

- The student understands the relationships among current, resistance, and voltage in a simple series electrical circuit.
- The student knows the significance of Presidents Kennedy, Johnson, and Nixon in involving the American people in the war in Vietnam.
- Students understand how developments in naval architecture prior to 1500 made possible the "discovery" and colonization of Africa below the Sahara and of both the Americas.

Examples of Skill/Process Outcomes

- The student demonstrates satisfactory competence in using the Internet as a research resource.
- Each student uses appropriate skill in gathering and classifying data to make inferences for a history project.
- The student states an appropriate series of steps in diagnosing and repairing an automobile that won't start.

Examples of Attitude Outcomes

- Students show progress (indicated by the teacher's anecdotal records) in delaying a decision until sufficient data have been assembled.
- Students achieve a level of personal satisfaction (indicated in self-reports) from completing the history project.
- Students apply a "decision tree" (evidenced by student journals and self-reports) in making several personal decisions.

much as three or four weeks. A unit lasting longer than this should have logical dividing points, both for understanding and manageability. The example outcomes in the box above are typical.

The example outcomes imply that at least several lessons will be required to achieve the level of competence indicated. Notice also that from the wording, both the necessary instruction and the proper evidence of achievement (for evaluation) are implied. For attitudinal outcomes, evaluation tools are indicated, since these outcome goals are less frequently seen in unit plans (and, in some locales, might be subject to citizen criticism for encroaching on personal thoughts or feelings).

In summary, your unit objectives will target specific contents, skills/processes, and attitudes. It is useful to state content objectives as concepts, questions, or generalizations. Skills/processes should include those related to learning, communicating, thinking, decision making, and relationships with other people. Attitudinal objectives, particularly concerning self-esteem and relating oneself to others, need to be deliberately built into unit plans so students can be "set up" for success. Finally, objectives are statements of *student outcomes,* not teacher behaviors. "In this unit I will teach about time zones" is a statement of teacher intent, not a student learning outcome (see Yelon 1996; Zemelman, Daniels, and Hyde 1998).

Selecting Resources and Materials   Since we discussed resources in Section 1 of this chapter as part of the preparation stage, we only remind you here of their importance. Each unit you create should have as many appropriate resources as you can find to support your instruction and to provide as many ways as possible for students to connect their experiences to the unit. By the way, keep an index of the resources you use; as you gain teaching experience, you can save yourself many hours of searching by having a handy record of sources and items you have used in the past. Resources are entered into the unit plan most conveniently as a list, with perhaps a note about location or intended use.

You plan for computer or other technology usage.

School districts are now purchasing more than $7 billion worth of computers and high-technology hardware and courseware per year for instructional and administrative purposes. You will be expected to have basic computer literacy to apply in your lesson-planning activities. You may even be assigned to one of the lucky schools that are "wired." That is, all teachers and students can interact on an established network. Your students can work in teams or contact students across the hall or across the oceans. These are not spontaneous events. You plan for computer use just as you plan for the daily assignments. "High tech" just adds one more dimension to your planning efforts (see Lovely 1997; Utley and Mortweet 1997).

Creating Learning Activities   Learning activities were introduced briefly in the discussion on preplanning. Like resources, however, they play an important part in the unit-planning process. This section will give you some specific aids in creating and finding activities beyond the textbook that will reinforce your instruction.

Learning best takes place when everyone is actively engaged in planned school work.
© Robert Llewellyn.

As much as possible, learning activities should reach students through the several intelligences that Howard Gardner has brought to our attention (see Lazear 1999a and 1999b). Gardner and other researchers have made it clear that students learn in a variety of ways; they have also provided us with useful tools and techniques to plan instruction that recognizes this variety. Specific suggestions for using Lazear's findings to create learning activities will be given later in this section.

One of the most useful aids in planning unit and lesson activities is the **Kaplan Matrix,** created by Sandra Kaplan (1979). The matrix is illustrated in Table 4.1; notice that the intent is to plan outcomes and activities at the several levels of Bloom's cognitive taxonomy. Such planning is extremely important if you are to avoid presenting most instruction and assessing at the knowledge level. Use of this matrix forces you at least to consider the other taxonomic levels; if you then choose to remain at the knowledge level, it will be intentional rather than an oversight.

The matrix idea can be used in many ways. Table 4.2 shows it in use as a work plan, indicating objective levels, teacher activities, learning experiences, and student products. Again, the act of making such a planning document is itself a positive planning activity—it forces you to think about student outcomes and the types and levels of activities that will most likely help students achieve those outcomes.

A further extension of the matrix idea is to combine it with multiple intelligences. Table 4.3 shows the eight intelligences outlined by Howard Gardner and elaborated on in detail by David Lazear. Beneath each intelligence is a list of associated indicators and activities. One way to use this in concert with the matrix would be to list major concepts vertically on your plan, with the intelligences across the top of the plan. Then search for ways to include as many intelligences as possible with each concept.

Learning activities are what you use to get your students involved—in as many ways and through as many senses as possible. Your imagination (right hemisphere) is the key, but a planning matrix (left hemisphere) will help you organize and sequence this important piece of your teaching.

Formulating Assessment Tools   The final portion of your unit plan is assessment of student progress. Since planning is a recursive activity, you need to consider assessment throughout the planning process. Indeed, some teachers find it useful to consider it first—"How will I measure what my students can do?"—and then create appropriate instruction and activities. In other words, they create a test and teach to it. We urge you to consider assessment throughout your planning. Good instruction entails appropriate assessment.

Assessment refers to all the ways teachers monitor student progress.

Since Chapter 10 focuses in detail on assessment, we will provide only some general guidelines here. First, perhaps most important, is to remember that the purpose of assessment is to provide evidence of the degree of achievement *each* student has made toward *each* objective. Whatever your system, it must provide that type of individual data.

Second, it is important to think of assessment as occurring throughout your units—it is not simply "a big test at the end." If your units include some skills/processes as objectives (and they should), you can assess these as students complete them, using rating scales or checklists. Attitudes can be assessed with your own anecdotal records throughout the unit and periodically

TABLE 4.1

The Kaplan Matrix for Extending the Curriculum

Content or Concepts	Performance Objectives and Related Student Activities				
	Knowledge	Comprehension	Application	Analysis	Synthesis
Volcanoes	List facts about Mt. Saint Helens's devastation.	Compare Mt. Saint Helens to the volcanoes of Hawaii.	How could we use the piles of volcanic ash?	What do the people near Mt. Saint Helens feel?	Make a volcano model for our class.
Minerals and gems	List the important gems found in the Northeast.	Contrast the hardness of the minerals found in the Northeast.	Field test the hardness of ten minerals.	What would happen if the government imposed tougher mining regulations?	Grow crystals of various shapes and colors.
Space travel	Name all the people who have gone to the moon.	Compare the Russian space program to the U.S. space program.	If you were an astronaut, what would you study about space?	What do you think would happen if we found life elsewhere?	Make a rocket and fly it.
Weather and climate	Name the different types of clouds.	Contrast the climates of the Southwest and the Southeast.	Chart the amount of rainfall for the next week.	What effect did La Niña have on the world's weather?	Create a wind generator.

SOURCE: Adapted from Kaplan 1979, with the permission of the author.

TABLE 4.2

Teacher-Student Work Plan

Content	Level of Objective	Teaching Activity	Learning Experiences	Student Product
Places of origin	K	Lecture/recitation Reading assignment Worksheet	Note taking Reading	Completed worksheet
Places of origin	C	Demonstration of how to construct graphs	Note taking Constructing a graph	Graph
Places of origin	AP	Small-group presentation	Each group makes a prediction and presents to the class.	Presentation by small groups to whole class
Places of origin	AN	Presentation of assignment Discussion of resources Description of final product Breaking class into groups	Each group focuses on one immigrant group and is responsible for explaining its motives for coming to the United States, using references, film strips, and other resources.	Report to class

SOURCE: Adapted from Kaplan 1979, with permission of the author.

TABLE 4.3

Lazear's Multiple Intelligences Toolbox

Logical/Mathematical

- Abstract Symbols/ Formulas
- Calculation
- Deciphering Codes
- Forcing Relationships
- Graphic/Cognitive Organizers
- Logic/Pattern Games
- Number Sequences/ Patterns
- Outlining
- Problem Solving
- Syllogisms

Verbal/Linguistic

- Creative Writing
- Formal Speaking
- Humor/Jokes
- Impromptu Speaking
- Journal/Diary Keeping
- Poetry
- Reading
- Storytelling/Story Creation
- Verbal Debate
- Vocabulary

Visual/Spatial

- Active Imagination
- Color/Texture Schemes
- Drawing
- Guided Imagery/ Visualizing
- Mind Mapping
- Montage/Collage
- Painting
- Patterns/Designs
- Pretending/Fantasy
- Sculpting

Musical/Rhythmic

- Environmental Sounds
- Instrumental Sounds
- Music Composition/ Creation
- Music Performance
- Percussion Vibrations
- Rapping
- Rhythmic Patterns
- Singing/Humming
- Tonal Patterns
- Vocal Sounds/Tones

Interpersonal

- Collaborative Skills Teaching
- Cooperative Learning Strategies
- Empathy Practices
- Giving Feedback
- Group Projects
- Intuiting Others' Feelings
- Jigsaw
- Person-to-Person Communication
- Receiving Feedback
- Sensing Others' Motives

Naturalist

- Archetypal Pattern Recognition
- Caring for Plants/Animals
- Conservation Practices
- Environment Feedback
- Hands-On Labs
- Nature Encounters/Field Trips
- Nature Observation
- Natural World Simulations
- Species Classification (organic/inorganic)
- Sensory Stimulation Exercises

Bodily/Kinesthetic

- Body Language/Physical Gestures
- Body Sculpture/Tableaus
- Dramatic Enactment
- Folk/Creative Dance
- Gymnastic Routines
- Human Graph
- Inventing
- Physical Exercise/Martial Arts
- Role Playing/Mime
- Sports Games

Intrapersonal

- Altered States of Consciousness Practices
- Emotional Processing
- Focusing/Concentration Skills
- Higher-Order Reasoning
- Independent Studies/Projects
- Know Thyself Procedures
- Metacognition Techniques
- Mindfulness Practices
- Silent Reflection Methods
- Thinking Strategies

SOURCE: Eight Ways of Knowing, Third Edition, by David Lazear. Copyright © 1999 Skylight Training and Publishing, Inc. Arlington Heights, Illinois. Reprinted with permission.

by student self-report forms. Particularly for a unit that includes many concepts or much complex information, understanding of content should be assessed with short quizzes at several points during the unit rather than all at once at the end.

Finally, explain your assessment methods to your students—they want and need to know how their performance will be judged. Knowing the ground rules helps them clarify their efforts and will probably result in higher achievement.

Reflect Reflect Reflect

- We usually think of assessment as tests of subject matter knowledge. What other areas of student progress are important for you to monitor?
- For the eight areas identified by Lazear, what types of assessment tools, other than subject matter tests, would be useful?

Lesson Planning

General Plans Although it is often considered as a separate topic, lesson planning is simply an extension of unit planning. Individual lessons are one means we use to help students achieve desired unit learning outcomes (objectives). We will show you what elements a lesson plan should include and some ways to arrange those elements, but you must be the one to determine what methods work best for you.

Much confusion can be avoided if you think of a **lesson** as a piece of a unit, not as a block of time (see Kagan and Tippins 1992). Lesson plans are not the same as activity schedules for the school day. Student teachers are often confused when they see their cooperating teacher's "lesson plan" book and note that it contains mostly words and phrases like the following:

Tuesday, 8th-grade English, 1st period

1. Review spelling words.
2. Dictate test—be sure students make answer sheet first.
3. Introduce Poe's "Tell-Tale Heart." Discuss mental aspects first.
4. Silent reading, Poe.
5. Announce preparations for dismissal at 9:55.

Well-designed lesson plans are a unit's building blocks.

This example is not a lesson plan; it is a schedule of what the teacher intends to do during a class. Lesson plans, like unit plans, are statements of what *students* will do. A good lesson plan will contain most of the elements of a unit plan, just on a reduced scale. See the Instructional Strategies box on 148.

Experienced teachers frequently do not write lesson plans, although they may expect you, as a student teacher or novice, to do so. An experienced teacher probably spent several years writing similar plans but now has them largely in his or her head, jotted down in margin notes in textbooks, and

Instructional

Strategies

A Model Lesson Plan

Teacher _____

Course Title _____

1. Unit _____

2. General Instructional Objectives _____

3. Specific Learning Outcomes _____

4. Rationale _____

   _____

5. Content and Skills/Processes _____

   _____

6. Instructional Procedures

   (a) Focusing Event

   (b) Teaching Procedures

   (c) Student Participation and Activities

   (d) Formative Check

   (e) Closure

   _____

7. Assessment _____

8. Materials, Aids, and Computer Needs_____

9. Notes/File Comments _____

(*The intent of each part is probably clear to you, but some amplification of several parts may help and is provided below.*)

1. *Unit:* Record your unit title here.

2. *General Instructional Objectives:* As discussed earlier, these are the *unit* outcomes that this lesson is meant to reinforce. A general instructional objective might be "Each student will understand the relationships among voltage, resistance, and current in an electrical circuit." A lesson will typically reinforce several objectives. Thus, this lesson might focus on content but could also reinforce skills and attitudes.

3. *Specific Learning Outcomes:* These are the specific objectives of this *lesson.* You might have several in a lesson. An example might be "Using Ohm's Law for calculations, the student will correctly determine the needed values in each of the following circuits: (a) Current is 3.0 amps; resistance is 5,000 ohms. (b) Voltage is 9 volts; current is 0.3 amps. (c) Resistance is 10k ohms; voltage is 6 volts."

Instructional

Strategies

A Model Lesson Plan (continued)

4. *Rationale:* This is the same as the rationale for the unit plan but stated in a way that relates this lesson to the unit. That is, a rationale for a lesson would explain why this particular lesson is important in achieving the unit goals: "To use electricity safely in the home, shop, and business, it is necessary to understand how current, voltage, and resistance are related. The physical relationship can in part be understood mathematically. This lesson will help the student achieve this understanding."

5. *Content and Skills/Processes:* It is important to separate in your mind (and on paper) the content and skills you want students to learn and the procedures or techniques you will use to teach them that content and those skills. This lesson plan format helps you do that. Under "Content" you would list the specific concepts or ideas you want students to learn in the lesson. Content for the above lesson in electrical circuits might include working with the following:

Circuits	Ohm's law	Resistance
EMF	Currents	Amperage
Volts	Inverse ratios	Ohms

6. *Instructional Procedures:* In this section, you list the specific methods you will use to teach each part of the lesson. For our lesson on electrical circuits, for example, some parts might be done by questioning to review an earlier lesson and establish focus on this one. Other parts might have students experiment with a circuit in small groups or view a video and take notes. Your efforts to find activities for the several intelligences should appear here.

7. *Assessment Procedures:* Include a brief explanation of what you will do to determine whether students have reached the objectives. For our sample lesson, students' answers to the computations and explanations of how the problems were solved would be sufficient for assessment.

Content and instructional procedures should be separate parts of your lesson plans.

summarized in brief notes on the several activities a lesson might contain. Also, an experienced teacher's unit plan or outline may contain much of what a novice would put into lesson plans. Thus, even if an individual teacher's lesson plan book looks much like the above example, he or she probably did do the planning.

There are many different lesson plan formats from which to choose; the best one to use is determined by your specific instructional goals and teaching strategies. The authors of this text, and many of their students, have found the format of this lesson plan to be useful. The importance of lesson plans and the unit plans they support cannot be overstated for professional instruction. As one high school teacher put it, "The better the teacher plans, the better the teacher" (Walsh 1992, p. 97). (Excellent examples of lesson plan formats are found in Arends 1997; Kauchak and Eggen 1998; Price and Nelson 1999; and Martinello and Cook 2000.)

Constructing IEPs   In Chapter 1, we briefly noted that all children with disabilities, by federal law, must have Individual Education Plans (IEP's) *written* for them. The IEP is a special and extended adaptation of a lesson plan. We

TABLE 4.4

Elements of an IEP Required in Washington State

General

- Student's personal information (age)
- Grade level
- IEP date
- Statement that **parent or surrogate** agrees or disagrees with plan
- Date of IEP review
- Signatures (parent, student, teacher, district, representative)

Services

- Special service needed
- Frequency—hours or times per week
- Projected starting date
- Expected duration
- Responsible persons by position or title
- Special media and materials or modifications
- Adaptations for physical education
- Need for extended year service (rationale, goals, time)

Placement (Least Restrictive Environment)

- General education class
- General education class with consulting services
- General education class with in-class special education instruction
- General education class with pull-out related services
- General education class with pull-out special education services
- Special education class with integration into general education class and/or community
- Self-contained special education class
- Residential school
- Home instruction
- Hospital instruction
- Other

TABLE 4.4

Elements of an IEP Required in Washington State (continued)

Recommendations and Placement

- Program placement
- Rationale
- Location
- Neighborhood school or close to student's home
- Opportunities for extracurricular or school-sponsored nonacademic activities
- Transportation
- Degree of general education participation

Levels of Performance

- Present levels of performance
- Annual goals
- Short-term objectives
- Objective criteria
- Evaluation procedures to be used
- Schedule to determine how often objective is achieved
- Objectives achieved

have seen them typed in as few as four pages and as many as twenty! Your employing school district will provide the specified format for you to follow. However, just to illustrate their complexity and attention to detail, we present Table 4.4 that simply lists all the key descriptors or key elements mandated by Washington's Office of the State Superintendent of Public Instruction. As you examine Table 4.4, keep in mind that for each item listed, a complete justification or detailed description is required. Did we mention that IEPs are labor intensive?

Don't give up in despair! There will be specialists available to help with the planning and delivery of services. You aren't alone. (See Ysseldyke and Algozzine 1995 and Bateman 1996 for detailed models of IEPs.) And remember, at least 12 percent of your students will be legally classified as being disabled! You will do IEPs.

Postlesson Activities

Evaluating Unit and Lesson Plans   Up to this point in this chapter, we have used the term *assessment* several times to indicate monitoring of student progress. However, we also wish to monitor our own progress as teachers. In this section we will use the term **evaluation** for this process.

At the conclusion of every class session, ask yourself a series of questions about the effectiveness of your lesson and unit plans: Were the objectives realistic and appropriate? Did the instructional methods work? For which learn-

Reflect Reflect ~~Reflect~~

Instructional planning can be envisioned as a grid with a series of principles and strategies. This grid includes deciding what to teach, how to teach, and how to communicate realistic expectations as key principles for instructional planning (Ysseldyke and Elliott 1999).

Under the component of managing instruction, the grid highlights instructional preparations, productive use of time, and the establishment of a positive classroom environment. Obviously, we concur. Do you? List several specific classroom management benefits you believe might flow from good instructional planning.

ers and to what degree? What components of the lesson succeeded? What aspects could be improved? Write your thoughts in a journal or in your textbook's margins to help you identify difficulties experienced by learners and to relate these problems to specific elements of the lesson and unit.

Keeping Planning Notes and Reflecting on Future Planning Needs   Also jot down any notes or comments about the lesson or unit that will help you the next time you teach it. Master teachers refer to the previous year's notes and resource files as they plan their lessons (Walsh 1992). In fact, one of the greatest distinctions between novice and expert teachers is that the experts have large quantities of previously gathered material to draw on—*and they use it continually.*

Lesson and unit plans should be thought of as *emerging documents;* the first ones you construct will be at only the earliest stage of development. After your initial use of these plans, the actual classroom conditions (learner entry skills, teaching procedures, and learner outcomes) need to be compared to the planned situation. The resulting data will allow for refinement and recycling, making the unit and lesson plans more effective instructional tools. You will continually evaluate your instructional plans each time you use them, always attempting to improve content, activities, and methods.

Section 3: How Expert Teachers Plan

We will close this chapter by describing some planning behaviors that separate expert and novice teachers. If you are aware of these when you begin to teach, you will have less to learn through experience to become an efficient and effective classroom planner and teacher.

Planning methods of master teachers differ from those of novice teachers.

In general, four areas separate the novice and expert planner: (1) planning routines, (2) reflective practice, (3) interdependent planning levels (Clark and Peterson 1986; Sardo-Brown 1988; Walsh 1992; Ornstein 1997), and (4) a treasury of teaching materials (Walsh 1992, pp. 12–24). We will consider each of these in some detail.

Planning Routines

Many repetitive tasks will confront you each day as a teacher. These **routines** include activities such as gathering and dispensing papers, recording tardies and absences, recording participation in activities, checking assignments, and giving all students an equal chance to respond to questions. Expert teachers devise and revise plans to simplify and systematize the accomplishment of such tasks. For instance, students can be assigned on a rotating schedule to distribute papers and to take roll. A student can be assigned to mark on a class roster which students you call on to help you avoid missing any or calling on some too often.

Expert teachers work out many aids such as these, frequently involving student help when appropriate, and thus save a few (or perhaps quite a few) minutes of instructional time each day. Consider: five minutes saved daily is twenty-five minutes a week, or nine hundred minutes in a 180-day school year. Your students deserve an extra fifteen hours of instructional time.

Reflective Practice

Donald A. Schön (1995) examined how various professionals—architects, physicians, engineers, and educators—actually practice. He discovered that competent professionals usually know a great deal more than they verbalize. That is, they have a depth of knowledge; in their professional lives they reflect upon that knowledge and then apply it to new or unusual problems. Schön encourages professionals to think, ponder, and reflect about past, present, and future actions as a means of designing productive, problem-solving strategies.

Applying Schön's postulates to education has encouraged many educators and educational researchers to promote reflection as a key element in stimulating professional growth and improving professional practice. Reflection is an active mental process that master teachers use consistently as they interact with students and the curriculum (see Osterman 1990; Canning 1991; Sparks-Langer and Colton 1991; Panasuk and Sullivan 1998).

Walsh (1992) observed evidence of "reflective dialogue" in the planning behaviors of award-winning teachers. The ones he interviewed stated that they consistently rehearsed classroom scenarios before teaching, frequently talking to themselves about what they wanted to have happen in class. These rehearsals included consideration of the best instructional options and methods for handling anticipated classroom dilemmas, such as a class that doesn't respond as expected to a lesson. Furthermore, they followed each lesson, as soon as possible, with a period of reflection, taking quick notes on what worked well and what didn't.

Interdependent Planning Levels

Expert teachers consistently implement several distinct planning levels—long range, unit, and daily—as an interdependent set of routines (Walsh 1992). These routines help convert long-range plans into daily and weekly schedules and keep short-term instruction aligned with long-range goals and the overall school calendar (Sadro-Brown 1988; Walsh 1992; Glatthorn 1993; Ornstein 1997).

Planning is the heart of instruction.

Treasury of Teaching Materials

Much of planning confidence and expertise stems from two sources that all master teachers possess: (1) file cabinets full of valuable resources collected over the years and (2) last year's plan book. These two sources constitute part of an experienced teacher's planning edge over new teachers.

There is no way the novice can compensate for the full file cabinets. Novices who want to become excellent teachers simply have to become savers and collectors (and develop a retrieval system that allows them to find what they have). What do you save? Virtually anything that relates to your instruction, but especially successful learning activities, tests, quizzes, magazine articles and pictures, bulletin board materials, computer and Internet resources, assignments, study guides—the list becomes almost endless.

Having last year's plans obviously simplifies this year's planning—much of the groundwork has been done. This is one part of teaching the student teacher usually doesn't see. However, don't be misled into believing that master teachers just reuse their old plans each year. Those plans are only the starting point for current lessons. True professionals are always thinking about and planning how to update content, find more effective instructional methods, and devise better activities to help their students succeed. As three recognized classroom observers have stressed, it is the lesson that transforms

---

A Closing Reflection Reflection Reflection

- What strengths do you see in yourself that will make you a successful planner?
- What limitations must you work around?
- How can you build a resource file when you haven't yet been hired?
- To what extent have you had to justify your content selection by specifying a written rationale?
- What criteria would you generate to critique your lesson plans in the post-lesson evaluation?
- Ask your instructor for models of IEPs. Do you observe any commonalities?

youngsters into students (Mitchell, Ortiz, and Mitchell 1987). Learning is the primary goal of the schools. Your job is to make planning decisions that ensure learning is always *intentionally inviting*.

Planning is the heart of teaching. To the degree that you can become a successful planner, you will become a successful teacher.

Summary

1. The preplanning phase is essentially one of teacher reflection.
2. Planning decisions are often influenced by what content is not included, as there is so much.
3. Textbook publishers and state education agencies supply more than adequate instructional guides and resources.
4. Long-range planning is simplified by use of a school day activity calendar.
5. Student readiness is critical for content mastery.
6. Unit planning makes learning manageable.
7. Each lesson is designed and executed to achieve desired learning outcomes and instructional objectives.
8. Learning activities provide students with hands-on experiences.
9. Assessment is essential to determine students' levels of achievement.

Key Terms

concept (p.138)

curriculum guides (p. 129)

entry skills (p. 135)

evaluation (p. 151)

generalization (p. 139)

interdisciplinary unit (p. 139)

Kaplan Matrix (p. 144)

learning activities (p. 136)

lesson (p. 147)

manageable (p. 136)

motivation (p. 140)

rationale (p. 140)

readiness levels (p. 135)

routines (p. 153)

topics (p. 137)

understandable (p. 136)

units (p. 136)

Helpful Resources

Campbell, B. *The Multiple Intelligences Handbook: Lesson Plans and More.* Stanwood, WA: Campbell and Associates, 1994, 170 pp.

Here you will find classroom-tested lessons and themes for elementary grades that use the multiple intelligences perspective.

Cheros, P., et al. *The Golden Age of Greece: Imperial Democracy 500–400 B.C.: A Unit of Study for Grades 6–12.* Los Angeles: University of California at Los Angeles, National Center for History in Schools, 1991, 168 pp.

Lesson plans are illustrated for the major topics often studied for this period of ancient history.

Johnson, D. H., and R. T. Johnson, editors. *Learning Mathematics and Cooperative Learning: Lesson Plans for Teachers.* Edina, MN: Interaction Book Company, 1991, 173 pp.

After you digest Chapter 8, you'll have a handy reference from which to adapt math lesson plans that are structured about cooperative learning.

Needler, T., and B. Goodman. *Exploring Global Art.* New York: American Forum for Global Education, 1991, 185 pp.

The authors illustrate sets of lesson plans that were designed as part of the multicultural arts curriculum at Washington Irving High School in New York City.

Wresch, W., editor. *The English Classroom in the Computer Age: Thirty Lesson Plans.* Urbana, IL: National Council of Teachers of English, 1991, 145 pp.

This handy book gives you a set of lesson plans that you can adopt or adapt plus a directory of software sources.

Internet Resources

❖ The following will direct you to many of the best lesson-planning sites:

❖ "Ask Eric Lesson Plans" will open a listing of 358 Web pages devoted to lesson plans for all grades and subjects.

   http://www.askeric.org/Virtual/Lessons/

❖ The Los Angeles County Office of Education offers lesson plans in all areas of K–12 education at its Web site:

   http://teams.lacoe.edu/documentation/places/lessons.html

❖ The Eisenhower National Clearinghouse, funded through the U.S. Department of Education's Office of Educational Research and Improvement, is a source of curricular materials for K–12 science and math teachers.

   Http://www.enc.org

References

Arends, R. *Classroom Instruction and Management.* New York: McGraw Hill, 1997.

Bateman, B. D. *Better IEPs,* (2nd edition). Longmont, CO: Sopris West, 1996.

Bloom, B. S. *Human Characteristics and School Learning.* New York: McGraw Hill Book Company, 1976, p. 167.

Brophy, J., and J. Alleman. "Activities as Instructional Tools: A Framework for Analysis and Evaluation." *Educational Researcher* 20(4) (1991): 9–23.

Canning, C. "What Teachers Say About Reflection." *Educational Leadership* 48(6) (1991): 18–21.

Castanos, J. "Interdisciplinary Instruction." *Thrust for Educational Leadership* 26(6) (1997): 33–38.

Clark, C. M., and P. L. Peterson. "Teachers' Thought Processes." In *Handbook of Research on Teaching* (3rd edition). M. C. Wittrock, editor. New York: Macmillan, 1986.

English, F. W. "It's Time to Abolish Conventional Curriculum Guides." *Educational Leadership* 44(4) (December 1986/January 1987): 50–52.

Gettinger, M., and K. C. Stoiber. "Excellence in Teaching: Review of Instructional and Environmental Variables." In *The Handbook of School Psychology* (3rd edition). Cecil R. Reynolds and Terry B. Gutkin, editors. New York: John Wiley & Sons, 1999, pp. 933–958.

Glatthorn, A. "Teaching Planning: A Foundation for Effective Instruction." *NASSP Bulletin* 77(551) (1993): 1–7.

House, J. D., R. S. Hurst, and E. J. Keely. "Relationship Between Learner Attitudes, Prior Achievement, and Performance in a General Education Course: A Multi-Institutional Study." *International Journal of Instructional Media* 23(3) (1996): 257–271.

Kagan, D. M., and D. J. Tippins. "The Evolution of Functional Lesson Plans Among Twelve Elementary and Secondary Student Teachers." *Elementary School Journal* 92(4) (1992): 477–489.

Kaplan, S. M. *Inservice Training Manual: Activities for Development Curriculum for the Gifted/Talented.* Ventura, CA: Ventura County Schools, 1979.

Kauchak, D. P., and P. D. Eggen. *Learning and Teaching: Research-Based Methods, 3rd edition.* Needham Heights, MA: Allyn and Bacon, 1998.

Lang, H. R., A. McBeath, and J. Hébert. *Teaching Strategies and Methods for Student-Centered Instruction.* New York: Harcourt Brace, 1995.

Lazear, D. G. *Eight Ways of Knowing: The Artistry of Teaching with Multiple Intelligences* (3rd edition). Arlington Heights, IL: Skylight Training and Publishing, Inc., 1999(a).

Lazear, D. G. *Multiple Intelligence Approaches to Assessment: Solving the Assessment Conundrum* (revised edition). Tucson, AZ: Zephyr Press, 1999(b).

Lovely, G. "Need Lesson Plans? They're Ready for You on the Net!" *Instructor* 107(5) (1997): 102–103.

McDonald, J., and C. Czerniak. "Developing Interdisciplinary Units: Strategies and Examples." *School Science and Mathematics* 94(1) (1994): 5–10.

Martin, P. L. "Creating Lesson Blocks: A Multi-Discipline Team Effort." *Schools in the Middle* 5(11) (1995): 22–24.

Martinello, M. L., and G. E. Cook. *Interdisciplinary Inquiry in Teaching and Learning* (3rd edition). Upper Saddle River, NJ: Merrill, 2000.

Mitchell, D. E., F. I. Ortiz, and T. K. Mitchell. *Work Orientations and Job Performance: The Cultural Basis of Teaching Rewards and Incentives.* Albany: State University of New York Press, 1987.

National Center for History in the Schools. *National Standards for United States History: Exploring the American Experience, Grades 5–12.* Los Angeles: University of California at Los Angeles, 1995.

National Council of Teachers of Mathematics. *Curriculum and Evaluation Standards for School Mathematics.* Reston, VA: The National Council of Teachers of Mathematics, Inc., 1989.

Ornstein, A. C. "How Teachers Plan Lessons." *High School Journal* 80(4) (1997): 227–238.

Osterman, K. F. "Reflective Practice: A New Agenda for Education." *Education and Urban Society* 22(2) (1990): 133–152.

Panasuk, R. M., and M. M. Sullivan. "Need for Lesson Analysis in Effective Lesson Planning." *Education* 118(3) (1998): 330–345.

Pressman, H., and P. Dublin. *Accommodating Learning Style Differences in Elementary Classrooms.* New York: Harcourt Brace College Publishers, 1995.

Price, K. M., and K. L. Nelson. *Daily Planning for Today's Classroom.* Belmont, CA: Wadsworth Publishing Company, 1999.

Roskos, K. "When Two Heads Are Better Than One: Beginning Teachers' Planning Processes in an Integrated Instruction Planning Task." *Journal of Teacher Education* 47(2) (1996): 120–130.

Sardo-Brown, D. S. "Twelve Middle-School Teachers' Planning." *The Elementary School Journal* 89(1) (1988): 69–87.

Schön, D. A. *The Reflective Practitioner: How Professionals Think in Action.* Aldershot, England: Arena, 1995.

Sizer, T. R. *Horace's Hope: What Works for the American High School.* Boston: Houghton Mifflin Company, 1996.

Sparks-Langer, G. D., and A. B. Colton. "Synthesis of Research on Teachers' Reflective Thinking." *Educational Leadership* 48(6) (1991): 37–44.

Tyler, R. W. *Basic Principles of Curriculum and Instruction.* Chicago: University of Chicago Press, 1949.

Utley, C. A., and S. L. Mortweet. "Peer-Mediated Instruction and Interventions." *Focus on Exceptional Children* 29(5) (1997): 1–24.

Walsh, F. M. *Planning Behaviors of Distinguished and Award-Winning High School Teachers.* Unpublished Doctoral Dissertation. Pullman: Washington State University, 1992.

Washington State Commission on Student Learning. *Revised Essential Learnings: Reading, Writing, Communication, Mathematics.* Olympia, WA: Commission on Student Learning, 1996.

Wiggins, G., and J. McTighe. *Understanding by Design.* Alexandria, VA: ASCD, 1998.

Wolcott, L. L. "Understanding How Teachers Plan: Strategies for Successful Instructional Partnerships." *School Library Media Quarterly* 22(3) (1994): 161–165.

Yelon, S. L. *Powerful Principles of Instruction.* White Plains, NY: Longman Publishers, 1996.

Ysseldyke, J. E., and B. Algozzine. *Special Education: A Practical Approach for Teachers* (3rd edition). Boston: Houghton Mifflin, 1995.

Ysseldyke, J. E., and J. Elliott. "Effective Instructional Practices: Implications for Assessing Educational Environments." In *The Handbook of School Psychology* (3rd edition). Cecil R. Reynolds and Terry B. Gutkin, editors. New York: John Wiley & Sons, 1999, pp. 497–518.

Zemelman, S., H. Daniels, and A. Hyde. *Best Practice: New Standards for Teaching and Learning in America's Schools* (2nd edition). Portsmouth, NH: Heinemann, 1998.

Sequencing and Organizing Instruction

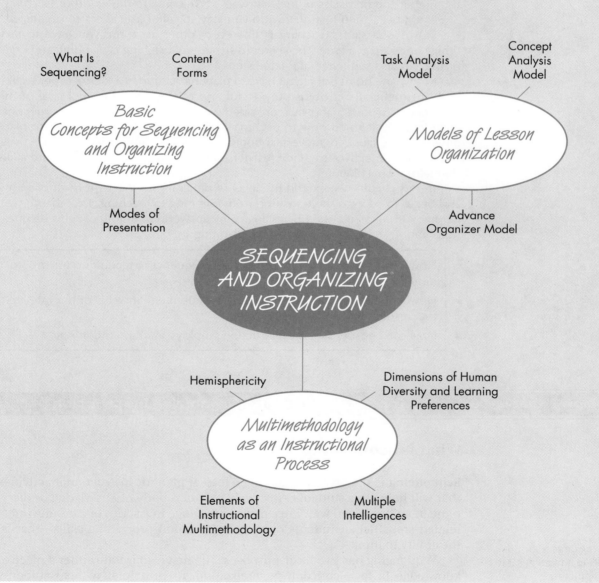

Although Ms. Chan was a demanding teacher, her students found her English composition classes very enjoyable. They completed their assignments on time, seemed to know what Ms. Chan expected of them, and took pride in their work. Josh, a new English teacher at West Central High School, heard that students respected Ms. Chan. He wanted to observe how she taught her courses. What was her secret? Josh felt a bit intimidated by her, but he also felt lucky to be assigned to the room next door to such a good teacher.

Planning, teaching, grading, attending meetings—all new responsibilities for Josh—contributed to a hectic and sometimes chaotic first week of school. In contrast to how he felt, Josh noticed that Ms. Chan, although busy, was much calmer and organized. "Josh, you seem very tired," said Ms. Chan as she entered his room after the first class of the first week. "Welcome to the world of teaching."

"I am beat," said Josh. "How do you stay so calm? You seem so organized."

"Josh," she said, "teaching is like every other art form: you have to take things one step at a time. The secret to successful teaching is planning and organizing a logical sequence of related steps."

Ms. Chan's point is that you have to plan instruction in a logical order so that each instructional activity is purposeful and related to the overall goal of the course. In Chapters 3 and 4 we provided you with a framework for instructional planning. You learned how to use goals and standards as guideposts for planning, how to use a cognitive taxonomy when translating goals into objectives, how to use objectives to guide learners, and how to use procedures and skills for instructional planning.

In this chapter we extend the level of detail in our discussions of planning and begin to address the transition from planning to teaching. This chapter will help you understand Ms. Chan's advice by answering the following three questions about sequencing instructional planning:

- How can I select the most appropriate sequencing technique for my students?
- How can I determine if I am helping a student enhance his or her intellectual resources?
- How can I ensure that my instruction employs "multimethodology"?

Section 1: Basic Concepts for Sequencing and Organizing Instruction

What Is Sequencing?

Sequencing is the art of developing a logical plan for instructional activities that will help your students effectively master a body of knowledge or discipline in an organized way. Presenting knowledge in a series of carefully interrelated steps helps students develop information-processing skills—that is, the ability to think.

Sequencing targets specific information and relates it to the bigger picture.

Sequencing has two basic purposes. The first is to isolate either a piece of knowledge (a fact, concept, generalization, or principle) to help students learn and understand its unique characteristics or a thinking process to help students master it under varying conditions. The second is to relate the knowledge or process being taught to a larger organized body of knowledge. The first function—isolating what is being taught—helps make learning more manageable. The second function—relating the information to the bigger picture—makes learning more meaningful.

For example, to teach the concept of a metaphor, first teach the characteristics of a metaphor by providing examples of metaphors. This gives students a manageable amount of information and a focus for their study. You can then teach a second figure of speech—a simile—in the same way. After the students have mastered both concepts, you can show that similes and metaphors have common characteristics; that is, they are both figures of speech. In this way you relate the lesson content to a larger body of knowledge. This example shows the relationship between instructional sequencing and hierarchies of knowledge. A sequence is an instructionally related process, because it establishes a schedule for learning the various parts of the related content. In a subject area such as mathematics, in which there is an accepted hierarchy of knowledge, the sequence and hierarchy are very similar, because the relationships among the content components usually dictate a sequence of learning activities. Thus everyone learns to add before learning to multiply. In a subject such as social studies, on the other hand, in which it is difficult to agree on an established hierarchy of information, the sequencing of learning is usually established by either the interest or the experience of the teacher. If a **content hierarchy** exists, it influences the instructional sequence. If a content hierarchy does not exist, the sequence of instruction establishes a hierarchy for the student.

To teach effectively, you must sequence learning objectives in a way that reflects the relationships between the various components of the curriculum. This allows you to identify and teach prerequisite or entry-level skills and competencies at the appropriate stage. For meaningful learning to take place, the sequenced objectives should be communicated to students so they will understand the relationships among the various components of the unit or the overall curriculum.

General Principles of Sequencing   Four general principles apply to all kinds of sequencing. The first principle is that you always *begin with a simple step.* This does not mean that you "talk down" to your students. Rather, it means that you structure your lessons so that learners can understand easily identified characteristics of the content. At this step you should provide numerous examples. Using analogies often helps. In a biology class, you could start by stating, "The circulatory system is similar to a river system in that it carries both food and waste and can be overused and misused." Since your students studied river systems in a previous year, you have provided them with a simple beginning to understanding the circulatory system through an analogy.

The second principle is to *use concrete examples.* This means that you use materials, simulations, models, or artifacts that illustrate the fact, concept, or generalization being taught. Let's stay with the biology class example. You call your student's attention to the circulatory system on the life-size plastic human body at the front of the classroom. You point out major arteries and discuss their similarity to major rivers such as the Mississippi and Columbia.

Then you proceed to identify and name the major arteries and veins, discussing the primary functions of each one.

The third principle is to *add complexity to the lesson.* Sequence the learning experience so that it becomes more and more complex as you progress. Additional variables may be introduced, new sets of criteria may be generated, and relationships may be established between the content of the lesson and other content. For example, you may add the function of the heart, liver, and other organs of the circulatory system to the discussion. The topic now becomes significantly more complex; as you add the organs one at a time, explaining the function of each, you may need to go back to the first step (the river–circulatory system analogy) or the second (the plastic human model).

Finally, the fourth principle is to *introduce abstractions.* You might want to do this with a question: "When you are sick, why does the doctor start an examination by checking your blood pressure and listening to your heart beat?"

Again, you may need to go back to previous steps. For example, you might point out that blocking a river tributary produces pressure on the banks and that this is similar to what happens when a vein or artery becomes blocked. Or you might note that by testing water systems for contaminants, you can determine the health of an ecosystem, which is similar to what blood testing does.

The four steps or principles of sequencing (see the box below) are useful in that they provide a logical progression of learning. They are interactive, though, in that you may need to go back to a previous step to help explain the idea currently under discussion.

Although we have divided sequencing into four steps, don't be fooled into thinking that on Monday your lesson should be "simple," on Tuesday it should be "concrete," on Wednesday you should address "complex" issues, on Thursday you should deal with the "abstract" issues, and on Friday you should test. It may take years to apply all four principles in the teaching of certain complex topics—for example, the basic concept of democracy is never completely taught and mastered. The process of teaching the concept of democracy begins at the preschool level and is continued throughout the entire educational system, becoming more complex and abstract at each successive level. Or you may use all four principles in a single lesson such as the circulatory system. Each discipline or area of the study has similar core facts, concepts, and generalizations that permeate the entire curriculum. What we wish to stress is that understanding the interrelationships of these four principles helps teachers teach. Using this instructional technique will remind you of the sequential nature of learning and thus help you incorporate appropriate learning experiences for each instructional objective. Figure 5.1 provides a visual model of the technique.

Sequencing integrates complexity and abstraction.

Four Principles of Sequencing

- Begin with a simple step.
- Use concrete examples.
- Add complexity to the lesson.
- Introduce abstractions.

FIGURE 5.1

A Hierarchy for Student Success

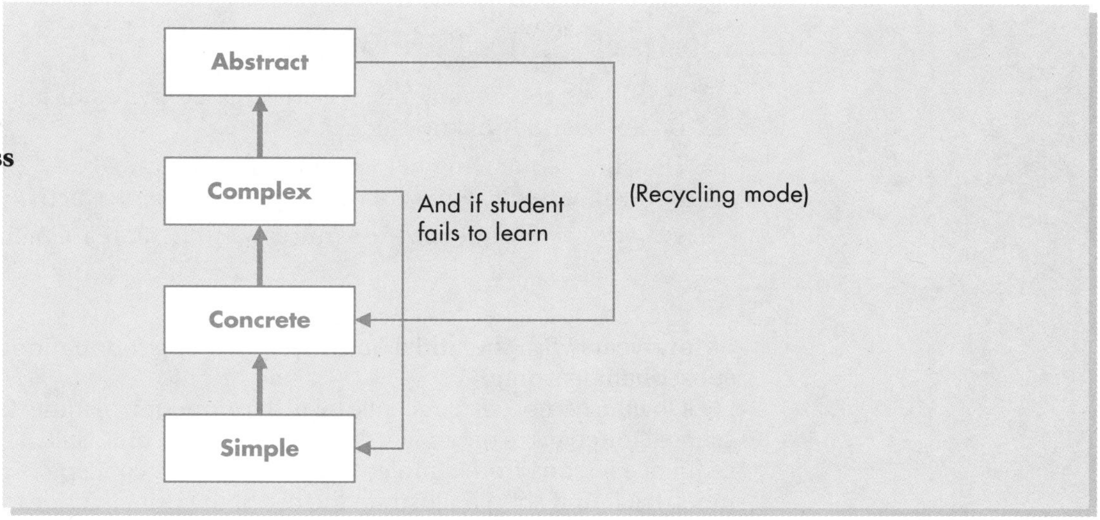

A Concrete Example: Graphing To illustrate the long-term nature of sequencing, let's examine a concrete example. In the first grade, teachers introduce the concept of graphing. The overall goal is to provide a series of experiences through which the concept of graphing will emerge. The complete sequence of instruction, which includes all types and levels of difficulty of graphs, may take ten years or more.

The sequence begins with a first-grade science lesson. The children plant bean seeds to study plant growth. The teacher raises the idea of regularly measuring the growth of the plants (say, every Friday). All plants are watered as uniformly as possible. As the seeds germinate, the teacher gives each child a strip of paper. The child places the paper next to the seedling and tears the strip to equal the height of the plant on the prescribed day. (This measuring technique uses a 1:1 scale, or one-to-one correspondence.)

Each child glues his or her strip to a large piece of paper, with a date label. This process continues each week until the unit has been completed. The teacher asks the children to observe the changes in plant height, which are discussed. Everyone has a concrete graph of the changes over time—a simple histogram. The teacher has the class discuss how they made the histograms and then introduces the concept of one-to-one correspondence.

The next year the teacher continues to use histograms but makes them more complex. Finally the teacher can show that if a dot is placed at the top of the piece of paper and scales are made (labeling the axes), all the information will be available in a form that is easier to use. This will take us through the second or maybe the third grade. Remember that some learning tasks take a long time to develop.

At the next grade level the teacher provides other data, such as daily maximum temperatures and, later, minimum temperatures. The graphing concepts thus become more complex and abstract; yet these activities provide a concrete experience that the class shares in common. The culmination of this set of experiences would be to have the children obtain data of their own choosing and make graphs of them. Such a graphing sequence may take three

Reflect Reflect Reflect

■ How does sequencing help relate isolated pieces of information to an organized body of knowledge?

■ How has sequencing helped your learning processes? Do you remember teachers who were good at sequencing course activities?

■ Why can you sequence the same content in more than one way?

or four years with the initial activities providing foundational knowledge for subsequent learning.

Obviously, not all concepts take that amount of time to teach. In high school it often takes only a few days to complete a unit. Still, it is often helpful to sequence lessons from simpler to more complex concepts, even in very short units. Each unit should illustrate the use of the principles described previously. Our main point is that you, the teacher, control the learning environment.

Content Forms

You want your students to understand both content and processes as well as the relationship between the two. **Content** is the information you want them to learn; processes are the thinking skills you want them to acquire. For example, in a geography course you want students to understand that there are different kinds of land forms, such as mountains, plateaus, and valleys, and to recognize the characteristics of each. The processes you want them to acquire will involve map-reading skills, reference skills, and information-gathering and organizing techniques. We will focus on your instruction of skills and processes in Part 3, especially in Chapters 7, 8, and 9. In this section, we will concentrate on content.

Although terms may occasionally differ, educators agree that content exists in three primary forms: facts, concepts, and generalizations (see Figure 5.2).

Facts   The most fundamental piece of information is called a **fact**. It is a type of content that is singular in occurrence, that occurs or exists in the present time, that has no predictive value, and that is acquired solely through the process of observation. The following are examples of facts:

1. Olympia is the capital city of the state of Washington.
2. President Clinton was governor of the state of Arkansas.
3. The sun set at 4:15 P.M. today.

The primary means of learning facts is through memorization and recall. One of the most effective ways of learning facts is verbal repetition. It is also easier to remember facts that are related to other content. A program of studies built on facts is at the lowest level of Bloom's taxonomy, knowledge (see Chapter 3). Facts are fundamental to learning, but learning is limited if teaching does not go beyond facts. Facts are often confused with generalizations, the third type of content (defined in the "Generalizations" section).

Facts are not the same thing as generalizations.

FIGURE 5.2

Hierarchy of Content Forms

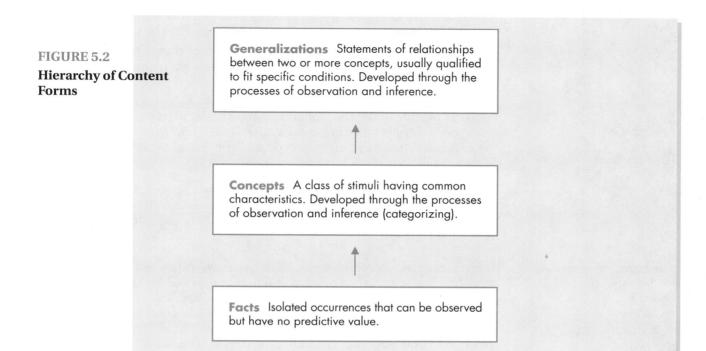

Generalizations Statements of relationships between two or more concepts, usually qualified to fit specific conditions. Developed through the processes of observation and inference.

Concepts A class of stimuli having common characteristics. Developed through the processes of observation and inference (categorizing).

Facts Isolated occurrences that can be observed but have no predictive value.

Concepts   **Concepts** are expressions, usually consisting of one or two words, of stimuli having common characteristics. We defined them in Chapter 4 as category words that we use to group objects as ideas. They are the result of categorization of a number of observations. Forming concepts seems to be a natural process in the human brain. For example, young children form concepts of what cats and dogs are like based on their observations of these familiar animals. Children learn to differentiate between dogs and cats because of the distinctive behavior of each species, the sound each produces, the distinctive shape of their heads, and perhaps some other characteristics. They do not rely on a single characteristic, such as size. Thus, for example, even though a particular cat may be larger than a particular dog, any child would be able to tell the difference between them.

Much of schooling consists of learning concepts. For example, in a beginning class on parts of speech, students learn that a noun is a "person, place, or thing." Throughout their schooling, students are required to understand and remember many such concepts. All concepts have the following five components:

1. **Name.** For example, *noun* is the name, or label, of a concept. It refers to a part of speech, and when it is used, people who have learned the concept understand what is being communicated. The name is more efficient to use than a lengthy definition.

2. **Definition.** A definition is a statement about the concept's characteristics. For example, "a noun is a person, place, or thing."

3. **Characteristics.** Characteristics are qualities that must be present for the concept to apply. For example, the characteristics of a noun are "person, place, or thing." One, but not all, of these must apply to a word for it to be

considered a noun. For some concepts—for example, democracy—a number of characteristics must be present for the concept to apply.

4. **Examples.** Examples are members of a class of things that show a concept's essential characteristics. *Tom* is an example of a noun; so are *car* and *Iceland.*

5. **Place in a hierarchy.** Most concepts are part of a content hierarchy that gives meaning to the concept and makes it easier to learn. Related, or coordinate, concepts to *noun* are *verb, adverb,* and *adjective.* Subordinate concepts are *common noun, proper noun,* and *pronoun.* The superordinate concept is parts of speech.

In Section 2 of this chapter, you will learn about concept analysis, an approach for the sequencing of concepts. This approach will teach you to relate all five components to develop lessons that will help your students learn and remember concepts.

Generalizations   As defined in Chapter 4, a **generalization** is an inferential statement that expresses a relationship between two or more concepts. It applies to more than one event and has predictive and explanatory value. For example: "People who smoke have a higher incidence of lung cancer than those who don't" is a generalization. It states a relationship between smoking (a concept) and lung cancer (another concept). The statement is predictive and applies to anyone who smokes. A good example of the use of generalizations in teaching is given in James A. Banks's book *Teaching Strategies for Ethnic Studies* (1997). Banks presents the following generalizations about immigration and migration: "In all cultures, individuals and groups have moved to different regions in order to seek better economic, political and social opportunities. However, movements of individuals and groups have been both voluntary and forced" (p. 112).

Given this general statement, students would expect, regardless of the country being studied, evidence of both forced and voluntary migration. Therefore, Banks's statement has predictive value and applies to more than one event. The statement also contains many concepts—*cultures; individuals and groups; economic, political, and social opportunities;* and *voluntary and forced.* The statement suggests relationships among these many concepts.

As students proceed from facts to concepts and then to generalizations, the amount of information increases and becomes more complex. Using Bloom's taxonomy, facts are at the knowledge level, concepts are at the comprehension level, and generalizations are at the application and analysis levels. Students can recall facts, concepts, and generalizations, but facts and concepts are not adequate for application and analysis, since neither has predictive or explanatory value.

As we close this discussion, we want to elaborate on a point we made earlier. Facts are often confused with generalizations, but the important differences between facts and generalizations follow:

1. Generalizations are inferences that condense a large amount of data; facts are statements that are singular in occurrence. For example, the statement "Sunset occurs earlier every day between June 21 and December 21 in the

Generalizations express the relationships between concepts.

Facts are not the same thing as generalizations.

Northern hemisphere" is a generalization. "The sun set at 4:15 P.M. today" is a fact.

2. Facts are statements of events that occurred in the past or exist in the present, whereas generalizations are statements about general trends or patterns. For example, "Governors often choose to run for the U.S. presidency" is a generalization; "Gary Locke is governor of the state of Washington" is a fact.

3. Generalizations have predictive value, whereas facts, because they are singular in occurrence, do not have predictive value. For example, "Studying enhances learning" is a generalization, because it makes a prediction. By contrast, "Liza is studying for her calculus test" is a statement of fact because it does not predict Liza's performance.

At this point we would like to briefly introduce two modes of presenting cognitive information that will influence sequencing of activities within a lesson.

Modes of Presentation

In general there are two basic modes of thinking: deductive reasoning and inductive reasoning. **Deductive reasoning** moves from the general to the specific; **inductive reasoning** proceeds from the specific to the general.

The primary modes of presentation are based on these modes of thinking. As a teacher, you have options: you can teach students a concept or a generalization by providing them with a definition followed by examples, or you can help students form the concepts or generalizations themselves based on observation or examples. The type of reasoning you select will determine the sequence of lesson activities. The scenarios in the box on page 168 illustrate the different approaches.

Mr. Hall and Miss Stewart were teaching the same content, and both wanted their students to learn the same generalization: "Magnets attract objects made of metal." Additional similarities in their approaches are using magnets and examples and asking questions.

However, there were major differences. Mr. Hall initiated the activity with a generalization while Miss Stewart started the activity by asking students to make observations. The two examples illustrate the essential difference between inductive and deductive reasoning and how this difference influences sequencing within a lesson. They also illustrate that sequencing is influenced by things other than content since the content was the same in both cases.

Different instructional approaches may stress inductive or deductive reasoning.

Reflect Reflect Reflect

- Name the primary modes of presentation. What are they based on?
- Remember your best teachers. Did they use both modes of presentation?
- Why is it important for teachers to understand the processes by which facts, concepts, and generalizations are formed?

Instructional

Strategies

Modes of Lesson Presentation

Mode 1: Deductive Reasoning

Mr. Hall began a lesson on magnetism by giving each student a handout. On the handout was this statement: "Magnets are attracted to some objects and not to others, and the things magnets are attracted to are called metals."

After a brief discussion regarding the concepts in the statement (such as *attraction*), Mr. Hall asked, "Will a magnet pick up your textbook?"

"No," responded the class.

"Why?"

"Because it is not a metal."

Mr. Hall gave each student a magnet and asked the class to use their magnets on objects on their desks. The discussion continued.

Mode 2: Inductive Reasoning

Miss Stewart wanted her students to understand magnetism. She began the lesson by handing out a magnet and an envelope to each student. In each envelope were objects—paper clips, plastic buttons, an iron nail, a penny, a plastic chip, an aluminum nail, a pencil. She asked the students to observe what happened when the magnet was applied to each object or other objects on their desks. After allowing a brief time of exploring, she called the class to order by saying, "Let's describe some observations you made about the magnet."

After a brief discussion that ranged from color and size of magnets to objects that were picked up by magnets, one of the students said, "It seems that magnets pick up some things but not others."

"Fine," said Miss Stewart. "Let's organize what we have observed into lists. One list is for the objects that magnets pick up, and one list is of those objects that the magnet does not pick up."

After students made lists and discussed the characteristics of each object, Miss Stewart asked, "Would someone summarize in statements what we have discovered?"

Angelica raised her hand and said, "We found that magnets pick up things that are called metals and do not pick up things like plastic and wood."

Your choice of mode of presentation is often determined by the lesson objectives. If you want your students to understand the process by which a generalization is formed, you may want to use the inductive approach. If your primary concern is only that your students know a particular concept or generalization, you may want to use the deductive approach. The next section provides more examples of inductive and deductive teaching.

Section 2: Models of Lesson Organization

In Section 1 of this chapter, the following components of instructional planning were discussed: sequencing, content forms, and modes of presentation. In this section we will describe how these components are integrated into three models of lesson or unit organization: the *task analysis, concept analysis,* and *advance organizer* models.

Each model of lesson organization has intrinsic strengths.

Each model presents a guideline for sequencing objectives and activities and establishes a hierarchy or relationship of knowledge. Each model has unique characteristics that assist the teacher in selecting a planning model. For example, content is the guiding force in the concept analysis model. The models and their primary characteristics are described in Table 5.1. Although each model has intrinsic strengths, no model is inherently superior. The teacher, as a decision maker, should choose the one that provides the greatest assistance in lesson planning, organizing, and implementing.

Each group of students, because of previous experiences or different levels of maturity, provides a different challenge to the teacher. Every discipline has different types of learning problems. Mathematics is very different from social studies and English. Thus the instructional planning models presented in this chapter must be adapted for specific situations. Perhaps the one valid generalization that can be made about planning is that, more often than not, teachers assume students have the prerequisite knowledge when in fact they do not. Some students may have already mastered the intended lesson, whereas other students in the same class do not have the requisite experiences and academic background for success.

Task Analysis Model

Consider the following none-too-uncommon scenario: You have taught a lesson, and you assume that your students will be able to answer successfully nearly all the questions you plan to ask on an examination covering that lesson. From all indications your students enjoyed the lesson, and you anticipate no

TABLE 5.1

Models of Lesson or Unit Organization	
Model	**Primary Characteristics**
Task analysis	Careful sequencing of intermediate and terminal objectives
Concept analysis	Sequencing of concept characteristics or examples that relate to the concept or to a concept hierarchy
Advance organizer	Use of an "identical scaffold" to teach the interrelationships within an organized body of knowledge

problems at assessment time. To your dismay, the class performs poorly on the examination. Was the test poorly conducted, or was the instruction lacking? An incident similar to this happened to one of America's foremost learning theorists, Robert M. Gagné (1992). The lesson was in subtraction, but the content could have been high school chemistry, college calculus, or even English, physical education, or any subject at any level. What is important is that Gagné was not satisfied with the results and wanted to determine why.

Task Analysis and Sequencing   Gagné began to study the sequence in which his learning activities were planned. He concluded that some instructional elements should have preceded others and that some concepts he had omitted should have been introduced. This initial study led Gagné to rearrange some of the learning sequences and try the lesson again. The result was a dramatic change in student success as measured by test results.

Gagné arranged the concomitant learning experiences in his lesson in a chart (see Figure 5.3). The top of the chart contained the end of the instructional sequence, usually called the *terminal objective*. Below the terminal objective he listed the *intermediate objectives*. The terminal objective is what students finally should achieve after a series of planned instructional encounters (in this case, "subtract whole numbers of any size"). Until students master the basic skills (the bottom half of the chart), they probably will not be able to reach the learning objectives at the higher levels (the top half of the chart). In Figure 5.3, the roman numerals refer to the order of presentation, and the lines illustrate the relationships between each cell.

Typically, a lesson on subtraction would begin with "simple subtraction" (facts). As a teacher, you have two options. You can prepare activities that teach "simple subtraction," or, as we discussed in Chapter 4, you can first identify your students' entry skills with a brief test. The benefit of using a concept hierarchy chart is that through testing, you can ensure that students have the requisite necessary skills to be successful learners.

To study the effects of a hierarchical structure on learning, Gagné employed the **task analysis model,** which subdivides a lesson's content, concepts, or processes into smaller, sequential steps beginning with the least complex and progressing to the most complex. This model has long proved valuable in business and industry. Careful sequencing of tasks has been and continues to be a critical element of efficient production in education, as it is in the industrial and technological sectors. You can imagine how chaotic and costly education would be if there were no grade levels and no methods for

To use the task analysis model, identify and sequence the terminal and intermediate objectives.

Reflect Reflect Reflect

- Select a complex topic such as lasers or capitalism. Create a chart showing all the prerequisite facts, concepts, and generalizations a student must learn to successfully master the topic.
- Examine some complex textbook in your area. To what extent is the content structured hierarchically?

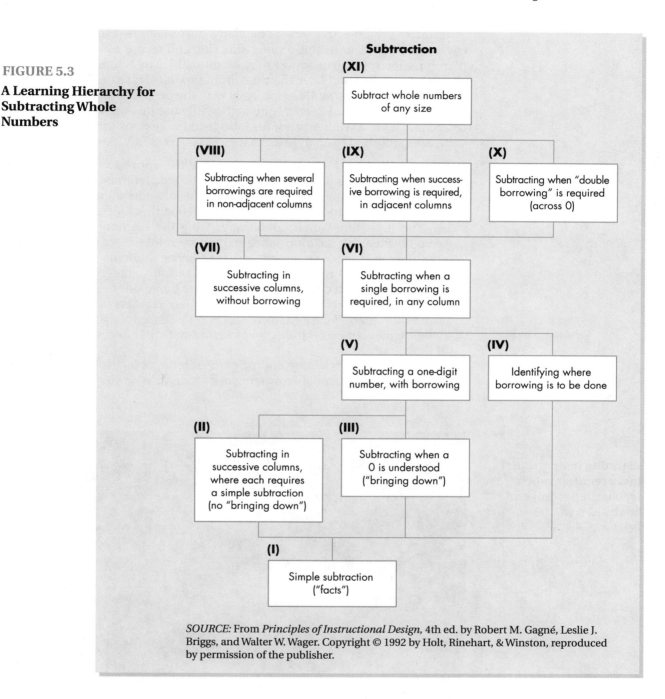

FIGURE 5.3

A Learning Hierarchy for Subtracting Whole Numbers

SOURCE: From *Principles of Instructional Design,* 4th ed. by Robert M. Gagné, Leslie J. Briggs, and Walter W. Wager. Copyright © 1992 by Holt, Rinehart, & Winston, reproduced by permission of the publisher.

identifying the difficulty level of university courses. If you think your program of studies seems disorganized, think of the problems you would have if each piece of information you learned were taught in isolation and not as part of a course or if your courses had no titles or identifying numbers. You can arrange almost any set of facts, concepts, or generalizations into the Gagné system.

Procedures for Task Analysis   The major purpose of task analysis is to discover the interrelationships among subskills and to use this information to plan for effective instruction. It may be unrealistic to assume that you, as a classroom teacher, will have the time or methodological expertise to identify and validate **enabling skills** empirically with the perception of Gagné's investigations, but you can effectively and efficiently use task analysis in your own teaching. The following procedures (also listed in the box on page 173) need to be accomplished to analyze learning tasks successfully.

1. **Select an instructional objective that is at the appropriate level of difficulty.** To make this initial determination, the teacher must know the structure of the content area (such as physics, health, education, mathematics, or social studies) and what the learner has already achieved.

   The first step, which entails specifying the learning objective, may seem obvious, but its importance is often overlooked. For example, teachers sometimes make statements such as "when students are in the ninth grade they should read *Julius Caesar*" or "seventh-graders should master percentages." Such curriculum decisions are based on the incremental nature of content, but they fail to identify where learners are located in the curriculum plan. For example, it makes little sense to teach students how to figure percentages if they do not first understand decimals—regardless of their grade level.

   Therefore, in selecting appropriate learning objectives, you will need to identify the general area where your students' knowledge ends. This is

Planning instructional tasks requires much teacher reflection and analysis. © Susan Lapides/ Design Conceptions.

Analyzing Learning Tasks

1. Select an appropriately difficult instructional objective.
2. Identify enabling skills.
3. Subdivide independent and dependent skills and sequences.
4. Arrange independent and dependent sequences in order.
5. Sequence specific tasks for students.

---

the point at which you should formulate new learning objectives and analyze the subskills that lead to the attainment of these objectives. We will refer later to the importance of using *diagnostic vigilance* when you help learners achieve an objective through a classroom lesson. The technique of diagnostic vigilance allows the teacher to check on whether the original objective is, in fact, at the right level of difficulty.

Students must possess the required enabling skills to attain a specific objective.

2. **Identify the enabling skills students need to attain the objective.** Enabling skills are those thinking processes that must be mastered and the information that must be understood for students to achieve the objective. For example, in a physical education class, students are being taught the golf skill of putting. Without regard to sequencing, the teacher lists the skills necessary for putting: gripping the club, maintaining the proper stance, positioning the club face correctly, executing the backswing, following through, and mentally visualizing the ball's trajectory. These are the specific skills that must be mastered to putt successfully.

3. **Subdivide independent and dependent enabling skills and learning sequences.** For any given objective, there are two basic types of enabling skills: independent and dependent. (Sometimes an objective requires both.) Learning these skills can be thought of in terms of sequencing: in an independent sequence, the enabling skills are not incremental. For example, when you learned to tie your shoes, it did not matter whether you started with the right or the left shoe. These activities are independent of each other. Similarly, in constructing a house, it does not make any appreciable difference if one starts by laying the foundation for the garage or for the main part of the house.

   In the dependent sequence, on the other hand, accomplishment of one skill is essential before attainment of the next skill in the series. When you put on your shoes and socks, the ordering of the tasks does make a difference. In the same way, the construction company would be remiss in attempting to shingle the roof before raising the walls of the structure.

4. **Arrange the independent and dependent sequences in order.** Perform the task yourself to identify steps that may have been omitted. Use this sequence to construct a lesson that will systematically facilitate the learning of the terminal objective. Once you have analyzed the objective and discovered its component parts (independent and dependent enabling skills or learning sequences), these parts will provide an entry point of learning for all students. The enabling skills themselves become objectives that you use to help students learn the terminal objective. As an example, let's

return to the putting problem. The teacher determines that the grip and stance are **independent skills** that can be learned in any order but should be mastered before the backswing and follow through, since you need to know how to grip the club and how to stand in order to practice these **dependent skills.** Since the grip and stance are independent skills, the teacher may decide to teach the grip first because it may be easier to teach the stance when students are holding a golf club.

It is doubtful that you will be able to identify all the prerequisite enabling skills before implementing a lesson and consistently emphasize the most important ones. As you teach, your judgment will allow you to adjust, to add other skills to the list, and to emphasize certain skills with particular students. Keep notes about such skills in your daily lesson plan book. These notes will be a handy reference for your next class.

5. **Sequence specific tasks for students.** Before you do this step, you must first plan the sequence in which you will conduct the class. As we saw in Chapters 3 and 4, there are some tasks that you must accomplish every time you prepare and implement a lesson. You must (1) identify the instructional objectives, (2) plan the appropriate educational activities or experiences, (3) obtain the materials, (4) read the materials yourself, (5) plan the strategies that you will employ in the teaching act, (6) evaluate the students, and (7) critique the lesson—that is, decide how you would improve it. But now you need to establish the sequence or order in which specific dependent tasks will be taught. This sequencing plan ensures student success.

Task analysis is an especially useful tool for planning instruction for children with special needs, integrating topics in a multidisciplinary unit, and designing multicultural activities. As you identify each task, you can analyze it for content that is culturally biased, skills that are difficult for students with special physical or learning needs to accomplish, and skills and knowledge that were not covered previously. You might even be surprised to learn that a task analysis approach can be used to help college students write better history papers (Simon 1991). In the same vein, task analysis principles are used for teaching music to non-music majors (Duke and Madsen 1991). Because it looks directly at the classroom and the functions of work within it, task analysis can help students better understand their role as "workers" in a school environment (Munson and Rubenstein 1992).

A Concrete Example: Task Analysis for the Concept of Density   One of the authors of this text, a science teacher, has observed that teachers often have difficulty teaching the concept of density. By observing student errors, he inferred that if the tasks associated with learning the concept of density were identified and structured, some of the problems could be reduced. Table 5.2 lists the various tasks or elements that are prerequisites to mastering the concept of density.

On examining Table 5.2 carefully, are you surprised at the number of operations and prerequisite skills that are needed to learn about density? Several teachers were, and so were we.

After all the major tasks were listed, they were sequenced using Gagné's

---

(margin notes)

Students can learn difficult concepts if teachers use task analysis

Task analysis has many useful applications.

TABLE 5.2

Task Analysis for Teaching the Concept of Density

I. Using the metric system
   A. Weight
   B. Linear measurements

II. Understanding two-dimensional measurements: computing the area of a rectangle and a circle

III. Computing volumes
   A. Rectangular objects
   B. Cylindrical objects
   C. Irregularly shaped objects
      1. Those that float in water
      2. Those that sink in water

IV. Defining and using a "unit standard"
   A. Linear
   B. Volumetric

V. Using mathematics skills
   A. Division
   B. Multiplication
   C. Linear equations ($a = b/c$)

VI. Knowing that the mass of water in grams approximates the volume of water in cubic centimeters (cc)

VII. Deriving that density is mass per unit of volume.

approach. Figure 5.4 illustrates a simplified task analysis and hierarchy chart for the concept of density. Once this chart was created, it became apparent that it is useless to teach this concept before the seventh grade. Students simply do not have the necessary intellectual background until that time—and some may not until one year later.

As researchers and teachers, we often wonder why students cannot learn certain concepts or principles. The truth is that in many cases teachers have to revise even the order of the text pages students read so that it is understandable. To maximize the benefits to the learner, you may have to sketch rough hierarchy charts for every chapter, unit, or module you teach. Thus it is

Reflect Reflect Reflect

- Why would you take the effort to use task analysis? What benefits would you expect to derive from it?
- Prepare a chart showing the relationships of various facts, concepts, and generalizations you have learned in previous education courses. Use the concept of dependent and independent sequencing.

FIGURE 5.4

Simplified Task Analysis and Hierarchy Chart for Concept of Density

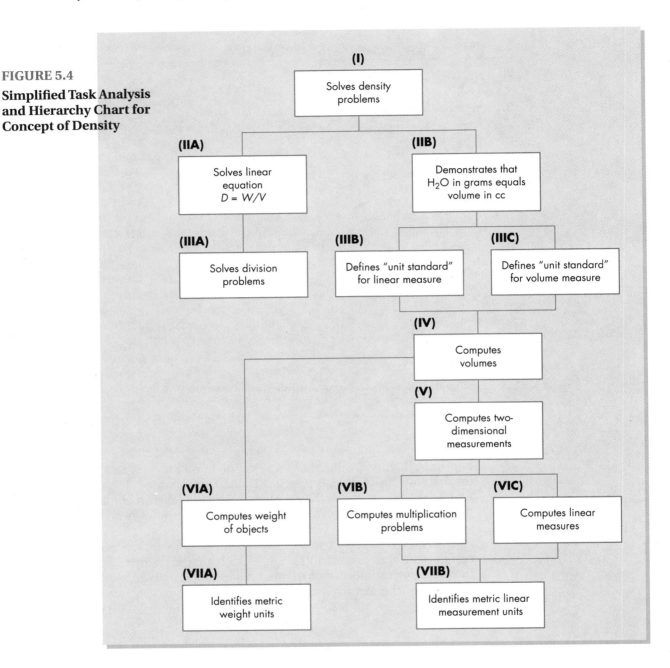

beneficial to set aside a few minutes to prepare a task analysis chart for each new unit you plan.

When you observe student **learning deficits,** you can construct your own hierarchy chart to determine whether key elements of instruction are missing. No doubt other charting modifications can be devised using three techniques. Try your hand at creating such a chart for, say, a concept in English grammar, biology, mathematics, or social studies. We believe that if more teachers used this technique, teaching would improve immeasurably. Both teachers and students would be happier in school—and more successful!

Concept Analysis Model

Task analysis allows you to arrange any number of learning components or tasks into a "map" or plan to be accomplished. As we have observed, students often do not understand concepts because the teacher makes too large an intellectual leap. A concept analysis will help the teacher address such planning deficiencies before lessons are assigned by identifying the characteristics that need to be considered.

The teaching of concepts encompasses a substantial portion of all instruction. For example, science requires students to understand the concepts of matter, energy, plants, and animals; language arts applies the concepts of communication, paragraphs, parts of speech, and punctuation; mathematics requires students to apply the concepts of sets, commutative property, and inverse operations. A lengthy list could be compiled for every subject area.

When you teach concepts, you must use both sequencing and task analysis. As the example of the magnetism lesson illustrated, you have two sequencing options: (1) start the lesson by describing the concept and follow this with an analysis of characteristics (facts) and a series of illustrations or examples (facts) so that the students gain a thorough understanding of the concept or (2) provide examples (facts) related to the concept and allow students to discover the concept themselves. As we observed earlier, when you start the lesson by defining the concept, you are teaching deductively; when you begin with examples and expect students to discover the concept, you are teaching inductively. In either instance, a procedure called concept analysis is helpful. For example, if you were teaching the concept *proper noun,* it would be helpful to develop a conceptual hierarchy of the content to illustrate the characteristics of the concept (show its uniqueness) and its relationship to the larger body of content covered by the course. An example of this kind of chart is shown in Figure 5.5.

A concept hierarchy provides the teacher with a sequencing technique. To teach the concept *proper noun,* for example, the teacher must demonstrate the characteristics that make a proper noun both "proper" and a "noun" (see Figure 5.5). Thus the teacher provides examples that illustrate the characteristics of a proper noun—in this case, the names of two *persons,* Jim and Mary.

One way to describe the relationship of concepts formed using a concept hierarchy is in terms of *superordinate, coordinate,* and *subordinate* concepts. These terms refer not only to the scope of inclusiveness of a concept but also to its relationship to other concepts. For example, the concept of *parts of speech* is inclusive and subsumes the concept of *noun,* which, in turn, subsumes the concept of *proper.* In this respect, *proper* is a type of *noun,* which is a part of speech. Related concepts such as these form a hierarchy, or ordered arrangement.

In Figure 5.5, the concept *parts of speech* is superordinate to the concepts *noun, verb, adverb,* and *adjective.* The concepts *common, proper,* and *pronoun* are subordinate to the concept *noun.* The connection between the concepts *noun, verb, adverb,* and *adjective* is called a coordinate relationship.

Use both sequencing and task analysis to teach concepts.

FIGURE 5.5

Concept Analysis

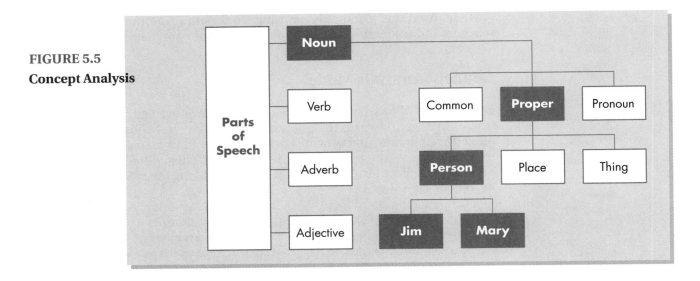

Concept Analysis Components

1. Concept name
2. Definition
3. Characteristics
4. Exemplars
5. Superordinate concept(s)
6. Subordinate concept(s)
7. Coordinate concept(s)

In preparing to teach a concept, the teacher must have a thorough understanding of that concept. A **concept analysis** is a thorough examination of the different aspects of a concept, which is described earlier in this chapter, plus the concept hierarchy. A concept analysis includes the components listed in the box above. Concept analysis is a planning tool that has proved valuable to teachers in structuring their concept-learning activities.

Each dimension of concept learning describes a different and unique aspect of the concept. This process not only provides teachers with a thorough understanding of the concept to be taught but also can serve as a plan for instruction. An example of concept analysis for the concept "parallelogram" is provided in Figure 5.6, which shows each step.

In the second phase of teaching a concept, the teacher determines whether the lesson should be taught inductively or deductively. Should the students be given the concept and then be provided with examples of its characteristics, or should they be given examples from which to induce the concept? Whether the lesson is taught inductively or deductively, a thorough analysis of concept characteristics and examples is necessary. The concept analysis hierarchy is an excellent procedure for accomplishing this task.

FIGURE 5.6

Concept Analysis for Parallelogram

Concept Name:	Parallelogram
Definition:	A parallelogram is a four-sided geometric figure whose opposite sides are parallel.
Characteristics:	Four-sided, opposite sides parallel, opposite angles equal
Exemplars:	
Superordinate Concept:	Geometric shapes or quadrilaterals
Subordinate Concept:	Rhombus, Square
Coordinate Concept:	Trapezoid

SOURCE: From *Strategies for Teachers: Information Processing Modes in the Classroom* by P. D. Eggen, D. P. Kauchak, and R. J. Harder. Copyright © 1979 by Prentice-Hall. Used with permission.

The teaching of concepts is often a prerequisite for the teaching of generalizations. For example, a civics teacher might want to use the generalization "incumbents usually win elections" in a unit on politics. For students to understand this generalization, they must understand the concept *incumbent*. Although incumbents may be older or wealthier or even more experienced than challengers, these are not characteristics of the *concept* of incumbency. If the students don't correctly understand the concept, they will not correctly understand the generalization; they may think incumbents usually win because they are older rather than simply because they are incumbents.

One of the most effective methods for teaching concepts is the use of examples. In planning a lesson, the teacher must have come up with enough examples to illustrate all the dominant characteristics adequately. For concrete concepts such as *dog* or *verb*, it is easy to find good examples. For concepts such as *anger, justice,* or *poetic*, the teacher must spend considerable time developing good exemplars. Providing examples of coordinate concepts often helps students understand the characteristics of the concept being taught. For example, you might give the examples of *hostility, indignation,* and *wrath* to help students understand the concept anger. Negative examples (opposites) can also be used.

Advance Organizer Model

The advance organizer model is useful for teaching abstract and complex concepts.

Teaching abstract and complex concepts such as *hate, bigotry, ecosystems, diversity,* and *democracy* can be a great challenge. Often students confuse such concepts. For example, many students believe that *democracy* and *capitalism* are the same concept, not realizing that one is a political concept and the other is an economic concept. The advance organizer model is an effective tool for teaching such concepts. This model is based on an **advance organizer,** which is a statement of those elements that the learner will be required to master in the lesson. You can use this model to compare capitalism to the coordinate concepts socialism and communism, for example. One of the model's primary purposes is to teach the relationships between such concepts.

The advance organizer model is based on Ausubel's explication of deductive learning (1968). The deductive mode of inquiry includes three basic components: advance organizers, progressive differentiation, and integrative reconciliation. It requires a body of knowledge that can be organized hierarchically. The purpose of the advance organizer model is to provide students with a structure so that they understand each part of the hierarchy of knowledge in the lesson as well as the relationships among the parts. The model consists of three phases, listed in the box below and explained in the following sections.

Advance Organizer   As an example of an advance organizer, an English teacher who is starting a unit on metaphors, similes, and personification would start the lesson with a *definition of* or *generalization about* figures of speech. The teacher might follow a simple hierarchy chart like the one shown in Figure 5.7.

If each student understands the advance organizer, it will provide a frame of reference for the lesson so that each part of the lesson can be more easily understood. The organizer enables the learner to relate the lesson materials to previous knowledge. The teacher's task is to develop an abstract statement that encompasses all aspects of the lesson and that the student can relate to previously learned material.

Steps in the Advance Organizer Model

1. ***Advance Organizer.*** Abstract introductory statement related to previously learned material that encompasses all aspects of the lesson
2. ***Progressive Differentiation.*** Process of subdividing broad ideas into narrower, less inclusive ones
3. ***Integrative Reconciliation.*** Process of examining similarities and differences among related concepts

---

FIGURE 5.7

Hierarchy Chart for Figures of Speech

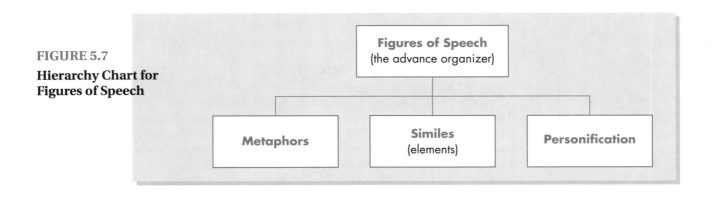

The teacher then has considerable latitude in organizing and developing the lesson. Therefore, two teachers using the same advance organizer may develop and teach the lesson differently. A practical note is helpful here: record the advance organizer and brief hierarchy chart on a transparency or large sheet of paper. This allows students to refer to it throughout the lesson and thus provides direction and focus.

Progressive Differentiation   After you have presented the advance organizer and you are sure your students understand it, the second phase of the model begins. This phase, progressive differentiation, is the process by which the content is subdivided into narrower, less inclusive ideas. The English teacher can start a lesson on metaphors with the statement, "A metaphor is one kind of figure of speech. The primary characteristics of a metaphor are. . . ." The teacher has used a broad, abstract concept (*figure of speech*) and taken from it a narrower, more concrete concept (*metaphor*). **Progressive differentiation** is the process of isolating each fact, concept, or generalization within a hierarchy of knowledge so that it can be learned independently. Highlighting the unique and discrete characteristics of an element of information makes it easier to learn.

Integrative Reconciliation   The third component of the advance organizer model is **integrative reconciliation,** which is the process of teaching students how main concepts and underlying facts are related or how underlying facts are different or similar. In this phase you make a deliberate attempt to help students understand similarities and differences among the components of the hierarchy of knowledge and to reconcile real or apparent inconsistencies between the ideas presented. In our English lesson example, the teacher makes certain that students understand the relationship between figures of speech and metaphors (vertical reconciliation) and that they comprehend the differences and similarities between metaphors and similes (lateral reconciliation). We use the terms *vertical* and *horizontal* because in most hierarchy charts (such as Figure 5.7), broader, more abstract, more inclusive concepts (in this instance, *figures of speech*) are placed above less inclusive, narrower concepts (*metaphors*). Notice that *metaphors, similes,* and *personification* are on the same horizontal level.

The advance organizer model provides both vertical and horizontal reconciliation.

In summary, the advance organizer model is designed to teach organized bodies of content deductively (based on Ausubel's conception of deductive learning). The advance organizer provides the students with an overview and focus; progressive differentiation provides items of information that can be more easily understood, and integrative reconciliation provides meaningful learning by helping students understand the relationships among the elements of the content being taught.

Interactive Nature of This Model   Although the three components are presented here as sequential, in reality they are interactive (especially progressive differentiation and integrative reconciliation). If the comparison and differentiation discussion develops students' understanding of a specific concept or generalization, then the teacher should not hesitate to use the two steps concurrently. As with any teaching model, the teacher should use the model and its components in the way that most effectively helps his or her

---

Tips for Deductive Lessons

1. Have students verify an understanding of the advance organizer by providing examples, definitions, and characteristics of it.

2. Whenever appropriate, students should help with progressive differentiation by providing definitions, characteristics, or examples.

3. Develop a chart that illustrates both the relationship among ideas and their uniqueness.

---

students learn. The model should be applied with flexibility and not become a straitjacket.

The advance organizer model promotes deductive interaction.

Be careful not to confuse deductive teaching with lecturing. Often lectures are neither deductive nor inductive. A deductive lesson can contain as much teacher-student or student-student interaction as an inductive lesson does. After presenting the advance organizer, the teacher can hold students responsible for progressive differentiation and integrative reconciliation by having them provide characteristics and examples and explain relationships (Ausubel 1968). In this instance the teacher becomes the facilitator of the learning process, much in the same manner as in an inductive lesson. The box above provides a few suggestions for teaching deductive lessons.

Instructional Strategies

Teaching the Concepts of Government

This is a lesson on government and the concepts associated with it. The class has already studied basic forms of government; the current topic is the functions of government. To understand how government functions, the students need to understand the relationship of government to other societal institutions. Thus the teacher might introduce the lesson with the following advance organizer:

> Government is but one of the institutions serving society. The state or government is essential to civilization, yet it cannot do the whole job by itself. Many human needs are met by the home, the church, the press, and private business.

With the presentation of the advance organizer, the teacher is ready to proceed with the progressive differentiation component of the lesson. Materials are made available to students so that they may begin their investigations into human needs that are met by different institutions. First, the teacher and the class prepare a list of different problems that can be studied. As an alternative, they might list steps they could take to identify areas in which various institutions serve society and in which institutional functions overlap. Functions that are not covered by any institution would also be listed. As the students gather material and present it to the class, the teacher leads them in the progressive differentiation and integrative reconciliation processes. The result is an interactive, deductive lesson.

Begin lessons with an advance organizer.

For the advance organizer model to work effectively, the teacher must prepare an advance organizer that provides students with an understandable focus for the lesson and a visual representation that illustrates the relationships among the information to be taught. When you bridge previous knowledge and materials to new learning, there are important achievement gains (Walberg 1991, p. 38). If you use advance organizers systematically, along with continuous reviews, your students will outperform others. Thus this model is a valuable addition to your knowledge base of teaching.

Examples of lessons planned according to the advance organizer model are presented in the boxes on pages 183 and 184.

Instructional Strategies

An Ausubelian Lesson Plan About Verbs

Advance Organizer

1. Review sentence elements to demonstrate that the *subject* is one of the two basic elements of a sentence.
2. "What is the function of the subject in a sentence?"
3. "After we have a subject, what is the second basic element of a sentence?"
4. "Usually there are more than two words in a sentence. But we will concentrate on these two most basic sentence elements, because they are necessary in writing a sentence."

Progressive Differentiation

5. "Today we will talk specifically about verbs."
6. "What is the primary function of a verb?"
7. "There are many types of verbs, but today we will want to focus specifically on action verbs."
8. "Why is it important that we use action verbs in our writing?"
9. Administer list of verbs to determine how much the students might already know about verbs. Tell them to circle action verbs.
10. Ask students to read those verbs that they did not circle.
11. Tell students that these verbs are called "forms of the verb *to be*" and are used to show being or existence.
12. Tell students that if teachers have ever told them their writing was lifeless or dry, it could be that they were not using enough action verbs.

Instructional

Strategies

An Ausubelian Lesson Plan About Verbs (cont.)	
Integrative Reconciliation	13. "A verb is one of the two basic what?" 14. "How is a verb related to a subject?" 15. "When can one of these basic sentence elements be left out of a sentence and the sentence still be considered correct?" (Awareness of inconsistencies) 16. Put a box on the table. Ask the students to list at least three actions that can be done to the box or that the box performs. 17. Review the importance of action verbs in writing. 18. Give the next day's assignment—to write a paper that describes the student's favorite sport and that uses ten action verbs.
SOURCE: Adapted from a lesson plan prepared by Cathy Valencsin Duffy. Used with permission.	

Graphic Organizers   Observe the introduction of each chapter in this book. We use a graphic organizer called a concept map or web. In this chapter alone, we used a variety of **graphic organizers** to illustrate learning hierarchies, principles of sequencing, the list of items in a task analysis for density, and the concept analysis for parts of speech. As you read the text, you will

Examples of Graphic Organizers

- Historical timelines
- Flow charts
- Bar graphs
- Pie graphs
- Networks
- Taxonomic keys
- Tables
- Continuum scales
- Family trees
- Venn diagrams
- Cyclic diagrams
- Content outlines

observe others that we incorporate with the written text. The box on page 184 lists several common graphic organizers.

Many researchers have verified the effectiveness of graphic organizers for students at all grade levels. The use of concept maps shows promise in determining whether students relate prior knowledge more efficiently and thus expedite current learning (Dochy and Alexander 1995). Concept maps have a long history of helping students absorb content at higher levels, from kindergarten to the university (see Heinze-Fry and Novak 1990; Liu 1994; Novak 1993; and Novak and Musonda 1991).

Other types of graphic organizers, such as pictures, have enhanced student learning in geography (Fitzhugh 1995). Explicit graphic organizers facilitated information retrieval processes by fifth graders (Griffin and Malone 1995). The use of graphic organizers in college writing classes helped students craft essays of higher quality (Robinson and Kiewra 1995). Significant student improvements were reported in fourth-grade writing test scores when different forms of concept maps were used when presenting instruction (Hyerle 1995–96). By using graphic organizers in your teaching, you may help your students reach a level of understanding they would not reach without the organizers.

Each group of students, because of previous experiences or different levels of maturity, provides a different challenge to the teacher. Every discipline has different types of learning problems. Mathematics is very different from social studies or English.

Graphic organizers are *right-brain hemisphere* related, a topic that will be discussed in Section 3 of this chapter. Thus, while you stress left-brain hemisphere content or processes, you reinforce the learning by using techniques that incorporate right-brain hemisphere learning. Graphic organizers provide an instructional *double wammy*. (What's a *double wammy*? Refer to *'Lil Abner* comic strips for *Evil Eye Fleagle's* famous look.)

Teach your students how to use graphic organizers as they study for your lessons. You can use them as advance organizers. Their use provides another way to enrich the classroom environment. (See Hyerle 1996 and Robinson 1998.)

Because graphic organizers have a positive impact on student achievement, we stress their utilization. For example, their use, plus the use of other interactive teaching methods, helps increase reading comprehension (Bowman, Carpenter, and Paone 1998). Likewise, teachers report increased comprehension in K–8 schools where graphic organizers are appropriately used (Culbert et al. 1998). Leticia Ekhaml (1998) describes a wide variety of graphic organizers that aid both teaching and learning.

Thus the instructional planning models presented in this chapter must be adapted for specific situations. Perhaps the one valid generalization that can be made about planning is that, more often than not, teachers assume students have the prerequisite knowledge when in fact they do not. Some students may have already mastered the intended lesson, whereas other students in the same class do not have the requisite experiences and academic background for success.

Graphic organizers expedite student learning.

> ## Reflect Reflect Reflect
>
> - How is the relationship between ideas illustrated by progressive differentiation and integrative reconciliation?
> - How can inductive and deductive lessons be crafted to create student involvement?
> - What graphic organizers could you use to instruct concepts in your teaching field?

Section 3: Multimethodology as an Instructional Process

We begin this section on instructional **multimethodology** by briefly introducing three topics that lend theoretical credence to our thesis of providing an instructionally rich teaching repertoire. The first topic relates to the functions of the right- and left-brain hemispheres in information processing; the second to learning preferences; and the third to multiple intelligences. With those as your advance organizers, we'll fully develop the idea of multimethodology.

Hemisphericity

Over the past several decades, a major theory about how the brain works, called hemisphericity, has given teachers another tool to use in planning instructional experiences. **Hemisphericity** is the study of where in the brain—in the left hemisphere or the right hemisphere—different types of mental functions occur. Research suggests that the right cerebral hemisphere is involved in visual, nonverbal, spatial, divergent, and intuitive thinking. The left cerebral hemisphere is involved in verbal, logical, categorical, detail-oriented, and convergent thinking. The right brain works more with approximations and creativity, whereas the left brain works more with specifics and analysis. For example, the right side of the brain processes the visual information that allows you to recognize a face, but the left side provides the name to go with the face. The facts that allow us to understand the kinds of functions that occur on each side of the brain are important because they help educators understand that instruction must be planned to enhance both hemispheres.

Schooling overemphasizes left-hemisphere functions.

Research conducted over many years has demonstrated that teachers persistently emphasize objectives and instruction that focus on the left side of the brain. The vast majority of objectives focus on the cognitive, analytical, and convergent functions dominated by the left side of the brain (Sylwester 1995; Caine and Caine 1997; Jensen 1998).

Research also tells us that although each side of the brain tends to emphasize a specific kind of function, the most productive intellectual functioning occurs when there is cooperation between both sides of the brain. Learning exercises that are focused on the left side of the brain (the majority of the learning objectives and instructional experiences we plan for students) are enhanced when the right side of the brain is included in the experience. So, not only have we largely ignored the right-side functions of the brain in devising instructional experiences, but also we have limited the effectiveness of left-side functions in students learning. To teach most effectively to either side of the brain, we must balance outcomes and learning experiences to involve *both* sides whenever possible (Baker and Martin 1998).

It is important to plan for right-hemisphere activities.

Including Creativity in Instructional Plans   It is important to plan learning experiences that use the right side of the brain, but a brief caution applies. Because objectives or outcomes for the right side of the brain emphasize creative functions, the criterion of any outcome for the right side of the brain can be difficult to write. By their nature, the more creative functions of the brain are less measurable in terms of quantity and quality. For example, suppose you assign your students the problem of designing a novel use for plastic soda pop bottles. How do you define an objective for such an assignment? How do you quantify or define creativity? Remember that effective instruction includes a balance between left- and right-brain emphasis, and you will have taken care of most of your problem. Objectives are not presented in isolation; rather, as this chapter shows, they are presented as sequences of expectations that lead to a general outcome. If you write carefully constructed objectives that allow students to master left-brain activities, you can also construct a framework to define and assess right-brain objectives so that they are part of the whole sequence of learning. Such a framework could resemble the Kaplan Matrix (see Chapter 4). We offer in the box below a brief sample of objectives that emphasize right-brain functions.

One cannot assume that stressing right-hemisphere activities automatically enhances creativity. There is a lack of clear evidence that there is a close relationship between creativity and brain hemispheres (Hines 1991). Hemispheric differences tend to be relative rather than absolute, and implications for schooling may yet be speculative (Hellige 1988). We strongly suggest that

---

Right-Hemisphere Objectives

1. Using only a pencil and a blank sheet of paper, draw a caricature of a fellow class member that is recognizable by the majority of the class.

2. Presented with ten objects of different size, shape, and texture, develop a scheme that will enable another person to classify all ten objects, using only the senses.

3. Given a story starter, create a short story in which all the physical elements of the story starter are incorporated into the plot.

4. Using only the three primary colors, create a painting that includes all the elements of the modern style.

5. Using the computer simulation "Oregon Trail" as a model, construct a simulation for travel from an earth-orbit space station to the moon that adheres to the physical principles regulating movement in an airless and weightless environment.

Reflect Reflect Reflect

- Prepare a lesson plan that includes right-brain student activities.
- Examine a set of textbooks or computer programs for your intended grade level. What hemisphericity traits do you recognize?
- Obtain a set of your state's standards for any curricular area. Apply the test of hemisphericity to those standards.

you study Robert Sylwester's *A Celebration of Neurons: An Educator's Guide to the Human Brain* (1995). He provides an excellent overview of how the brain functions.

Dimensions of Human Diversity and Learning Preferences

Our second topic in the discussion of multimethodology concerns how individuals learn. No two people think exactly alike, and it is safe to say that no two people learn in exactly the same way either. Teachers respond to this diversity in a number of ways, one of the most prevalent being grouping (Slavin 2000). At the elementary level, grouping often means dividing classes into subgroups on the basis of students' skills and abilities, particularly in math and reading. At the high school level, grouping often results in tracks, with the curriculum in each track aimed at different educational and vocational goals. But students differ in other, more subtle ways than aptitude and ability. In this section we will consider some factors that may have a positive or negative effect on student learning; then we will present a few techniques you can use to accommodate individual learning styles.

Students bring varying cultural backgrounds to school.

Students' cultural and background experiences influence how they understand new material and how they respond to, and benefit from, instruction. Differences in background, experience, socioeconomic status, culture, and language all influence learning (Banks 1997; Bennett 1999). For example, teachers who move from a rural setting to a big city school will find that they need to adapt how they teach. A simple question to first-graders about where milk comes from will elicit one response from farm kids (cows) and a completely different one from suburban or inner-city kids (the store).

Educators have recognized the impact of experiential and cultural differences on student success for some time (Cushner, McClelland, and Safford 1996), and most teacher education programs contain courses or units on multiculturalism to help teachers become sensitive to the powerful effect of background experiences. But more recently, considerable attention has been focused on other, less apparent dimensions of individual differences.

Researchers in this area have termed this dimension "learning style" and have developed instructional programs to meet the needs of different groups of students. Learning style is usually defined as the cognitive, affective, and physiological traits that learners exhibit as they interact in the classroom

---

Sternberg's Summary of Thinking Styles

- Styles are preferences, not abilities.
- Matching style with ability creates a synergy.
- Each individual develops patterns of styles, not just one.
- Styles vary across tasks and situations.
- Style preferences differ according to the individual.
- Stylistic ability differs for individuals.
- Styles are socialized.
- Styles are teachable.
- Styles are not universal.
- Culture, gender, age, and education influence styles.

---

environment. Students with different learning styles understand problems in different ways, and they try to solve them in different ways.

Assuming that you think before you learn, Robert J. Sternberg's (1997) concept of thinking styles is very appropriate to our discussion. He postulates that any style of learning is *a preference, not an innate ability*. Thus learning styles are not fixed but are conditions of one's environment. This statement tends to support the popularity of the constructivist perspective. In the box above we summarize several of Sternberg's main points that apply to our plea for instructional multimethodology.

At this point you might be saying to yourself, "Hey, this is very close to schema theory, which we studied in psychology." In one sense it is. As students of any age or learning style study something, they fit what they learn into a meaningful pattern, or schema. When students are introduced to a new concept, their schema for it might be disorganized, irrational, or just plain wrong. Such a schema will obviously hinder learning. Similarly, in terms of learning styles, students' individual and environmental attributes can help or hinder learning (see Wilson 1996).

Learning styles are simply tendencies or preferences.

Researchers and advocates in the area of learning styles think of these styles as being on the borderline between mental abilities and personality. Learning styles fall between these two areas and are the individual's preferred way to learn new skills, knowledge, or techniques. In the remainder of this chapter we will illustrate how to accommodate all students by using a diverse array of teaching styles.

Multiple Intelligences

There are at least three key findings about human intelligence that relate to our current discussion. First, intelligence is a dynamic quality not fixed at birth. Second, through appropriate learning experiences, intelligence can be enhanced. Third, intelligence has many different attributes (Gardner 1993).

> ### Gardner's Eight Intelligences
> - Verbal/linguistic
> - Logical/mathematical
> - Visual/spatial
> - Body/kinesthetic
> - Musical/rhythmic
> - Interpersonal
> - Intrapersonal
> - Naturalist

The latter finding is the key element for instructional planning and sequencing; that is, intelligence is a multiple facet, not a singular one associated only with verbal or quantitative aptitudes. This notion has led to a novel idea called **multiple intelligences.** The chief proponent of the concept of multiple intelligences is Howard Gardner (1985, 1991, 1999). Gardner's work is applicable in the school setting because of its ease of use for planning. He identifies eight basic intelligences. These are listed in the box above.

Multiple intelligences may encompass learning styles.

Gardner asserts that we all possess these eight intelligences, but schools tend to develop only the first two to any extent. As a consequence, six areas of intelligence are consciously depressed (discriminated against) by schooling. The notion of treating these multiple intelligences as learning styles may cause educational psychologists to shudder, because there are so many different variables to control. We believe it is helpful at least for teachers to make themselves aware of these different intelligences. Refer back to the chart in Table 4.3 in Chapter 4 showing what kinds of *activities* you can use to accommodate the eight intelligences (Lazear 1992).

As you begin planning for student outcomes, you need to be cognizant of how many ways school learning can be approached. Verbal/linguistic learning will undoubtedly remain the area that receives the most attention in schools. There are many more cognitive and affective dimensions of the brain (see Guilford 1967), but in a classroom environment, you can have only so many balls up in the air at once! Nevertheless, by being aware of the other seven intelligences, verbal/linguistic learning can be greatly enhanced, and you can plan to provide multimethodological experiences for all your students.

Elements of Instructional Multimethodology

At this point you are probably second-guessing what we will discuss as an element of multimethodology. Yes, we know that effective teachers use a wide variety of teaching methods and techniques. For example, if you want to use an inductive presentation mode, then your lesson will include at least the following elements (that we greatly expand in Chapters 7, 8, and 9).

- Teaching questioning
- Data of some nature
- Student research
- Applied or laboratory exercises
- Lists of student generalizations

If you plan to use a deductive mode of presentation for some topic, then you'll be using other elements.

- Demonstrations
- Videos or films
- Student activities
- Guest speakers
- Assigned readings
- Student reports

You might not be using either inductive or deductive modes of instruction but one or more of the following instructional methods:

- Direct instruction
- Whole-class recitation
- Computer-related instruction
- Internet-generated research reports
- Simulations or games
- Class projects
- Book reports

Obviously, the range of instructional strategies that you can use in the classroom is limitless. Our plea to you is to plan your objectives or *what to teach* and then plan *how to teach it*. By using a wide variety of instructional techniques, you will appeal to every child's **learning modality.** By varying your weekly calendar of activities, you will accommodate the spectrum of individual learning differences in your classroom. By using multimethodology, you do not get *stuck in the proverbial rut*. If you have to lecture, then break it up with activities, questions, or student-elicited summaries every ten minutes. Keep the focus on the content, but vary the pace and the instructional method of the lesson. Recall John Goodlad's description of American classrooms as being flat? If you adopt the concept of multimethodology, you'll have an *instructionally rich classroom environment*. (See Walberg 1991, pp. 33–62 for a discussion of effect sizes computed for various instructional methods.)

Before closing, we need to add a general caveat. Teachers often feel compelled to "cover all the materials," but this is not a function of any style. One young middle school student made a profound observation: "Kids never really get to do anything with new school learning, except just get more of it." Textbooks set the pace for most teachers and learners, the Internet not withstanding. But you will probably supplement the text with short presentations or demonstrations that provide students with missing skills or background information. Once you are able to sequence major blocks of information while keeping in mind all the differences in your students' learning and abilities, you will be able to implement any planning or learning model.

You have been introduced to instructional sequencing, organizing, and multimethodology, but to use them appropriately, you will need additional training and classroom experiences in the specifics. Difficult and challenging instructional concepts can be taught and understood if you structure your lessons to be intentionally inviting to learners. It is your decision.

Multimethodology means using a variety of teaching procedures.

Instructional richness is a key to motivate students to want to learn.

A Closing Reflection Reflection Reflection

- Using one of the instructional modes, outline how you would teach one major concept in your teaching area.
- Select one major concept that is not usually taught but that you feel is important. Create a set of advance organizers and a hierarchy chart for it.
- How can task analysis be used to plan a daily lesson?
- Concepts are the intellectual pieces of learning. Design a lesson that incorporates a concept with graphic organizers.
- To what extent have you seen or been exposed to the concept of thinking styles and multimethodology?

Summary

1. Sequencing instructional activities provides a ladder for student success.
2. Facts, concepts, and generalizations form the basis of most content.
3. Inductive modes of presentation lead the student to generalizations by providing specifics first.
4. Deductive modes of presentation begin with a generalization and follow with specific points.
5. Task analysis allows you to determine what components of more complex instruction are needed for student success.
6. Sequencing isolated tasks provides a meaningful or logical pathway for student success.
7. Hierarchy charts and graphic organizers help teachers plan and students learn.
8. Advance organizers provide students with an instructional map of what is to be learned.
9. You need to plan instruction to incorporate both right- and left-brain activities.
10. Multimethodology is primarily a planning tool that accommodates individualization.
11. Planning, organizing, and sequencing instruction are fluid and flexible processes, not static ones.
12. Graphic organizers are intentionally inviting.

Key Terms

advance organizer (p. 179)   **content** (p. 164)

concept (p. 165)   **content hierarchy** (p. 161)

concept analysis (p. 178)   **deductive reasoning** (p. 167)

dependent skills (p. 174)

enabling skills (p. 172)

fact (p. 164)

generalization (p. 166)

graphic organizer (p. 184)

hemisphericity (p. 186)

independent skills (p.174)

inductive reasoning (p. 167)

integrative reconciliation (p. 181)

learning deficits (p. 176)

learning modality (p. 191)

multimethodology (p. 186)

multiple intelligences (p. 190)

progressive differentiation (p. 181)

sequencing (p. 160)

task analysis model (p. 170)

Helpful Resources

Hyerle, D. *Visual Tools for Constructing Knowledge.* Alexandra, VA: Association for Supervision and Curriculum Development, 1996, 139pp.

This small book presents an example of just about every type of graphic organizer you can use. It's one for your professional library.

Irvine, J. J., and D. E. York. "Learning Styles and Culturally Diverse Students: A Literature Review." In *Handbook of Research on Multicultural Education.* J. A. Banks and C. A. McGee Banks, editors. New York: Macmillan Publishing USA, 1995, pp. 484–497.

This singular chapter on the learning styles of culturally diverse students is mandatory reading and discussing for both students and instructors in any instructional methods course! The authors illustrate the complexity of the entire concept of styles and enumerate the "preferences" of African American, Hispanic, and Indian students. *Caveat emptor* seems to be the implied message.

Lazear, D. G. *Teaching for Multiple Intelligences.* Bloomington, IN: Phi Delta Kappa Educational Foundation, Fastback. No. 342, 1992.

In just a few pages, you'll be oriented to the concept of using Howard Gardner's theory of multiple intelligences. There are practical applications for teachers. We caution that the treatment is by an advocate.

Sylwester, R. *A Celebration of Neurons: An Educator's Guide to the Human Brain.* Alexandria, VA: Association for Supervision and Curriculum Development, 1995, 167pp.

After you read this book you'll have an excellent understanding of the chemistry and environment under which the brain functions. This is a technical piece and might make a good discussion stimulus for you and a few peers.

Internet Resources

❖ The URL below will provide information and a list of several other Internet sites all relating to Bloom's taxonomy.

http://www.uct.ac.za.projects/cbe/mcqman/mcqappc.html

❖ The current status of Goals 2000 and related educational issues are provided via an on-line database managed by the U.S. Department of Education.

http://www.ed.gov/

❖ Information about state standards and related educational research can be obtained from the University of Minnesota National Center for Applied Research and Educational Improvement.

http://carei.coled.umn.edu/Default.html

References

Ausubel, D. P. *Educational Psychology: A Cognitive View.* New York: Holt, Rinehart & Winston, 1968.

Baker, J. C., and F. G. Martin. *A Neural Network Guide to Teaching.* Fastback 431. Bloomington, IN: Phi Delta Kappa Education Foundation, 1998.

Banks, J. A. *Teaching Strategies for Ethnic Studies* (6th edition). Boston: Allyn & Bacon, 1997.

Bennett, C. I. *Comprehensive Multicultural Education: Theory and Practice.* Boston: Allyn & Bacon, 1999.

Bowman, L. A., J. Carpenter, and R. A. Paone. *Using Graphic Organizers, Cooperative Learning Groups, and Higher Order Thinking Skills to Improve Reading Comprehension.* Unpublished Action Research Project. St. Xavier University, 1998. ED 420 842.

Caine, R. M., and G. Caine. *Education on the Edge of Possibility.* Alexandria, VA: Association for Supervision and Curriculum Development, 1997.

Culbert, E., M. Flood, R. Windler, and D. Work. *A Qualitative Investigation of the Use of Graphic Organizers.* Paper presented at the Sony-Geneseo Annual Reading and Literacy Symposium. Geneseo, NY: May 1998. ED 418 381.

Cushner, K., A. McClelland, and P. Safford. *Human Diversity in Education: An Integrative Approach,* (2nd edition). New York: McGraw-Hill, 1996.

Dochy, F. J. R., and P. A. Alexander. "Mapping Prior Knowledge: A Framework for Discussion Among Researchers." *European Journal of Psychology of Education* 10(3) (1995): 225–242.

Duke, R. A., and C. K. Madsen. "Proactive Versus Reactive Teaching: Focusing Observations on Specific Aspects of Instruction." *Bulletin of the Council for Research in Music Education* 108 (1991): 1–14.

Eggen, P. D., D. P. Kauchak, and R. J. Harder. *Strategies for Teachers: Information Processing Models in the Classroom.* Englewood Cliffs, NJ: Prentice-Hall, 1979.

Ekhaml, L. "Graphic Organizers: Outlets for Your Thoughts." *School Library Media Activities Monthly* 14(5) (1998): 29–33.

Fitzhugh, W. P. "Magazine Geography: Using Magazine Pictures to Enhance Social Studies Instruction," 1995. ERIC Document Reproduction Service No. ED 390 784.

Gagné, R. M., L. J. Briggs, and W. W. Wager. *Principles of Instructional Design* (4th edition). Orlando, FL: Harcourt Brace Javanovich, 1992.

Gardner, H. *Frames of Mind: The Theory of Multiple Intelligences.* New York: Basic Books, 1985.

Gardner, H. *The Unschooled Mind: How Children Think and How Schools Should Teach.* New York: Basic Books, 1991.

Gardner, H. *Multiple Intelligences: The Theory in Practice.* New York: Basic Books, 1993.

Gardner, H. "Who Owns Intelligence?" *The Atlantic Monthly* 283(2)(1999): 67–76.

Griffin, C. C., and L. Malone. "Effects of Graphic Organizer Instruction on Fifth-Grade Students." *Journal of Educational Research* 89(2) (1995): 98–107.

Guilford, J. P. *The Nature of Human Intelligence.* New York: McGraw-Hill, 1967.

Heinze-Fry, J. A., and J. D. Novak. "Concept Mapping Brings Long-Term Movement Toward Meaningful Learning." *Science Education* 74(4) (1990): 461–472.

Hellige, J. P. "Split-Brain Controversy." In *Encyclopedia of School Administration and Supervision.* R. A. Gorton, G. T. Schneider, and J. J. Fisher, editors. Phoenix: Oryx Press, 1988.

Hines, T. "The Myth of Right Hemisphere Creativity." *Journal of Creative Behavior* 25 (1991): 223–227.

Hyerle, D. "Thinking Maps: Seeing Is Understanding." *Educational Leadership* 53(4) (1995-96): 85–89.

Hyerle, D. *Visual Tools for Constructing Knowledge.* Alexandria, VA: Association for Supervision and Curriculum Development, 1996.

Jensen, E. *Teaching with the Brain in Mind.* Alexandria, VA: Association for Supervision and Curriculum Development, 1998.

Lazear, D. G. *Teaching for Multiple Intelligences.* Bloomington, IN: Phi Delta Kappa Educational Foundation, Fastback, No. 342, 1992.

Liu, X. *The Validity and Reliability of Concept Mapping as an Alternative Science Assessment When Item Response Theory Is Used for Scoring.* Paper presented to the Annual Meeting of the American Educational Research Association, New Orleans, April 4–8, 1994.

Munson, H. L., and B. J. Rubenstein. "School Is Work: Task Learning in the Classroom." *Journal of Career Development* 18(4) (1992): 289–297.

Novak, J. D., "How Do We Learn Our Lesson?" *Science Teacher* 60(3) (1993): 50–55.

Novak, J. D., and D. Musona. "A Twelve-Year Longitudinal Study of Science Concept Learning." *American Educational Research Journal* 28(1) (1991): 117–153.

Robinson, H. "Graphic Organizers as Aids to Text Learning." *Reading Research and Instruction* 37(2) (1998): 85–105.

Robinson, D. H., and K. A. Kiewra. "Visual Argument: Graphic Organizers Are Superior to Outlines in Improving Learning from Text." *Journal of Educational Psychology* 87(3) (1995): 455–467.

Simon, L. "De-Coding Writing Assignments." *History Teacher* 24(2) (1991): 149–155.

Slavin, R. E. *Educational Psychology: Theory and Practice,* (6th edition). Boston: Allyn & Bacon, 2000.

Sternberg, R. J. *Thinking Styles.* New York: Cambridge University Press, 1997.

Sylwester, R. *A Celebration of Neurons: An Educator's Guide to the Human Brain.* Alexandria, VA: ASCD, 1995.

Walberg, H. J. "Productive Teaching and Instruction: Assessing the Knowledge Base." In *Effective Teaching: Current Research.* H. C. Waxman and H. J. Walberg, editors. Berkeley, CA: McCutchin Publishing Co., 1991.

Wilson, W. J. *When Work Disappears: The World of the New Urban Poor.* New York: Knopf, 1996.

Instruction as a Dynamic Process in Classrooms

In Parts 1 and 2 of this text we discussed the vitally important, yet somewhat passive, areas of preparation and instructional planning. We say these subjects are passive because the work is often done in isolation, after school, or with colleagues; it does not involve interacting with students. Now we present the dynamic parts of teaching, where students and teachers interact. In Part 3 we show you how to create an environment for learning. Chapter 6, "Managing the Classroom Environment," shows you how to keep the classroom ethos positive. Questioning and conducting highly involved recitations are the topics of Chapter 7. Conducting authentic small-group discussions is the principal subject of Chapter 8. In addition, we introduce you to a cooperative learning model that fosters learning for all in a small-group configuration.

Chapter 9 adds the complete inquiry model to your teaching repertoire. Here are methods that will help you teach students how to think. We close Part 3 with Chapter 10 on monitoring student work. All of these strategies will help you create a classroom that intentionally invites everyone to engage in learning at the highest possible level.

Managing the Classroom Environment

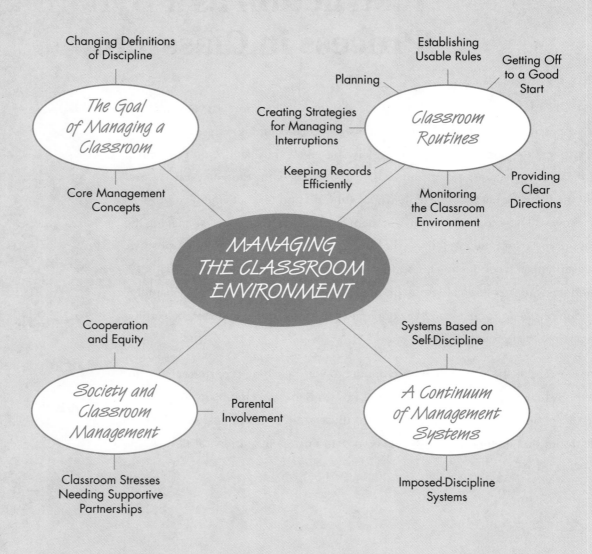

Changing Definitions
of Discipline

The Goal
of Managing a
Classroom

Core Management
Concepts

Establishing
Usable Rules

Getting Off
to a Good
Start

Planning

Creating Strategies
for Managing
Interruptions

Classroom
Routines

Keeping Records
Efficiently

Providing
Clear
Directions

Monitoring
the Classroom
Environment

MANAGING
THE CLASSROOM
ENVIRONMENT

Cooperation
and Equity

Systems Based on
Self-Discipline

Society and
Classroom
Management

Parental
Involvement

A Continuum
of Management
Systems

Classroom Stresses
Needing Supportive
Partnerships

Imposed-Discipline
Systems

Today's math lesson in Mr. Jamal's fourth-grade class involves adding three-digit numbers, with regrouping. Working with manipulatives, all the students are busy writing puzzle problems for each other to solve. As each child comes up with a problem and a solution, Mr. Jamal checks it for accuracy, and the child then challenges another student to solve the problem. As the students become increasingly involved in this activity and move around the room to challenge and be challenged, the murmur of activity gradually rises. The steady, loud drone is continually punctuated by cries of "Let me try!" "You got it!" "Who wants to try this one?" "Wow! That's not the solution I came up with, but you're right, too!" A stranger walking into the classroom would think that pandemonium reigned here.

What's going on in this classroom?

Some educators might consider this classroom to be out of control! Does Mr. Jamal have a classroom management problem in this noisy, active place? Is he using a conscious classroom management approach? Is this a good environment for all learners? Is this approach suitable for boys and girls? How would Mr. Jamal handle an emergency such as a fire alarm in such circumstances? This chapter will help you assess and learn to apply positive classroom management techniques to achieve desirable learning outcomes. As you move through this chapter, think about how you would answer the following questions.

- How will you establish a classroom environment that rewards appropriate behavior and deters inappropriate behavior?

- How can you tell when to intervene to prevent discipline problems?

- Which student-to-student behaviors do you believe are harassing? Abusive?

- How can you analyze a classroom management technique to determine its impact on student learning?

- How important are parents to achieving your goals as a teacher?

- How can you manage your classroom so that the learning environment is fair to all your students?

Section 1: The Goal of Managing a Classroom

Prospective teachers tend to focus their attention on preparing subject matter. Yet according to a 1998 survey of more than 4,000 teachers, many feel inadequately prepared to maintain order and discipline in the classroom and even fewer feel competent to address the needs of students from diverse cultural backgrounds (Loehrke 1999). This finding comes as little surprise since the related elements of **classroom management** (see Table 6.1) were essential for Margaret C. Wang, Geneva D. Haertel, and Herbert J. Walberg (1993) to establish a knowledge base for classroom teachers. Additionally, Charlotte Danielson (1996) identifies "The Classroom Environment" as one of her four critical domains for professional practice. In this domain, she includes the elements of management of instructional groups, transitions, materials and supplies, and non-instructional duties—topics covered in Chapter 6.

Effective classroom management programs promote successful classroom experience.

In this chapter we present a variety of classroom management strategies for your analysis. Your task is to formulate a classroom management program that fits your teaching style and philosophy and that will promote successful classroom experiences. As you gain experience, you will observe more experienced teachers using the same tested techniques that are presented here.

Changing Definitions of Discipline

Why are classroom management issues of such concern? Two events in the late 1990s might illustrate the increased concern. The *Davis vs. Monroe County School Board* decision and the fatal shootings at Columbine High School in Colorado may or may not be familiar events to you. However, these two events shook the pillars of education throughout the country. In *Davis vs. Monroe County,* the U.S. Supreme Court ruled that educators who are deliberately indifferent to student-to-student sexual harassment might be liable under a federal antibias law (Greenberger 1999). If you, as a teacher, overlook some "children just being children" behavior that others deem harassment, you may be liable.

The Columbine High School shootings displayed the gross inadequacies of educational institutions to address planned violence. The U.S. Department of Education's National Center for Educational Statistics showed that in the 1996–1997 school year, metal detectors were permanently installed in 1 percent of schools, 4 percent used handheld metal detectors, 19 percent had drug sweeps, 24 percent controlled access to the grounds, 53 percent controlled access to the building, 80 percent had closed lunch (prohibiting students from leaving campus for lunch), and 96 percent required visitors to sign in. Yet Education Department statistics showed that the overall crime rate in schools was 128 crimes per 1,000 students in 1996 (Henry 1999).

Your essential tools to prevent and mitigate such events are observation and preparation. Know what to look for and what to do when you identify potential problems.

Discipline is usually defined as the preservation of order and the maintenance of control—the two traditional outcomes of classroom management techniques. However, this view of discipline is far too narrow. Teachers must make on-the-spot, split-second decisions and must react spontaneously when using classroom management techniques to solve problems that arise in the classroom. Classroom management techniques are determined by *teacher–student–situation* factors. The attitudes students develop in formal classroom settings are influenced by the teacher's classroom management skills. Your ideas about what a classroom should look like and how it should function will determine your classroom's atmosphere. Recall Mr. Jamal's classroom. The box on page 202 indicates how experienced and inexperienced teachers might view its environment.

The classroom management elements listed in Table 6.1 were found to be essential ingredients to effective student learning outcomes and teacher preparation.

Initially, the major emphasis of teacher preparation programs was classroom control. Accepted ideas about "mental discipline," physical punishment, order, and obedience provided educators with a consistent frame of

TABLE 6.1

Seven of Thirty Selected Categories for Emergent Knowledge Base for School Learning

Category	(Indicates Ranking)
Classroom management	1
Student and teacher social interactions	5
Social and behavioral	6
School culture	10
Classroom climate	11
Student and teacher academic interactions	14
Teacher/Administrator decision making	18

SOURCE: Wang, Haertel, and Walberg, 1993, Table 4.

Note: This Table 6.1 is a truncated list. Our purpose is to illustrate the importance given to management criteria as components for classroom teachers' knowledge base.

Principles of Democratic Discipline

- As the adult member of the class, the teacher must add the rational dimension to the rule-making capacities of the group.
- Rules administered by the teacher should reflect the wisdom and fairness of a judge who participates in a trial as an impartial observer and arbiter.

---

reference. Later, school administrators began to shift more of the burden for establishing classroom climate and managing student conduct to the individual teacher. While this shift in responsibility was occurring, the results of relevant studies of discipline by social and behavioral scientists began to be applied in the schools. The shift to individual responsibility, combined with social and behavioral research, set the stage for **"democratic discipline"** (see the box above).

Classrooms began to change even more dramatically during the 1970s and 1980s. Four changes have had a distinct effect on classroom management. First, families have become very mobile. It is not uncommon for even rather stable schools to show a 25 percent annual student turnover. Such a high degree of turnover impacts both the learning environment and the expected patterns of student behavior and classroom systems. Thus today's classrooms tend to be relatively unstable social systems.

The second phenomenon is the so-called breakup of the nuclear family. More students now live with single parents than at any other time in history, and this number is increasing. Only about 6 percent of all families now resemble the classic two-parent model: father as breadwinner, mother at home, and two children in school (Dwyer 1999).

> ### Reflect Reflect Reflect
>
> Experienced teachers would recognize the quality of learning going on in Mr. Jamal's classroom. However, novice teachers tend to be concerned about the need to get their students' attention for emergencies and to maintain authority. What would be your own concerns, if any, in a classroom like Mr. Jamal's? How might Mr. Jamal regain his students' attention if necessary? Discuss the possibilities in a small group.

Third, an ethos has developed among many students that views school as a place to "get through." Social promotion (promoting failing students with their age group) has firmly taken hold; as a result, students feel entitled to advancement. How can teachers motivate students if there is little threat of failure and little reward for achievement?

Fourth, urban schools developed a distinct set of problems (gangs, violence, high dropout rates, poverty) that are quite different from the problems facing suburban and rural schools. One can no longer compile a singular list of rules and expect it to apply to all schools.

Core Management Concepts

Our approach to classroom management is based on a **humanistic orientation** toward the classroom environment that views students as diverse individuals seeking acceptance and fulfillment. Teachers must be mindful of the fact that young minds and attitudes are shaped by overt and covert teacher behaviors. Thus in this section we discuss three concepts that are both central to the principles of classroom management and an important influence on student development norms, power, and awareness.

The most successful teachers are those who make deliberate decisions based on sound educational principles.

A **norm** is usually defined as a behavioral rule or pattern accepted to some degree by most members of a group. For example, raising one's hand before speaking is a norm in many classrooms. All group members feel some obligation to adhere to the behavioral rule, so it introduces a high degree of regularity and predictability into their social interaction (see the box below). Norms are not recorded, like the laws of a country. However, there exists in the minds of group members an ideal standard directing how each member

---

Norms

- Are valuable to social relationships
- Reduce necessity for direct, informal, and personal influence
- Adherence provides for the control of individual and group behavior without anyone overtly exerting power

TABLE 6.2

Change in Percentage of High School Seniors Who Reported Being Victimized (Nationally), by Race, 1993 vs. 1997

Offense Reported	Black		White	
	1993	1997	1993	1997
Experienced stolen property	46.0	42.8	41.6	37.6
Experienced property deliberately damaged	26.3	18.8	25.8	25.5
Injured with a weapon	6.4	7.1	4.3	4.3
Threatened with a weapon	23.5	13.7	13.8	9.6
Injured without a weapon	11.5	11.1	11.0	12.0
Threatened without a weapon	22.3	19.3	23.8	22.4

SOURCE: U.S. Department of Education 1999, *The Condition of Education 1999,* Supplemental Table 26-1.

ought to behave under specific conditions. Norms are part of the culture and are tacitly understood by all members. An observed deviation from the norm usually results in a negative response.

By virtue of your role and position in the classroom, you as teacher have influence, or **power.** Unrestrained use of that power creates insecurities and resistance among students, adversely affecting their learning. Students can retaliate against the teacher (and other students) by forming cliques, creating irritating disturbances, and making threats (see Table 6.2). To be an effective classroom manager, you must learn to exercise the least amount of power necessary to accomplish the desired result (see Leriche 1992).

Being aware and alert to classroom interactions is critical.

We use the term **awareness** to refer to a teacher's attention to and insight about the classroom environment. A class constantly gives its teacher verbal and nonverbal cues. Children's behaviors also offer insights regarding student-to-student interactions (Power 1992). Furthermore, communication occurs both between the teacher and individual students and between the teacher and the class as a whole. The master teacher understands how to handle this mix of communication. Knowing which communications to ignore and which to quickly attend to separates the pros and the rookies.

Initially, a teacher must determine how his or her class presents cues. The teacher who simply complains that "my class was particularly lousy today" has not adequately analyzed the information provided by the class. This teacher must define with some precision what is meant by *lousy.* What behaviors did the class exhibit that led to the inference that the class was lousy? Did students recite inappropriately, not pay attention, or not accomplish the work requested? The teacher must be able to specify what behaviors are being alluded to when the class is identified as "lousy" and how students can model the appropriate behaviors (Evertson 1995).

We use the terms *discipline* and *classroom management* throughout this chapter. The Instructional Strategies box describes how the two concepts differ operationally. The list for discipline may be summarized as showing reactive teacher behaviors. The classroom management behaviors illustrate

Instructional Strategies

Teacher Strategies for Discipline Versus Classroom Management

Discipline

Giving in-school suspensions
Sending misbehaving students to the office
Contacting parents
Using a check or demerit system
Lowering grades
Taking away privileges

Classroom Management

Emphasizing rules at the start of the school year
Planning for smooth transitions; leaving minimal time between activities
Paying attention to the entire class; continuously scanning the group
Pacing activities effectively
Giving clear and concise instructions
Carefully designing the classroom environment
Organizing activities in advance

SOURCE: Based on information from Rita Seedorf. Used with permission.

Reflect Reflect Reflect

■ How might classroom norms, power relationships, and teacher awareness affect a teacher's implementation of a planned lesson?

proactive teacher actions. This comparison shows how much management differs from discipline. Being proactive reduces the need to be reactive.

Section 2: Classroom Routines

Classroom management systems include routine ways of managing instructional and behavioral interactions in the classroom (see Table 6.3). The research on teacher effectiveness gives us a perspective through which to synthesize management strategies. We will focus here on the seven key elements the "pros" use to effectively manage their classrooms (see the box on page 206).

TABLE 6.3

Selected Problems Associated with Classroom Management

Motivation Problems

Insufficient activity for students
Student apathy
Difficulty getting students involved
Negative student attitudes
Daydreaming
Lack of student success
Negative teacher attitudes

Instructional Problems

Lack of variety in instructional techniques
Inadequately communicated goals and objectives
Bad pacing (too fast or too slow)
Lack of prerequisite skills, causing student failure
Student distress or anger over evaluations
Students not following directions
Failure to complete all assignments

Procedural Problems

Unclear assignments
Moving the class to a different room
Lack of a systematic routine for procedural activities
Failing to reserve a special room or space for an activity
Forgetting to check out projector or AV equipment
Failing to preview media, resulting in presentation of inappropriate material
Not having the necessary materials in the classroom
Failure to plan discussion groups in advance

Disruptive Problems

Excessive talking at beginning of class
Note passing
Cheating
Stealing
Vandalism
Attention seeking
Arriving late for class
Racial tensions
Teacher making value judgments about students' dress, home life, or parents
Teacher making unenforceable threats
Obscene language or gestures

> ## Seven Key Elements of Effective Classroom Management
>
> - Planning
> - Establishing usable rules
> - Getting off to a good start
> - Providing clear directions
> - Monitoring the classroom environment
> - Keeping records efficiently
> - Creating strategies for managing interruptions

Planning

Detailed planning is initially time consuming, but teachers who make explicit plans are better organized and see the worth of these plans (Walsh 1992). Teachers who plan and communicate their expectations to their students promote academic achievement. For example, effective teachers know what, whom, and how they will teach; they have materials ready for their students; they plan for smooth transitions between classes and activities; and they have additional activities ready for students who finish early.

Effective teachers plan ahead and critique their lessons.

Well-prepared teachers keep lessons moving at a brisk pace but do not ignore students who are having difficulties. They do not allow interruptions during a lesson, and they stress the importance of every lesson. Our observations have shown that good teachers are efficient in their planning and in critiquing their day's work. They jot a few notes into their lesson planning books to act as tips for future lessons. Their lesson plans are very brief and are conceptual in nature. But they do carry out formal planning, a process considered top priority (see Ysseldyke and Elliott 1999).

Establishing Usable Rules

The purpose of rules is to enhance students' academic and social achievement (Cangelosi 1990). Teachers who are effective managers teach students how to follow rules and procedures and begin with the rules that are of the most immediate importance. (How do I get permission to leave the room? How do I ask a question?) They state rules clearly and enforce them consistently. On-again, off-again enforcement contributes to student behavior problems.

Effective teachers also make rules that are not related to discipline. These cover classroom routines for distributing materials, progressing to new activities, starting and ending class, obtaining permission to use the bathroom, and accomplishing tasks such as sharpening pencils (Doyle 1985). Simplicity is the hallmark of effective rules. If your rules are complicated, you will not be able to enforce them and students will become confused. Thus simplicity will allow you to easily explain and enforce your rules.

Getting Off to a Good Start

Effective classroom managers discuss classroom procedures with their students at the beginning of the school year and provide opportunities for students to practice them to ensure understanding (Lombardi 1992; Tauber 1999). During the first few days of school, much feedback is needed. State your expectations frequently and give students positive or corrective feedback. By the end of the third or fourth week of school, you can anticipate that transitions will be smoother and shorter and that reminders to your students on class routines can be greatly reduced (Evertson, Emmer, and Worsham 2000). It is much easier to be firm and precise in the beginning and then relax as you observe that students have adopted your rules. It is almost impossible to gain control once chaos reigns.

Providing Clear Directions

Giving directions is a critical part of a teacher's function (Long 1985). Whether the directions concern instruction or classroom procedures, they must be given clearly and succinctly. Even more important, their orientation must be positive. Directions such as "stop that" or "cut that out" given to disruptive students omit the most important part: *what is the student to do after he or she stops or "cuts out" the disruptive behavior?* It is much more accurate and meaningful to give directions in a positive form. Provide the student with a constructive alternative. For example, you might suggest that the student return to work, or you might provide some instructionally related activity to replace the disruptive behavior. For example, you might say, "Sam, please reduce your volume; turn to page 72 in your book and complete the questions following the unit's reading. I will grade your answers in ten minutes."

Monitoring the Classroom Environment

Effective teachers hold students accountable for their behavior and for learning.

Effective teachers monitor student behavior in the classroom. They make each student responsible for some work during the learning activity and then monitor to see that it was actually accomplished. These teachers are strong student motivators (Malm 1992).

Room arrangement is an important part of a monitoring strategy. An orderly arrangement of desks and tables in a classroom contributes to a smooth, businesslike atmosphere that promotes effective use of instructional time. Two aspects of room arrangement are critical: (1) your ability to see all students at all times and (2) the circulation patterns that you establish. It is important to be able to monitor all students from your desk and from all other areas where you are likely to be. Simply being visually close to a student can prevent many problems. This is your greatest deterrent against harassing and bullying behavior.

Questioning is also an effective monitoring strategy (Dillon 1988). During learning activities, effective teachers ask questions and then look around the room before calling on a student. They call on volunteers as well as others and seem to get around to everyone but not in a predictable manner. Effective teachers intersperse calls for group answers with solicitations of individual responses and occasionally throw out challenging statements such as, "I don't think anyone can get this!" Finally, effective teachers monitor their classes by asking students to react to the answers of others. Such monitoring strategies as questioning techniques and classroom arrangements promote a smooth-flowing, highly interactive learning environment with a high percentage of on-task student behavior.

Keeping Records Efficiently

Every teacher faces the tasks of recording grades, taking attendance, keeping track of students' class participation, recording disciplinary actions, and documenting other aspects of classroom life. For legality, fairness, and consistency, you need a comprehensive and systematic approach to record keeping.

Records management is an extremely important part of maintaining a fair and equitable grading system. After you have established reasonable guidelines for standards, quality, late work, missed assignments, bonus work, makeup tests, and class participation, you must be prepared to track each student's performance in each area reliably and consistently.

In addition, anecdotal records should be objectively maintained to document classroom incidents such as fights, inappropriate behavior, and cheating. Of course, you should also record acts of courage, ingenuity, and creativity. If you notice a rapid change in a student's dress, friends, language, or attitude, you should note the change and closely monitor it. Such behavioral change frequently indicates abuse of some nature (physical, gang, or drug). Record these acts when they happen. This record will provide you with a chronicle that may provide evidence to support or confront a student at some later date.

Creating Strategies for Managing Interruptions

Thirty percent of the instructional day is lost to interruptions.

Teachers spend a tremendous amount of time planning instruction: preparing lesson plans, selecting support materials, creating student activities, designing tests, and so on. Yet all too often the anticipated instructional period is drastically reduced by interruptions. Lost time! Studies have demonstrated that frequently 30 percent or more of the instructional day is lost to anticipated and unanticipated interruptions. These interruptions range from student misbehavior to announcements over the intercom. (We heard of one example of thirty such announcements in one day!) Whatever its cause, lost time has a negative impact on student academic achievement and creates the conditions for student behavior problems (see Ysseldyke and Elliott 1999).

The ability to manage most interruptions is fully within teachers' control (Crosser 1992). You simply need to anticipate and plan for them. You must plan for transitions in instruction (anticipated interruptions), and you must establish firm expectations regarding student behavior to avoid as many unanticipated interruptions as possible. Table 6.4 uses some examples of anticipated and unanticipated interruptions. The list is not exhaustive, but it provides a starting point for planning when "fillers" are likely to be required to avoid lost learning time.

TABLE 6.4

Anticipated and Unanticipated Interruptions

Anticipated Interruptions

Transitions between and during instructional episodes

Equipment setup and take-down

Materials distribution/collection

Changing from teacher- to student-centered activity

Beginning/end of class or school day

Unanticipated Interruptions

Student illness

Visitors

Announcements/messages

Student behavioral problems

Equipment malfunctions

Fire alarms/classroom evacuations

Materials shortages

Anticipated Interruptions   Twenty-one percent of class time is spent on transitions (Gump 1982), on ending one lesson or activity and beginning another. Effective teachers prepare their students for transitions (Evertson 1986). Besides making transitions from one activity to the next quickly, they are especially careful not to end one activity and begin a second and then return to the first. Abrupt endings to activities set the stage for numerous behavior problems. To become more efficient, give signals, set time limits, and provide very clear instructions—even modeling them as needed (Gump 1982).

"Fillers" are student activities or routines that teachers use to fill the gaps created by transitions between instructional episodes and administrative activities. Let us discuss things you can do to solve traditional problems.

Gaps in teacher directions before and after an instructional episode are a frequent cause both of classroom management problems and of lost instructional opportunities. Frequently teachers get caught up in the physical requirements of lesson setup or breakdown, materials handling, and student assessment. While the teacher is focusing on these tasks, the class is left to their imaginations and machinations, which causes problems! Thus teachers must develop strategies for managing prelesson transitions, transitions that occur during a lesson, and postlesson transitions:

1. **Prelesson transitions.** Delegate administrative tasks to students whenever possible. A routine should be made for managing attendance, announcements, materials distribution and collection, and special activities as much as possible. Create a routine in which homework is checked by a peer or teacher's aide and deposited in student files. Rotate the students selected for such administrative support activities. Many teachers use the

first few minutes of class and the last few minutes to encourage creative thinking activities, which are repeated each day. Puzzles, thought problems, computer games, or related art and media projects that can be quickly started and stopped are good "fillers." Naturally, it is important to assign some value to these activities in terms of student grades (Friedman and Judson 1991).

You can predict problems well ahead by planning.

2. **Transitions that occur during a lesson.** Students rarely complete an activity in a uniform time span. A prepared teacher will recognize the likelihood of this and prepare supplementary activities or additional resources for the fast workers. Many teachers use peer tutor strategies or have fast finishers assist with administrative tasks (such as correcting tests) or prepare for the next instructional episode. The transition from a regular to a supplementary activity must be carefully thought out and the procedures explained to the class in advance. If you develop activities that can be used on a regular basis, be sure to state your expectations for their use clearly and then reinforce appropriate student behaviors.

3. **Postlesson transitions.** Teacher control of the classroom can easily break down at the end of an instructional episode, due to the many details a teacher must attend to before the class moves on. Frequently you will be involved with materials collection, equipment management, individual student assignments, or administrative chores. Prepare for such demands by developing routine student activities. Create a routine for the last five minutes of each class period or instructional episode. The routine will give you time to shift from one class or activity to the next. The ending activity should be self-paced and self-instructional for the students. The teacher should merely announce the beginning of the "curtain" (ending) activity, and everyone should know what to do. For such curtain activities, avoid student movement, materials distribution, and teaming. The activities should focus on the individual and provide an opportunity for relaxed exploration. Reading, writing, drawing, student planning, or journal writing are appropriate for the closing minutes. Avoid the rigorous, the active, the involved. *Slow things down. Your students need a breather before moving on to the next instructional episode,* just as you do.

Summary
for motivies
guided practice/homework
demonstration

Unanticipated Interruptions   During the course of a typical day, many unanticipated events occur. These events may be initiated by students, school personnel, visitors, or others. They include fire alarms, intercom announcements, broken equipment, problems with the school building, messages from the office, and untold other attention breaks. You can anticipate that such events will occur each day; however, you cannot anticipate when they will occur or how long they will last. For example, loss of electrical power is always an interesting instructional interruption with which to cope. All you can do is prepare yourself and your classes for such eventualities. During the initial weeks of the school year, you should explain your expectations for how the class is to deal with unanticipated interruptions. Provide specific instructions concerning what students should do in an emergency (fire, injury, chemical spill, accident, electrical failure, earthquake), how they should behave for a visitor (parent, student, other), and how the class is to manage itself if your attention is required to resolve another issue or if you must leave the room.

Reflect Reflect Reflect

The *Encyclopedia Britannica* (*EB*) provides a comprehensive guide to women in American history. Included are recordings, art, and writings from early to modern America. Use the following *EB* net site to develop enrichment activities that build knowledge and increase student value for gender diversity. How could such materials prove useful in complementing the general curriculum?

women.eb.com

You may want to simulate these events. The expected behaviors should become part of your classroom's norms.

When explaining your expectations for interruptions and transitions, be sure to provide a detailed explanation of the importance of good behavior and ongoing academic effort. All too frequently a teacher will establish a set of classroom rules but fail to explain their importance to classroom citizenship and learning.

Some classroom interruptions cannot be foreseen.

The specific way you approach planning for interruptions will obviously vary according to your students' maturity level. Individual planning can help reduce the time loss caused by anticipated interruptions; however, many unanticipated interruptions are schoolwide or otherwise beyond the teacher's control (intercom messages, inappropriate classroom visitors). The teachers in a school must band together to address such interruptions and suggest ways to stop or greatly reduce them.

Section 3: A Continuum of Management Systems

As you strive to maximize learning time for your students, you must choose from among a large number of classroom management strategies. We have arranged these strategies along a continuum ranging from those that rely on self-discipline to those that involve imposing discipline on your students (see Figure 6.1). Self-discipline implies voluntary adherence to norms that promote students' self-interest and protect the welfare of others. Imposed discipline suggests a student code of conduct prescribed by the teacher in the best interests of individual students and the class as a whole. Between self-discipline and imposed discipline there are numerous choices.

To provide you with an overview of selected classroom management systems, we will discuss three strategies that lean toward self-discipline, with a special focus on reality therapy. On the imposed-discipline side, we will discuss desist strategies and behavior modification. Reality therapy, desist strategies, and behavior modification are highlighted because they are generic (that is, other systems have been developed from them).

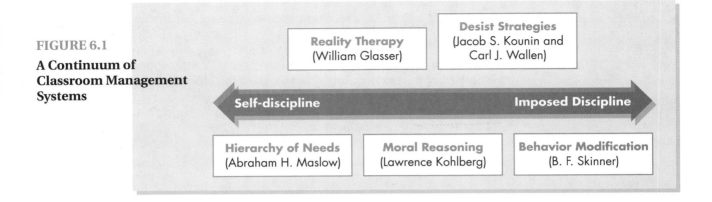

FIGURE 6.1

A Continuum of Classroom Management Systems

Reality Therapy (William Glasser)

Desist Strategies (Jacob S. Kounin and Carl J. Wallen)

Self-discipline ← → Imposed Discipline

Hierarchy of Needs (Abraham H. Maslow)

Moral Reasoning (Lawrence Kohlberg)

Behavior Modification (B. F. Skinner)

Systems Based on Self-Discipline

These three strategies are based on the premise that self-discipline on the part of students depends heavily on effective teacher-student and student-student relationships. Advocates of self-discipline as a classroom management tool argue that to facilitate learning, teachers need to adopt the following attitudes: genuineness, empathy toward the student, as well as acceptance and trust of the student.

While success is attained with involvement, teacher involvement means working with individual students on a personal level to address behavioral or academic problems. While remaining in the "teacher role," the teacher

The school environment sets the circumstances for positive classroom management. © Smiley/ Texas Stock.

helps the student make plans, carry them out, revise them, and strive continually for success. Involvement means that the teacher helps the student become more responsible for his or her behavior by having the student constantly state what he or she is doing. Involvement also means meeting with parents or guardians, if possible, and seeking their cooperation. Furthermore, it means meeting with other teachers to discuss the welfare of certain students.

Additionally, self-discipline requires a positive perspective and *positive expectations,* even though some *classroom management* techniques may fail. Through involvement, teachers demonstrate genuineness, acceptance, and empathy toward students. And through positive regard, self-discipline is expected and achieved by students (McDaniel 1987). With these prerequisites in mind, let us examine classroom management strategies that focus on self-discipline.

Maslow's Hierarchy of Needs   Abraham H. Maslow's humanistic approach (1968) has had a major impact on educational theory and classroom management for decades. Maslow is best known for his "hierarchy of needs" (see Figure 6.2). Maslow's theory assumes that an individual's behavior at any time is determined by his or her needs. For example, a hungry student will have a hard time focusing on learning skills. An effective teacher tries to determine what need might be causing a behavior problem and then addresses that need. Naturally, teachers would like for self-esteem and self-actualization to direct student behavior, for then students could be truly self-regulated.

To use Maslow's ideas, you must truly *believe* in your students. Students need to be shown that they are valued and respected and are really important in the class. Structure, routines, and consistency are all hallmarks of this strategy. You help all students to develop a positive, constructive self-image. The classroom environment must be structured to be supportive. Even when someone is "in trouble," *it is always the act that is corrected, not the person.*

Always correct the act, not the person.

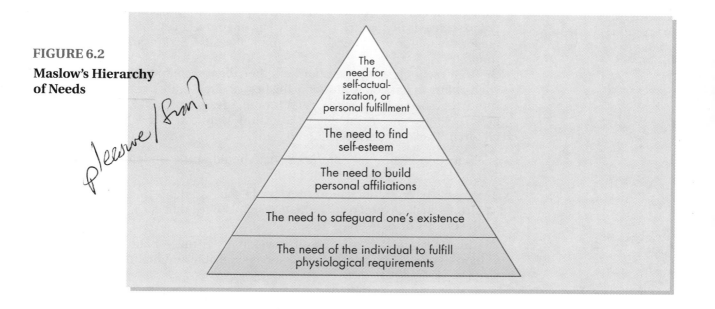

FIGURE 6.2

Maslow's Hierarchy of Needs

Teachers stress the intrinsic value of each student and attempt to motivate all students to do the best they possibly can. Implementing Maslow's system requires a long-term commitment to classroom structure and routines consistent with students' self-actualization.

Moral Reasoning and Character Development   Many recent calls for educational reform have come from parents and community leaders who believe that the schools have ignored a responsibility to build the character and moral values of students. Researchers have also argued that the schools should focus more on students' moral reasoning and character development (Kohlberg 1975; Power, Higgins, and Kohlberg 1989; Ryan and Bohlin 1999). Others argue that the public schools have no role in character development and moral education and that they should concentrate exclusively on developing students' cognitive skills. We believe that the process of schooling necessarily affects the way children think about issues of right and wrong, so it is important to purposefully address those issues. Developing character is an essential part of educating a child: "Character development is the effort to help the young acquire a 'moral compass,' the sense of right and wrong and the enduring habits necessary to live a good life" (Ryan and Cooper 1998). No education is complete without it. Kevin Ryan (1997) calls it the "missing link" in American education.

> *Moral and character education are important.*

A model for providing a moral education was developed by Lawrence Kohlberg (1975; Power, Higgins, Kohlberg 1989). His model presents "moral dilemmas" in which students are faced with a personal choice. One such dilemma might be a group of students that is aware that a friend has a gun in his locker and recently threatened another student. What action should the group take? How would the students feel if someone were injured or killed by the gun? Such an exercise forces students to work through their values and develop and apply their moral compasses.

For such an exercise, the class is divided into groups for discussion. Kohlberg believes that these discussions will help students raise their consciousness and come to understand the motivation of others better. He stresses that the classroom should be a "just community" in which a democratic society is the model. Obviously, the dilemmas posed must be appropriate for the maturity of the class members. (See also Etzioni's *The New Golden Rule,* 1997.)

If the schools are to be reformed, they must reclaim their traditional responsibility to pass on to students the best of our culture's values. With this in mind, the Boston University Center for the Advancement of Ethics and Character (1997) wrote a Character Education Manifesto for America's schoolchildren. The following are adapted from its seven guiding principles:

1. Education is a moral enterprise that should guide students to know and pursue what is good and worthwhile.

2. Schools have an obligation to foster in their students' personal and civic virtues such as integrity, courage, responsibility, diligence, and respect for the dignity of all people.

3. Character education is about developing virtues—habits and dispositions—that lead students to become responsible and mature adults.

4. All adults in a school must embody and reflect the moral authority that has been invested in them by parents and the community.

5. Schools must become communities of virtue in which responsibility and kindness are modeled, taught, expected, celebrated, and continually practiced.

6. Teachers and students must draw from the human community's reservoir of moral wisdom, much of which exists in our great stories, works of art, literature, history, and biographies.

7. Young people need to realize that forging their own character is an essential and demanding life task.

For an elaborating discussion on this entire subject we refer you to Sizer and Sizer 1999.

Reality Therapy   Reality therapy is an approach that helps individuals take responsibility for solving their own problems. As humans, we have the ability to determine our own personal destiny. We are not victims of circumstance. Reality therapy leads all people toward reality, toward grappling successfully with the many aspects of the real world (Glasser 1965). Reality therapy requires positive, genuine, human involvement that allows people to recognize their own reality and to begin to reshape their own behaviors to meet selected needs.

The main premise is that an individual must acknowledge his or her own failures and be personally responsible for becoming successful. Toward this end, teachers must avoid labeling inappropriate behaviors with interesting-sounding tags—for example, *disadvantaged, dysfunctional,* or *disabled.* Another premise is that examination of family or personal histories is not essential.

> An individual must perceive his or her own failures and be personally responsible for becoming successful.

Principle 1   The first principle of reality therapy is human involvement. Essentially, Glasser (1986) notes that we are always involved with other people—at the very minimum with one other person, and ideally with many more.

In the classroom setting this means devising a structure that facilitates teacher–student and student–student involvement. Classroom management problems can then be solved in ways that express care and concern on the part of the teacher with direct student involvement. Thus small group instruction on self-regulated learning is very much in concert with reality therapy.

Principle 2   While reality therapy does not deny emotions and their importance, its success depends on focusing on current behaviors—on what the student is doing *now.* Thus the teacher should ask a misbehaving student what he or she is doing. Teachers tend to recall previous behavior: "Well, that's the seventh time today that you've interrupted without raising your hand." Instead the teacher should ask, "What are you doing?" Note that the emphasis is on the statement (*you*); there can be no misunderstanding concerning who is responsible for the misbehavior.

Principle 3   Reality therapy requires the student to examine his or her current behavior, evaluate it, and determine for himself or herself that the current behavior is not beneficial or appropriate. This means that the student who constantly misbehaves must be made to discuss his or her behavior and come to the conclusion that another type of behavior would be more appropriate. The teacher does not evaluate or label behaviors as good or bad, but, without moralizing, simply indicates whether behaviors are appropriate or inappropriate.

Principle 4   Once a student makes a judgment about his or her behavior, the teacher helps the student make realistic plans to change it. The student must take small, individually positive steps to attain success.

For example, a student who never studies should not be expected to begin studying two hours a night. Fifteen-minute sessions a few times a week would be more appropriate. Be certain that remedial plans are realistic for the particular student.

Reality therapy emphasizes making student contracts. The student, with the help of the teacher, develops a plan to help meet his or her personal or educational goals. This plan becomes a contract between the student and the teacher.

Principle 5   Reality therapy demands a commitment from the student. After a reasonable plan has been devised, it must be carried out. Typically, the student prepares a plan in writing and signs it as a means of increasing personal motivation to maintain and fulfill the plan. This kind of commitment intensifies and accelerates the student's behavioral change.

Principle 6   There are no excuses when a student fails to change his or her behavior. The student has expressed a commitment in the form of a written plan and cannot be excused for not fulfilling the plan. However, it is essential that both the teacher and the student be willing to reexamine the plan and renew or change it if it is in some way inappropriate. This does not mean that the teacher excuses the student's failure. When failure occurs, it must be mutually recognized that the responsibility lies with the student, either for not having fulfilled the plan or for not having planned appropriately in the first place.

In the reality therapy model, the teacher *helps* the student; the teacher's praise of student success increases the involvement between the teacher and student and leads to more responsible student behaviors (Glasser 1972).

Principle 7   The final principle of reality therapy is the absence of punishment. Glasser believes that punishment hinders the personal involvement that is essential between the teacher and the student. The purpose of punishment is to change an individual's behavior through fear or pain. Rather than punishment, Glasser suggests using a program of positive reinforcements to achieve contract success. If you are philosophically against punishment, reality therapy may be a classroom management approach that you should explore further. Please glance through the reference section at the end of this chapter for additional reading.

Reality Therapy and the Entire Class   Reality therapy may also be applied to an entire class through classroom meetings. As social problem–solving meet-

Reality therapy can be used for whole-group sessions.

Instructional

Strategies

Social Problem–Solving Meetings

1. All group and individual problems in the class are eligible for discussion.
2. The session focuses on solving the problem, not finding faults or specifying punishment.
3. Meetings are conducted with all individuals positioned in a tight circle to foster interaction.

ing involves a group discussion of classroom problems with the goal of reaching a mutually agreed upon solution (see the box above).

Such a meeting may be an extremely useful first step in resolving a seemingly intractable problem. For example, students in an eighth-grade class were truant at an increasing rate as the warm days came in the spring term (Glasser 1969). A social problem–solving meeting was called, and the teacher asked if everyone was there. In the discussion, the class admitted that eight of thirty-five were absent. The class was then asked why the others were absent. Most student responses included terms such as *dull* and *boring*. With the "problem" exposed, the teacher then pressed for a solution. The students were asked to make value judgments on the worth of school. They were asked to sign a statement promising to come to school the next day. Only one-third of the class would sign. Next they were asked to sign a paper stating that they

TABLE 6.5

Absenteeism and Tardiness in U.S. Schools*

Type of Community	Public School Level		
	Elementary	Middle	High
Absenteeism			
Central city	11.9	18.1	45.5
Urban fringe/large town	5.8	8.6	30.6
Rural/small town	3.8	7.8	19.6
Total	**6.8**	**10.9**	**29.0**
Tardiness			
Central city	10.7	18.0	33.0
Urban fringe/large town	5.8	7.8	20.0
Rural/small town	1.8	5.5	12.1
Total	**5.7**	**9.7**	**19.4**

SOURCE: U.S. Department of Education, 1996, p. 138.

*Figures indicate percentage of teachers reporting that absenteeism or tardiness is a serious problem in their school, by type of community. (Latest data published as of year 2000.)

Reflect Reflect Reflect

- When can a written promise or contract from the teacher be effective?
- How is such a contract consistent with the principles of reality therapy?
- Reality therapy stresses teacher involvement. To what extent is it reasonable or unreasonable to expect a teacher to become involved with the problems of every student?

---

would not sign the promise. This was to cause the students to make some type of commitment. Once again, only one-third of the students would sign, which left one-third who would sign nothing. This last group was then asked to allow their names to be placed on a paper stating that they would not sign anything, and to this they agreed.

There was little improvement in student behavior as a result of this meeting; however, the problem of truancy became a principal topic of general class discussion, setting the stage for additional meetings that eventually resolved the problem. In this particular case, the general class discussion eventually focused on the teacher's responsibility for stimulating student interest through a variety of teaching strategies and materials. (See Table 6.5 on page 217 for data indicating that absenteeism and tardiness are serious problems.)

Teachers can use many individual and group techniques in implementing a program of reality therapy. However, one requirement is essential to all of these techniques: being involved yourself. This takes training, patience, and, above all, perseverance.

Imposed-Discipline Systems

Imposed-discipline systems are based on teachers' recognized authority to maintain group norms within the classroom and to dictate appropriate classroom behaviors and consequences of misbehavior. Teachers' authority resides in the definition of the role of teacher, which is traditionally determined by societal expectations. Occasionally, a teacher's authority is challenged. When this happens, the teacher's role can include the power to reward and punish.

In the following discussion we describe two imposed-discipline strategies, *desist strategies* and *behavior modification.* Each of these strategies use a variety of methods to exercise the teacher's authority within the classroom.

Desist Strategies   Of the classroom management techniques we discuss here, the desist strategy is the most traditional. The term is derived from "desist techniques" suggested by Jacob S. Kounin and Paul V. Gump (1959). The **desist strategy** is a means of systematically communicating the teacher's desire for a student's behavior to stop or change. The communication may be accomplished by a command such as "Stop that!" or by a glance or movement.

Desist strategies offer a systematic framework for applying the teacher's authority to maintain group norms. The technique of desist strategies involves two basic concepts. First, there are three levels of force—low, moderate, and high. Second, there are two types of communication of teacher desires—public and private.

In dealing with classroom discipline, it is usually best to use a low rather than a high level of force, and it is always better to use a private rather than a public form of communication. Occasionally, however, a situation calls for a high-level, public display of force. A classroom fight would be an example. In the vast majority of cases, though, you will find it best to use private displays and low levels of force to handle "normal" discipline problems. Desist strategies are further explained in Tables 6.6 and 6.7.

The concept of the desist strategy is summarized by two principles first presented by Carl J. Wallen in 1968 (see the box on page 220).

It is important that you specify the appropriate behavior for a particular activity. During a test, for example, you may decide that students should not speak out unless they raise their hands and are called on. During small-group activities, students may be permitted to speak quietly. Your verbal statement of the appropriate behavior is the expected norm.

In handling discipline problems, it is always better to use a private rather than a public form of communication.

Appropriateness is a primary rule.

TABLE 6.6

Examples of Desist Strategies

Level of Force	Definition	Desist Strategy
Low	Nonverbal, a signal or movement	Glancing at child, shaking head, moving over to child unobtrusively in the instructional activity
Moderate	Verbal, conversational, no coercion	Appealing to a child to act reasonably, removing disturbing objects, commanding the child to stop
High	Verbal and nonverbal, changed voice pitch, may use coercion	Raising voice and commanding child to stop, removing the child from group, threatening, punishing, physically restraining the child

Type	Definition	Desist Strategy
Public	Intended to be noticed by most of the children in a class	Acting and/or speaking in a way that commands attention
Private	Intended to be noticed only by small groups of children	Using unobtrusive actions or moving close to a child when speaking

SOURCE: From Wallen 1968, Appendix A, p. 15.

TABLE 6.7

Desist Strategies in Combination		
Level	Private	Public
1. Glance (low level)	Teacher shakes head so only one or two other children notice the action.	Teacher shakes head dramatically so most of class notices the action.
2. Appeal (moderate level)	Teacher moves close to child, asks child to act reasonably, and uses voice and manner so only one or two other children notice the action.	Teacher asks children to act reasonably, in a manner that most of the class notices.
3. Threat (high level)	Teacher moves close to child, tells what will happen if misbehavior continues, and uses voice and manner so only one or two other children notice.	Teacher tells what will happen if misbehavior continues, uses a loud and commanding voice that most of the class notices.

SOURCE: From Wallen 1968, Appendix A, pp. 15–16.

Principles of Desist Strategies

1. If a classroom activity is about to occur and you have not previously established standards of student behavior and your expectations, specify these expectations and behavioral standards before you begin the activity.

2. If in a continuing activity a student or group of students behaves in a manner contrary to specific expectations, use a desist strategy aimed at reaching the level of expectations while causing the least possible disruption to the classroom setting.

Punishments   In contrast to reality therapy, desist strategies allow some form of punishment to be administered to nonresponsive students. Punishment entails consequences that reduce the future rate of undesirable behavior (Skinner 1953, 1974). *Loss of privilege* is the most common form (for example, loss of recess, sports pass, or an assembly).

George Sugai emphasizes, however, that "we also know that increasing the intensity of sanctions and excluding students for rule violations are insufficient solutions. Problem behavior often increases when only punitive discipline practices are used" (1996, p. 10).

Observations about Desist Strategies   We should not leave the topic of desist strategies without including a short summary of one of the more important works on the topic. Jacob S. Kounin (1970) reported that more than half (55.2) percent of perceived student misbehavior can be categorized as talking or other noisy behaviors. Off-task behaviors—for example, gum chewing—accounted for 17.2 percent of the total, and all other deviations from accepted norms—being late, not having homework, moving about the room without permission—accounted for the remainder (27.6 percent). According to Kounin's categories, the bulk of student misbehaviors would be regarded as low-level discipline problems.

Yet when teachers were given the options of punishing, providing a suitable desist, or prescribing another form of productive activity in reaction to these misbehaviors, over half opted for high-level, public desists. The most interesting, or perhaps sad, finding in Kounin's study is that in 92 percent of the cases, the teachers could give no reason for perceiving student behavior as being bad. Furthermore, in 95.6 percent of the cases, the teacher never provided the class with any knowledge of expected standards. This, of course, is an indictment of the teacher, not the students.

In another study, Kounin noted the effects on the class of the way in which teachers either punished students or provided desists when a student or group misbehaved. After observing students in kindergarten through college, he collected data based on experimental conditions to show that the way the teacher provided a desist had, in fact, an accompanying effect on all of the class members. Kounin called this the *ripple effect.* As the students in a class observe the teacher confronting a student for apparent misbehavior, all other class members tend to be adversely affected as well. Kounin reported that the angry desist did not motivate the other students to behave better or to attend to the task; rather, it made them anxious, restless, and uninvolved.

The ultimate goal of classroom management is to change behavior with the least effort possible.

Behavior Modification   **Behavior modification** refers to the process of changing behavior by rewarding desired actions and ignoring or punishing undesired actions. It is a set of strategies you can use in establishing effective classroom management. The classroom teacher can select components of the behavioral approach while retaining a humanistic approach to learning and students. The basic steps in the technique are listed in the box on page 222 (adapted from Ysseldyke and Marston 1990).

Phase 1: Charting Baseline Behaviors   During the baseline period, the teacher observes and records instances of the target behavior (the behavior to be changed). This phase provides evidence of whether or not the problem actually exists. Systematic observation may reveal that a student who has been labeled "disruptive" does not exhibit disruptive behavior more often than his peers. All data are recorded and tallied so that an established rate of

Reflect Reflect Reflect

The use of punishment as a classroom management tool has its proponents and opponents. How would the supporters of desist strategies and reality therapy defend their positions as to punishment? What is your position as a teacher?

Instructional

Strategies

Basic Steps in Behavior Modification

1. Chart baseline behavior.
2. Use an intervention in which contingencies are changed or manipulated.
3. To test the intervention, revert to the baseline conditions by reinstating original contingencies.
4. Return to the intervention condition.

occurrence may be determined. (See Figure 6.3, which illustrates one example of charting.)

Phase 2: Intervention or Experimentation   The chart serves as a baseline in choosing an appropriate strategy and determining its effectiveness. For example, if the behavior occurs only two or three times during silent reading, you may select ways to increase the student's ability to read silently. Structure the day so that during these periods you are positioned near the student to administer verbal praise when the appropriate behavior (silent reading) occurs. During this time, continue to record the student's behavior to determine whether or not the intervention is effective. If after a few days of your increased attention, there is a decrease in the number of times the student talks to neighbors during a silent reading period, you can assume that the strategy is having a positive effect. In most cases you will try to reinforce an appropriate behavior while ignoring or not responding to inappropriate ones.

Charting very specific behaviors establishes a base for comparison.

FIGURE 6.3

"Turning in Homework" Behaviors

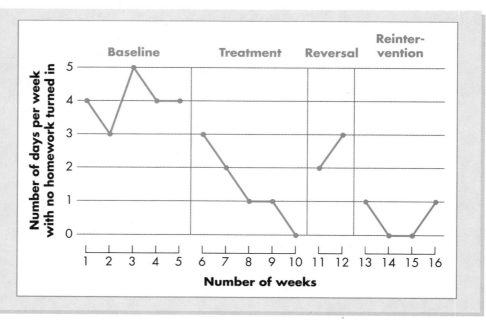

Sample Reinforcers for Classroom Situations

1. Recognition
2. Tangible rewards
3. Classroom learning activities
4. Classroom and school responsibilities
5. Status indicators
6. Incentive feedback
7. Personal activities
8. Social activities
9. Relief from aversive policies or procedures
10. Relief from aversive classroom environments

Often student problem behaviors result in more teacher or peer attention than usual. If a student is withdrawing from classroom participation, for example, the teacher may encourage the student to interact with other class members and reward him or her for doing so (the contingency strategy).

Intervention can also be applied to other inappropriate behaviors. A math teacher might reinforce completion of assignments; a science teacher might simultaneously reinforce "attending" behaviors. The participation of the key people with whom the student interacts (other teachers, counselor, parents) will help you identify and implement an effective plan of reinforcement.

Sometimes verbal reinforcers are adequate to modify the student's behavior. You may need to experiment to determine the set of reinforcers that change the student's behavior with the least effort. In some cases you need visible or material reinforcers such as stars on the student's papers, the student's name on the class "honor list," tokens, pencils, or special privileges. Whatever the reward, it is absolutely imperative that it follow the appropriate behavior immediately.

The use of **reinforcers,** or rewards that encourage students to repeat positive behaviors, is a critical component of behavior modification (see the box above). *Reinforcement* is defined as consequences that increase the future rate of a behavior. If you use the same set of reinforcers over an extended time, you may find that they lose their impact. After studying this problem, Roger Addison and Donald T. Tosti (1979) compiled a system and a list of reinforcers that can be applied with various motivational strategies in an education environment.

Reinforcers are very personal; a teacher may have to try various reinforcers with a specific student before finding the most powerful one (Addison and Tosti 1979). Obviously, there is no one universal reinforcer. Several of the above activities have been classified as being aspects of *student recognition programs* (Lockwood 1988). Such programs emphasize student success. Recognition helps create a positive climate and makes schooling intentionally inviting.

Recognition helps create a positive climate and makes schools intentionally inviting.

Phase 3: Reversal to Baseline Conditions   For most teachers, no further class manipulation is necessary once the appropriate reward or reinforcer is determined. However, to follow the behavior modification paradigm completely, you should return from the Phase 2 conditions to those classroom conditions that were present during the original baseline period. Teachers often resist this requirement, since it means returning to the original conditions that seemingly prompted the undesired behavior.

As in Phases 1 and 2, in Phase 3 data are consistently tabulated so that the behavioral patterns are quickly discernible. Phase 3 usually is conducted only long enough to effect a reversal of behavior to the baseline type. When you have again observed such behavior, go on to Phase 4.

Phase 4: Reinstating the Intervention Conditions   The final stage reinstates the conditions used during Phase 2. If the intervention caused a change in behaviors during the second phase, it should do so again at this time. But if there is no change toward the desired behaviors, then you were just lucky in Phase 2, and you will have to start all over again. Now you can understand why teachers dislike Phase 3.

Try to be positive at all times.

Principles for Classroom Use   Several general principles can help the teacher apply behavior modification in the classroom.

1. **Accentuate the positive.** Schools have been criticized for being too "unpleasant" and teachers for being far too negative toward students. To change this image, the teacher must praise students, even if it is for the most inconsequential matter. Admittedly, it may be difficult to praise a student who continually disrupts the class, but it has been frequently demonstrated that simply admonishing a student will not reduce the inappropriate behavior. Praising some positive aspect of the student's behavior is more likely to bring about change (see Ellett 1993).

    How does the teacher use different forms of praise or social reinforcement? There are verbal, nonverbal, and tactile reinforcers. Several examples of positive verbal and nonverbal praise are listed in the box on page 225. We comment on tactile reinforcers in the next section.

2. **Identify productive behavior for the class.** Praise provides reinforcement not only for the student to whom it is directed but also for the entire class. Praise provides students with an explicit model of what you expect of them. To be sure, public praise can be embarrassing as well as reinforcing; therefore, you must learn what technique works best for each student— and, hence, for the whole class.

3. **Start small.** In most cases, students view major changes in behavior as unachievable. If a student hands in about 25 percent of the required homework assignments, there is little chance that reinforcement will result in 100 percent completion right away. However, you can still establish a definite contingency schedule by making a behavioral contract with the student. The student may complete two of five assignments in the first week. If so, move up the requirement to three of five assignments for the next week. Remember that the student probably did not reach the present level of academic deficiency in one step. Therefore, do not expect to remedy the problem in one great leap. Take small initial steps by increasing the quantity or the quality until the student reaches the agreed-upon criterion. This requires you to be patient and to give constant positive feedback to the student.

4. **Be consistent.** As you begin to use behavior modification in the classroom, whether on an individual or a group basis, keep your own behavior consis-

Examples of Praise

Verbal Praise

- All right
- Great
- Very interesting
- Really great
- Fantastic
- Nice work
- Dynamite
- Wonderful
- Mighty fine
- Terrific
- Keep it up
- Fabulous
- Splendid
- Clever
- Quite nice
- Marvelous
- Awesome
- Ideal
- A winner
- Yes
- Neat
- Unreal
- Excellent
- Wow
- Super
- Good job
- Lovely
- Beautiful

Nonverbal Praise

- Laughing
- Thumbs-up signal
- Pointing with a smile
- Moving toward student
- Smiling
- Signaling by lifting the palms
- Looking with interest
- Winking
- Raising the eyebrows
- Nodding approval
- High-five

Reflect Reflect Reflect

Susan Bolotin has written an interesting debate between imposed discipline and self-discipline advocates in the February 14, 1999, issue of *The New York Times Magazine* entitled "The Disciplines of Discipline." Question: Which strategies identified in the article would be appropriate for parents and which might work for you as a teacher?

tent and predictable. If you remain consistent in your responses to student stimuli, then you can better predict the reactions of class members. For example, ask that every student always raise his or her hand and wait to be called on to answer a question, and always wait until students do so before calling on them.

Section 4: Society and Classroom Management

Successful classroom management requires a productive working environment in which students feel safe and accepted. "Attempting to view each student in your classroom as an individual should not be seen as a hopeless or

Successful teaching requires a productive environment in which students feel safe and accepted.

frustrating task. The old way of attempting to stuff kids into predetermined categories or molds is a much more frustrating and failure-ridden task than taking them as they arrive and moving on from there" (Zabel and Zabel 1996, p. 108).

Teachers sometimes must deal with classroom management problems that are severe by any standards (Columbine High School is a prime example). To be effective, schools will need to maintain an environment that underscores safety, cooperation, and commitment. Every teacher must be committed to ensuring that such characteristics are primary to the classroom and school. Teachers must now teach and model basic social skills—even in high school. These skills help adolescents accept others, cope with interpersonal differences, and simply learn how to behave in social settings (see Iannaccone, Wienke, and Cosden 1992). Teachers today spend fully one-third of their work day on such nonteaching activities (Caudell 1992). This fact provides the rationale for developing a philosophy on equity and management. Effective school organization has a positive impact on student life (see Table 6.8).

The classroom is a social and emotional environment as well as a learning environment. As teachers, we need to be certain that *all* students play a role in learning and participatory activities. If boys are always asked to lead or to set up schoolroom apparatus, or if girls are always asked to take notes and arrange things, then both boys and girls are being unfairly typecast. The manner in which a teacher engages every student has potential learning and

TABLE 6.8

Selected Traits of Effective Schools

Academic Characteristics

- Clear instructional focus
- High academic time on task
- Frequent monitoring of student progress
- High school expectations
- Appropriate award structures
- Active teaching
- Few student absences

School Climate Indicators

- Orderly and safe environment
- Minimal instructional interruptions
- Few discipline problems
- Little time spent on classroom management
- Friendly ambience
- No graffiti
- Frequent contact with parents

SOURCE: Teddlie and Stringfield 1993; Bickel 1999, pp. 959–983.

achievement overtones. This means you must consciously address many of your personal mores and habits and avoid reinforcing social barriers and stereotypes. Helping every student feel the thrill of success is what teaching is all about. And that goes for girls, boys, minorities, children with disabilities, and non-English speakers. It is a great and worthy challenge.

Cooperation and Equity

When you establish classroom management strategies, remember that students are, for the most part, reasonable human beings who are anxious to make their classrooms cooperative and pleasant places in which to be (Johnson and Johnson 1989). By enlisting student aid in the formulation of classroom activities and regulations, you help prevent classroom management problems in three ways: (1) you are setting the stage for classroom equity through a process of respect and understanding, (2) students tend to have a greater interest in the maintenance of these regulations when they have had a part in generating them, and (3) they have a greater understanding of the need for and the meaning of regulations when they help to develop them.

Equity is a classroom value.

Gender and Race Issues   Teachers are often unaware that they project a bias toward or against some students because of sex, race, ethnic background, or intelligence level. This bias is most obvious in science classes. As a consequence, female students have more negative attitudes toward high school science than do males (Baker 1988).

Several studies have shown that teachers reward boys more than girls in secondary science classes, girl-initiated science interactions *decline* during the middle school years, teacher expectations favor boys, and racial minorities tend to be rejected more by teachers than are majority students (Good and Brophy 2000). These situations are all *intentionally disinviting* to female and minority learners.

What can you do to be an unbiased teacher? First, you or someone else can chart your interactions with students. Tabulate positive and negative feedback, nonverbal cues, use of male pronouns, and male bias. If bias is apparent, use a list of student names to conduct recitations on a regular schedule. Change your verbal and written communication patterns to use inclusionary language. (In case you need a model, this textbook is written with inclusionary, gender-neutral language.) Provide an equitable number of leadership positions to males, females, minority students, and students with disabilities. In short, become proactive by making the classroom environment equitable to all.

Use inclusionary language in all classroom communication.

To enhance equity and promote achievement, Sam Kerman (1979) perfected a series of fifteen strategies that are collectively labeled TESA, "Teacher Expectations and Student Achievement" (see the box on page 228 and Phi Delta Kappa 1993).

As you examine these fifteen elements, you will see that in this chapter we have stressed all but touch. Very young pupils do touch their teachers and vice versa; but we suggest that, beginning at middle school, you do not touch students, especially members of the opposite sex. The best intentions may be misinterpreted and lead to charges of sexual harassment or physical abuse.

Instructional

Strategies

The TESA Program

Response Opportunities

1. Equitable distribution of participation
2. Individual help
3. Latency or wait time
4. Delving
5. Higher-level questions

Feedback

1. Affirmation of correct responses
2. Praise
3. Reasons for praise
4. Listening
5. Accepting feelings

Personal Regard

1. Proximity of teacher to student
2. Courtesy
3. Personal interest and compliments
4. Touching (as a positive gesture)
5. Desist strategies

Chapter 2 provides additional insights into issues impacting gender and racial equity. The most critical point is to be fair, impartial, and intentionally inviting to every student.

Student Tracking   Most teachers particularly enjoy working with their top students. And why not? After all, academically capable students virtually teach themselves. So some teachers use tracking. However, too frequently low-track students are not expected to amount to much. And once put in this track, they

Homogeneous grouping may be intentionally disinviting.

Reflect Reflect Reflect

Use the following Internet resource to explore your attitudes toward equity. The *Long Walk of Nelson Mandela* provides the essentials of the life and character of one of the twentieth century's greatest leaders as he faced a life of inequity. How could you use this Internet resource in your classroom?

http://www.pbs.org/wgbh/pages/frontline/shows/mandela

will probably stay there for all twelve years of their education. Teachers expect them to do poorly. (What an example of being intentionally disinviting!)

The most compelling evidence against tracking comes from a 1988 study by Adam Gamoran and Mark Berends. They concluded that tracking favors students in the high track, accounts for disparities in student achievement, produces a cycle of low expectations for low-track students, and creates poor morale among teachers and students.

Evidence supporting academic tracking at both the elementary and secondary levels, especially over long periods of time, has been inconclusive. Teachers have reported, however, that they *dislike* teaching low-ability classes, spend less time preparing for them, and schedule less interesting or less challenging activities for them (Good and Brophy 2000). Students in low-track classes are merely kept busy with mundane, irrelevant work. Not surprisingly, students in high-track classes have better attitudes toward school and better work habits, and they assume positions of greater leadership.

And as we stated above, there is little advancement among low-tracked students—what movement there is tends to be downward. Many problems with tracking reflect poor placement. For example, one middle school girl was placed in the school's slow reading track for three years. The teachers and principal were quite unaware that during these years, this young adolescent had read on her own *every* Nancy Drew mystery book that had ever been published. So much for objective placement in tracks!

We recognize that specific classes will automatically draw the top academic students in high school (advanced mathematics, physics, and chemistry; advanced foreign language study). Of course, many teachers in these classes will discourage girls, children with disabilities, or minority students from entering. Or worse, advisers will tell them not to enroll in prerequisite classes. Such incidents are commonly reported by university undergraduate students. Gender bias is closely related to tracking and, in our opinion, is extremely unprofessional teacher behavior.

Robert E. Slavin (1991) provides the best interpretation of the evidence *against* tracking. His findings are summarized in the box below.

This analysis will not receive rave reviews in most public schools—it runs counter to the myths that educators and school board members perpetrate about tracking. A 1992 report from the National Assessment of Educational

---

Slavin's Findings Against Tracking

- The top 3 to 5 percent of students benefit from acceleration but not enrichment.
- Enrichment programs may benefit very slightly from homogeneous placement, but such enrichments are beneficial to all students, not just the top 5 percent or top one-third of them.
- Low-track students tend to drop out of school more frequently than lower-achieving students in heterogeneous classes.
- Ethnic minority students tend to make up a disproportionate number of low-track classes.

Progress noted that while approximately 25 percent of tested eight-grade students were grouped by ability, their average proficiency score was not higher in any educationally significant manner than scores of students not grouped by ability. Significant differences did appear when the top 16 percent of eighth graders were compared to the lowest 11 percent.

In middle and elementary schools, tracking has no professional defense (see Becker 1988). Review Chapter 8 for several tested strategies that will have a far more effective impact on student achievement, attitude, and quality of work in these grades. These include cross-age peer tutoring, cooperative learning, feedback, reinforcement, and mastery learning. To be sure, there are gifted-and-talented programs in most schools. Several use the "pull-out" model; that is, they pull these students out of regular classes for enrichment experiences. That such a model disrupts the regular class is often ignored. The real challenge is how to provide all children with that elusive "best of educations."

Parental Involvement

Do you want to provide a pleasing, enriching, successful classroom experience? The path to such a learning experience is well known: get parents involved. Active parents follow the development of their children, reinforce the expectations of the schools, and monitor student behavior and participation. Getting the parents into the schools is so important that it is the eighth goal in Goals 2000: "Every school will promote parental involvement and participation to promote social, emotional, and academic growth of children."

The parents of problem students rarely follow their children's educational achievement.

It is rare for the parents of problem students to closely follow their children's educational achievement. There are few models parents can follow in deciding just what role they should play in their children's educational career. It is exactly this lack of direction, coupled with the demands of two-career and single-parent homes, that fosters poor parent participation.

Working Parents   Two working parents now represent the norm. This leaves little time and even less energy for oversight of children's schooling. Today's parents tend not to ask for school reports, monitor class assignments, or attend school activities. If you are a primary teacher, you have a good chance of encouraging parents to build an active school attendance resume along with their children. However, you must call, call, call! Don't wait for participation; go out and get it. Such extra work will pay off in fewer classroom disruptions and better achievement.

Secondary teachers face too many years of parental inactivity to hope for much parental participation. Yet the teacher still has an obligation to keep parents informed. There are those committed parents who actively pursue a good education along with their children. These folks will demand your attention, and you will be glad to give it. Rejoice in this rarity. Table 6.9 shows various reasons that parents of twelfth-graders were contacted by their school.

The Single Parent   In urban areas, the single parent is the norm. These parents work double-time to keep up with all the demands of their job, parenting, and personal life. Don't jump to the conclusion that the single parent is always female or young. Many parents share the custody of their children, so

TABLE 6.9

Reasons for Contacting Parents of Twelfth-Graders

Reason School Personnel Contacted Parents	Control of School			
	Total	Public	Catholic	Other Private
Student's academic performance	52.7	52.5	48.5	60.8
Student's academic program	43.8	42.9	46.1	59.0
Student's post–high school plans	37.1	34.9	50.0	69.1
Student's attendance	37.0	38.7	17.5	25.7
Student's behavior	20.1	20.5	14.6	18.5
To request parent volunteer time at school	55.0	51.9	82.9	86.2
To inform parents how to help student with schoolwork	22.3	21.5	29.3	31.8

SOURCE: U.S. Department of Education, 1995, p. 128. (Most current data as of year 2000.)

you may find a different parent present at consecutive school activities. Confusion for you and the student may be a frequent result.

No Parent Available   Many children are being raised today by members of their extended family. This might be a grandmother, uncle, sister, or cousin. Don't ask questions; just build a relationship with any "parental" figure who demonstrates an interest in your student. *Concern* is the operable word here.

Classroom Stresses Needing Supportive Partnerships

Child Abuse   All schools have policies relating to the role of the police in the schools and court referral systems. Teachers are not usually involved with these agencies, but you need to know about them, especially when child abuse is suspected. You are never wrong to request that any police action or directive first receive approval from the principal. Your principal is trained in such law-enforcement agency interaction and has prescribed procedures to follow. Obviously, concerns about a life-threatening situation overrule any prior-notice issues.

Every school has a strict written policy outlining the steps to be taken if child abuse is suspected by a teacher or reported to school personnel. These policies have been developed in conjunction with the courts to protect our most vulnerable citizens. A teacher has little recourse but to follow such policies exactly. Most school districts will provide an orientation to all new teachers regarding the policy and procedure for handling such cases and will expect all personnel to follow the guidelines rigorously. States such as Washington have laws requiring all school personnel to report suspected child abuse. Discuss this point with your principal on the first day of school!

Alcohol and Drug Abuse   In today's schools, you will almost certainly come in contact with drug and alcohol abuse among your students (see Table 6.10). According to the Federal Substance Abuse and Mental Health Services Administration, any school of 1,500 can expect to have 195 students (13 percent of the student population) with serious emotional and/or drug problems, which block success and increase feelings of hopelessness. Without help, as many as 56 percent drop out and become adults with problems such as underemployment or unemployment.

You are responsible for encouraging students to understand and value our system of government and laws.

TABLE 6.10

Drug Use Among High School Seniors*			
Type of Drug	**1978**	**1988**	**1998**
Alcohol	87.8	85.3	74.3
Marijuana	50.2	33.1	37.5
Any illicit drug other than marijuana	27.1	21.1	20.2
Stimulants	17.1	10.9	10.1
Inhalants	4.1	6.5	6.2
LSD	6.3	4.8	7.6
Cocaine	9.0	7.9	5.7
Sedatives	9.9	3.7	6.0
Tranquilizers	9.9	4.8	5.5

SOURCE: U.S. Department of Education, 1999, Supplemental Table 27-1, p. 185.

*Figures are percentage of high school seniors who reported using drugs or alcohol any time during the previous year.

As a teacher, you are responsible for encouraging students to understand and value our system of government and laws. Your role demands that you exhibit high ethical standards, because the community has given you charge of its youth. Furthermore, professional ethics preclude your support of student use of alcohol or illegal drugs. On a personal level, we must do a better job of listening to and making time for our students. Plan regularly for after-school conference time to talk with your students. Encourage those you feel are at risk to "drop by" for a chat. Encourage at-risk students to become involved in after-school activities. Too frequently, children are raising themselves and are alone after school when the riskiest behaviors, including drug and alcohol use, sexual activity, and criminal activities, surface. The box on page 233 lists several early warning signs of alcohol and drug abuse.

All teachers must be cautious in handling students suspected of drug or alcohol abuse. An accusation may lead to a lawsuit by the student or his or her parents. Our advice is to check with school administrators on the accepted protocol for dealing with such problems (Zabel and Zabel 1996). The alcohol and drug problem is not simply critical—it is pandemic!

Early Warning Signs of Alcohol or Drug Abuse

- *Sudden behavioral changes.* Homework is lost, not turned in, copied, or declines in quality.
- *Attitude changes.* Comments are made to hurt others' feelings, or an "I-don't-care" demeanor emerges.
- *School problems.* Grades decline, difficulties with other teachers and school personnel appear, fights and arguments occur.
- *Changes in social relationships.* Student abandons old friends, becomes involved in a different social scene.
- *Self-destructive behavior.* Student develops injuries from "falls" or "fights" that he or she has difficulty recounting.
- *Avoidance.* Student withdraws or refuses to communicate, spends an inappropriate amount of time in isolation.

Reflect Reflect Reflect

- In your state, what laws relating to reports of alleged child abuse are enforced in the schools?
- Gather a few of your classmates to examine and discuss the National Center of Educational Statistic's URL (http://nces.ed.gov/pubs98/violence/tab14.html) relating to violence and discipline in the schools. Any surprises?

Bullies and Harassers   A 1991 study of U.S. school children found that 81 percent of boys and 72 percent of girls from seven to twelve years old reported being bullied. One of ten elementary school children had been bullied at least once a week during a three-month period in a South Carolina study of 6,500 students. "Bullying is one of the most serious and yet underrated problems in school today," said Ronald Stephens, executive director of the National School Safety Center, a California nonprofit group that researches school crime and violence (Wicker 1999).

Educators are redefining violence to include all the time-honored tools of the schoolyard bully—ridicule and jokes, mean tricks, and exclusion. Bullying is a power issue. All kids try bullying strategies at some time, but some use them regularly. Girls typically bully with insults and rejection, they ostracize, gossip, and use secrets. Boys typically use physical tactics. Although much of the bad behavior is limited to bathrooms, hallways, and the playground, it is also prevalent in the classroom. Elementary school bullies generally pick targets of their own gender, but as early as the fifth grade, bullies begin to target the opposite sex. Young bullies, left unchecked, are likely to move on to sexual harassment or physical violence when they get older. Children who seem friendless are such magnets for bullying that even one friend can make a difference.

Teacher intervention must be consistent, thoughtful, and skilled (see the box on page 234). Teachers should establish classroom rules regarding

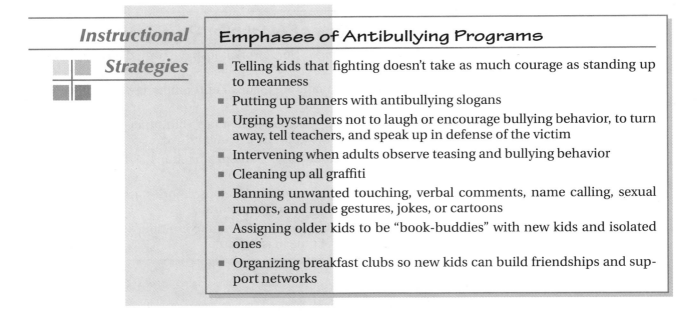

Instructional

Strategies

Emphases of Antibullying Programs

- Telling kids that fighting doesn't take as much courage as standing up to meanness
- Putting up banners with antibullying slogans
- Urging bystanders not to laugh or encourage bullying behavior, to turn away, tell teachers, and speak up in defense of the victim
- Intervening when adults observe teasing and bullying behavior
- Cleaning up all graffiti
- Banning unwanted touching, verbal comments, name calling, sexual rumors, and rude gestures, jokes, or cartoons
- Assigning older kids to be "book-buddies" with new kids and isolated ones
- Organizing breakfast clubs so new kids can build friendships and support networks

bullying and harassing behavior and enforce them. Inappropriate behavior should draw consequences designed to be as calm as possible. Remember, the bully wants attention! Don't argue with the bully; instead, state the consequences for the action and walk away. Avoid eye contact. Immediately praise someone for good behavior. When bullying becomes boring, the bully will change. Would you call this behavior modification?

The effectiveness of any strategy depends on commitment.

One more caution should be given. The effectiveness of any classroom management strategy depends on how much time, energy, and confidence you invest in it. A possible pitfall is moving quickly from one technique to another without expending the necessary time and energy to make any strategy succeed. Such efforts are likely to be counterproductive, thus confusing the student and making management problems more severe. The final selection and implementation of any one strategy or combination of strategies rest solely with you. But the ultimate criterion is student success.

Only you can transform the classroom into an interesting and positive learning environment. Structure that environment so that everyone is highly motivated to learn. It is the very least that you can do; perhaps the very most!

A Closing Reflection Reflection Reflection

- Would you confront a bully? Discuss the implications of your decision with a group of peers.
- How would you create a classroom management system if you have not experienced one in operation? Discuss this question with a group of peers as well.

Summary

1. A positive classroom environment is based on adherence to norms and your awareness of and insight into the classroom environment.

2. The seven core concepts of classroom routines are planning, establishing rules, getting a good start, providing clear direction, monitoring the environment, keeping essential records, and creating strategies for managing interruptions.

3. Self-discipline systems, which include the hierarchy of needs, moral reasoning, and teacher effectiveness training, stress personal responsibilities.

4. Imposed-discipline systems, such as desist strategies and behavior modification, stress teacher authority.

5. Behavorial systems require pinpointing specific behaviors and using reinforcers.

6. To apply behavior modification strategies in the classroom, it is necessary to identify positive behavior and use rewards consistently.

7. A positive environment stresses equity as a major principle.

8. Homogeneous grouping may not be instructionally effective.

9. Parental involvement aids in achieving school expectations, so teachers should build positive relationships with parents.

10. Teachers must learn to recognize the signs of child abuse, drug and alcohol abuse, and bullying so that they can work with the proper authorities.

Key Terms

awareness (p. 203)

behavior modification (p. 221)

classroom management (p. 199)

democratic discipline (p. 201)

desist strategy (p. 218)

discipline (p. 200)

humanistic orientation (p. 202)

imposed-discipline systems (p. 218)

norm (p. 202)

power (p. 203)

reinforcers (p. 223)

Helpful Resources

Daniels, V. I. "How to Manage Disruptive Behavior in Inclusive Classrooms." *Teaching Exceptional Children* 30(4) (1998): 26–31.

This short article provides very helpful tools for teachers with mainstreamed or inclusive students.

The Journal of Moral Education

For detailed discussions about moral and character education, refer to current issues of this journal.

Prosise, R. D. *Beyond Rules and Consequences for Classrooom Management.* Bloomington, IN: Phi Delta Kappa Educational Foundation, Fastback No. 401, 1996, 37 pp.

In just a few pages you gain valuable insights on positive approaches to manage your classes.

Zabel, R. H., and M. K. Zabel. *Classroom Management in Context: Orchestrating Positive Learning Environments.* Boston: Houghton Mifflin, 1996, 395 pp.

These authors give a complete treatment to our points of view on classroom management.

Internet Resources

❖ The AskERIC online database contains a large number of resources relating to classroom management.

http://ericir.sun.site.syr.educ/

❖ The Education Commission of the States provides a comprehensive list of information sources pertaining to school safety policies, practices, and resources.

http://www.ecs.org

❖ The Boston University Center for the Advancement of Ethics and Character Web site is rich with information relating to moral and character education.

http://education.bu.edu/CharacterEd/

❖ The National Association for School Psychologists provides an excellent site for exploring issues surrounding abuse, harassment, and violence in the schools.

http://www.naspweb.org

❖ Finally, the following Web site provides access to Teacher Talk, an on-line journal with articles on many topics, including classroom management.

http://education.indiana.edu/cas/tt/tthmpg.html

References

Addison, R., and D. T. Tosti. "Taxonomy of Educational Reinforcement." *Educational Technology* 19 (1979): 24–25.

Baker, D. "Teaching for Gender Differences." *NARST News* 30(1) (April 1988).

Becker, H. J. *Addressing the Needs of Different Groups of Early Adolescents.* Baltimore, MD: Johns Hopkins University Center for Research on Elementary and Middle Schools, 1988.

Bickel, W. E. "The Implications of the Effective Schools Literature for School Restructuring." In *The Handbook of School Psychology* (3rd edition). C. R. Reynolds and T. B. Gutkin, editors. New York: John Wiley, 1999, 959–983.

Bolotin, S. "The Disciplines of Discipline." *The New York Times Magazine* (February 14, 1999): 32–37.

Boston University Center for the Advancement of Ethics and Character: Character Education Manifesto. Boston: April 13, 1997.

Brophy, J. "Classroom Management Techniques." *Education and Urban Society* 18 (1986): 182–194.

Cangelosi, J. S. *Cooperation in the Classroom: Students and Teachers Together* (2nd edition). Washington, DC: National Education Association, 1990.

Caudell, L. S. "The Jobs of Teaching." *The Northwest Teacher/NWREL Report* (January 1992): T3.

Cramer, K. "Poll Says Education Reform Depends Mostly on Teacher Quality." *The Salt Lake Tribune* (November 22, 1998): A19.

Crosser, S. "Managing the Early Childhood Classroom." *Young Children* 47(2) (1992): 23–29.

Danielson, C. *Enhancing Professional Practice: A Framework for Teaching*. Alexandria, VA: Association of Supervision and Curriculum Development, 1996.

Dillon, J. T. *Questioning and Discussion: A Multidisciplinary Study*. Norwood, NJ: Ablex Publishing, 1988.

Doyle, W. "Recent Research on Classroom Management: Implications for Teacher Preparation." *Journal of Teacher Education* 36 (1985): 31–35.

Dwyer, K. "Troubled Students Lack Easy Access to Adults and Psychologists." *USA Today* (June 30, 1999): 15A.

Ellett, L. "Instructional Practices in Mainstreamed Secondary Classrooms." *Journal of Learning Disabilities* 26(1) (1993): 57–64.

Etzioni, A. *The New Golden Rule: Morality and Community in a Democratic Society*. New York: Basic Books, 1997.

Evertson, C. M. "Do Teachers Make a Difference?: Issues for the Eighties." *Education and Urban Society* 18 (1986): 195–210.

Evertson, C. M. "Classroom Rules and Routines." In *International Encyclopedia of Teaching and Teacher Education* (2nd edition). L. W. Anderson, editor. Tarrytown, NY: Elsevier Science, 1995, pp. 215–219.

Evertson, C. M., E. T. Emmer, and M. E. Worsham. *Classroom Management for Elementary Teachers* (5th edition). Boston: Allyn & Bacon, 2000.

Friedman, M. L., and C. Judson. "Tips for Beginners." *Mathematics Teacher* 84(7) (1991): 538–539.

Gamoran, A., and M. Berends. *The Effects of Stratification in Secondary Schools: Synthesis of Survey and Ethnographic Research*. Madison, WI: University of Wisconsin at Madison National Center for Effective Secondary Schools, 1988.

Gettinger, M., and K. C. Stoiber. "Excellence in Teaching: Review of Instructional and Environmental Variables." In *The Handbook of School Psychology* (3rd edition). C. R. Reynolds and T. B. Gutkin, editors. New York: John Wiley, 1999, 933–958.

Glasser, W. *Reality Therapy*. New York: Harper & Row, 1965.

Glasser, W. *Schools Without Failure*. New York: Harper & Row, 1969.

Glasser, W. "Reality Therapy: An Anti-Failure Approach." *Impact* 2 (1972): 6–9.

Glasser, W. *Control Therapy in the Classroom*. New York: Harper & Row, 1986.

Good, T. L. and J. E. Brophy. *Looking in Classrooms* (8th edition). New York: Longman, 2000.

Gorney, C. "Teaching Johnny the Appropriate Way to Flirt." *The New York Times Magazine* (June 13, 1999): 43–83.

Greenberger, R. S. "Justice Rules on School Bias and Land Use." *The Wall Street Journal* (May 25, 1999): A3.

Gump, P. V. "School Settings and Their Keeping." In *Helping Teachers Manage Classrooms*. D. Duke, editor. Alexandria, VA: Association for Supervision and Curriculum Development, 1982.

Henry, T. "Suburban Schools Eye Urban Solutions." *USA Today* (April 26, 1999): 6D.

Iannaccone, C. J., W. D. Wienke, and M. A. Cosden. "Special Skills Instruction in Secondary Schools: Factors Effecting Its Implementation." *The High School Journal* 75(2) (1992): 111–118.

Johnson, D. W., and R. T. Johnson. *Cooperation and Competition: Theory and Research*. Edina, MN: Interaction Book, 1989.

Kerman, S. "Teacher Expectations and Student Achievement." *Phi Delta Kappan* 60 (1979): 716–718.

Kohlberg, L. "The Cognitive-Developmental Approach to Moral Education." *Phi Delta Kappan* 56 (1975): 670–677.

Kounin, J. S. *Discipline and Group Management in Classrooms*. New York: Holt, Rinehart and Winston, 1970.

Kounin, J. S., and P. V. Gump. "The Ripple Effect in Discipline." *Educational Digest* 24 (1959): 43–45.

Leriche, L. "The Sociology of Classroom Discipline." *The High School Journal* 75(2) (1992): 77–89.

Lockwood, A. T. "Student Recognition Programs." *Resource Bulletin* 5 (Fall 1988). University of Wisconsin at Madison National Center on Effective Secondary Schools.

Loehrke, J. "Teacher Quality Trumps Quantity When It Comes to Helping Kids." *USA Today* (January 29, 1999): 13A.

Lombardi, T. P. *Learning Strategies for Problem Learners*. Bloomington, IN: Phi Delta Kappa Educational Foundation. Fastback No. 345, 1992.

Long, J. D. "Troubleshooters' Guide to Classroom Discipline." *Instructor* 95 (1985): 122–124.

McDaniel, T. R. "Practicing Positive Reinforcement: Ten Behavior Management Techniques." *Clearing House* 60 (1987): 389–392.

Malm, K. *Behavior Management in K–6 Classrooms.* Washington, DC: National Educational Association, 1992.

Maslow, A. H. *Motivation and Personality.* New York: D. Van Nostrand, 1968.

Phi Delta Kappa. *TE&SA: Teaching Expectations and Student Achievement.* Bloomington, IN: Phi Delta Kappa, 1993.

Power, B. M. "Rules Made to Be Broken: Literacy and Play in a Fourth-Grade Setting." *Journal of Education* 174(1) (1992): 70–86.

Power, F. C., A. Higgins, and L. Kohlberg. *Lawrence Kohlberg's Approach to Moral Education.* New York: Columbia University Press, 1989.

Ryan, K. "The Missing Link's Missing Link." *Journal of Education* 179(2) (1997): 81–90.

Ryan, K., and K. E. Bohlin. *Building Character in Schools: Practical Ways to Bring Moral Instruction to Life.* San Francisco: Jossey-Bass, 1999.

Ryan, K., and J. M. Cooper. *Those Who Can, Teach* (8th edition). Boston: Houghton Mifflin, 1998.

Sizer, T. R., and N. F. Sizer. "Grappling." *Phi Delta Kappan* 81(3) (1999): 184–190.

Skinner, B. F. *Science and Human Behavior.* New York: Macmillan, 1953.

Skinner, B. F. *About Behaviorism.* New York: Knopf, 1974.

Slavin, R. E. "Are Cooperative Learning and 'Untracking' Harmful to the Gifted?" *Educational Leadership* 48(6) (1991): 68–71.

Sugai, G. "UO and Public Schools Design Just-In-Time Learning Approaches to Find Solutions to Rising Student Discipline Problems." *Education Matters* 3(1) (Fall-Winter 1996): 10–11.

Tauber, R. T. *Classroom Management: Sound Theory and Effective Practice* (3rd edition). Westport, CT: Bergin and Garvey, 1999.

Teddlie, C., and S. Stringfield. *Schools Make a Difference.* New York: Teachers College Press, 1993.

U.S. Department of Education. National Center for Educational Statistics. *The Condition of Education 1995.* Washington, DC: 1995.

U.S. Department of Education. National Center for Educational Statistics. *The Condition of Education 1996.* NCES 93-304. Washington, DC: 1996.

U.S. Department of Education. National Center for Educational Statistics. *The Condition of Education 1998.* Washington, DC: 1998.

U.S. Department of Education. National Center for Educational Statistics. *The Condition of Education 1999.* NCES 1999-022. Washington, DC: 1999.

U.S. Department of Education. *The 1990 Science Report Card.* Washington, DC: Office of Educational Research and Improvement, 1992. (See especially Table 5.1, p. 90.)

Wallen, C. J. "Establishing Teaching Principles in the Area of Classroom Management." In *Low Cost Instruction Simulation Materials for Teacher Education.* Monmouth, OR: Teaching Research, 1968. (U.S. Department of Health, Education and Welfare, Office of Education, Bureau of Research.)

Walsh, F. M. *Planning Behaviors of Distinguished and Award-Winning High School Teachers.* Unpublished Doctoral Dissertation. Pullman: Washington State University, 1992.

Wang, M. C., G. D. Haertel, and H. J. Walberg. "Toward a Knowledge Base for School Learning." *Review of Educational Research* 63(3) (1993): 249–294.

Wicker, C. "Educators Work to Rid Schools of Bullying Behavior." *The Salt Lake Tribune* (April 4, 1999): A14.

Ysseldyke, J., and J. Elliott. "Effective Instructional Practices: Implications for Assessing Educational Environments." In *The Handbook of School Psychology* (3rd edition). C. R. Reynolds and T. B. Gutkin, editors. New York: John Wiley, 1999, pp. 497–518.

Ysseldyke, J. E., and D. Marston. "The Use of Assessment Information to Plan Instructional Interventions: A Review of the Research." In *The Handbook of School Psychology* (2nd edition). T. B. Gutkin and C. R. Reynolds, editors. New York: John Wiley, 1990.

Zabel, R. H., and M. K. Zabel. *Classroom Management in Context: Orchestrating Positive Learning Environments.* Boston: Houghton Mifflin, 1996.

The Process of Questioning

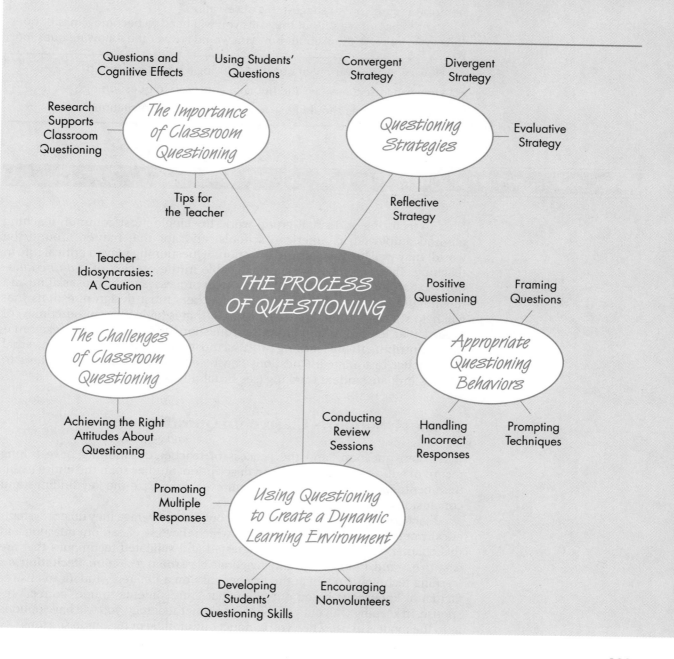

Your mentor has suggested that you observe another teacher, Dee Ryan, because she is a master of the questioning technique. Dee begins her class with a series of questions and in a businesslike manner calls on a number of students for responses. She calls on as many as four students to respond to the same question. The students respond eagerly. Their responses are lengthy and thoughtful, and they seem to be carrying on the recitation among themselves with few verbal cues from the teacher.

"Wow," you say to yourself, "I'd like to know how to use this technique. My mentor was sure cool to suggest this observation."

In this chapter we set out the skills you will need to become a master questioner. As you read, think about how you would answer the following questions:

- How can I ask a variety of questions during a recitation period?
- How can I use a positive and humane approach to questioning?
- What techniques should I use to conduct effective recitations?

Section 1: The Importance of Classroom Questioning

Next to lecturing and small-group work, the single most common teaching method employed in American schools (and, for that matter, around the world) may well be the asking of questions. Questioning plays a critical role in teaching. Teachers must be knowledgeable in the process of *framing questions* so that they can guide student thought processes in the most skillful and meaningful manner. This implies that teachers must design questions that will help students attain the specific goals (that is, objectives or outcomes) of a particular lesson. Although written questions in textbooks and examinations contribute to the learning process, most classroom questions are verbal and teacher formulated. Questions can be critical elements for teachers to use to stimulate student thinking (see Brualdi 1998).

Research Supports Classroom Questioning

Classroom questions and the process of teacher questioning have a long record of educational research and description. Studies span the entire twentieth century. Rather than listing them, we summarize the key findings and conclusions in the box on the next page.

Teachers ask a plethora of questions, but on the average they do not systematically organize or classify the ways in which they ask classroom questions. In this chapter, we provide empirically tested and validated techniques that are easy to use and, more important, invigorate classroom recitation. **Recitation** is a learning technique in which the teacher calls on a different student to answer factual or knowledge-based questions that limit students to one "correct" response. In keeping with our concept of multimethodology, you will have options as to the models to use when you conduct questioning or recitation sessions.

Twentieth-Century Research Findings on Questioning

- Questioning tends to be a universal teaching strategy.
- A broad range of questioning options is open to you.
- Being systematic in the use and development of questioning tends to improve student learning.
- By classifying questions according to a particular system, you may determine the cognitive or affective level at which your class is working and make adjustments as needed.
- Through systematic questioning, you may determine students' entry skill and knowledge levels for specific content areas.
- Questions should be developed logically and sequentially.
- Students should be encouraged to ask questions.
- A written plan with key questions provides lesson structure and direction.
- Questions should be adapted to the students' level of ability.
- Questioning techniques that encourage the widest spectrum of student participation should be used.
- Statements rather than questions should also be used to promote student reactions.
- No one questioning strategy is applicable to all teaching situations.

Questioning is a highly interpersonal and interactive teaching strategy. © Tom McCarthy/ *Photo Edit*

Questions and Cognitive Effects

Before we initiate the presentation on improving your questioning skills, let's briefly summarize the hundreds of published studies on questioning to determine which levels of questioning are used in the classroom and how these levels of questioning affect student thinking. Studies of questions asked by social studies, science, middle, elementary, and high school teachers show that the bulk of questions asked are at the lowest levels of Bloom's cognitive taxonomy. Seldom do teachers ask students to relate newly acquired information to previously learned information. Thus, students at all levels do not have experience in responding systematically to higher-level questions (see Brualdi 1998; Glover and Corkill 1990; Swift, Gooding, and Swift 1988; Wilen 1989; Wood and Muth 1991).

Textbook questions tend to be low level or knowledge based.

The blame for the prevalence of low-level questioning in U.S. classrooms does not rest completely with teachers. One study compared the fifth-grade elementary science textbooks published by the three biggest textbook publishers in the United States between 1983 and 1989. The new editions had, in two or three cases, almost doubled the number of knowledge-based student questions compared to the earlier editions. No more than 10 percent of the six hundred sampled questions could be classified as application level or above (Risner, Skeel, and Nicholson 1992). (Is it any wonder that children in the United States score so low on the higher–thinking level science portion of the National Assessment of Educational Progress?) If you want to use higher-level questions in your classroom, you will have to prepare them yourself.

We add a caution here, however: there is no guarantee that a higher-level question will elicit a higher-level student response. In fact, one of the world-class researchers in the field of questioning, J. T. Dillon (1982a, 1982b), reported wide discrepancies between the cognitive level of teachers' questions and that of students' responses. There is a 50 percent chance that a student will respond with a lower-level response when asked a higher-level question and vice versa. In another study, twenty-two student teachers of high school English, social studies, and science were observed for their questioning patterns; 63 percent of them asked questions that were at the lowest cognitive level. These questions had a 100 percent correspondence rate; that is, when the teachers asked low-level questions, students responded 100 percent of the time with a low-level response. For higher-level questions, there was 76 percent correspondence; about one-fourth of the students still responded at levels lower than that of the question (Dantonio and Paradise 1988).

Ask a low-level question and you'll get a low-level response.

These facts are important reminders that merely asking questions is not causal to student thinking. More important, you should realize that your higher-level questions do act to *invite* and *encourage* higher levels of critical thinking in students. Furthermore, it appears that if teachers *systematically* raise the level of their questioning, students raise the level of their responses correspondingly (Fillippone 1998). Of course, this implies a carefully planned questioning strategy, probably spanning several weeks of instruction. The major caution is not to jump haphazardly into high-level questions without making the necessary teacher-student attitude adjustments. This means that you must plan how to ask appropriate questions (van Zee and Minstrell 1997).

Use declarative statements rather than asking questions.

You should also consider an alternative to asking questions to stimulate student responses and thinking: using *declarative statements*. This technique elicits longer and more complex student responses. Teachers should keep such statements short—about one sentence—and, when appropriate, seek comments from students. There is some evidence that students' verbal responses are of higher quality when they respond to statements rather than to questions alone (Dillon 1990). For example, statewide testing has improved students' attitude toward school subjects. Another might be laboratory-based science instruction helps students to learn. Using this technique requires some practice. An ideal way to acquire such practice is through microteaching or peer coaching (Joyce and Showers 1995).

Using Students' Questions

Even when your questions are higher level, it is important not to let yourself "dominate the scene." It appears that teachers may have become doctrinaire in their almost exclusive use of teacher questioning at the expense of more student participation. Question-and-answer periods seldom lead to meaningful classroom discussion since recitations tend not to encourage others to participate.

Encourage students to ask questions.

This leads us to another major and important source of questions that is often overlooked: the students. Classes should be oriented toward student communication, that is, toward giving students a chance to express their opinions and ideas. As we have seen, however, the evidence shows that teachers do most of the talking and questioning. Disturbingly few students ask questions during recitations, "nor are they encouraged to do so" (Swift, Gooding, and Swift 1992). (What an example of being intentionally disinviting!) This is particularly unfortunate, since encouraging student questions leads to higher-level questions, stimulates more students to interact, provides positive cognitive effects, and promotes analytic reasoning (see Gall and Artero-Boname 1995, Koegel et al. 1998). (Student questioning as a teaching technique is expanded later in this chapter.)

Reflect Reflect Reflect

- What benefits should students derive from asking questions?
- In one of your methods classes, practice making declarative statements rather than asking questions. What reactions do you receive?
- In another class, tabulate the number of questions asked and then classify them using Bloom's taxonomy.

Tips for the Teacher

These studies have many implications for your decision making. First, if you want your students to develop higher levels of thinking, to evaluate information, to achieve more, and to be more interested, you must learn to ask higher-level questions. Chapter 9 explores the development of higher-level thinking and inquiry-based teaching. Second, you must encourage your students to ask more questions—and more thought-provoking ones—themselves, especially if you want to increase student involvement in the process of learning.

If you desire to stimulate critical thinking among your students, another important consideration is the way to use textbooks. Be aware of the advantages and disadvantages of your textbook materials. To attain the objective desired, you may have to supplement the materials provided. For example, you might teach lessons with focused questions that require students to compare or contrast items, persuade others, or determine cause and effect. These processes are crucial to developing thinking skills (Barr and Dailey 1996). Finally, you can use questions to diagnose student progress, determine entry-level competence, prescribe additional study, and enrich an area (Gibson 1998).

Classroom questions can be classified by one of seven different systems.

Lelia Christenbury and Patricia P. Kelly (1983) have discussed seven different taxonomies or hierarchies of learning that can be used in formulating questions. One of these seven is Bloom's cognitive taxonomy, and three others are also "sequential hierarchies" with stages similar to his. Thus, for our purposes and for the sake of uniformity, we will simply rely on using Bloom's (1956) cognitive taxonomy as a means for classifying questions and their responses. Refer to Chapter 3, Section 2, to review the six categories.

Although, as we pointed out earlier, your higher-level questions do not *guarantee* higher-level responses, they open a very important door to critical thinking for your students. Thus we want you to become aware of the kinds of questions you ask and the kinds of responses these questions elicit. The cognitive level of your questions must always be taken into account. Remember: *If you want to encourage a response at a particular level of thinking, you must frame the question accordingly.* This simple application of the "if-then" strategy will give you the necessary awareness of the intellectual level at which you are conducting your class. This strategy also requires concomitant and continuous decision making and evaluation. Furthermore, the technique can be applied to *all* levels of instruction and with *all* types of students.

To instruct at higher cognitive levels, use a questioning hierarchy as a plan for your recitations and discussion. This will allow you to structure facts, concepts, and generalizations within a framework for thinking—the hierarchy becomes a visible blueprint for action (see Beamon 1997). Note that a "questioning" hierarchy can also be used to plan declarative statements and to structure them in a hierarchical manner to elicit higher-level student responses. You'll find yourself asking fewer questions (see Barnette et al. 1995).

Finally, we want to underscore that teachers need to try hard not to dominate classroom verbal interactions and thereby cause class members to become passive and dependent on the teacher. Student passivity hardly fosters ingenuity, creativity, or critical thinking—traits we all consider desirable. Nor

Reflect Reflect Reflect

- Using Bloom's taxonomy, frame a question or declarative statement at each level for a lesson of your choice.

is passive student behavior appropriate for a constructivist method of teaching; rather, the classroom should be highly interactive (Rallis et al. 1995).

Section 2: Questioning Strategies

There are four distinct questioning strategies.

In this part of the chapter we will describe four basic questioning strategies: *convergent, divergent, evaluative* (Verduin 1967), and a fourth strategy that we have synthesized especially for this edition—*reflective questioning*. If you assign a particular importance to the different types of questions you ask, then you will need a method for verifying that you are indeed using the desired questioning patterns. The classification scheme we present here will help you conduct goal-specific recitation periods.

Convergent Strategy

The convergent questioning strategy focuses on a narrow objective. When using a convergent strategy, you encourage student responses to converge, or focus, on a central theme. **Convergent questions,** for the most part, elicit short responses from students and focus on the lower levels of thinking—that is, the knowledge or comprehension levels. This does not mean that using a convergent technique is "bad" per se. In many situations you will decide that your students need to demonstrate a knowledge of specifics; in such cases, lower-level questioning strategies are appropriate. Remember that the appropriateness of any questioning strategy must be judged solely on the basis of its ability to fulfill your predetermined objectives.

Convergent questions lead to a common set of responses.

So when might convergent questioning be the appropriate choice? If you use an inductive teaching style (proceeding from a set of specific data to a student-derived conclusion), then you will use a large proportion of convergent-type questions. Or you may wish to use short-response questions as rapid-fire warm-up exercises (for example, when you are building vocabulary skills). Teachers in foreign language classes may use a convergent, rapid-fire pattern to help develop students' oral, vocabulary, and spelling skills. This technique also allows all students to participate. The same method may be used by a science teacher to build technical vocabulary. Thus, a biology teacher may wish to use a convergent technique for the first few minutes of class to maximize participation and to generate constructive verbal motivation among the students.

The basic convergent pattern allows you to "dominate" the thinking of

Examples of Convergent Questions

- In what works did Robert Browning use the dramatic monologue as a form for his poems?
- Under what conditions will water boil at less than 100°C?
- What helps bread dough rise?
- What rights are ensured by the First Amendment?
- Why do relatively few people live in the deserts of any country?
- Where and when was Fort Ticonderoga built?
- What's the present tense first-person plural form of *estar*?
- What's 5 to the third power?

Reflect Reflect Reflect

- Give an example from your own teaching area of an objective for which you would use sets of convergent questions.

students by asking for short, low-level responses (such as a single response or a limited number of logical responses). You should understand that a convergent questioning pattern is not an appropriate means of stimulating thought-provoking responses or classroom discussions; rather, it stresses the knowledge level (see Rowe 1996). The convergent technique is an ideal application of "teacher-directed instruction," or *direct instruction*, in which all students in class respond in unison to teacher-asked questions. Everyone participates.

The box above includes examples of convergent questions. Note that these questions all meet the criterion of limiting student responses to a narrow spectrum of possible options and are more recall oriented than analytical.

Divergent Strategy

Divergent questions lead to a wide array of responses.

Divergent questions are the opposite of convergent questions. Rather than seeking a single focus, the goal in using a divergent questioning strategy is to evoke a wide range of student responses. Divergent questions also elicit longer student responses. Thus, if you wish to evoke several different responses from your class, ask a divergent question. The divergent technique is ideal for building the confidence of children with learning difficulties, because divergent questions do not always have right or wrong answers (see Beamon 1997).

Eliciting Multiple Responses   If you want to elicit multiple responses, then you will want to use a multiple-response questioning technique. After asking a question, call on three or four students, and then assume a passive role in the ensuing discussion. Such a technique teaches students to conduct a classroom recitation themselves. It is a rather sophisticated teaching strategy when used properly. The multiple-response technique also sharpens students' listening skills.

Divergent questions are ideal for eliciting many responses for the same question.

Accepting Diverse Responses   If encouraging creative responses to questions and novel solutions to problems is your goal, then the divergent method is appropriate. Remember, though, that if you elicit diverse responses from students, you have a professional obligation to accept them. This is a very important component of the art of questioning: to reinforce appropriate response behavior, you must demonstrate a high degree of acceptance for the responses of each student (van Zee and Minstrell 1997). This means that you may not use subtle put-down tactics, regardless of how outlandish a student's point of view may seem (or how different from what you expected). When you ask divergent questions, you must allow free responses by students. Again, this is a great technique for students with some learning difficulties as they get to become "stars" in the classroom.

The Technique in Action   When you begin to use divergent questions, you will find it helpful to write out the questions ahead of time. Then examine them to ensure that they are clearly stated and convey the precise meanings you intend. You will probably find your initial class experience with divergent questions difficult or even disappointing, usually because students are not oriented toward giving longer or higher-level responses (see Savage 1998).

It takes a good deal of reshaping of student behavior patterns to elicit high-level student thinking and responses. From grade school through high school, over thousands of classroom hours, students have been conditioned to give short, low-level responses. When you begin to ask divergent questions, you must let your students know that the level of questions is changing and that you want the level of their responses also to change, quite drastically. You will soon find that students' responses will demonstrate higher-level thinking—application, analysis, and synthesis. Thus, if you want your students to be prepared to conduct discussions and to give longer and more diverse oral or written responses, then the divergent technique is the appropriate one to use.

You should also inform the class that you expect multiple responses, with each student taking cues from other students' responses. This means that you do not repeat student responses to other class members (except when a student speaks too quickly or softly to be heard). The rationale for not repeating responses is that if students know that the teacher will repeat the previous response, they become conditioned to listening only for the teacher's repetition of the response.

When using the divergent strategy, you should allow all students to present their responses without your interference. This has a positive effect on the class. In general, we find that teachers tend to interrupt their students before students have fully explained their positions. If the teacher avoids interrupting students, then students will realize that their responses are important and that they must take their cues from one another rather than from the teacher. Students will realize that they must be responsive to one another, and, as a result, the class's attending behavior will improve. It does little good for a teacher continually to remind students that they are not paying attention; such negative comments only make a class less attentive. By encouraging students to listen to one another, you encourage them to participate in a

Examples of Divergent Questions

- What type of social and cultural development might have taken place if Christopher Columbus had landed on Manhattan Island on October 12, 1492?
- What would happen in a school if it had no personal computers?
- Explain the attitude that the Romantic poets had toward nature.
- What do you think are other effective methods of organic gardening that are not listed in the textbook?
- How does the environment affect human shelter building?
- Why would you select arc welding over gas welding in creating art objects?
- What kinds of evidence would you seek if you were an opponent of the "Big Bang" theory?
- How would a government organized according to a parliamentary system have reacted to the Iran-Contra incident in the 1980s?
- Why was Fort Ticonderoga built where it was on Lake Champlain?
- Under what conditions are First Amendment rights abridged?

Reflect Reflect Reflect

- For which content areas are divergent questions most appropriate? For which are they least appropriate?

dynamic fashion. You also encourage peer reinforcement of positive, constructive classroom behavior.

Use of the divergent strategy to encourage higher-level thinking skills requires planning. Your emphasis must be on systematic development of questions over an extended time, with well-conceived, appropriate learning objectives. Do not expect overnight miracles, however: it takes weeks, even months, to incorporate these techniques into the usual repertoire of teaching strategies.

Use of divergent questions requires you to help students locate different sources of information so that they can share a variety of viewpoints in class. The box above lists examples of divergent questions. Note that we have adapted a few of these from the previous list of convergent questions.

Evaluative Strategy

The third questioning strategy is based on the divergent strategy, but with one added component—evaluation. The basic difference between a divergent

Using evaluative questions helps students generate criteria for making judgments.

question and an **evaluative question** is that the evaluative question has a built-in set of **evaluative criteria.** For example, an evaluative question might ask why something is good or bad, why something is important, or why one theory explains the facts better than another. When you frame an evaluative question, emphasize the specific criteria on which students should base their judgments. As with divergent questions, you should accept all student responses to evaluative questions.

A major component of the teacher's role in the evaluative strategy is to help students develop a logical basis for establishing evaluative criteria. To illustrate this, we'll give you a classic negative example. You ask a question, and a student presents a response. You next ask, "Why?" and the student replies, "Because." You should recognize immediately from this response that the student does not understand how to frame a logical, consistent set of evaluative criteria. Once again, we caution that you must never use sarcasm or any other disparaging approach; instead, reinforce the student in an environment conducive to the development of logical evaluative criteria. For example, you might suggest a number of criteria: "What happens when someone is convicted of a crime? What about situations of national emergency?" Provide a specific set of criteria from which students may develop their own criteria. Some students might be intimidated if you ask "Why?" It has been suggested that instead of asking why, use the word *What.* This is a subtle form of shifting the burden of proof from the student to the topic (see Dana et al. 1992). As an introduction to the evaluative technique, we recommend a joint writing session, with the teacher and small groups of students collaboratively listing criteria. Then, as you pose evaluative questions and students make responses, you and the students can classify the evaluative responses along a continuum ranging from "inappropriate" or "illogical" to "appropriate" or "logically developed" (see Figure 7.1).

Note that we have been using the term *responses,* not *answers. Answers* carry the connotation of being final, complete, or the last word. To be sure, convergent questioning patterns may elicit such answers, but when you ask divergent and evaluative questions, students will not be giving you definitive or absolute answers. They will be providing responses that tend to be relative, tentative, or less than certain (see Martinello 1998).

FIGURE 7.1

Classification Criteria for Evaluative Responses

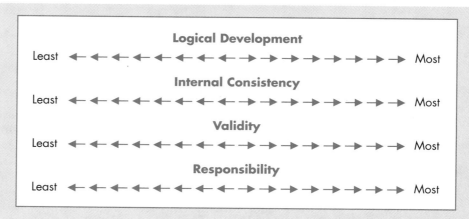

Evaluative Questions

- Why is the parliamentary system of government more responsive to citizens than our legislative system?
- Why is the world a better (or worse) place because of computers?
- What rationale is there that all teachers strive to be aware of the types of questions they ask?
- Why will the federal position on welfare reform affect social and moral attitudes and behaviors?
- What reasons could be given to switch to either gasohol or hydrogen as fuel for our automobiles?
- What evidence is there that the federal system of interstate highways harmed our city environments?
- Defend (or criticize) the strip mining of coal in eastern Montana.
- Why is the "Big Bang" theory a more viable one than the "Cold Start" theory?
- What made the location of Fort Ticonderoga critical to early colonial development?

Most student responses to evaluative questions will demonstrate a broad range of thought when rated on a set of evaluative criteria. You can classify them according to their logical development, internal consistency, validity, and perhaps responsibility (from least to most logical, least to most consistent, and so on; see Figure 7.1). Again we suggest that you accept all student responses. When apparent logical inconsistencies develop, discuss them *after* the student has had an opportunity to participate in classroom discourse.

The box above provides examples of evaluative questions. Some of the questions we previously designated as divergent have been converted now into evaluative questions. Remember that most evaluative questions are also divergent. The one characteristic that separates divergent questions from evaluative ones is that the latter rely on established judgmental criteria.

Evaluative questions are divergent, but divergent questions are not evaluative.

Reflective Strategy

We now present our newest addition to the list, reflective questioning strategy. This strategy draws its historical perspective from the classical Socratic method of questioning (Elder and Richard 1998). Reflective questions stimulate the wide range of student responses, as do divergent questions. Reflective questions also have an evaluative element. The major difference between these three techniques is that the **reflective question** attempts to elicit motives, inferences, speculations, impact, and contemplation. A divergent question attempts to gather a wide variety of responses, while an evaluative question seeks primarily to obtain student rationales or reasoning. The goal of using the reflective strategy is to require your students to develop higher-order thinking. Rather than asking a student a "why" or

---

Stimulating Thinking Process with Reflective Questions

- Seeking motives
- Expanding a vision
- Listing implications
- Searching for unintended consequences
- Identifying issues
- Analyzing persuasive techniques
- Making unique interpretations
- Inferring values
- Challenging assumptions
- Seeking meanings

"what," as we suggested in the *evaluative strategy,* you want the student to ponder, to think of implications, to search for unintended consequences (see Traver 1998; Ward 1997; van Zee and Minstrell 1997). The box above includes the types of thought processes that can be stimulated through reflective questions.

Note that the listing in the box indicates that reflective questions definitely initiate the process that we call *critical* or *analytical thinking!* Obviously, you don't get to this stage of intellectual development without carefully shaping the classroom environment and instructing your students as to what the process entails. Jim Minstrell (van Zee and Minstrell 1997) uses a technique that he calls the "reflective bounce." He bounces questions from the student back to the student so that the student needs to provide an expanded version

---

Reflective Questions

- What were some implications of Manifest Destiny?
- What issues are unresolved by having security persons in our high school?
- What rationale is given to support interscholastic activities?
- What problems might you anticipate if algebra were to be made a required course for all eighth graders?
- What values can we imply are important in our school by examining its entry showcase?
- What assumptions did we make when we constructed the interstate highway system?
- What impact have personal computers made on our school courses?
- What metaphors do your teachers use when describing school?

> ## Reflect Reflect Reflect
>
> - How can you provide students with content knowledge so that they can respond to evaluative and reflective questions?
> - Reflect on the techniques discussed here. Please contact the authors with your thoughts.

of a previous response—the reflective dimension we are advocating. The box on page 251 includes a few examples of reflective questions.

Using reflective questions requires a bit more planning than using convergent or divergent ones. We recommend that you write out a cluster of reflective questions that would be relevant to the content being taught and learned. In some cases, the reflective strategy approaches a constructivist perspective; that is, the students must construct their own meanings to the questions. We even suggest that you organize student teams to write a few reflective questions. This approach gives you double value: students work cooperatively, and they have to think.

Section 3: Appropriate Questioning Behaviors

To develop a repertoire of questioning skills, you must be aware of a wide spectrum of questioning techniques that may elicit appropriate responses from students. Our descriptions of questioning skills that follow address specific kinds of problems that may arise in any class using questioning strategies.

Positive Questioning

The questioning in a recitation period, a tutorial period, or an inductive session is always predicated on the assumption that some meaningful or purposeful learning activity will take place, allowing the student to gain another learning experience. For this to happen, questions must be asked in a positive, reinforcing manner—that is, so that the student will enjoy learning and responding. All students should receive positive reinforcement from the questions being asked as well as for the responses elicited. Thus questions should *never* be used for punitive purposes. The teacher who asks a question to punish a student is turning a positive learning situation into a negatively reinforcing one. The result is that the teacher not only "turns off" the learner but also shuts down the learning process. This is extremely critical, especially when working with students with learning disabilities or young students. In short, our philosophy is that questioning must be used only in ways that are meaningful, purposeful, and positively reinforcing.

Questioning must serve purposeful ends.

Framing Questions

The basic rule for asking questions is as follows: *ask the question, pause, and then call on a student.*

This rule is grounded in the psychological truism that when a question is asked, followed by a short pause, all students will "attend" to the communication. The nonverbal message—the pause—communicates that any student in the class may be selected for a response; thus the attention level of the class remains high. If you reverse this pattern by calling on a particular student before you ask a question, all the other students may ignore the question.

To be an effective questioner, you must be able to frame clear, concise, succinct questions. For this reason teachers have been cautioned against using "uhs," false starts, uncertain pauses, and ineffective transitions between topics. All such verbal behaviors by teachers ultimately cause student uncertainty (see Gettinger and Stoiber 1999). Of all the virtues of good questioning, clarity is one of the highest on the list.

The formula for asking questions is A + P + C: ask, pause, and call on a student.

Thus the technique of **framing** (that is, of asking a question very precisely) entails asking a question, pausing, and then calling on a student. You can use this same technique even when you intend to select several students to respond. Furthermore, once you and the students have mastered this technique, you can modify the third element to the nonverbal action of simply pointing or nodding to a student for a response. This technique becomes easy with a little practice.

Wait time is essential for thoughtful student responses.

Wait Time 1   There are several reasons to use the second element in framing, the pause. First, this pause, called **Wait Time 1,** is the time between when you first ask a question and when you call on a student. It gives students a chance to think about their responses to the question. This is especially important when you ask higher-level questions.

Second, this pause gives you time to read students' nonverbal cues. With some practice you can readily observe nonverbal signals indicating pleasure, apprehension, fright, excitement, joy, or shame. As you become more sensitive to humanitarian considerations in the classroom, this dimension of teaching becomes very important.

Wait Time 2   We have described the importance of Wait Time 1. **Wait Time 2,** the pause to allow the student you have called on to respond, is equally important, since it gives the student time to think or allows other students to respond as well (Rowe 1969, 1980). Furthermore, if the teacher waits a while to respond after the initial student response, students will continue to respond—without prompting. Figure 7.2 illustrates the use of wait time.

Many teachers are impatient with students when asking questions (Rowe 1969, 1974, 1978). The wait time between asking a question and either answering it for the student or calling on another student was found to be only a few fractions of a second! Is it any wonder, then, that some students dread to be called on? They know that being called on will elicit impatient behaviors from the teacher and that they will simply be "in hot water" again.

The effectiveness of wait time has been well documented (see Stahl 1994).

FIGURE 7.2

Wait Times 1 and 2

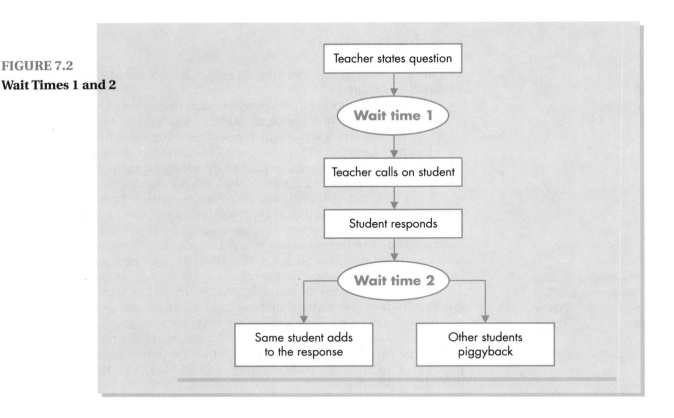

The box on page 255 lists the benefits to both teachers and students (Tobin 1987).

We do add one cautionary comment. Wait time has no effect on student responses to lower-level questions (Riley 1986), but it has a significant effect on responses to higher-level questions. Lack of wait time with higher-level questions can lead to low-level student responses.

Remember that classroom silence is not all bad—even when you are asking questions. So make the decision to wait—not only once, but twice, even three times, if students are interacting. With practice, you'll develop *the art of staying silent.*

Reflect Reflect Reflect

■ Recall your experiences as a high school or middle school student. What questioning strategies did your teachers use? Did they ever use wait time? Have you observed this technique in your most recent observations of classroom teachers?

Benefits of Wait Time

For the Teacher
- Less teacher talking
- Less repetition of questions
- Fewer questions per period
- More questions with multiple responses
- Fewer lower-level questions asked
- More probing
- Less repetition of students' responses
- More application-level questions asked
- Less disciplinary action

For the Students
- Longer responses
- More student discourse and questions
- Fewer nonresponding students
- More student involvement in lessons
- Increased complexity of answers and improved reasoning
- More responses from slower students
- More peer interaction and fewer peer interruptions
- Less confusion
- More confidence
- Higher achievement

The use of wait time provides many educational benefits.

Prompting Techniques

Once you have asked a question and called on a student to respond, the student may not answer the question the way you want him or her to, or he or she may not answer at all. When this happens, you should prompt the student. You may do this by clarifying the question, by eliciting a fuller response, or by eliciting additional responses from the student to allow you to verify whether he or she comprehends the material (Dann 1995). As you develop prompting skills, you can follow many rules. However, to simplify matters, keep one rule foremost in mind: *prompt in a positive manner.*

You may have to prompt a student many times during a questioning session to evoke a more complete or logical response. Always provide positive reinforcement so that the student will be encouraged to complete an incomplete response or revise an incorrect one. In many cases a student will answer with a *partially* correct response. When you hear such a response, immediately begin to prompt the student so that the response can be completed, be made more logical, be reexamined, or be stated more appropriately.

Instructional

Strategies

Prompting Techniques

Example 1

Teacher: What did the English citizens and American colonists think a constitution should be like? (Pause) Hector?

Hector: Well . . . um . . . they figured it was a bunch of laws all written down in one place.

Teacher: That's a good description of the American point of view. Now . . . what did the English think?

Hector: They thought the laws should be written down in different places . . . sort of.

Teacher: Okay . . . that's part of the answer. Now, did *all* the laws for the English constitution have to be written down?

Hector: Some stuff was just rules that had been set up, and everybody knew what they were and followed them. But others were written down in many different . . . ah . . . documents.

Teacher: Fine! Now, how about going back and listing the main points on what you've worked out so far?

Example 2

Teacher: Class, now let's examine the data that we collected on our experiment on absorption and radiation. What differences did you observe between the covered and uncovered shiny pans? (Three- to five-second pause.) Angela?

Angela: The water in the covered pan had a temperature of 96 degrees.

Teacher: At what point in the experiment was that temperature measured?

Angela: After the pan had been covered for 10 minutes.

Teacher: What was the temperature of the water when you took the first reading?

The teacher prompts the student in a nonthreatening or neutral verbal tone (including all the nonverbal cues). The episode continues until the student provides all the necessary information for an appropriate closure.

Use prompting to help support a struggling student.

The Instructional Strategies box above illustrates two possible prompting techniques. Observe that in the first example, the teacher tries to focus the student's ideas. In the second example, the student's response is recast to answer the question that was asked. In both cases the teacher is trying to use some aspect of the student's responses to keep the episode positive.

Handling Incorrect Responses

No matter how skillful a teacher is at motivating students, providing adequate and relevant instructional materials, and asking high-quality questions, one continual problem will detract from both the intellectual and the interpersonal aspects of classroom questioning sessions—incorrect student responses.

As we discussed previously, you may use prompting techniques when students' responses are partially correct or stated incompletely. Prompting is an easy technique, because you can reinforce the positive aspect of a student's response while ignoring the negative or incomplete component. However, when a student gives a totally incorrect response, a more complex interpersonal situation arises. First, it's hard to reinforce positively in such a case. But comments such as "No," "You are *way* off," or "That is incorrect" should be avoided because they all act as negative reinforcers and may reduce that student's desire to participate in a verbal classroom interaction. This is critical, especially with students whose first language is not English.

Second, if you respond negatively to an incorrect student response, there is a high probability that a **ripple effect** will occur (Kounin 1970). This effect describes the way in which students who are not themselves the target of a teacher's negative behavior are still negatively affected by what the teacher says or does to another class member. Therefore, when a student gives an incorrect response, try to move to a neutral prompting technique rather than responding with, "No, that is not at all correct."

How should you do this? Because the entire approach to this method is to stress the positive, you might first analyze the student's verbal response to determine whether any portion of it can be classified as valid, appropriate, or correct. After you make this split-second decision, you then provide positive reinforcement or praise for the correct portion of the response. For example, if you ask a general mathematics question and the student gives a totally incorrect answer, then you might state, "Your response is in the magnitude of the answer," "Could you tell us how you arrived at your answer?" or "Could you rethink your solution and take another try at it?" These responses are *neutral*, not negative.

Another strategy is to rephrase the question, to remove from the student the onus for incorrectly answering the original question. You can carefully lead the student to a correct response with a set of convergent questions.

Always avoid being sarcastic or punishing. If you use a punishing verbal response, then you are, in fact, using a "put-down" strategy. Such a strategy provides negative reinforcers and ultimately has unpleasant residual effects, because it causes students to ignore opportunities to respond verbally. Verbal abuse is never an appropriate or professional response.

When carrying out this strategy, you must be careful that nonverbal cues—such as frowning—do not show that you are upset or angered by the incorrect response. You must maintain congruency between your verbal and nonverbal behaviors when handling incorrect responses. (See Chapter 6 for a list of positive verbal and nonverbal responses.)

Another strategy for helping a student correct a response is to immediately

Be patient and thoughtful in responding to incorrect student answers.

Avoid giving negative nonverbal signals.

assess the type and level of question you asked and then ask the student a similar but less difficult question, without making any other comments. Always react flexibly; give students the opportunity to show that they know *some* answer.

Interpersonal relationships between teachers and students are delicate and take time to build. After you have assessed each student's personality type, you may find that it is appropriate to use some negative as well as positive reinforcers with certain students. It is not uncommon for better students to clown or joke with the teacher or to kid the teacher. When you see such situations developing, you can predict fairly accurately how a specific student will react, and you can then humor that student.

The Instructional Strategies box below illustrates a number of different ways to handle incorrect responses.

In these examples, the teacher's response does not criticize the student. A primary goal of schooling is to provide a positive and stimulating environ-

Learning can be impeded by insults or put-downs from the teacher.

Instructional *Strategies*

Handling Incorrect Responses

Example 1

Teacher: What relationships did we find between the hypotenuse and sides of a right triangle? (Pause) Peggy?

Peggy: Well, we did some squaring of a side. I forgot.

Teacher: Okay. Now think of the model that the class constructed. Can you visualize it in your mind? What did those constructions look like?

Example 2

Teacher: What was one of the military reforms instituted by Senator Harry Truman? (Pause) Joe?

Joe: Didn't he want to stop building forts?

Teacher: What was it about building the forts that he challenged?

Joe: Was it something about costs and waste?

Teacher: You're on the right track now. What were some of the wasteful practices that he uncovered?

Example 3

Teacher: In this house plan, the living room windows face west. Is that a good idea? (Pause) Isadore?

Isadore: I think it's great. You can see the sunset straight on.

Teacher: Izzy's answer is a good example of individual priorities in house design. To some people, the advantage of being able to view sunsets is very important. What kinds of weather-related problems might be created, though, Izzy, if the large windows face west?

Reflect Reflect Reflect

- Recall your own experiences as a student. To what extent did your teachers employ the positive behaviors discussed here?
- Participate with a group of peers in a role-playing exercise in which you have to respond to incorrect or completely illogical student responses. Do you find it difficult to prompt positively? Why?

ment in which learning can take place. Learning is blocked by insults and negative teacher responses. The student learns nothing by humiliation—except to despise the teacher and to hate school. We hope you will create an atmosphere in your classes that is supportive—one in which students can react freely without the fear of being wrong. Again, you must be *aware* of how you behave.

Section 4: Using Questioning to Create a Dynamic Learning Environment

In Section 3 of this chapter, we discussed some prompting techniques you can use to help your students become more successful. Now let's focus on how you increase student verbal interaction and reduce yours. You see, we want your students to go home tired from thinking and working—and you to go home refreshed.

Promoting Multiple Responses

As noted earlier, teachers typically conduct recitation periods by questioning: they ask one student to respond, than another student to respond, and so on. For the most part the teacher does the talking. Few students, if any, listen carefully to their peers' responses, because at any one time there is a closed communication circuit between two individuals: the teacher and one student. We recommend that you avoid this closed technique and instead use **multiple-response questions,** which are questions to which at least three or four students respond. The key to increasing the number of students who respond to each question is to emphasize divergent and evaluative questions. These types of questions allow for many different responses. In the multiple-response technique, you ask a question, pause, and then call on three or four students to respond.

Of course, before you use the multiple-response technique, you must carefully explain it to the class. Also caution students that you will not repeat any student responses. Thus students must listen carefully to their peers' responses so that they will not repeat them.

The multiple-response strategy allows for longer student responses,

The multiple-response technique shifts more activity to the students.

greater depth in student statements, and greater challenges for all students. Thus the use of multiple-response techniques is a logical precursor to student-conducted **discussions.** Student discussions are extremely difficult to conduct effectively, because many students do not demonstrate the needed behaviors or skills. By using multiple-response questions, you subtly condition students to accept more responsibility for listening to one another and to modify their responses based on previous ones.

The multiple-response strategy also allows the teacher to speak less. It is difficult for you to be an empirical observer of student behavior, direct a question-and-answer period, manage the classroom, and plan for appropriate questions—all at the same time. You cannot listen and talk simultaneously. But if you use divergent or evaluative questions coupled with the multiple-response strategy, you will have time to analyze the responses that are being given. In short, you will be able to make a qualitative evaluation of each student's response.

In a slight modification of the technique, you can subdivide the class into teams of three, four, or five students to add the motivating factors of small-group solidarity and identification. You ask a divergent or evaluative question of the class. Each group discusses it and then a spokesperson responds. This situation increases student-to-student verbal interaction. (You can further facilitate students' interaction by rearranging their desks.) Any competition that develops within the class will be peer oriented rather than between teacher and student. Friendly intraclassroom competition can be established by incorporating some type of "game" into the lesson.

Teachers tend to be parsimonious with rewards. But by using this variation of the multiple-response strategy, you can reward one group for providing the most novel responses, another for the best responses obtained from an encyclopedia, another for the best nonverbal responses (pictures, cartoons, posters), and another for the best multimedia presentation. All these are motivational strategies that help make the classroom an enjoyable, creative, and interesting place.

The Instructional Strategies box on page 261 illustrates the multiple-response technique. Notice how the teacher frames a question and then calls on three or four students to answer it.

When you use the multiple-response technique, you also build other communication skills in students. For example, when you start using this technique, you can ask students to write one-sentence summaries of each response given by their peers. Think of the implications of this simple teaching technique for improving listening skills; structuring logical discussions; identifying the main points in an oral discourse; enabling students to classify arguments, positions, or statements systematically; and learning to outline. Since questioning is such a widely used communication technique in the classroom, it follows that teachers should maximize the usefulness of questioning so that it improves other cognitive skills and processes as well.

Again, the use of the multiple-response technique is an excellent way to ease the class into student-led discussion. We recommend, however, that such discussions be postponed until the multiple-response technique is mastered by teachers and students alike.

Instructional

Strategies

The Multiple Response Technique

Teacher: Today I'm going to use a new technique that we'll continue using from here on. I'll ask you a question, pause for a few seconds, and then call on three or four of you for responses. Listen carefully, because I won't repeat the question. Furthermore, listen to your classmates as they respond, because I will not repeat any of their responses either. Any questions? Okay? Where might Christopher Columbus have landed if he had set sail from London and headed due west? (Pause) Trudy, Raphael, Billy, Tommie.

Trudy: He'd have landed in Canada.

Teacher: (Smiles and points, without comment, to Raphael)

Raphael: I think he would miss Canada and land near Boston, because the Pilgrims landed in that area.

Teacher: (Nods head and points to Billy, without verbal comment)

Billy: You're both off. He'd have been blown to Greenland.

Tommie: That would not happen, either. Christopher Columbus would have been blown by the Gulf Stream winds right back to England.

Teacher: Those are all interesting ideas. Class, let's check the direction of the Gulf Stream and the air currents. Hermie, will you please get the big map of ocean and air currents from the closet and give us a reading?

Hermie: Okay.

Reflect Reflect Reflect

- Select a favorite teaching topic and write two questions to use with the multiple-response technique.

- In your next class, tabulate the number of responses that are teacher initiated and those that are student initiated.

- What topics might be inappropriate for interactive questioning techniques?

Conducting Review Sessions

How can you review previously taught concepts using questioning strategies? One successful method is to reintroduce previously discussed concepts in the context of newly presented material. For example, if you are teaching a unit on transportation and you wish to review the topic of railroads, which has already been covered, you could compare the placement of airports and bus stations with that of railroad stations as part of a discussion on transportation infrastructures. Through questioning, you could elicit from students the fact that most railroad terminals, like airports, were initially built at the edges of cities. Students would then have the opportunity to demonstrate their comprehension of city growth, noting that transportation terminals become engulfed as cities expanded and that this, in turn, causes a set of problems unique to cities and the transportation industry.

What we are suggesting, as a viable alternative to dedicated review sessions, is continual review. Such review may be conducted at any level of Bloom's taxonomy. As students begin to relate previously learned skills or concepts to new ones, they may begin to perceive the relationships between old and new material. If you wish to use the true basic liberal arts approach, then you should relate the ideas of one discipline to those of other disciplines. But instead of *telling* students about subtle interdisciplinary relationships, you can direct them to the library or the Internet so that they may discover them on their own and report them to the class. This is particularly useful for those students who are always finished with their work and have "nothing to do"—except disrupt the class. (See Gagliardi 1996 for other examples.)

Build in concept review questions each week and each month.

To use the **concept review questioning technique**, you must always be on the alert for instances that will allow you to establish meaningful relationships,

Instructional Strategies

Concept Review Questioning Technique

Teacher: How does the taxonomy of the cognitive domain, which we studied last month, differ from the taxonomy of the affective domain? (Pause) Bill?

Bill: The cognitive domain is concerned with the intellectual aspects of learning, while the affective domain is more concerned with emotional outcomes.

Teacher: Good. Can you list some examples of these "emotional outcomes"? (Pause) Mary?

Mary: Attitudes and values?

Teacher: Fine. Now, going back to my original question, how are the two taxonomies similar? (Pause) Sally?

Sally: Well, because they both are called taxonomies, they both are classification systems, and both are hierarchical in nature.

Teacher: Excellent. What do we mean by "hierarchical" in nature? (Pause) Bill?

Bill: I think it means that each category builds on the ones below it.

Teacher: Okay, could you give us an example of another kind of taxonomy that would illustrate your point?

Instructional

Strategies

Concept Review Questioning Technique (cont.)

Bill: Sure, the taxonomy of the animal kingdom. Each phylum supposedly is related in some evolutionary fashion to the one below it.

Teacher: Good. Does everyone see how that example applies to Bloom's taxonomy? Okay, let's take a second now and try to relate the module on the taxonomy to previous modules. In other words, how could we use the taxonomy with some of the other ideas we've talked about? (Pregnant silence, which does not last for long.) Let me try to be more specific. How could the taxonomy be used in constructing better lesson plans? (Pause) Jim? Mary?

Jim: You can use the taxonomy to look at your performance objective and see if your procedure correlates with the terminal behavior.

Mary: (With emotion) You could also use the taxonomy to kind of judge whether the lesson is worth doing at all.

Teacher: How do you mean, Mary?

Mary: Well, if the lesson consists of nothing more than transmitting a lot of facts, maybe the teacher should ask if these facts are ever going to be used again in one of the higher categories. And if the facts are important, there are more effective ways of having the students master them than by recitation.

Teacher: Good. Anything else? (Pause) How about the discussion module? Can you make any connections with the taxonomy? (Pause) Al?

Al: Kind of going along with what we said about lesson plans, the taxonomy might give teachers some new ideas about discussion topics.

Teacher: Could you elaborate?

Al: Well, sometimes it's easy to get in a rut. Though teachers aren't likely to use discussions with performance objectives at the knowledge level, they may not be aware of the full range of possibilities open for discussion topics.

Teacher: Excellent. Anyone else?

Tina: Also, the taxonomy might be useful in analyzing why discussions bog down.

Teacher: In what respect?

Tina: If the students are attempting thought processes at the higher levels and don't have the background at the lower levels, there's likely to be a lot of confusion because the students don't "know" or "comprehend" what they're talking about.

> ## Reflect Reflect Reflect
>
> ■ What topics were reviewed in the preceding example? How could you design lessons that would incorporate concept review as a regular component?
>
> ■ Give an example of a lesson you could design that would incorporate concept review. List the main topic and other topics you would review.

reinforce previously learned concepts, or synthesize students' knowledge, and thereby create added motivation for the class. More importantly, you will be using the technique of "ideational scaffolding," or "bridging," that is, diagramming a concept map on the chalk board and showing how other ideas or concepts relate to it.

The boxes on pages 262 and 263 illustrates the concept review questioning technique. The class is studying the affective domain.

Encouraging Nonvolunteers

In most situations you will not have much problem encouraging students to respond to questions. To be sure, if you kept careful records of which students respond to questions, you would find that a few students dominate recitation sessions. Furthermore, observation of any class tends to show that there are several students who do not volunteer responses. If your goal is to encourage verbal responses, then you must encourage nonvolunteers to respond. Such encouragement is most difficult at the beginning of a new term, when you are relatively new to the students. As you become more knowledgeable about your students' interests, it becomes easier to prompt nonvolunteers, because you can ask questions that relate to their individual areas of interest. What, then, are some helpful strategies to motivate nonvolunteers to respond during questioning sessions?

Maintain a highly positive attitude toward nonvolunteering students. Allow them to respond appropriately or correctly each time they are called on. In other words, ask nonvolunteers questions that they will be likely to answer successfully. Once the student has responded appropriately, give generous positive feedback to encourage him or her to continue responding. Ask questions that require short responses *but lead to other questions that require longer responses*. Thus you will progress from a convergent frame of reference to a more divergent one. You may even begin by using easy evaluative questions, because most students respond readily to questions that concern judgment, standards, or opinions.

You should attempt to determine why each nonvolunteer remains quiet. Is the student merely shy, or is there a language disability? We do not mean that you should play the role of an amateur psychologist, but you should determine whether a specific student manifests a speech deficit and, if necessary, make an appropriate referral.

Another method for increasing nonvolunteer participation is to occasionally make a game out of questioning. For example, place each student's name on a card and draw cards at random to select respondents. Or if certain students always raise their hands when you ask a question, you can politely ask these students to "hold all hands for the next three minutes" so that other students may have an opportunity to respond. In this way you can shape the behavior of those students who are already adequately reinforced through verbal participation to allow other students to respond.

In addition, there is nothing wrong with giving each nonvolunteering student a card with a question on it the day before the intended oral recitation period. Very quietly, hand these students their cards and tell them they may review the assignment so that they can summarize their responses for the next class period. This method begins to build a trusting relationship between teacher and student.

You can provide prompts to encourage shy students.

Implicit in this technique is the task of systematically recording who is volunteering responses in class recitations, and in what class situations. If time permits, it would even be desirable to keep a daily record of each student's verbal activity. You could appoint one member of the class to keep such a tally each day. At the end of a week, you will begin to see patterns for each student.

Again, we condemn the technique of calling on nonvolunteers as punishment. Schooling ought to be a positive, enjoyable experience that makes students *want* to learn. As a general rule, the most effective way to encourage nonvolunteers to participate is to treat each student sincerely and as a human being. Many nonvolunteers have learned—sometimes painfully—that it does not pay to say anything in class because the teacher will put them down. No one likes to put a hand in a hot fire. No student will volunteer if his or her response will be met with sarcasm, witty innuendoes, snide remarks, or hostility. Be highly considerate and approving at all times.

Developing Students' Questioning Skills

The techniques discussed so far all have been oriented toward improving your questioning skills. The following technique is an attempt to teach students how to frame their *own* questions.

For the most part, teachers neither encourage nor teach their students to ask questions. Some teachers are even upset when students do ask questions (see Commeyras 1995). However, if you, as an educator, desire to encourage critical or reflective thinking, or thinking of any sort, then you must develop your students' skill at framing questions (Ciardiello 1993). To aid in such a strategy, we refer to a game made famous many years ago on radio—Twenty Questions.

In Twenty Questions, participants ask questions in order to identify something. The teacher thinks of some problem or concept, and students attempt to discover it through questioning. Initially you will conduct the session, but as students master the technique and develop their questioning skills, you can let them conduct the entire session. This will leave you free to analyze their interactions.

Twenty Questions is similar to the Inquiry Development Program (Suchmann 1966), which emphasizes the development of student questioning skills. In the Inquiry Development Program the teacher presents some problem or question to students and then plays a passive role, responding only with yes or no to students' questions as they attempt to solve the problem or answer the question. This means that students must learn how to ask questions on which they can build a pyramid of knowledge that ultimately leads to a convergent response. Consider this example: a group of students has just watched a multimedia presentation showing a baseball catcher and a baseball that takes very wide curves. The teacher asks for explanations.

Student: Is that a real baseball?
Teacher: Yes.
Student: Is that magic?
Teacher: No.
Student: How does it work?
Teacher: I can only answer a "yes" or "no" question.
Student: Is the catcher standing still?
Teacher: Yes.
Student: Is the catcher on a moving platform?
Teacher: Yes.
Student: Is the pitcher on the moving platform?
Teacher: No.
Student: Is this an example of relative motion?
Teacher: Yes.
Student: Is there more to this discussion?
Teacher: Yes.

This line of questioning would continue until a student or group of students could explain the entire event.

When this technique is first used, students tend not to ask the teacher logical questions, since much of schooling requires little logic, causing initial results to be discouraging. However, the teacher should review each lesson and then give students precise and detailed directions on how their questioning logic can be improved. As one alternative, if it will not be too slow, the teacher may write each student's question on a chalkboard or transparency. This will allow students to accumulate information and skills gradually and in a systematic manner. (See Chahrour 1994 for an extension of this technique.)

Of course, to develop effective questioning skills it is imperative that students have the ability to formulate questions that address a specific point, not some vague one. The teacher can demonstrate how to develop this ability by moving from a general point of reference to a specific one. (In other words, use a deductive logic questioning process, and encourage students to do the same.)

Another method of developing students' questioning skills is to have them prepare study or recitation questions ahead of time about the subject being studied. Select a few students each day to prepare a series of questions for their peers. You might even share with students a few of the questioning techniques discussed here, such as following Bloom's taxonomy. To be sure, most students will be oriented only toward the knowledge level, because that is what is reinforced the most in their schooling. But a skillful teacher will continually reinforce those questions that are aimed at higher-level thinking skills and will ultimately help students prepare appropriate higher-level questions.

Make every effort to encourage students to ask questions.

Multiple question technique is a first step toward conducting authentic classroom discussions.

As you begin to encourage class members to ask questions of one another, there is a subtle shift of responsibility away from the teacher and toward the students (Rallis et al. 1995). This shift implies that responsibility is a learned behavior. As a teacher, you owe it to your students to help them become articulate and thinking individuals. You have a splendid opportunity to do so when you transfer more responsibility for classroom questioning to them (see Richetti and Sheerin 1999). Additionally, you will be creating the conditions necessary for student-initiated learning (Commeyras and Sumner 1996; Callison 1997).

Like all new methods, this one must be explained carefully to students and then practiced for a few class periods. Then, once a week or more often, students can conduct questioning sessions on their own. This method is a prerequisite experience to student-led discussions. If you teach children with learning disabilities or exceptional children, they can display their responses (and questions) on cards (Heward 1996).

A very novel technique for creating a more interactive questioning session is to have the students *question the author.* Isabel L. Beck and her colleagues (1997) illustrate how you can encourage students to ask questions of the texts that they read, just as if the author of the text were standing in the classroom. Students are shown how to initiate queries in three forms (Beck et al. 1997, p. 34):

1. What is the author trying to say here?
2. What is the author's message?
3. What is the author talking about?

These queries are then followed with other student questions as they construct the author's meaning (see Kucan and Beck 1997). This technique is very handy when you study complex topics or the textbook is difficult to comprehend. Now you have one more way to create an active learning environment in what is traditionally a dull one!

You and the class may generate a set of criteria on which to base student-framed questions. The criteria may also be applied to a broader context. Students can be requested to evaluate the kinds of questions that are asked on various television quiz shows as a means of improving their own skills in data collection and interpretation.

Include student-led questioning periods as part of your unit plans.

All the teachers we have worked with since 1968 have been pleased with the results of the techniques described here. More important, they were all amazed at how much they had underestimated their students' potential. We are not suggesting that these techniques are simple to implement; they take much work and planning. But the attendant rewards make both teaching and learning more worthwhile.

Reflect Reflect Reflect

- With a small group of your peers, discuss how you can incorporate many different questioning techniques during your first year on the job.

Teacher Idiosyncrasies: A Caution

Up to this point we have been discussing only those teacher behaviors associated with questioning that are positive and encouraging. We hope we haven't made you think that you need only a few tricks and a smile to achieve instant success. Unfortunately, inappropriate teacher behaviors can interfere with smooth verbal interaction in the classroom. These behaviors, or **idiosyncrasies,** include repeating the question, repeating all student responses, answering the question yourself, not allowing a student to complete a long response, not attending to the responding student, and always selecting the same student respondents. Each of these behaviors is analyzed in the following sections:

Repeating the Question   A common error often made by teachers is the regular repetition of each question. This habit conditions students to catch the "replay" of the question instead of attending to it the first time, either cognitively or intuitively. Moreover, this habit causes a loss of valuable time and does not help the teacher efficiently manage the classroom. To be sure, there are appropriate times to repeat questions: when the class is in a very large room with poor acoustics, when the question is multifaceted, when the question was not adequately framed the first time, or when you are dictating a question to the class. We do caution that beginning teachers often have difficulty framing verbal questions that students will understand. In such cases, rephrase the question for added clarity. Repeating a question may also be appropriate when you use divergent questions. In most cases, though, avoid repeating a question.

Read the following two sets of repeated questions aloud to friends or colleagues and obtain their reactions.

> **Teacher:** What is the main set of criteria by which to frame questions? What main set of criteria can be used by which to frame questions?
> **Teacher:** What is the population of Boston? What is Boston's population? How many people live in Boston?

How did they respond to these repetitious questions? Listen to teachers or professors in oral discourse to determine whether they repeat their questions. If you have not observed this idiosyncratic pattern, then obtain a tape recorder, tape a simulated version of the pattern (that is, of a teacher repeating questions), and play it back to a small group of peers. We will wager that after listening to a few of these simulated episodes, your audience will be highly amused. This may make a creative term project for your methods class.

Repeating Students' Responses   An equally distracting and time-wasting habit is that of repeating all or nearly all of your students' verbal responses. Not only is this a waste of time, it causes class members to ignore their peers as sources of information, and it subtly conditions them to wait until the word comes from the "fount of all wisdom." Students do not attend to their peers' initial responses; instead they wait for the "instant replay" from the teacher. If you are sensitive to the need to build positive student self-images, you will not want to be the center of verbal interaction: you will keep the focus on the responding student. After all, if it is important to call on a student and require a response, then it ought to be equally important to listen to that response.

This general rule does not hold for large-group sessions, however. Because most large-group rooms or halls have poor seating arrangements, you must almost always repeat student responses so that all can hear. The same is true for students with very soft voices. But in the vast majority of cases, there is no need to repeat student responses.

If students are to develop prediscussion behaviors, then they must learn to take cues from one another. You must establish the appropriate climate for this to occur. The introduction of true discussions is then the next logical step.

Answering the Question   Have you ever observed or participated in a class in which the teacher carefully frames a question, pauses, calls on a student, and then answers the question himself? This idiosyncrasy is a morale defeater. How can students be encouraged to think when they know that the teacher will not allow them to voice their opinions? This behavior tends to discourage volunteering and causes students to be negatively reinforced. If a question is so complex that no student can answer it, rephrase it, begin prompting, or assign it as a research project.

Not Allowing a Student to Complete a Long Response   One very distracting, inappropriate, and rude teacher idiosyncrasy is to ask a question and then interrupt the student by completing the response or by adding personal comments without attempting to elicit other student responses. Consider the following example:

> **Teacher:** What impact did the Vietnam War have on our young people? (Pause) Arnie?
> **Arnie:**   Well, I sure don't trust . . .
> **Teacher:** Right, you kids really don't have the confidence in our government that my generation did. Why, I can remember when I was in high school. . . .

Teachers who suffer from excessive verbosity frustrate students. Worse, they do not allow students to develop logical response systems. Interrupting students discourages them from even participating in the recitation period.

Not Attending to the Responding Student   When you call on a student, show courtesy to that student by attending to (that is, listening to) him or her. After all, if you expect to instill attending habits in students, this habit should be reciprocated during verbal interactions with them. How would you feel if you were responding in class and the teacher was gazing out the window or counting some loose change? Teachers often fail to reinforce appropriate stu-

Repeating questions reinforces inattentive student behaviors.

Not attending is simply rude teacher behavior.

dent behaviors in class simply because they are being insensitive to the feelings of others.

Always Selecting the Same Student Respondents   One frequently heard student complaint is that "my teacher never calls on me" or that "the teacher has a few pets who are always being called on." These statements typify the frustrations of students who recognize partiality when they see it. The teacher who calls on only a few (usually highly verbal and successful) students provides a negative reinforcer to the majority of the class members, makes them lose interest in the subject, and causes serious erosion of group morale.

If you are skeptical, let us remind you of a classic study conducted in a Chicago elementary school. A teacher in a primary grade exhibited great bias in selecting students for class recitations (Rist 1970). Fewer and fewer individuals were called on by the teacher, until only a select few were. To make matters worse, the teacher began to move the responding pupils up to the front seats and the nonrespondents to the rear of the room. Needless to say, there were tremendous disparities between the educational achievement of the students in the front rows and that of the other students. The teacher and pupils were all of the same ethnic group, so racism can be eliminated as the basis for bias. This may be an extreme case, but in general such situations exist to varying degrees. For example, in mathematics classes there is a tendency to call on boys more than girls. You can avoid bias by giving equal opportunity to every student in the conduct of recitations, regardless of what questioning technique you use.

Be cognizant of instructional equity.

How Teachers Treat Low Achievers

- Giving them less time to answer a question.
- Giving them answers, or calling on others rather than trying to improve the low achievers' responses by giving clues or repeating or rephrasing questions.
- Reinforcing inappropriately: rewarding their inappropriate behavior or incorrect answers.
- Criticizing them more often for failure.
- Praising them less frequently than high achievers for success.
- Failing to give feedback to their public responses.
- Paying less attention to them or interacting with them less frequently.
- Calling on them less often to respond to questions or asking them easier, nonanalytical questions.
- Seating them at a distance from the teacher.
- Using less eye contact and other nonverbal means of communicating attention and responsiveness (such as leaning forward and nodding the head) in interactions with them.

SOURCE: T. L. Good and J. E. Brophy, *Looking in Classrooms* (8th edition). Copyright © 2000 by Longman. Reprinted by permission of Longman Publishers, Inc.

You can show your expectations in many ways.

Many teachers exhibit strong biases against "academically poorer" students. The box on page 270 lists a few of the *intentionally disinviting* teacher behaviors exhibited toward these students.

A quick way to determine whether you show bias is to ask a different student each day to list the number of times that you call on each student. A quick tally at the end of the week will provide the data.

It is tempting to call on students who often volunteer and who will give you the "right" answer, so that you will appear to be an effective teacher. But if you wish to encourage all your students to be winners, then you must accord them an equal opportunity to respond. One motto is fairly accurate in this case: "Nothing breeds success like success." If students are hesitant about responding verbally, then you must gear your questions to their needs and abilities so that they too can enjoy the feeling of success and positive reinforcement.

Achieving the Right Attitudes About Questioning

Using systematic questioning is a pathway to instructional equity.

If you perceive that we are attempting to make a "game" of schooling, then you may be absolutely correct. School ought to be a place in which one may have fun or at least have a positive experience while learning. The idea that if something is fun it must be bad is totally inappropriate. If learning can be made meaningful and relevant, then students will enjoy it. A great deal of research has demonstrated that students have a strong interest in, and like, those areas in which they are successful. If mathematics is distasteful to some students, it is because, for the most part, they have been unsuccessful at it. Such an attitude can be rectified easily by making mathematics, or any other subject, success-oriented. The essence of mastery learning is that interest is a function of success.

All these questioning strategies provide you with important tools of the trade. But they are just that—tools. Each technique must be used appropriately and must be congruent with your objective for a specified student, group of students, or class.

Because questions play such an important part in the learning process, we have attempted to provide you with a cognitively ordered set of questioning alternatives based on "if-then" logic. Our goal is to increase the number of techniques available to you so that whenever you pose a question, you cognitively and automatically know what you are attempting to do with the students. We also believe that questioning sessions in classrooms ought to be constructive and cheerful experiences in which students' opinions are respected, their interests stimulated, and their minds challenged. And questioning is another tool that ensures that quality that we strongly advocate—*instructional equity.*

These techniques are empirically validated!

Speaking of challenges, despite the fact that the techniques described in this chapter have powerful effects on student achievement, thousands of teachers and principals refuse to adopt them. Unquestionably, school culture can be very anti-intellectual and way behind the times in helping kids to learn. Maybe you can help by demonstrating the efficacy of this empirically validated interactive method!

A Closing Reflection Reflection Reflection

- Describe the questioning techniques you have observed in your teacher education courses. Do they match the techniques described here?
- Arrange to microteach lessons to practice the art of questioning.
- What kinds of lessons lend themselves to convergent, divergent, evaluative, and reflective questions?
- Why is it useful to apply a taxonomy to your questions?
- Examine the effects on students of Wait Time 1 and Wait Time 2 in your classes by collecting data on student responses. Do students provide higher-level responses when teachers use wait time?
- Review a few studies relating to teacher responses to incorrect student answers. Are there any conclusions that differ from ours?
- What is equity in questioning?

Summary

1. The convergent strategy elicits short or even one-word responses.
2. The divergent strategy elicits varied student responses.
3. The evaluative strategy elicits a divergent response plus a rationale.
4. The reflective strategy helps students actively develop a concept.
5. Hierarchies or taxonomies may be used to categorize questions.
6. Students need to be encouraged to ask questions in class.
7. Using wait time is a powerful technique to aid student learning.
8. Teachers need to develop skills in prompting, handling incorrect responses, prompting multiple responses, framing review questions, and encouraging nonvolunteers.
9. Positive responses to incorrect answers encourage continued student participation.
10. Teacher idiosyncrasies can interfere with student learning.
11. Stress the positive and avoid sarcasm and cynicism.
12. Provide opportunities for equity in responding.

Key Terms

concept review questioning technique (p. 262)

convergent questions (p. 245)

discussions (p. 260)

divergent questions (p. 246)

evaluative criteria (p. 249)

evaluative questions (p. 249)

framing (p. 253)

idiosyncrasies (p. 268)

multiple-response questions
    (p. 259)

recitation (p. 240)

reflective question (p. 250)

ripple effect (p. 257)

Wait Time 1 (p. 253)

Wait Time 2 (p. 253)

Helpful Resources

Below are three carefully selected resources that will provide you with an expanded knowledge base about the art of questioning.

Beck, I. L., M. G. McKeown, R. L. Hamilton, and L. Kucan. *Questioning the Author: An Approach for Enhancing Student Engagement with Text.* Newark, DE: International Reading Association, 1997, 122 pp.

The authors provide a teaching strategy for engaging students to interact with the text materials. This is an application of student-initiated questions.

Freedman, R. L. H. *Open-Ended Questioning: A Handbook for Educators.* Menlo Park, CA: Addison-Wesley, 1994, 81 pp.

The author provides an easy-to-use model for teachers who want to design classroom questions that encourage higher-level thinking. There are models of scoring rubrics and plenty of examples.

Morgan, N., and J. Saxton. *Teaching Questioning and Learning.* London and New York: Routledge, 1991, 151 pp.

This user-friendly manual will give you more ideas on how to use questioning in the classroom than you'd ever believe existed. There are models, activities, and practical hints that any teacher can adopt.

Internet Resources

❖ The following URL provides a review of nineteen different topics all associated with questioning. It is a handy review site.

> **http://www.utep.nursing/3547/quest/index.htm**

❖ Columbia University's Institute for Learning Technologies Web page features documents, papers, and projects on how to increase student motivation:

> **http://www.ilt.columbia.edu/K12/index.html**

❖ Northwestern University's Institute for Learning Science allows educators to pursue questions about students, learning environments, and successful teaching.

> **http://www.ils.nwu.edu**

References

Barnette, J. J., S. Orletsky, B. Sattes, and J. Walsh. *Wait-Time: Effective and Trainable*. Paper presented at the annual meeting of the American Educational Research Association, San Francisco, April 18–22, 1995. ED 383 706.

Barr, K., and B. Dailey. *From Teaching to Learning, From Managing to Leading: Facilitation Skills to Bridge the Gap*. ED 394 567, 1996.

Beamon, G. W. *Sparking the Thinking of Students, Ages 10–14: Strategies for Teachers*. Thousand Oaks, CA: Corwin Press, 1997.

Beck, I. L., M. G. McKeown, R. L. Hamilton, and L. Kucan. *Questioning the Author: An Approach for Enhancing Student Engagement with Text*. Newark, DE: International Reading Association, 1997.

Bloom, B. S., editor. *Taxonomy of Educational Objectives. Handbook I: Cognitive Domain*. New York: David McKay, 1956.

Brophy, J., and T. L. Good. "Teacher Behavior and Student Achievement." In *Handbook of Research on Teaching* (3rd edition). Merlin C. Wittrock, editor. New York: Macmillan, 1986.

Brualdi, A. C. *Classroom Questions. ERIC/AE Digest*. Washington, DC: ERIC Clearinghouse on Assessment and Evaluation, 1998. ED 422 407.

Callison, D. "Key Term: Questioning." *School Library Media Activities Monthly* 13(6) (1997): 30–32.

Chahrour, J. "Perfecting the Question." *Science Scope* 18(2) (1994): 8–11.

Christenbury, L., and P. P. Kelly. *Questioning: A Critical Path to Critical Thinking*. Urbana, IL: ERIC Clearinghouse on Reading and Communications Skills and the National Council of Teachers of English, 1983.

Ciardiello, A. V. "Training Students to Ask Reflective Questions." *The Clearing House* 66(5) (1993): 312–314.

Commeyras, M. "What Can We Learn from Students' Questions?" *Theory into Practice* 34(2) (1995): 101–106.

Commeyras, M., and G. Sumner. *Questions Children Want to Discuss About Literature: What Teachers and Students Learned in a Second-Grade Classroom*. Athens, GA: National Reading Research Center, 1996. ED No. 390 031.

Cruickshank, D. R., and K. K. Kennedy. "Explaining." In *International Encyclopedia of Teaching and Teacher Education* (2nd edition). L. W. Anderson, editor. Tarrytown, NY: Elsevier Science, 1995, pp. 232–238.

Dana, N. F., K. L. Kelsay, D. Thomas, and D. J. Tippins. *Qualitative Interviewing and the Art of Questioning: Promises, Possibilities, Problems and Pitfalls*. Paper presented at the Qualitative Research I Education Conference, Athens, GA, January 1992. Ed 343 308.

Dann, E. "Unconsciously Learning Something: A Focus on Teacher Questioning," 1995. ED No. 389 618.

Dantonio, M., and L. V. Paradise. "Teaching Question-Answer Strategy and the Cognitive Correspondence between Teacher Questions and Learner Responses." *Journal of Research and Development in Education* 21 (Spring 1988): 71–75.

Dillon, J. T. "Cognitive Correspondence Between Question/Statement and Response." *American Educational Research Journal* 19 (1982a): 540–551.

Dillon, J. T. "Do Your Questions Promote or Prevent Thinking?" *Learning* 11 (1982b): 56–57, 59.

Dillon, J. T. *Questioning and Teaching: A Manual of Practice*. London: Croom Helm, 1987.

Dillon, J. T. *The Practice of Questioning*. London and New York: Routledge, 1990.

Elder, L., and P. Richard. "The Role of Socratic Questioning in Thinking, Teaching and Learning." *Clearing House* 71(5) (1998): 297–301.

Filippone, M. *Questioning at the Elementary Level*. M. A. Research Project. Union, New Jersey: Kean University, 1998, 37 pp.

Gagliardi, C. "Changing the Rules (Teaching Idea)." *English Journal* 85(3) (1996): 86–90.

Gall, M. D., and M. T. Artero-Boname. "Questioning." In *International Encyclopedia of Teaching and Teacher Education* (2nd edition). L. W. Anderson, editor. Tarrytown, NY: Elsevier Science, 1995, pp. 242–248.

Gettinger, M., and K. C. Stoiber. "Excellence in Teaching: Review of Instructional and Environmental Variables." In *The Handbook of School Psychology*, (3rd edition). C. R. Reynolds and T. B. Gutkin, editors. New York: John Wiley, 1999, 933–958.

Gibson, J. "Any Questions, Any Answers?" *Primary Science Review* 51 (January–February 1998): 20–21.

Glover, J. A., and A. J. Korkill. "The Implications of Cognitive Psychology for School Psychology." In *Handbook of School Psychology* (2nd edition). T. B. Gutkin and G. R. Reynolds, editors. New York: John Wiley, 1990.

Good, T. L., and J. Brophy. *Looking in Classrooms* (8th edition). New York: Longman, 2000.

Heward, W. L. "Everyone Participates in This Class: Using Response Cards to Increase Active Student Response." *Teaching Exceptional Children* 28(2) (1996): 4–10.

Joyce, B., and B. Showers. *Student Achievement Through Staff Development* (2nd edition). White Plains, NY: Longman, 1995.

Koegel, L. K., S. M. Carmarata, M. Valdez-Menchaca, and R. L. Koegel. "Setting Generalization of Question-Asking by Children with Autism." *American Journal on Mental Retardation* 102(4) (1998): 346–357.

Kounin, J. S. *Discipline and Group Management in Classrooms.* New York: Holt, Rinehart & Winston, 1970.

Kucan, L., and I. L. Beck. "Thinking Aloud and Reading Comprehension Research: Inquiry, Instruction and Social Interaction." *Review of Educational Research* 67(3) (1997): 271–299.

Martinello, M. L. "Learning to Question for Inquiry." *Educational Forum* 62(2) (1998): 164–171.

Rallis, S. F., G. B. Rossman, J. M. Phlegar, and A. Abeille. *Dynamic Teachers: Leaders of Change.* Thousand Oaks, CA: Corwin Press, 1995.

Richetti, C., and J. Sheerin. "Helping Students Ask the Right Questions." *Educational Leadership* 57(3) (1999): 58–62.

Riley, J. P. II. "The Effects of Teachers' Wait-Time and Knowledge Comprehension Questioning on Science Achievement." *Journal of Research in Science Teaching* 23 (1986): 335–342.

Risner, G. P., D. J. Skeel, and J. I. Nicholson. "A Closer Look at Textbooks." *Science and Children* 30(1) (1992): 42–45, 73.

Rist, R. C. "Student Social Class and Teacher Expectations: The Self-Fulfilling Prophecy in Ghetto Education." *Harvard Educational Review* 40 (1970): 411–451.

Rowe, M. B. "Science, Silence and Sanctions." *Science and Children* 6(6) (1969): 11–13.

Rowe, M. B. "Wait-Time and Rewards as Instructional Variables, Their Influence on Language, Logic and Fate Control. Part I: Fate Control." *Journal of Research in Science Teaching* 11 (1974): 81–94.

Rowe, M. B. "Wait, Wait, Wait." *Science and Mathematics* 78 (1978): 207–216.

Rowe, M. B. "Pausing Principles and Their Effects on Reasoning in Science." *New Directions for Community Colleges* 31 (1980): 27–34.

Savage, L. B. "Eliciting Critical Thinking Skills Through Questioning." *Clearing House* 71(5) (1998): 291–293.

Shake, M. C. Teaching Questioning: Is There an Answer?" *Reading Research and Instruction* 27 (1988): 29–39.

Stahl, R. J. *Using "Think-Time" and "Wait-Time" Skillfully in the Classroom. ERIC Digest.* Bloomington, IN: ERIC Clearinghouse for Social Studies/Social Science Education, May 1994. ED 370 885.

Suchmann, J. R. *Inquiry Development Program in Physical Science.* Chicago: Science Research Associates, 1966.

Swift, J. N., C. T. Gooding, and P. R. Swift. "Questions and Wait Time." In *Questioning and Discussion: A Multidisciplinary Study.* J. T. Dillon, editor. Norwood, NJ: Ablex Publishing, 1988.

Swift, J. N., C. T. Gooding, and P. R. Swift. "Using Research to Improve the Quality of Classroom Discussions." *Research Matters . . . to the Science Teacher.* Cincinnati: The National Association for Research in Science Teaching, 1992.

Tobin, K. "The Role of Wait-Time in Higher Cognitive Level Learning." *Review of Educational Research* 57 (1987): 69–95.

Traver, B. "What Is a Good Guiding Question?" *Educational Leadership* 55(6) (1998): 70–73.

van Zee, E., and J. Minstrell. "Using Questions to Guide Student Thinking." *Journal of the Learning Sciences* 6(2) (1997): 227–269.

Verduin, J. R. Jr., editor. "Structure of the Intellect." In *Conceptual Models in Teacher Education.* Washington, DC: American Association of Colleges of Teacher Education, 1967.

Ward, C. "Never Give 'Em a Straight Answer." *Science and Children* 35(3) (1997): 46–49.

Wilen, W. W. "Questioning, Thinking and Effective Citizenship." *Social Studies Record* 22 (1989): 4–6.

Wilen, W. W. *Questioning Skills for Teachers* (3rd edition). Washington, DC: National Education Association, 1991.

Wood, K. D., and D. K. Muth. "The Case for Improved Instruction in the Middle Grades." *Journal of Reading* 35(2) (1991): 84–90.

8

Small-Group Discussions and Cooperative Learning

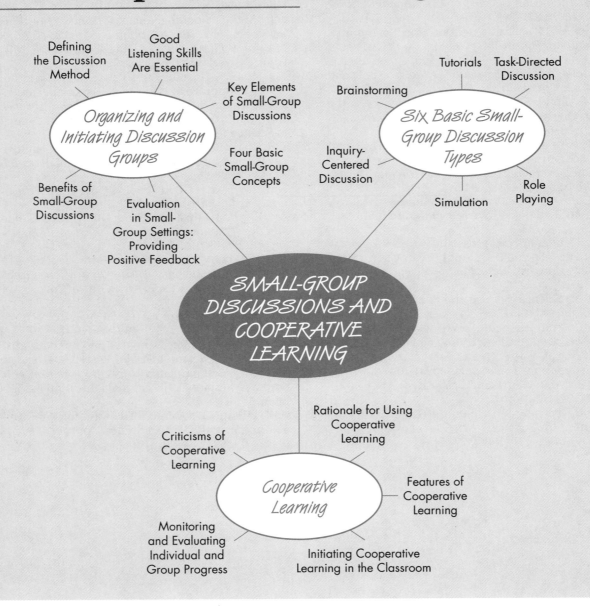

Your principal has just informed you that a demonstration lesson is being planned at the Harry S. Truman Professional Education Development Center. Your substitute takes over your class, and off you go.

On arrival and check-in you observe a classroom with thirty-two students. Their desks are arranged in circular groups, with eight students to a group. A buzz of meaningful noise emanates from the room. The teacher walks about the room, sitting in with each group but not participating verbally. After a bit, students begin to give reports to the class. Students then prepare summary statements on sheets of newsprint, and there is more interaction among them.

As the lesson ends, you are impressed with the level of responsibility and control the students have exhibited, as well as with the amount of real learning they have achieved. You wonder how to organize similar work groups in your classroom.

Using small groups is one of the best ways to promote student autonomy, cooperation, and learning in your classroom. This chapter will show you how to organize discussion, small-group, and cooperative learning experiences for your students. As you read, think about the following questions:

- How can I organize my class for small-group discussions?
- What kinds of small groups are there, and how can I use them in my classroom?
- How can I use cooperative learning in my classroom?

Section 1: Organizing and Initiating Discussion Groups

A major tenet of the constructivist philosophy of education is the importance of an active learning environment. If every student were always active in the classroom, however, chaos would soon reign. Therefore, we suggest implementing active learning by organizing the class into small groups of students who can work harmoniously, foster their own learning strategies, and create an atmosphere in which information sharing can take place. As you read this chapter, remember the following key definitions:

- *Discussions* are purposeful learning exchanges conducted by students in small groups.

Small groups are limited in size and are used for discussion, *not* recitation.

- *Small groups* are purposeful arrangements of up to six to eight students.
- *Cooperative learning* is an adaptation of the small-group teaching technique, used to promote individuals' and group members' achievement.

Defining the Discussion Method

What exactly do we mean by a "discussion" in the context of schooling? *A **discussion** is a teaching technique that involves an exchange of ideas, with active learning and participation by all concerned.*

Discussions *are not* traditional
recitation periods.

The discussion method requires the teacher to develop a viewpoint and
to tolerate and facilitate the exchange of a wide range of ideas. Discussion is
an active process of student-teacher involvement in the classroom environment. Discussion allows a student to discover and state a personal opinion or
perspective, not merely repeat what the teacher or text has already presented.
In one study, fifth-graders in discussion-based classes learned concepts and
vocabulary better than did students who only read instructional materials
(Stahl and Clark 1987). In discussion groups, students are *active learners*.

For example, a previously tracked advanced-placement high school English class was opened to all interested students. The teacher changed her
technique to use small groups, tutoring, and role playing (all discussed later).
These processes gave students more responsibility for learning and created
an opportunity for some to experience learning that had previously been denied to them (Cone 1992). This is an example of being intentionally inviting!

Besides promoting meaningful personal interaction, discussion promotes
a variety of learning, including content, skills, attitudes, and processes. It is an
appropriate way to improve both the thinking and the speaking skills of students. Discussions can also be a means of enhancing students' analytical
skills (Dillon 1994, 1995). If you desire to have different students doing different tasks or activities at the same time, all leading to meaningful goals, then
discussions are suitable. If you want to practice indirect control of learning,
then discussion is the technique to use.

Before we discuss the specific links between classroom discussion and
the use of small groups, we will focus on a fundamental skill that you and
your students must develop to participate in successful discussions.

Good Listening Skills Are Essential

All discussions involve verbal interaction. This means that without good listeners, a meaningful discussion cannot take place. Being a good listener is
partly a matter of attitude and partly a matter of skill, so you and your students have two things to practice—positive attitudes and listening skills. From
our work with students and others (Field 1998), we have gathered tips that
can help you become systematic and thorough in fostering listening in the
classroom.

Begin by modeling excellent listening habits for your students. Observe
yourself: Do you lean forward, make eye contact, and show interest in students? Or do you fidget, look away, show boredom, or walk around the classroom? The former behaviors are indicators of listening; the latter indicate that
you couldn't care less. You must give your students nonverbal feedback when
they talk to you. Your nonverbal posture is the only way that they have of determining if you really heard and understood what was said. Also observe
whether you reinforce students for listening to one another.

Listening skills must be taught
or at least reviewed.

Follow up the modeling tips with these tips on instructional practices.
First, use short and simple directions. Children in the early grades can usually
remember only one or two directions. Even older students forget if you give
long directions or a series of directions at a time. (Write detailed sets of directions on paper and hand them out to students.) Second, do not keep repeating and explaining the directions. Expect students to listen the first time.

Instructional

Strategies

Tips for Teaching Listening

- Deliver a short, well-organized lecture and have the class outline it. Review the content to identify main topics and main points.
- Ask a question. Have students paraphrase the question, and recite these paraphrases in class.
- Conduct oral tests frequently.
- Limit or avoid repetition of directions, questions, and comments.
- Allow students to conduct recitations.
- Have students summarize television programs they have seen.
- List good listening habits on the blackboard (at the end of each class, each student could list one good listening habit).
- Post a bulletin board display relating to listening skills.
- Appoint a class recorder to provide a summary of recitation or discussion activities.
- Appoint one or two students to listen for any grammatical errors spoken in a class.
- Ask a student to paraphrase a student's previous response to a question.

Third, to help students develop into listeners, check to see that unnecessary noises, such as talking and equipment noises, are reduced.

When students know that there are concrete reasons for listening, they will improve. If you give them practical listening experience, some of what they learn will show up in their discussion activities. Honing students' listening skills will improve their academic achievement in all subject areas. Carl Glickman (1998) suggests that teachers also develop these skills.

Listening is a learned behavior, and the teacher's attitude is what illustrates to the student that listening is important (see McCaslin and Good 1996). How can you teach attentive listening? We have already presented a few tips. The Instructional Strategies box above contains a number of additional techniques that teachers have told us work well.

Key Elements of Small-Group Discussions

Because they encourage interaction among students, small-group settings are particularly appropriate for the exchange of ideas and to provide a focus on processes—in short, for classroom discussion. In this section, we will discuss four key elements of organizing small groups in your classroom: goals and objectives, ideal size, room arrangement, and choice of topics and applications. First we will put this in a context for you and describe how long a time period you may typically expect this process to take. As you'll see, it doesn't happen overnight!

Successful Small-Group Discussions Take Time   Figure 8.1 illustrates the skills that *both teachers and students* must develop before implementing student-led discussion techniques effectively. As the figure shows, it takes ap-

FIGURE 8.1

Progression of Steps for Successful Small-Group Discussions

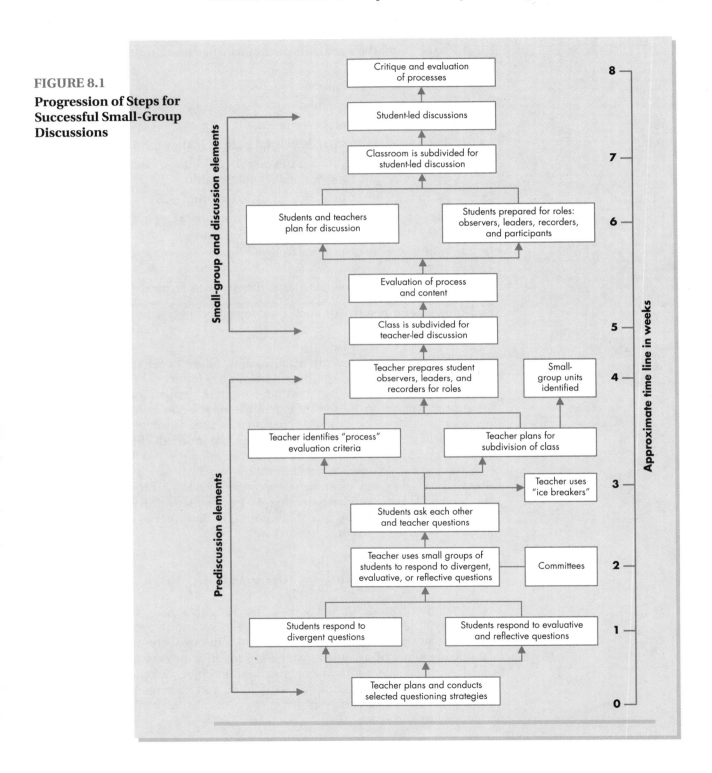

proximately eight weeks to practice all of the discussion elements (although it can be done in as little as four weeks). Note that the first steps in Figure 8.1 are based on the questioning strategies we considered in Chapter 7.

The Peavey Flour Milling Company's slogan for its Occident brand of flour ("Baking is no accident—it's *Occident*") implied that one had to select the right brand of flour to succeed at baking. The same logic may be applied to the use of discussions in the classroom. The correct skills must be identified, and they must be practiced repeatedly so that students will understand the routines and support one another's learning. By having students perform the process, the teacher can better discover problems and effectively resolve them.

The teacher who claims that small-group discussions just don't work ("I tried one once during the first week of school, and my students wouldn't even participate") does not understand them. *Effective* small-group discussions do not take place accidentally; they are learning activities that develop from carefully structured student behaviors. The teacher thus needs to learn what is involved in conducting successful **small-group discussions**—verbal exchanges of ideas and information in groups of four to eight students.

Goals and Objectives for Small-Group Learning   Study the list of learning processes in the box below. Note that the real value of each is in the *process* or *experience*. Small-group learning is especially suited to focus on processes such as these for which the most important learning outcome is the process itself, not its end result. For such outcomes, teachers write **process objectives,** which require the learner to participate in some technique, interaction, or strategy. Whereas performance objectives, which we discussed in Chapter 3, indicate a specific desired achievement, process objectives usually call for the gradual and more openly defined development of skills, attitudes, and strategies.

The first task in planning a successful process-oriented learning activity is to develop a set of long-range priorities or goals. From these you will derive process objectives, which will help you to focus individual lessons. Each process objective in turn will require carefully planned learning experiences and ample time for student practice. A teacher who wishes to develop students' writing skills, for example, must give them guidance, feedback, *and* repeated opportunities to practice their writing. The same applies to building students'

Using small groups requires teacher planning and analyzing.

Carefully and appropriately integrate process skills into your unit plans.

Examples of Learning Processes

- Kindergartners having a verbal sharing time.
- Second-graders growing plants.
- Fourth-graders making a time line.
- Sixth-grade teams brainstorming solutions.
- Eighth-graders setting up recycling stations.
- Tenth-graders observing a court session.
- Twelfth-graders exploring different ways to apply mathematics to physics problems.

discussion skills. Students need practice and cumulative experience within a carefully planned framework to gain the skills necessary to be successful in these areas (see Stahl 1994).

Ideal Size for Small Groups   In this chapter, we make a distinction between small-group discussions as opposed to whole-class recitations. Group size is an important variable that influences learner participation. There is no absolute minimum or maximum number of persons that must be included in a small group to ensure a successful discussion. **Small groups** can number anywhere from three to fifteen (Miller 1986). Some suggest that two to five is the ideal size (Cohen, Lotan, and Holthuis 1997; Schmuck and Schmuck 1997); others assert that six is the maximum (Johnson, Johnson, and Holubec 1994, 1998). Our own observations suggest that the optimal group size is from six to eight students. When four or fewer individuals are involved in a discussion group, the participants tend to pair off rather than to interact with all members.

The extent of student interaction in small groups is affected by the group's size.

We have found that when a group consists of ten or more participants, student interaction begins to diminish. With larger groups—that is, fifteen or more—a few students participate actively, a few participate in a more limited way, and most remain silent or passive. Therefore, we suggest that you divide the class into groups of not more than eight before you initiate a small-group discussion (see Wheelan, Tilin, and Sanford 1996).

Room Arrangement   Probably the optimal physical arrangement for small-group discussion consists of several discussion centers located within a large room. You can partially isolate the centers from the rest of the room with bookshelves or folding room dividers. Another, simpler way is to turn student desks so that participants face one another and are not distracted by activities in the rest of the room. Students will normally block out noise from the other groups if each circle is enclosed so that students make eye contact only with members of the same group. By converting the room into "centers," you can conduct several types of activities simultaneously without disruptions.

It is simple to rearrange most classrooms to promote discussion.

Circular or semicircular seating arrangements offer at least four advantages to small-group interaction (Book and Galvin 1975):

- They reduce the authority role of the teacher.
- They provide the idea that everyone is equal.
- They reduce the possibility that a student will be ignored by the group or withdraw from it.
- They create a setting that encourages listening and contributing to the discussion.

Seating arrangements, personal space, and interaction patterns are important variables in the process. Avoid rows or concentric circles—they inhibit personal interaction. At a rectangular table, students who sit at the corners are likely to contribute the least. Furthermore, individuals tend to sit in the same seat or proximity during every class (Beebe and Masterson 1986). Thus, you should rotate small-group members' seating positions to encourage interaction and to maintain a feeling of equity.

Choice of Topics and Applications   Discussion topics may arise from ongoing class work, or they may follow students' interest in a selected area. The usefulness of the discussion depends in large part on group members' ability and willingness to define the problem.

The topic chosen should both be pertinent to classroom studies and be able to hold students' interest. The issue being discussed should be sufficiently difficult to sustain interest and require serious, creative thinking. In short, the topic must have relevance to those discussing it. Sufficient information should be available to class members, either in print or via the Internet, to keep the discussion going. Controversial issues and moral dilemmas are excellent topics for small-group discussions (Simpson 1995).

Discussions can be held in any classroom, on appropriate subject matter, and among students of any age or developmental level. Students need to learn how to express their ideas effectively and to incorporate this skill into their personality. This learner goal is appropriate not only in subject areas for which discussions are easy to conduct, such as literature and social studies, but also in physics, chemistry, home and family studies, art, health, foreign languages, and physical education—in all courses taught in school. Discussions should be meaningful: for example, it would be inappropriate to tell students to "discuss the quadratic equation," but having them discuss methods of proving the equation or derivations of it would provide a mind-stretching experience for all concerned.

Consider the list of applications for small-group discussion in the Instructional Strategies box below, and reflect on the usefulness of this type of teaching strategy in your discipline or teaching area (see also Scotty-Ryan 1998).

Consider this question: what kinds of sharing experiences do you want your students to have? Some of you will probably focus immediately on multicultural experiences—on sharing customs related to dress, games and recreation, family activities, and religion. Or you might think about the need for students to display and share their unique talents, or the benefits of sharing the experiences of students who are socioeconomically impoverished or who have disabilities.

The preceding question is important because most of you will be teach-

Discussions are an effective means of encouraging all students to participate actively.

Instructional	**Applications for Small-Group Discussion**
Strategies	■ Stimulating students' interest when introducing a new topic.
	■ Identifying problems or issues to be studied or alternative ways to approach a topic already under consideration
	■ Exploring new ways to solve problems
	■ Evaluating data, opinions, and sources of information
	■ Structuring concepts for future study
	■ Allowing students to demonstrate individual strengths
	■ Learning and improving leadership, organization, and research skills
	■ Learning teamwork
	■ Learning to defend one's ideas and to respect the viewpoints of others
	■ Learning to accept and value various ethnic and cultural backgrounds

Reflect Reflect Reflect

- List as many reasons as you can think of to use small-group discussion in your subject area.
- How would you initiate instruction on process objectives?

ing in classes where mainstreaming or school policy mandates the placement of students with disabilities within regular class settings (see Chapter 1). Others of you will be involved with gifted and talented classes, and all of you will be faced with the challenge of providing a non-gender-biased, multiculturally oriented education for your students. Being adept at handling small-group discussions will help you meet these challenges.

Four Basic Small-Group Concepts

You will need to consider four basic concepts as you initiate small-group discussions: process, roles, leadership, and cohesion (see the box on page 285).

Process and Interaction   As we have already discussed in earlier sections of this chapter, the essence of *process* in small-group discussion is verbal interaction. Communication processes are most vital for successful discussion. Students must be taught and encouraged to listen to what each person is saying and to respond appropriately. Involvement by everyone is part of the process. As facilitator, you need to walk about the class, listening, observing, and encouraging every student to participate (Miles 1998).

A **facilitator** gives students the skills, materials, and opportunities they need to direct their own learning experiences.

Roles and Responsibilities   Every member of a discussion group has a **role.** Group members may be assigned roles by the teacher or by the group as it matures. Each role has specific attendant privileges, obligations, responsibilities, and powers. As the teacher, your own role can best be described by the term *facilitator.* The kind of development and cohesiveness we describe in this chapter cannot be decreed by the teacher; it must be facilitated. In other words, you enable your students to develop an effective group by helping them feel free to express themselves. This occurs most often when you facilitate the development of classroom norms that are conducive to student participation. Such norms foster the belief among students that it is okay for them to express their opinions, that it is okay to interact with their peers and with the teacher, and that their opinions have value.

In most discussion groups, other roles will typically include a leader and a recorder, for example, and additional roles may be assigned as needed. All class members must be rotated through the roles so that everyone has the experience of being the leader. It is your responsibility to provide all students with the opportunity to participate in a variety of roles (see Schmuck and Schmuck 1997). Roles are discussed in more depth in Section 3 of this chapter.

> ### The Four Basic Concepts Related to Small-Group Methods
>
> - *Process*—the interactions that take place within the group.
> - *Roles*—each group member's specific responsibilities within the group.
> - *Leadership*—the capacity to guide and direct others in a group setting.
> - *Cohesion*—group members' support for one another.

Leadership roles are developed for and taught to all students.

Leadership The single most important role in a small group is that of the *leader.* The leader is the person in authority—the spokesperson for the group. Leadership is a learned quality. So, as teacher, you have to model how a leader opens the discussion, calls on participants, clarifies statements, and seeks everyone's comments. Leaders have to be taught how to plan the discussion, organize the group for maximum efficiency, direct the discussion, and coordinate different individual assignments.

When you begin to use small-group discussions, you may choose the initial student leaders on the basis of leadership abilities already observed in class situations. Attributes that enhance leadership ability may include personal popularity, academic standing, temperament or sociability, thinking ability, and speaking ability.

Ideally, leadership develops through experience, but is it wise to discuss with the class early in the semester what qualities a leader must have *to help the group work together.* At first, appoint leaders. As leaders emerge, they should then be rotated. It is your responsibility to help students develop the desired leadership behaviors and competencies. For example, leaders will need time to learn how to ask questions, how to report a summary, how to involve nonvolunteers, and how to restrain dominating volunteers without using aversive techniques. Ultimately, every class member should have an opportunity to develop those skills and be a leader. This is the essence of *instructional equity.*

> ### Functions of the Discussion Leader
>
> - *Initiating.* Getting the group going and keeping it moving when it becomes bogged down or goes off on a dead-end tangent (for example, by clarifying certain statements or asking questions that call for more than a yes or no answer).
> - *Regulating.* Influencing the pace of the discussion (by summarizing or pointing out time limits).
> - *Informing.* Bringing new information to the group (but not by lecturing).
> - *Supporting.* Making it easier for members to contribute (by harmonizing opposing viewpoints, voicing group feelings, varying members' place in group, helping group members get acquainted).
> - *Evaluating.* Helping the group evaluate process goals (by testing for consensus or noting the group's progress in some area).

You must emphasize the main functions of the small-group leader and provide the leaders with special training (see Miles 1998). Leader functions are summarized in the box on page 285.

Cohesion: The "We" Attitude   The final concept is group **cohesion**—the tendency of a group to stick together and support members. A cohesive group displays a "we" attitude: the members support one another and show pride in belonging. The tone the teacher sets is all-important here. In fact, possibly the most important criterion for predicting your ability to facilitate small-group discussions is your own set of attitudes and feelings. Mastering small-group discussion methods requires an appreciation of the atmosphere or emotional setting of the classroom. As the teacher, you must believe that students can accept responsibility and that your actions are closely related to the manner in which the students respond.

It is your responsibility as teacher to establish the proper atmosphere in the classroom. You need to develop a "*we* attitude," to think in terms of working *with* your students, together. This attitude will help you establish positive goals concerning teacher-student relationships, student-student relationships, and the learning purposes of the classroom, and it will foster a supportive emotional climate. The classroom environment needs to be supportive of all persons so that students will learn to respect all other individuals and their ideas. Such an atmosphere is fostered through small-group learning experiences. But you, the teacher, must make the decisions that will shape the classroom into a supportive learning community.

Before we close this discussion, we want to add one other observation: yes, we realize that a group can become so cohesive that conformity is the norm and individualism is ignored. Thus another reason that you will want to attend to each group as discussions are conducted is to observe whether there is not enough cohesion or too much. (For detailed treatments on these four concepts, see Englberg and Hynn 1997; Tiberius 1999.)

Evaluation in Small-Group Settings: Providing Positive Feedback

Why use positive feedback? First, positive feedback increases responses. Many students do not respond because they are afraid of giving an incorrect reply and being subjected to a negative teacher reaction. If they give a partially correct response, some positive feedback from you or the leader will usually motivate the student to try again (see Chapter 7). To many students, especially at the middle and secondary levels, peer approval or feedback is even more important than teacher approval.

Second, students need to learn to cooperate with and support others. Students *can* and *will* learn to give positive feedback to one another, but only if you are not the only one giving feedback. Gradually shift the responsibility for providing feedback to the group. This helps to promote activity and harmony within the group as well as to give the students practice with the valuable leadership skill of providing feedback to others (see Weissglass 1996).

Evaluative processes should provide feedback concerning group members' progress in discussion skills and processes, and they should inform the

Discussion efforts need systematic evaluation for continued improvement

teacher about how the group is progressing in relation to process objectives and group goals. You (or the group leader) and each student need to assess individual group members' progress. At first this evaluation may be merely a matter of noting how many responses each student makes during a discussion session or recording some general impressions of each person. Later it may focus on specific functions that individual members need to master or on how each student can help the others be effective group members. Remember that you cannot abdicate your responsibility to help each student in your class. At times a group may not be having a positive influence on a particular student. When this occurs, you must bear the responsibility for correcting the student's behavior and work with the group to shape his or her long-term behavior. Evaluation should be nonthreatening and varied, and it should be based on specific learning objectives. Students need to know, before the discussion or group project, on what they are being evaluated.

To assist you in collecting feedback from small groups, we present Figures 8.2 and 8.3 as illustrations of forms we've used when conducting discussions.

FIGURE 8.2

Personal Data Check Instrument

PERSONAL DATA CHECK

Name _____

Directions: Keep track of the number of times that you participate orally in the small-group activity. Then insert the total number in the place provided in Item 1. After the discussion is over, place an X next to the statement that best describes your reaction to each of the questions.

1. Tally the number of times that you participated verbally in the small-group discussion.

_____ Your Tally

2. To what extent did you participate in the discussion?

_____ **a)** I really dominated it.

_____ **b)** I participated as much as the others did.

_____ **c)** I didn't participate as much as I would have liked.

3. To what extent would you like to contribute more to the group discussion?

_____ **a)** I'd like to contribute more.

_____ **b)** I'm contributing just about the amount I'd like.

_____ **c)** I'd like to contribute less.

4. How would you rate the extent to which your group encourages all of its members to participate fully?

_____ **a)** The group encourages everyone to participate fully.

_____ **b)** The group could encourage its members to participate more.

_____ **c)** The group discourages individuals from participating.

Modify the form to match your process objectives.

FIGURE 8.3

Discussion Evaluation Form: Individual Participant Rating

DISCUSSION EVALUATION FORM

Group _____

Participant's Name _____

Directions: Rate your own participation in your group by circling one of the numbers in the scales (from 1 to 5) for each criterion stated at the left.

Criteria	Very Ineffective	Somewhat Ineffective	Not Sure	Somewhat Effective	Very Effective
1. What overall rating of effectiveness would you give this discussion session?	1	2	3	4	5
2. How effective was the background event in getting you interested in the discussion topic?	1	2	3	4	5
3. How effectively did your group seem to be working together by the conclusion of the discussion?	1	2	3	4	5
4. How effective were the decisions your group reached?	1	2	3	4	5
5. How effective was the group in considering every idea that you contributed?	1	2	3	4	5
6. How effective was the leader in making it easier for you to say something?	1	2	3	4	5
7. How effective were you in encouraging others to speak or to become involved?	1	2	3	4	5

A simple form such as this gives each participant some idea of his or her strengths or weaknesses in the group activity. The recorded information can provide a focus for the improvement of small-group discussion processes. Modifications of the form can be made for specific needs.

The process is cyclical. You collect, tabulate, and summarize the data and then share the results with the entire class for its collective reaction. Remember that it takes planning, time, and experience to develop smoothly functioning small groups, whether it be schoolrooms or . . . boardrooms.

Benefits of Small-Group Discussions

Are we justified in claiming that small-group discussions are beneficial? Yes, particularly if the groups are involved in tasks requiring higher-level thinking, decision making, problem solving, or positive social behaviors and attitudes. One summary of several research studies noted significant gains by students who worked collaboratively in groups (Fillmore and Meyer 1992).

Studies have shown that small-group methods are superior *for selected purposes and when conducted under appropriate conditions*. There is evidence that changes in social adjustment and personality can be best facilitated through small-group instructional methods. Students who work together in a small group are likely to learn more quickly and with more accuracy than are students engaged in other learning methods (Race and Brown 1999).

Moreover, small-group discussions may be a way to turn on your turned-off students. Since small-group learning requires varied activities and interactions, it gives students more chances for success. For example, a student who is a flop at initiating discussion but is highly perceptive may be called on for analysis or to craft a compromise. The class member who is a poor reader has a chance to excel in reporting or visualizing.

The now classic HumRRO study noted five benefits to the learners associated with discussion (Olmstead 1970). These are listed in the box below.

The box below summarizes some of the important points we have discussed about small groups thus far. Section 2 of this chapter provides a select number of types you can use to implement small-group discussions.

Small-group methods cannot be used indiscriminately.

Learner Benefits from Discussion

- Increased depth of understanding and grasp of course content.
- Enhanced motivation and greater involvement with the course.
- Positive attitudes toward later use of material presented in the course.
- Problem-solving skills specific to content of the course.
- Practice in the application of concepts and information to practical problems.

A Quick Summary of Key Points

- Active learning can be implemented in small groups of students (preferably six to eight).
- Achieving process objectives requires active student involvement and interaction.
- Discussions are highly interactive, not teacher-led recitations.
- Discussions cannot be used for any topic—they are selectively incorporated into teaching units.
- A positive classroom environment is essential for collaborative work.
- Everybody in a discussion group is assigned some responsibility.

> **Reflect Reflect Reflect**
>
> ■ How is your role as facilitator different from your usual role as teacher?
>
> ■ Parents are often concerned that small group learning destroys individual initiative. How would you address this issue?
>
> ■ Plan a unit that could be taught using discussions. How does the plan differ from one you might write if you were using other techniques?
>
> ■ How might you plan to include all students in a discussion?

Section 2: Six Basic Small-Group Discussion Types

In this part of the chapter, we present six basic types of small-group discussion: brainstorming, tutorials, task-directed discussion, role playing, simulations, and inquiry-centered discussion. From this list you should be able to find at least one type of discussion that will fit your instructional and process objectives at any given time.

One method for classifying (and remembering) discussion types is to use the variable of control or domination. When implementing small-group discussions, you must decide on the proper amount of teacher control for the activity: you can dominate the activities of the groups almost totally, you can act in an egalitarian manner, or you can choose not to participate at all. Likewise, you must decide how much control you want the group leaders to exert within their groups. Table 8.1 illustrates the basic types of discussion groups we have identified viewed along a continuum from greater control (at the top) to lesser control (at the bottom).

In addition to deciding on the proper amount of control, there are two other important decisions you must make when choosing a discussion type for a particular situation: the desired or anticipated process or skill to be learned, and the desired or anticipated product of the discussion. Group work always has a goal, such as the completion of a given task. This goal is the *product*. How the members interact with one another during the discussion is the *process*. These two objectives must be taught to the students so that they will know how to "play the game." Let us now proceed to those basic techniques.

Brainstorming

Brainstorming is a simple and effective skill-building technique to use when a high level of creativity is desired. Any number of students can participate in a brainstorming activity, but the shorter the time available for discussion, the smaller should be the number of participants (which should, in any case, be within five to fifteen persons).

The leader begins the brainstorming session by briefly stating the problem under consideration. The problem may be as simple as "What topics would

TABLE 8.1

A Taxonomy of Discussion Groups

Type of Discussion	General Instructional Purposes	Orientation	Knowledge, Skills, and Control Continuum
Brainstorming	Creativity Stimulation Idea generation Role building Listening	Processes	Lowest need of discussion skills and moderate probability for teacher control.
Tutorial	Individual skills Questioning Basic competencies	Processes and products	
Task group	Delegation of responsibility Initiative Achievement Planning skills Group learning Affective consequences Reflection Evaluation	Product and processes	
Role playing	Issue clarification Evaluation Reflective thinking Values analysis Situation presentation	Processes	
Simulation	Inquiry Decision-making Application of skills	Processes and product	
Inquiry group	Analysis Synthesis Evaluation Student initiative	Processes	Highest need of discussion skills and lowest probability for teacher control.

Brainstorming gives everyone an opportunity to participate.

the group like to consider this semester?" or as complex as "How can the personal computers of secretaries and junior executives be arranged to maximize efficiency?" Every school subject has some elements that require students to do some freewheeling thinking. This is when you want to use a brainstorming group.

After the topic has been stated and before interaction starts, it is crucial to select a method of recording the discussion. It can be taped, or one or two students who write quickly can serve as recorders. The leader should stress to the group that *all* ideas need to be expressed. All group participants need to realize that *quantity* of suggestions is paramount. Refer to Chapter 5 to review

---

Rules for Brainstorming

- All ideas, except for obvious jokes, should be acknowledged.
- No criticism is to be made of any suggestion.
- Members should build on one another's ideas. In the final analysis, no idea belongs to any individual, so encourage "piggybacking."
- The leader should solicit ideas or opinions from silent members, and then give them positive reinforcement.
- Quality is less important than quantity, but this does not relieve group members of the need to think creatively and intelligently.

Reflect Reflect Reflect

- List some potential brainstorming topics from your teaching specialty.

---

the topic of graphic organizing because it is an effective way to display and organize participants' suggestions.

There are some very important rules to follow for brainstorming sessions. All the students should be oriented to the rules ahead of time, and the student leader should enforce them. The box above summarizes them.

Brainstorming is an initiating process; it must be followed by some other activity. For example, the group might use the ideas generated in the brainstorming session as the basis for another type of discussion. After the brainstorming session, the ideas should be categorized and evaluated, and as many as possible should be used by students in follow-up activities. The group may arrange the elements in priority order; for example, members may evaluate the suggested topics according to their importance for future study.

Evaluation of the generated ideas should be short and nonthreatening to the participants. Remember that you want all to contribute, regardless of their current level of academic ability. Although you may be making some private assessments about academic levels, levels of inhibition, the pecking order, and who is bored in class, all your "public" evaluations must be highly positive or at least neutral. We recommend using brainstorming as a training technique for leaders and especially for recorders.

> Ideas generated in brainstorming sessions must be categorized before action is taken.

Tutorials

The **tutorial discussion group** is most frequently used to help students who have difficulties learning or processing information at a satisfactory rate. The group is very small (usually four or fewer) and focuses on a narrow range of materials. Teachers of such subjects as reading, mathematics, home economics, art, and business often use the tutorial group for remedial instruction. In the social studies, language arts, and sciences, the tutorial group is often used to help students grasp a concept, again with the purpose of remedying a learning difficulty (see Lowery 1998). Physical education and primary grade teachers employ a tutorial mode frequently in the area of motor development. It is an excellent way to facilitate student handling of manipulatives, allowing the teacher to evaluate students' motor skills, and helping students understand the relationships between movement and body functions (see Davies 1999).

The tutorial leader performs three major functions: questioning the students to pinpoint the exact problem that has blocked learning, providing feedback or skills to facilitate learning, and encouraging the students to ask questions and to seek answers among themselves. It has been demonstrated that students often learn as well as from one another as they do from the teacher (Cohen, Kulik, and Kulik 1982)! We caution, however, that before you use student tutors, you must be satisfied that each potential student tutor has mastered the necessary competencies—such as the skills of questioning, giving positive reinforcement, and analyzing work tasks.

Many school districts currently use student tutors and are finding them to be invaluable resources for the classroom teacher. Although it is most often used for remedial work, the tutorial discussion group is also an excellent method by which to encourage independent projects or advanced learning. Many gifted students find it a challenge to explain their projects to other students.

The person who leads the tutorial discussion needs skills in giving feedback and encouragement. The leader must also keep the group moving toward its goal, accept feedback from students who learn slowly, and prod group members who do not contribute. It may be a helpful to give your student leaders a brief review of the questioning techniques we covered in Chapter 7.

Figure 8.4 illustrates two excellent spatial arrangements for the participants in a tutorial group. Note that either arrangement provides easy "eyeball-to-eyeball" contact. Such visual contact helps facilitate the flow of communication between all group members. Also note that the leader is clearly identified by his or her spatial placement.

Tutoring that combines feedback and formative evaluation is such a powerful instructional technique that tutored students can gain 98 percent more than students in conventional classes, as measured by achievement tests

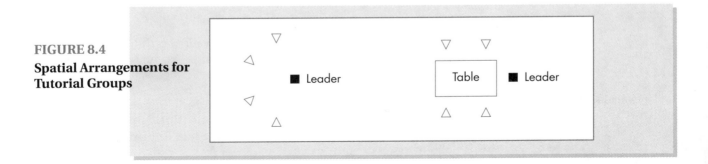

FIGURE 8.4

Spatial Arrangements for Tutorial Groups

Reflect Reflect Reflect

■ Under what circumstances might you use tutors in your classes?

Productive learning takes place in well-organized small-group discussions.
© Elizabeth Crews/The Image Works.

Tutors can be peers, older students, adults, or even computers!

(Bloom 1984; Walberg 1991). This critical finding validates the instructional efficacy of the tutorial. No other instructional variable—homework, advance organizers, conventional classes—surpasses tutoring in increasing achievement.

We have been discussing the use of adults, peers, or older students as tutors. However, several computer-assisted tutorials may be used for drill, practice, or remediation. (See Grabe and Grabe 2001 for details.) By using computer-assisted systems, you provide a private and individualized tutorial to any child who needs some extra help.

Reflect Reflect Reflect

■ How is individual autonomy reinforced when you use task groups?

Task-Directed Discussion

One of the least complex types of small groups used for discussion is the **task group.** Each student in a task group can make significant contributions to the discussion. A prerequisite to using task groups is to specify clearly defined tasks for all group members. A task group has clearly defined goals and clearly identified individual assignments and roles—for example, recorder, library researcher, artist, leader, and evaluator. It may be beneficial for you to establish a work schedule for the groups and a way to internally monitor participants' achievements and, initially, even to provide all the learning resources that are necessary to accomplish the identified tasks.

Task groups tend to begin as teacher-dominated groups, insofar as the teacher usually selects the tasks and assigns each group member to accomplish a specific role. You will find that this is an especially efficient group type for helping students learn to interact positively in small work groups. You may also observe how selected students work with one another and how responsibly they tend to accomplish the assigned task. Recall from Chapter 7 the *reflective questioning strategy* that we introduced. This is an ideal technique to use with task groups. Each team would be given the challenge to generate one reflective question on which the class could ponder—individually or in small groups.

We must end with a cautionary note. Even though you give a specific assignment to each task group member, do not assume that he or she will completely finish it. Students must ultimately learn to accept responsibility, but it is your job to help them set appropriate goals, to motivate them, and to monitor each student's activities to help all students achieve their assigned goals.

In task groups, tasks are assigned to each participant so that no one feels left out.

Role Playing

Role playing is a process-oriented group technique in which students act out or simulate a real-life situation. It may involve almost any number of participants, although seven to ten is ideal. To use this type of group, you should be well acquainted with role-playing techniques. Students also need some coaching to use the technique effectively. The box on page 296 lists the basic elements of role playing.

Thorough preparation will help students enjoy the process and experience of role playing and not be overly concerned about interactions that might, in other situations, be perceived as personal attacks. It is especially important for participants to understand the difference between regular acting and psychodrama. Role players and all students who participate in the follow-up discussion should abstain from psychoanalyzing anyone or pretending that they are psychologists. In role playing, as we are using the term, the emphasis is not on the psyche of any participant but on reenacting or dramatiz-

Elements of Role Playing

- *Briefing students*—explaining the topic and establishing the situation in understandable terms for each student.
- *Conducting the drama*—that is, behaving as an actor in the described situation.
- *Debriefing*—analyzing how the roles were played and identifying what concepts were learned.

Reflect Reflect Reflect

- For what topics in your teaching area might the use of role-playing groups be effective?
- How would you evaluate the process?

ing a situation and demonstrating how different characters would react in that situation.

Each role-playing group discussion is a unique experience, but there are some common criteria on which you can base your evaluation of a group's effort: Did students who are usually quiet take an active part? Did the role playing lead to a better understanding of the topic being investigated? Was the situation resolved (if the topic of study involved a problem)? Did the participants take their roles seriously? Did they avoid making self-serving comments during the discussion phase?

Role playing allows for some drama in the classroom.

Role playing can be used with students at all grade levels and all levels of academic achievement, and it can be used to investigate almost any situation or topic (see McCormick 1998). In a unit on environmental problems, for example, students can be assigned specific roles to play as they explore the complexities of scientific or mathematical issues (see Resnick and Wilensky 1998). The U.S. Constitution is a great topic for role-playing groups, especially the First Amendment and how it affects schooling (Vessels 1996). Role playing can also be effective in developing students' social skills (van Ments 1999). Teachers can also easily use role-playing groups to help assess students' competency levels. Your own creativity and that of your students are the only limits to using role playing as a powerful learning and evaluation tool.

Simulation

A **simulation** is a representation or re-creation of a real object, problem, event, or situation. Although it mirrors reality, a simulation removes the possibility of injury or risk to the participants. The learner is nevertheless an active participant, engaged in demonstrating a behavior or previously acquired skills or knowledge. Interactive simulations may be special cases of role playing. Simulations can be used to stimulate interest in a topic, provide information, enhance skill development, change attitudes, and assess performance by measuring it against an already established standard (see Ellington 1998).

While simulation groups have long been used in the military, in business, in medicine, and in administrative planning, their introduction into the schools is a more recent event. But we should remember that teachers have for years used play stores and school councils as instructional devices to reflect selected dimensions of reality. Some goals of instructional simulation are listed in the box below.

Simulation exercises should be selected for specific learning objectives for which they are appropriate. Usually you cannot achieve all of the goals listed in the box with a single simulation. All simulation exercises should stimulate learners to learn more through independent study or research, however. Furthermore, as students engage in relevant simulation exercises, they may begin to perceive that knowledge learned in one context can become valuable in different situations.

Simulations are selected to meet specific goals or purposes.

In our own use of simulations, we have observed that students become immersed in the activities almost immediately. Simulations are great icebreakers for diverse groups of students. There is also an element of risk taking for all participants. Even though there is no penalty for "wrong" answers, participants tend to view simulations in a serious, personal way, especially those that require decisions. For example, while middle and high school students *simulate* investment decisions as illustrated in the box, The D. A. Davidson Company of Great Falls, Montana, actually provides cash grants to several universities in the Northwest to learn about stock investing. In these instances, there is a reality of actually making (or losing) *real money!* The step from *classroom learning to capitalism* is just one grade level away (Davidson 1999). Simulations seem to be more easily applied to the study of issues than processes. The simulation encourages students to express, in their own words, the basic arguments for the various sides of an issue (see Boston 1998).

The box on page 298 provides three excellent examples of simulations. The examples in the box are computer oriented. Perhaps one of the better applications of computer technology is the use of simulations. A computer simulation can be "played" by just one student or a small group of students if the

---

Goals of Simulation

- Develop changes in students' attitudes
- Change specific behaviors
- Prepare participants for assuming new roles in the future
- Help individuals understand their current roles
- Increase students' ability to apply principles
- Reduce complex problems or situations to manageable elements
- Illustrate roles that may affect students' lives but that they may never assume
- Motivate learners
- Develop analytical processes
- Sensitize individuals to other persons' life roles

Decision-making skills are applied in simulations.

> ### Selected Examples of Simulations
>
> - *Comparing the United States and Europe.* Five data sets are provided by which to make comparisons—climatic, economic, political, demographic, and quality of life. Thinking, analyzing, and communications skills are stressed (Richburg and Nelson 1991).
> - *The Oregon Trail.* Students make a computer-simulated covered wagon adventure from Missouri to Oregon in 1865. Decision-making skills are applied (Grabe and Grabe 2001). Individuals could compare consequences of selected decisions.
> - *The Stock Market Game.* Students can make virtual fortunes in this simulation of the stock exchange. Analyses of data, predictions of trends, syntheses of information, and evaluating alternatives are all incorporated into this interactive game (Weiser and Schug 1992; Wood 1992; CNBC 2000).

Reflect Reflect Reflect

- Select and use a simulation appropriate to your teaching specialty. What specific skills or processes did it develop?

classroom has networking capabilities. One student could even play a simulation with students in several different classrooms.

While on the topic, let's note that "chat rooms" are now possible and can be used to provide a small-group discussion on a high-interest topic with schools within the city or in any city—anywhere. The computer offers one more dimension for human interactions.

Whether simulations will work for you depends on what your goals and objectives are. If you want to teach processes associated with decision making, then simulations provide alternatives to the usual classroom routines. Simulations are also appropriate if you wish to promote human interaction. If you want to provide experiences that students may not get from the routine application of learning skills or principles, then simulations can achieve this end. With some ingenuity, knowledge of your subject, initiative, and imagination, you too can design an effective small-group simulation.

Inquiry-Centered Discussion

If you wish to emphasize problem solving, then you will find the **inquiry discussion group** extremely valuable. Any number of students may be in the discussion group, but six students per team is ideal. The purposes of an inquiry discussion group are to stimulate scientific thinking, develop problem-solving skills, and foster the acquisition of new facts through a process of discovery

Selected Topics for Inquiry Groups

- How are the commercials on television framed?
- What major issues or topics occupy newspaper headlines?
- How much food is consumed or wasted in the school lunch room?
- Which school intersections carry the heaviest traffic when students arrive at or leave school?
- What themes are most repeated by persons seeking political offices?

and analysis (Sparapani 1998). The teacher may be the leader of this type of group. If, however, you have a student who has demonstrated good questioning skills and understands the concept under consideration, then allow that student to be the leader.

Inquiry groups are used to stimulate students to become skillful askers of questions. They also allow students to test the validity of hypotheses, to determine by direct experience whether they are valid. Inquiry groups are most appropriate for those disciplines that lend themselves to problem solving—science and social science (Yell 1998).

Before you introduce the inquiry-group technique, your students should have mastered the skills of observing and inferring. You can encourage these behaviors by having students ask questions based on selected observations of phenomena, by having them collect data, and by having them summarize and draw conclusions. After you and the students have identified the problems to be explored, subdivide the class into small inquiry groups to complete the investigation of each problem. In the box above are several suggestions for inquiry-group topics.

To make the inquiry-group exercise most meaningful, plan an activity that has some degree of authenticity. For example, the inquiry-group technique can be used effectively when students are studying about the general subject of human and civil rights. A group can role-play an episode in which a civil right has been violated and then, through inquiry discussion, isolate specific aspects of the violation or solve the problem in other ways. Student hypotheses

Instructional Strategies

Three Ways to Evaluate an Inquiry Group

1. Maintain a continuous checklist as each participant comments during the discussion (similar to taking minutes at a meeting).
2. Videotape the discussion and evaluate student performance during playback. Examine questioning skills and accuracy of information exchange.
3. Invite a colleague or train a student to tabulate selected behaviors during the discussion sessions.

Reflect Reflect Reflect

- How could you evaluate a simulation experience?
- Under what circumstances might you employ task groups when teaching?
- Which of the six discussion group techniques would be most desirable for your teaching content areas?

should be testable; for this reason, situations that affect students directly are excellent sources of material. For example, an inquiry group could study a specific area in which students' rights are seen as jeopardized.

Plan to evaluate every discussion so that all students may improve their skills or processes.

How to evaluate an inquiry group is fairly obvious. What you need to know, and what students need to know, is how well they ask questions. Were they able to ask higher-order questions that could lead to hypothesis making and testing? Of course, you also will want to know whether they learned the concept being discussed. How the students ask questions may be tabulated by listing higher-order questions, lower-order questions (refer to Chapter 7), formal statements of hypotheses, and miscellaneous statements. We suggest that the evaluation be accomplished simply. See the Instructional Strategies box on page 299 for suggestions.

Section 3: Cooperative Learning

So far we have described a variety of tested discussion methods. The purpose of all these methods is to involve students actively in thoughtful verbal exchanges. Cooperative learning, described in this part of the chapter, has much in common with the small-group methods already discussed. **Cooperative learning** is learning based on a small-group approach to teaching that holds students accountable for both individual and group achievement. Five characteristics of cooperative learning are shown in the box on page 301 (see Sharon 1995 and Jacob 1999).

Rationale for Using Cooperative Learning

Cooperative learning takes many forms within classrooms. Its essential characteristic is that it fosters positive interdependence by teaching students to work and learn together in a small-group setting. Traditional cooperative learning groups consist of three to four students who work on an assignment or project together in such a way that each group member contributes to the learning process and then learns all the basic concepts being taught. Both individual students and the group as a whole are held accountable for the outcome. Cooperative learning provides unique learning experiences for stu-

Characteristics of Cooperative Learning

- Uses small groups of three or four students (microgroups)
- Focuses on tasks to be accomplished
- Requires group cooperation and interaction
- Mandates individual responsibility to learn
- Supports division of labor

dents and offers an alternative to competitive models of education. It is especially beneficial to students who learn best through social or group learning processes (including a large number of students of color who come from cultures where learning most often takes place in social contexts). It offers opportunities for students to learn through speaking and listening processes (oral language) as well as through reading and writing processes (written language).

Cooperative learning enhances students' academic, management, and social skills.

Cooperative learning offers many benefits: for students, it improves both academic learning and social skills; for teachers, it is an aid to classroom management and instruction. Cooperative learning enhances students' enthusiasm for learning and their determination to achieve academic success (Lan and Repman 1995). It has been shown to increase the academic achievement of students of all ability levels (Stevens and Slavin 1995a, 1995b) in reading, writing, mathematics computation and application, comprehension, and critical thinking (Megnin 1995; Webb, Trooper, and Fall 1995; Bramlett 1994; Nattiv 1994; Hart 1993; Stevens and Slavin 1995a). Time on task and engagement increase in cooperative learning settings, because each student is a necessary part of the whole group's success (Mulryan 1995).

Cooperative learning is great for social studies classes (Morton 1998). For learning groups to be effective, students must learn to honor and respect one another's differences, to support one another through learning processes, to communicate effectively with one another, and to come to a consensus or understanding when needed. Thus cooperative learning provides valuable training in skills needed to become effective citizens, to engage in group problem solving, and to attain and keep employment. Cooperative learning has been shown to improve interpersonal relations and strengthen conflict resolution skills (Megnin 1995; Zhang 1994; Zuckerman 1994). It improves students' emotional well-being, self-esteem, coping skills, and attitudes toward schoolwork (Patterson 1994; Patrick 1994). Students engaged in cooperative learning experiences have been able to identify an increase in their own knowledge and self-esteem, trust of peers, problem-solving and communication skills (see Elliott, Busse, and Shapiro 1999), and technology proficiency (McGrath 1998).

Cooperative learning works well in multicultural classrooms.

African American, Hispanic, and Native American children often learn by socializing with their extended family and community members. Many cultures also have strong oral traditions that foster creativity, storytelling, and kinesthetic expression of language in students, skills that go unrecognized in those school settings where students are expected to work primarily as individuals through written work. While most cultures value cooperation, group loyalty, and caring for extended family and community members, these values may clash with the values of individual accomplishment, competition, productivity, and efficiency dominant in U.S. schools and workplaces. Cooperative learning has been specifically shown to increase school success for Hispanic students (Losey 1995). Cooperative and social learning is also the preferred learning style for many students of European descent. Obviously, students still learn by studying on their own. But some learn better in settings where they can share ideas, ask questions, and receive feedback.

Cooperative learning experiences have also been shown to improve the relationships among diverse students, when teachers are careful to construct groups of students from various cultures (Putnam 1997; Shulman, Lotan, and Whitcomb et al. 1998) and levels of physical need and ability (Stevens and Slavin 1995b). Cooperative learning benefits you as a teacher in terms of classroom management and instruction. When you teach the whole class and students are not allowed to interact or assist one another, it is up to you to provide individualized assistance to students who have not understood a given concept, have difficulty following directions, lack skills needed to begin a task, or have trouble following classroom routines. Much valuable student learning time is lost when students must wait for the teacher to circulate through the classroom.

Cooperative learning provides exciting learning opportunities across content areas. Students can work in cooperative groups to research topics, write reports, and plan and implement class discussions, debates, and panels. Students can also use cooperative groups to read materials, write summaries, find specific information, and answer questions. They can work together to study for tests, memorize information, and articulate concepts. Students can receive feedback and editing assistance from peers. They can engage in hands-on projects, experiments, and practical applications. They can design and implement school and community service projects. (For more examples, see Johnson and Johnson 1996; Webb, Trooper, and Fall 1995; Coelho 1998).

Increase students' learning time with cooperative small groups.

You can increase student learning time and reduce you own stress level and workload by teaching students to help one another with learning and organizational tasks and to monitor one another's progress. This allows you to become a facilitator of learning and allows students to become responsible for their own learning and that of their peers. Some other benefits of cooperative learning are listed in the box below.

Benefits of Cooperative Learning

- Improvement of comprehension of basic academic content
- Reinforcement of social skills
- Student decision making allowed
- Creation of active learning environment
- Boosted students' self-esteem
- Celebration of diverse learning styles
- Promotion of student responsibility
- Focus on success for everyone

Reflect Reflect Reflect

■ How is cooperative learning different from learning in a task group?

■ What major units of study could best be applied to a cooperative learning model?

Features of Cooperative Learning

Traditional models of cooperative learning include, at least, the following five distinct features (Johnson and Johnson 1999).

Positive Interdependence   In traditional classrooms, where competition is emphasized, students experience **negative interdependence**—a management system that encourages competing with one another for educational resources and academic recognition. Competition encourages better students to hoard knowledge and to celebrate their successes at the expense of other students. In cooperative learning classrooms, students work together to ensure the success of each student. **Positive interdependence** is a management system that encourages students to work together and teaches students that school life for each one of them is enhanced when everyone succeeds.

Face-to-Face Interaction   In cooperative learning situations, students interact, assist one another with learning tasks, and promote one another's success. The small-group setting allows students to work directly with one another, to share opinions and ideas, to come to common understandings, and to work as a team to ensure each member's success and acceptance.

In cooperative learning environments, individuals are held accountable for their learning.

Individual Accountability   In cooperative learning settings, each student is held accountable for his or her own academic progress and task completion, apart from the accomplishments of the group as a whole. In traditional models of cooperative learning, individuals are asked to sign statements describing their contribution to a particular project. Individuals may also be held accountable by means of grades based on their academic achievement and social skills and by evaluations conducted by the teacher, their peers, or themselves.

Development of Social Skills   Cooperative learning offers students a chance to develop the interpersonal skills needed to succeed at school, work, and within the community. Primary among these skills are effective communication, understanding and appreciation of others, decision making, problem solving, conflict resolution, and compromise. Students cannot simply be placed in a group and be expected to use these skills. As the teacher, you must actively teach and monitor the use of social skills. This requires articulation of social as well as academic goals to students. You need to actively teach social skills on a daily basis, ask students to practice those skills within their cooperative groups, and have students provide feedback on group interactions and social processes (Abruscato 1994; Kagan 1999).

Reflect Reflect Reflect

- How might you incorporate the five features of cooperative learning in our classroom?
- What reservations do you currently have about using cooperative learning in your classes?

Group Evaluation Groups of students need to evaluate and discuss how well they are meeting their goals, what actions help their group, and what actions seem to hurt group interactions. They may articulate these evaluations during class discussion or provide the teacher with written progress reports. Students should also have a way of alerting the teacher to group problems. As a teacher, you should develop plans for engaging students in problem solving and conflict resolution.

Initiating Cooperative Learning in the Classroom

Providing cooperative learning opportunities is not simply a matter of placing students in groups and assigning tasks. Teachers must carefully select student groups, plan cooperative learning activities, set both academic and social goals for group work, and monitor individual student progress and group learning and social processes. Finally, it will take you about one year or longer to master the model (see Ishler, Johnson, and Johnson 1998). The box below lists some of the keys to successful cooperative learning.

Cooperative small groups are established with specific goals in mind.

Selecting Student Groups Several details should be considered when you form cooperative learning groups. Groups may be formed on the basis of academic skill level, interests, personality characteristics, social skills, or a combination of these factors. Groups usually contain students of varying ability levels who support one another in multiple ways. Traditionally, cooperative learning groups have been set up to contain one above-average, two average, and one below-average student. One difficulty with this is that it blatantly cat-

---

Keys to Cooperative Learning

- Teacher planning is critical.
- Student engagement is mandatory.
- Assessment is vital.
- Quality work is essential.
- Constant student monitoring is required.
- Time requirements must be established.
- Trust, cohesiveness, and responsibility must be promoted.

egorizes students, when all students have areas of greater and lesser ability. In addition, it ignores the importance of considering the whole student. It ignores the fact that coping and social skills affect students' academic performance and that performance can vary from day to day based on emotional factors.

You might also form groups and have them pursue different activities based on students' interests. One group might paint pictures while others plan a play, develop a presentation, conduct experiments, surf the Internet, put on a debate, or work as a group of reporters. In reading, each group might choose a different novel to read. In history, groups might each choose to study a different aspect of World War II. In science, groups might each decide to spearhead a different project to increase environmental awareness. In home economics, each group might create a different portion of a menu. In art, each group might design a different project to beautify the city or town. Note how the above activities are applications of multiple intelligences that were highlighted in Chapters 4 and 5.

It is essential to group students carefully at the beginning of the year or whenever cooperative learning groups are first formed so student experiences can be positive and reinforcing. As the year progresses and students become accustomed to working together, group membership should become less of a factor in success. It also seems wise to capitalize on student strengths when groups are formed. Students should try as many roles as possible. In this way, they are allowed to share their strengths, learn new skills from peers, and then try them out in a small-group setting.

Cooperative learning groups often remain together for two to six weeks; at that time group membership changes to allow students to experience cooperation and caring with other peers. How long students should stay in a group depends on the characteristics of the students in the class and the nature of the tasks or projects on which they are working.

Every small-group member has a specific role to play.

You may assign specific roles to each group member. Typical roles might include *group leader* (facilitates group discussion, makes sure group sets goals and works to meet them), *monitor* (monitors time on task and ensures that everyone gets equal opportunity to participate), *resource manager* (gathers and organizes materials), *recorder* (keeps a written or taped record of group activities), and *reporter* (shares group findings and plans in whole-class discussions). Setting student roles allows teachers to influence the workings of the group, to capitalize on student strengths, and to encourage students to take risks by assuming new roles. On the other hand, group roles often evolve, with students falling into natural roles. While this may create spontaneous and natural interactions, it may also lock students into negative roles based on behaviors and social status. Keep in mind that it will take from three to nine weeks of experience before a class begins to maximize the benefits of cooperative learning.

Planning Cooperative Learning Activities Many types of learning can take place in cooperative settings. You, as the teacher, must decide if the particular skills and concepts to be taught are best learned in cooperative or individual settings. Many learning activities allow for both individual and collaborative work, for small-group interaction followed by whole-class discussion and analysis (see Zuckerman, Chudinova, and Khavkin 1998). For example, students

> ## Key Social Skills
>
> ■ Knowing how to brainstorm with others
> ■ Making sure each person has an equal opportunity to participate
> ■ Solving problems cooperatively
> ■ Choosing roles
> ■ Knowing what to do when one group member fails to contribute
> ■ Knowing how to handle conflict with other group members

might read a history text and articles as individuals, then convene in small groups to review the materials and discuss the causes of the Great Depression, and then share their findings with the whole class to generate a comprehensive list of causes. Later, students might be asked to write individual essays to show their understanding of the causes of the Great Depression.

Setting Academic and Social Goals   You must carefully set academic and social goals for cooperative groups and articulate these goals to students on a daily to weekly basis. Especially when first using cooperative learning, students will need specific training and monitoring. Seasoned teachers suggest that it is essential to teach social skills within the classroom and to model these before cooperative groups begin their work (Abruscato 1994). In addition, it is helpful to emphasize one or two social skills each day or week and to remind students to practice them within their group. Examples of such skills are listed in the box above.

Academic as well as social learning must be subdivided into meaningful tasks and goals. A teacher who wants students to choose a project, do research, write a report, and present the results to the class must teach students how to set group goals, brainstorm options, choose a viable topic, assign group member tasks, find and access resources, write meaningful and well-organized exposition, and execute effective oral presentations.

Monitoring and Evaluating Individual Group Progress

It is essential to monitor and evaluate the progress of both individual students and working groups as a whole. You need to assess the academic progress, social functioning, and emotional well-being of individual students and the productivity and social functioning of working groups. Individual academic progress may be measured by assessing the portion of the group project completed by a given student or by giving students individual assessments apart from their group work. Individual social functioning and emotional well-being may be assessed through teacher observation and group or self-evaluations that give feedback on how members are functioning within the group. Evaluations of group productivity may be made by assessing time logs, progress reports, and final group projects. Assessment of group social functioning may be made by teacher observations, conferencing with groups, group self-evaluations, or requests for teacher assistance.

All small-group progress must be evaluated.

Reflect Reflect Reflect

- Prepare a list of all the actions you would need to take to implement a cooperative learning strategy.
- Discuss with a small group of peers your own experiences with cooperative learning.

Cooperative learning supports the process of authentic assessment, in which students produce summative essays, creative works, and projects that allow them to use critical thinking, application, synthesis, analysis, and evaluation skills (Crotty 1994). Students might write essays, photo journals, or editorials; design public information pamphlets, posters, videos, or home pages; create works of visual or performing art; or design and implement community service projects.

Criticisms of Cooperative Learning

Cooperative groups should be presented with real challenges.

Several criticisms have been leveled at the concept of grouping together students of varying abilities. Advocates for gifted children believe that heterogeneous grouping may hold back those with the greatest academic talent. Advocates for students with learning difficulties state that children with disabilities may not get a chance to improve their reading, writing, and math skills when they receive so much assistance from peers. Research tends to refute this, showing significant academic gains for students who are gifted and students with learning disabilities in cooperative settings (Slavin 1990; Stevens and Slavin 1995a, 1995b; Johnson and Johnson 1992).

In addition, there are several counterpoints to these concerns. First, we must acknowledge that all students have areas of lesser and greater abilities—that academically gifted students may lack essential social skills, feel separate from peers because of unique abilities, or fear class presentations. Students with learning disabilities may lack essential reading and spelling skills yet have above-average intelligence and excel at oral language and listening comprehension skills. Cooperative learning allows students to share their diverse talents and learn new skills.

Second, it is essential to remember that cooperative learning provides benefits to students beyond academic learning, including the teaching of social skills essential to working with others in families, schools, communities, and workplaces. All students benefit from learning cooperative processes and social skills. Academically gifted students benefit by finding commonality with other students who seem distant in terms of academic skill (see Baloche 1998).

Third, the *type* of task assigned influences whether all students will benefit from a cooperative learning situation. Tasks that focus on finding information generally do not provide much benefit to gifted students. When students are asked simply to locate information, gifted students usually end up helping other students who have difficulty reading. But if the assignment also involves understanding essential concepts, exploring new meanings, thinking critically, and synthesizing information, it will likely benefit all students. Each group member can provide knowledge, perceptions, and ideas that will contribute to emergent, constructivist learning (see Vermette 1998).

Fourth, whether students benefit from group work or not seems to be a function of the classroom climate, which must be one of support, trust, and caring. Of greatest concern is whether students are building a sense of efficacy and self-esteem, both prerequisites to continued, successful academic learning.

Last, cooperative learning groups should not remain static, nor should they always be based on heterogeneous grouping. Certainly gifted students need opportunities to work, think, and learn together, and students with special needs need time to work together on essential reading, writing, and mathematics skills.

Another frequently heard criticism of traditional models of cooperative learning concerns the practice of rating, grading, or rewarding students on the basis of group accomplishment. Parents have been vociferous in criticizing this practice, citing instances where one student did his or her part of the group work but received a low grade because some other student in the group failed to follow through, thus bringing down the quality of the group's work. Such a system seems to foster an atmosphere of blame, of punishing students for situations beyond their control. In addition, awarding privileges on the basis of group performance once again sets up a competitive process, subtly undermining the ethic of cooperation and success for all (Kagan 1996). Although some students do need extrinsic rewards for work they accomplish, most can learn to appreciate the intrinsic benefits derived from group work.

Substantial research supports cooperative learning.

A Closing Reflection Reflection Reflection

- Parents are often concerned that cooperative learning destroys individual initiative. How would you address this issue?
- Plan a unit that could be taught using cooperative learning. How does the plan differ from one you might write if you were using other techniques?
- List the factors that will support your attempts to use small-group discussions and those that will hinder you.
- How can small-group activities be used with computers?

Summary

1. Using small-group discussions can promote student autonomy, cooperation, and learning.
2. Small-group discussions and cooperative learning are ideal for accomplishing process objectives.
3. The ideal size for a small group is six to eight students.
4. Students learn and gain experience by functioning in various roles within the group.
5. The six basic small-group discussion techniques are brainstorming, tutorials, task, role playing, simulations, and inquiry groups.
6. Cooperative learning requires much time, organization, and structure, but it is an ideal way to focus group work on specific tasks and to mandate individual responsibility.
7. Cooperative learning requires positive interdependence, face-to-face interaction, individual accountability, student involvement, and good listening skills.
8. Collect feedback to analyze small-group efforts.

Key Terms

brainstorming (p. 290)

cohesion (p. 286)

cooperative learning (p. 300)

discussion (p. 277)

facilitator (p. 284)

inquiry discussion group (p. 298)

negative interdependence (p. 303)

positive interdependence (p. 303)

process objectives (p. 281)

role (p. 284)

role playing (p. 295)

simulation (p. 296)

small-group discussions (p. 281)

small groups (p. 282)

task group (p. 294)

tutorial discussion group (p. 292)

Helpful Resources

We have listed some references below that will expand your knowledge base on cooperative learning, simulations, and discussions.

Johnson, D. W., R. T. Johnson, and E. J. Holubec. *The New Circles of Learning: Cooperation in the Classroom and School.* Alexandria, VA: Association for Supervision and Curriculum Development, 1994, 111 pp.

This is a handbook for any teacher who wants a practical lesson on initiating and maintaining cooperative learning.

Jones, K. *Simulations: A Handbook for Teachers and Trainers.* East Brunswick, NJ: Nichols Publishing Co., 1995, 145 pp.

This revised and improved handbook is a minilibrary for anyone who wants to use or design simulations in the classroom.

van Ments, M. *The Effective Use of Role-Play: Practical Techniques for Improving Learning* (2nd edition). London: Kogan Page, 1999, 196 pp.

The entire spectrum of role playing is presented in an easy-to-adopt format.

Internet Resources

❖ The Web site below has numerous tips on tutorial situations.

http://para.unl.edu/ServedDocuments/instruction/Presenting

❖ Two of the scores of URLs relating to cooperative learning follow:

http://www.ldonline.org/index.html

http://www.2emc.maricopa.edu/innovation/CCL/CCL.html

❖ The Institute for Learning Sciences at Northwestern University has a search engine providing several techniques relating to discussions.

http://www.ils.nwu.edu

❖ Another good source for information about discussions is

http://128.196.42.70/aed/aed695a/using/htm

References

Abruscato, J. "Boost Your Students' Social Skills with This 9-Step Plan." *Learning* 22(5) (1994): 60–61, 66.

Baloche, L. A. *The Cooperative Classroom: Empowering Learning.* Upper Saddle River, NJ: Prentice Hall, 1998.

Beebe, S. A., and J. T. Masterson. *Communicating in Small Groups: Principles and Practices* (2nd edition). Glenview, IL: Scott, Foresman, 1986.

Bloom, B. S. "The 2 Sigma Problem: The Search for Methods of Group Instruction as Effective as One-to-One Tutoring." *Educational Researcher* 13(6) (1984): 4–16.

Book, C., and K. Galvin. *Instruction In and About Small Group Discussion.* Urbana, IL: ERIC/ACS and SCA, ERIC DRS ED 113 773, 1975.

Boston, J. "Using Simulations." *Social Studies Review* 37(2) (1998): 31–32.

Bramlett, R. K. "Implementing Cooperative Learning: A Field Study Evaluating Issues for School-Based Consultants." *Journal of School Psychology* 32(1) (1994): 67–84.

CNBC. "Stock Market Game." CNBC.WSJ.Com, 2000.

Coelho, E. *All Sides of the Issue: Activities for Cooperative Jigsaw Groups.* San Francisco: Alta Book Center, 1998.

Cohen, E. G., R. A. Lotan, and N. C. Holthuis. "Organizing the Classroom for Learning." In *Working for Equity in Heterogeneous Classrooms: Sociological Theory in Practice.* E. G. Cohen and R. A. Lotan, editors. New York: Teachers College Press, 1997, 31–43.

Cohen, P. A., J. A. Kulik, and C. C. Kulik. "Educational Outcomes of Tutoring: A Meta-Analysis of Findings." *American Educational Research Journal* 19(2) (1982): 237–248.

Cone, J. K. "Untracking Advanced Placement English: Creating Opportunity Is not Enough." *Phi Delta Kappan* 73 (1992): 712–717.

Crotty, E. "The Role of Cooperative Learning in an Authentic Performance Assessment Approach." *Social Science Record* 31(1) (1994): 38–41.

Davidson, I. B. Personal Communication, October 8, 1999.

Davies, P. *70 Activities for Tutor Groups.* Brookfield, VT: Gower, 1999.

Dillon, J. T. *Using Discussions in Classrooms.* Philadelphia: Open University Press, 1994.

Dillon, J. T. "Discussion." In *International Encyclopedia of Teaching and Teacher Education* (2nd edition). L. W. Anderson, editor. Tarrytown, NY: Elsevier Science, 1995, pp. 251–255.

Elliott, S. M., R. T. Busse, and E. S. Shapiro. "Intervention Techniques for Academic Performance Problems." In *The Handbook of School Psychology* (2nd edition). C. R. Reynolds and T. B. Gutkin, editors. New York: John Wiley, 1999, pp. 664–685.

Englberg, N., and D. Hynn. *Working in Groups: Communication Principles and Strategies*. Boston: Houghton Mifflin, 1997.

Field, J. "Skills and Strategies: Towards a New Methodology for Listening." *ELT Journal* 52(2) (1998): 110–118.

Fillmore, L. W., and L. M. Meyer. "The Curriculum and Linguistic Minorities." In *Handbook of Research on Curriculum*. Philip W. Jackson, editor. New York: Macmillan, 1992.

Glickman, C. D. *Revolutionizing America's Schools*. San Francisco: Jossey-Bass, 1998.

Grabe, M., and C. Grabe. *Integrating Technology for Meaningful Learning* (3rd edition). Boston: Houghton Mifflin, 2001.

Hart, L. D. "Some Factors That Impede or Enhance Performance in Mathematical Problem Solving." *Journal for Research in Mathematics Education* 24(2) (1993): 167–171.

Ishler, A. L., R. T. Johnson, and D. W. Johnson. "Long-Term Effectiveness of a Statewide Staff Development Program or Cooperative Learning." *Teaching and Teacher Education* 14(3) (1998): 273–281.

Jacob, E. *Cooperative Learning in Context: An Educational Innovation in Everyday Classrooms*. Albany, NY: State University of New York Press, 1999.

Johnson, D. W., and R. T. Johnson. "What to Say to Advocates for the Gifted." *Educational Leadership* 50(2) (1992): 44–47.

Johnson, D. W., and R. T. Johnson. "Cooperative Learning and Traditional American Values: An Appreciation." *NASSP Bulletin* 80(579) (1996): 63–65.

Johnson, D. W., and R. T. Johnson. *Learning Together and Alone: Cooperative, Competitive and Individualistic Learning* (5th edition). Boston: Allyn & Bacon, 1999.

Johnson, D. W., R. T. Johnson, and E. J. Holubec. *The New Circles of Learning: Cooperation in the Classroom*. Alexandria, VA: ASCD, 1994.

Johnson, D. W., R. T. Johnson, and E. J. Holubec. *Cooperation in the Classroom*. Edina, MN: Interaction Book Company, 1998.

Kagan, S. "Avoiding the Group-Grades Trap." *Learning* 24(4) (1996): 56–58.

Kagan, S. *Building Character Through Cooperative Learning*. Port Chester, NY: National Professional Resources. Videocassette, 1999.

Lan, W. Y., and J. Repman. "The Effects of Social Learning Context and Modeling on Persistence and Dynamism in Academic Activities." *Journal of Experimental Education* 64(1) (1995): 53–67.

Losey, K. M. "Mexican-American Students and Classroom Interaction: An Overview and Critique." *Review of Educational Research* 65(3) (1995): 283–318.

Lowery, L. "Strategies for Instruction." *FOSS* (11) (1998): 6–9.

McCaslin, M. M., and T. L. Good. *Listening in Classrooms*. New York: HarperCollins, 1996.

McCormick, K. *Plays to Ponder for Grades 6–8: Prompting Classroom Discussion Through Dramatic Play*. Torrance, CA: Good Apple, 1998.

McGrath, B. "Partners in Learning: Twelve Ways Technology Changes the Teacher-Student Relationship." *T.H.E. Journal* 25(9) (1998): 58–61.

Megnin, J. K. "Combining Memory and Creativity in Teaching Math." *Teaching PreK–8* 25(6) (1995): 48–49.

Miles, M. B. *Learning to Work in Groups* (2nd edition). Troy, NY: Educator's International Press, 1998.

Miller, D. P. *Introduction to Small Group Discussion*. Urbana, IL: ERIC/RCS and SCA, DRS ED 278 037, 1986.

Morton, T. *Cooperative Learning and Social Studies: Towards Excellence to Equity*. San Clemente, CA: Kagan Cooperative Learning, 1998.

Mulryan, C. M. "Fifth and Sixth Graders' Involvement and Participation in Cooperative Small Groups in Mathematics." *Elementary School Journal* 95(4) (1995): 297–310.

Nattiv, A. "Helping Behaviors and Math Achievement Gain of Students Using Cooperative Learning." *Elementary School Journal* 94(3) (1994): 285–297.

Olmstead, J. A. *Theory and State of the Art of Small Group Methods of Instruction*. Alexandria, VA: Human Resources Research Organization, 1970.

Patrick, J. "Direct Teaching of Collaborative Skills in a Cooperative Learning Environment." *Teaching and Change* 1(2) (1994): 170–181.

Patterson, V. E. "Introducing Co-Operative Learning at Princess Elizabeth Elementary School." *Education Canada* 34(2) (1994): 36–41.

Putnam, J. W. *Cooperative Learning in Diverse Classrooms*. Upper Saddle River, NJ: Merrill, an Imprint of Prentice Hall, 1997.

Race, P., and S. Brown. *500 Tips on Group Learning*. London: Kogan Page, 1999.

Resnick, M., and U. Wilensky. "Diving into Complexity: Developing Probabilistic Decentralized Thinking Through Role-Playing Activities." *Journal of the Learning Sciences* 7(2) (1998): 153–172.

Richburg, R. W., and B. J. Nelson. "Where in Western Europe Would You Like to Live?" *The Social Studies* 82, No. 3 (1991): 97–106.

Schmuck, R. A., and P. A. Schmuck. *Group Processes in the Classroom* (7th edition). Madison, WI: Brown & Benchmark, 1997.

Scotty-Ryan, D. L. *An Investigative Study of How Cooperative Learning Can Benefit High-Achieving Students.* M.S. thesis, S.U.N.Y. at Brockport, 1998.

Sharon, S. "Teaching in Small Groups." In *International Encyclopedia of Teaching and Teacher Education* (2nd edition). Tarrytown, NY: Elsevier Science, 1995, pp. 255–259.

Shulman, J. H., R. A. Lotan, and J. A. Whitcomb, editors. *Groupwork in Diverse Classrooms: A Casebook for Educators.* New York: Teachers College Press, 1998.

Simpson, T. "Morality and the Social Studies: A Model for Addressing Those Difficult Topics." *Southern Social Studies Journal* 21(1) (1995): 65–73.

Slavin, R. E. *Cooperative Learning: Theory, Research and Practice.* Englewood Cliffs, NJ: Prentice Hall, 1990.

Sparapani, E. F. "Encouraging Thinking in High School and Middle School: Constraints and Possibilities." *Clearing House* 71(5) (1998): 274–276.

Stahl, R. J. "The Essential Elements of Cooperative Learning in the Classroom." *ERIC Digest.* Bloomington, IN: ERIC Clearinghouse for Social Studies/Social Science Education. ED 370 881. 1994.

Stahl, S. A., and C. H. Clark. "The Effects of Participatory Expectations in Classroom Discussion on the Learning of Science Vocabulary." *American Educational Research Journal* 24 (1987): 541–556.

Stevens, R. J., and R. E. Slavin. "The Cooperative Elementary School: Effects on Students' Achievement, Attitudes and Social Relations." *American Educational Research Journal* 32(2) (1995a): 321–351.

Stevens, R. J., and R. E. Slavin. "Effects of a Cooperative Learning Approach in Reading and Writing on Academically Handicapped and Non-Handicapped Students." *Elementary School Journal* 95(3) (1995b): 241–262.

Tiberius, R. G. *Small Group Teaching: A Trouble-Shooting Guide.* London: Kogan Page, 1999.

van Ments, M. *The Effective Use of Role-Play: Practical Techniques for Improving Learning* (2nd edition). London: Kogan Page, 1999.

Vermette, P. J. *Making Cooperative Learning Work: Student Teams in K–12 Classrooms.* Upper Saddle River, NJ: Merrill, an Imprint of Prentice Hall, 1998.

Vessels, G. "The First Amendment and Character Education." *Update on Law-Related Education* 20(1) (1996): 26–28.

Walberg, H. J. "Productive Teaching and Instruction: Assessing the Knowledge Base." In *Effective Teaching: Current Research.* H. C. Waxman and H. J. Walberg, editors. Berkeley, CA: McCutchan Publishers, 1991.

Webb, N. M., J. Trooper, and R. Fall. "Constructive Activity and Learning in Collaborative Small Groups." *Journal of Educational Psychology* 87(3) (1995): 406–423.

Weiser, L. A., and M. C. Schug. "Financial Market Simulations: Motivating Learning and Performance." *Social Studies* 83(6) (1992): 224–247.

Weissglass, J. "Transforming Schools into Caring Learning Communities." *Journal for a Just and Caring Education* 2(2) (1996): 175–189.

Wheelan, S. A., F. Tilin, and J. Sanford. "Small Group Effectiveness and Productivity." *Research Practice* 4(1) (1996): 1–3.

Wood, W. C. "The Stock Market Game: Classroom Use and Strategy." *Journal of Economic Education* 23(3) (1992): 236–246.

Yell, M. M. "The Time Before History: Thinking Like an Archaeologist." *Social Education* 62(1) (1998): 27–31.

Zhang, Q. "An Intervention Model of Constructive Conflict Resolution and Cooperative Learning." *Journal of Social Issues* 50(1) (1994): 99–116.

Zuckerman, G. A. "A Pilot Study of a Ten-Day Course in Cooperative Learning for Beginning Russian First Graders." *Elementary School Journal* 94(4) (1994): 405–420.

Zuckerman, G. A., E. V. Chudinova, and E. E. Khavkin. "Inquiry As a Pivotal Element of Knowledge Acquisition Within the Vogotskian Paradigm: Building a Science Curriculum for the Elementary School." *Cognition and Instruction* 16(2) (1998): 201–233.

9

Inquiry Teaching and Higher-Level Thinking

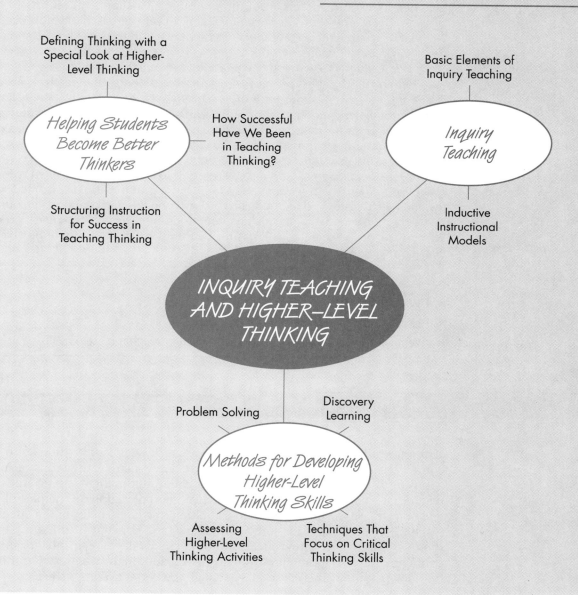

Defining Thinking with a
Special Look at Higher-
Level Thinking

Basic Elements of
Inquiry Teaching

*Helping Students
Become Better
Thinkers*

How Successful
Have We Been
in Teaching
Thinking?

*Inquiry
Teaching*

Structuring Instruction
for Success in
Teaching Thinking

Inductive
Instructional
Models

*INQUIRY TEACHING
AND HIGHER–LEVEL
THINKING*

Problem Solving

Discovery
Learning

*Methods for Developing
Higher-Level
Thinking Skills*

Assessing
Higher-Level
Thinking Activities

Techniques That
Focus on Critical
Thinking Skills

M r. Toshio Akiyama's social studies class is the designated site for your in-school observations. As you approach the room, you hear the buzz of meaningful noise. Students are working in small groups of three to five; a few students are at the computer center, which is neatly arranged in the far corner of the room; and the teacher is helping a small group of students with learning disabilities align their data on a large poster. The walls of the room are covered with the students' work. Their projects resemble the posters at a professional convention.

A student invites you to work with the group. You observe the division of labor among the students. After about thirty minutes, Mr. Akiyama calls everyone together, and the recorders from three groups give short oral reports to the class. Students question the presenters, and a lively verbal interaction occurs. The teacher then writes a few specific assignments on the chalkboard, and students begin individual seat-work.

"Wow," you say to yourself, "I wonder if I can pull this style off?"

Traditionally, teachers present knowledge to students, who passively absorb it, and this pattern becomes both the *means* and the *end* of education. Is it any wonder, then, that students get bored? As an alternative to routine lectures and recitations, we offer an instructional strategy that is not new but is centuries old. The generic term for the strategy is **inquiry teaching,** an investigative learning process that asks students to pose questions, analyze data, and develop conclusions or generalizations. It can also be referred to as *discovery, problem solving, reflective thinking,* and *inductive teaching,* among others. It is associated with teaching techniques and methods that all have one thing in common: encouraging higher-level thinking. In this chapter we discuss these techniques and describe their major characteristics. After you finish studying it, you'll be able to answer the following questions:

- Can we really teach kids how to think?
- What is inquiry teaching?
- How can I use it in my classroom?
- What techniques are associated with inquiry teaching?

Section 1: Helping Students Become Better Thinkers

While few people would argue with the idea that educating students to become good learners and responsible citizens means that they must also be good thinkers, the road toward that goal is not automatic. Helping students reach that goal takes knowledge, awareness, and planning on the part of the teacher. We use this first section to examine three key aspects of the effective teaching of thinking skills—first, we explore the concept of thinking itself; then we examine just how successful our schools have been thus far in encouraging the development of thinking skills; and finally we present our own framework for how this essential goal might be better accomplished.

Defining Thinking with a Special Look at Higher-Level Thinking

What do we mean by *thinking?* The word is a construct, a label we apply to processes we can observe only indirectly through actions or products. That is, when someone behaves in a careful, prudent manner, we infer that the behavior resulted from deliberate thought. When we observe an example of complex problem solving—space flight, for instance—we infer the incredible amounts of reasoning that were necessary.

Attempts to define thinking—beyond such synonyms as *reasoning* or *forming an idea*—become clouded by differences of psychological position. Despite the lack of consensus on the definition of thinking, we can still characterize it and suggest ways to make it more effective.

Thinking is a multifaceted process, not a singular one.

We propose that thinking is a combination of knowledge, skills or processes, and attitudes. Knowledge is involved, of course, because thinking requires an object. One must think about *something.* The more knowledge one has in any area, the more effectively one can think about it (Sternberg and Spear-Swerling 1996; Wright 1996).

Skills associated with effective thinking include

- Observing
- Identifying patterns, relationships, cause-and-effect relationships, assumptions, reasoning errors, logical fallacies, and bias
- Establishing criteria and classifying
- Comparing and contrasting
- Inferring and interpreting
- Summarizing
- Analyzing, synthesizing, and generalizing
- Hypothesizing and imagining
- Distinguishing relevant from irrelevant data, verifiable from nonverifiable data, and problems from irrelevant statements

Effective thinking also requires particular attitudes, such as a disposition to perceive and relate to one's surroundings in particular ways. Some people, for instance, are curious about their environment; others are not. Attitude determines in part *what* we think about and in *what ways* we think about it. But since attitudes tend to be learned responses, you can help students adopt appropriate attitudes for effective thinking (see the box below).

Attitudes That Promote Effective Thinking

- Willingness to suspend judgment until sufficient evidence is presented
- Tolerance for ambiguity
- A tendency to question rather than simply accept authority
- Willingness to believe credible evidence

Elements of Critical Thinking

- Identifying issues
- Identifying relationships between elements
- Deducing implications
- Inferring motives
- Combining independent elements to create new patterns of thought (creativity)
- Making original interpretations (creativity)

The cognitive taxonomy has relevance to enhancing critical thinking.

Thus we arrive at the following definition: *thinking is a complex act comprising attitudes, knowledge, and skills that allow the individual to shape his or her environment more effectively than intuition alone.*

Now let us focus on higher-level thinking skills, our particular concern in this chapter. Think back to our discussion of Bloom's cognitive taxonomy (Chapter 3). Recall that two of Bloom's higher levels are analysis and synthesis. Higher-level thinking skills, also known as "critical thinking," consist of the application of these two levels. Critical thinking is a multistage construction of meaning. It is rational and logical and results in high levels of student achievement (see Walberg 1991). To learn critical thinking skills, your students need to learn the skills listed in the box above.

It is one thing to identify and define thinking and higher-level thinking skills; it is quite another to teach them to students. How successful have our schools been in doing just that? We'll examine this question next.

How Successful Have We Been in Teaching Thinking?

As a nation, we want our schools to teach *thinking*. The authors of the SCANS Report (U.S. Department of Labor 1992) and *Work Force Education* (Imel 1999) stress that it is less important to provide a great deal of technical training in the schools than to develop students' ability to think and solve problems. To think, a student must learn to be actively involved with issues, data, materials, topics, concepts, and problems.

But are we succeeding in teaching students how to think? Pause for a moment to consider how you would answer this question: "What day follows the day before yesterday if two days from now will be Sunday?" Most likely you would think about the given information and try to arrange it in a way that would help you determine the answer. However, when Whimbey (1977) posed this and similar questions to numerous college classes, many students did not know how to proceed. They either guessed or gave up.

Now consider the following. The single best source for standardized and nationally collected data on the general topic comes from the National Assessment of Educational Progress (NAEP). Since 1969 the NAEP has intermittently tested nine-, thirteen-, and seventeen-year-olds (grades 4, 8, and 11) in

---

NAEP Key Findings for Civics, Science, Math, Reading, and Writing Grades 4, 8, and 11

1. All students do exceptionally well at Bloom's *knowledge* level with the correct responses ranging from 91 percent (grade 4 reading) to 100 percent (grades 8 and 11 all subjects).

2. At the *understanding* levels, the correct responses range from 68 percent (grade 4 science) to 100 percent (grade 11 math).

3. At the *application* levels, the correct responses range from 13 percent (grade 4 writing) to 97 percent (grade 11 math).

4. At the two higher NAEP levels, corresponding approximately to Bloom's *analysis and synthesis,* the correct responses ranged from 1 percent (grade 4 reading and writing) to 60 percent (grade 11 math).

5. The top NAEP standard, corresponding approximately to Bloom's *synthesis and evaluation* levels, shows the correct responses ranging from 0 percent (grade 4 all subjects) to 11 percent (grade 11 science).

6. The Civics Assessment showed 65 to 70 percent of students in these three grades to be at or above "basic," 22 to 26 percent at or above "proficient," and 2 to 4 percent at the "advanced" level. Between 30 and 35 percent of the students were judged at being "below basic."

---

civics, science, mathematics, reading, and writing. Data from the most recent NAEP publications are summarized in the box above (see Campbell, Voelkl, and Donahue 1998, pp. 9–12; *NAEP CIVICS Report Card Highlights,* November 1999, p. 8).

We recognize that fourth graders may not be cognitively developed to process formal thinking questions (see Chapter 2), which are posed at the three upper levels of Bloom's taxonomy and the NAEP levels. Fourth graders do very well, thank you, at the two lower cognitive levels, again corresponding developmentally to the concrete operations levels. Eighth and eleventh graders truly "shine" at these levels. However, one conclusion that may be drawn from America's acknowledged best achievement tests is that those students in grades eight and eleven are not being taught how to think!

We pause a moment to return to the Civics Assessment of those fourth graders. One advanced-level question required students to interpret a political cartoon that poked fun at "couch potatoes" and voter apathy. The cartoonist was showing the importance of civic participation to democracy. Answering the question correctly required fourth graders to (1) understand the cartoon, (2) infer a meaning from the drawing, (3) interpret the comment made by the couch potato, (4) analyze the message, and (5) select the correct response. Twenty-six percent of all fourth graders answered it correctly—which is about the "chance" level of 25 percent. (See Orlich 2000 for a critical analysis and interesting perspective about the issue of developmentally inappropriate tests.)

Now, reread the preceding paragraph and revisit the list at the beginning

Reflect Reflect Reflect

- Examine your local school district's test scores and compare them to the data sources presented in this section.

of this chapter that shows nine skills associated with thinking. We point this out so that you understand that national test scores and associated data need to be interpreted critically.

But wait, there is a ray of hope. *The Condition of Education 1999—Section I* provided national data showing slight or even moderate improvements between 1970 and 1998 for all students in grades 4, 8, and 11 and for every age, race, or ethnic origin for science, mathematics, and reading. There was a very slight decrease in test scores on writing. With the advent of the personal computer, we predict that writing will show major gains in the future. So teachers must be doing something right. We'll spend some time in the following discussion examining what you as a teacher can and should do "right" as you approach the teaching of thinking skills.

Structuring Instruction for Success in Teaching Thinking

First, what does it mean to *teach thinking?* Nearly all writers agree on the generic aspects of thinking highlighted in the box below (Beyer 1997; Holcomb 1999; Sternberg and Spear-Swerling 1996). These five skills are core skills. To build these skills requires careful teacher planning, appropriate sequencing, and a continuous building of cognitive and attitudinal factors.

The preceding statements about structuring instruction and the list focus our attention on those aspects of thinking that can be identified and taught to students—knowledge, skills, and attitudes. The assumption is, of course, that students will think more effectively as a result—that they will be able to relate to and alter their environment better than they otherwise would. Considerable empirical evidence supports this view (see Wakefield 1996; Winne 1995). In fact, we would go as far as saying that helping students identify and use these skills must be a basic part of instruction in *all* classes if students are to benefit from schooling.

Core Skills of Thinking

- Perception of a problem or issue
- Ability to gather relevant information
- Competence in organizing data
- Analysis of data patterns, inferences, sources of errors
- Communication of the results

So, more specifically, what do we mean when we say we will help students become more effective thinkers? Will we add a new course in thinking to the curriculum? Will we teach a new content area or a new group of process skills?

The answer isn't simple. Instead, we believe that teachers need to take a threefold approach to the teaching of thinking, especially the teaching of higher-level or critical thinking. First, you need to develop an overall awareness—a kind of infusion of the need to focus on thinking in all classes at all times. In other words, you must systematically and continually instruct them in ways to think more effectively. Thinking must be taught across all subjects and all grade levels. Teachers must stress meaningfulness, but children must be taught how to understand and think (see Beyer 1997 for a rich resource). For example, you might have the students ask one *reflective question* (Chapter 7) after they read some passage for study. Or after you have introduced concepts, such as *infer, classify, hypothesize,* you challenge the class to use those process skills in some pending assignment. By continuously reviewing thinking skills, you establish a base of knowledge and an attitude of inquiry (see Adey and Shayer 1994).

Our second point could be seen as an "operationalizing" of the first point, but we mention it separately to emphasize it: we believe the adoption of an inquiry-based teaching strategy will greatly facilitate your teaching of thinking skills. At the core of this approach is an emphasis on student exploration and understanding; for that reason, we spend a good deal of this chapter explaining and demonstrating that strategy. Third, you should know how to use some specific methods and teaching techniques that are themselves offshoots or "relatives" of the inquiry model; we present a number of these at the end of the chapter.

We want to offer a few other observations before we close this discussion. First, you should always bear in mind that the teacher is the most important factor in thinking instruction (Ennis 1985). Prepared texts, workbooks, pre-planned programs, and drill exercises may be useful instructional aids, but by themselves they are insufficient to induce thinking abilities. The most effective instruction emanates from a teacher who is knowledgeable about both subject matter and thinking processes, who continually demonstrates the skills and attitudes involved in thinking, and who demands systematic, rigorous thought from students—both in speaking and in writing. In this regard, it is the teacher who can add the dimension of meaning. Make your students think about what meaning they might derive from school subjects. It is up to you to provide the bases for meaning when new topics and concepts are introduced. For example, Carole L. Hahn (1996) shows how easy it is to use political issues as means to develop student critical thinking skills.

Also, realize that many—perhaps most—of the students you will teach will belong to minority ethnic or cultural groups. You can help them achieve at the highest academic levels if you demand it *and* if you try to relate the content, skills, or knowledge you are teaching to some artifact in their culture. Meaning is derived by moving from the known to the unknown. Be sensitive to the needs of all students, and be aware of teachable moments for students you may label "minorities" (see Banks 1997).

Finally, you need to reflect on how we have incorporated our concept of *multimethodology* into the entire realm of inquiry and critical thinking. There is really no limit to the number of ways that you may approach these powerful teaching strategies.

Teachers can establish a positive classroom environment that promotes critical thinking.

Every student must be encouraged to develop critical thinking skills.

> ### Reflect Reflect Reflect
>
> - What topics or units in your teaching field would be appropriate to stress thinking processes?
> - Examine your state's NAEP data for selected subjects. What can you conclude about the level of thinking skills shown?
> - How can you structure classroom questions to stimulate student thinking development?

Section 2: Inquiry Teaching

In this section, we first present several underlying bases for inquiry-based teaching and take a brief look at its relationship to the constructivist philosophy. We then explore in detail how two different instructional models based on the inquiry strategy can be used for instruction in your classroom.

The Basic Elements of Inquiry Teaching

There is a strong research base supporting inquiry teaching.

Theoretical Bases of Inquiry Methods   All inquiry methods are predicated on specific assumptions about both learning and learners. The box on page 321 provides a synthesis of the views on the subject by several scholars (Bigge and Shermis 1999; Holcomb 1999; Joyce and Calhoun 1998; Parker and Jarolimek 1997; Snowman, Biehler, and Bonk 2000).

Inquiry teaching is rather difficult to define in nonoperational terms—that is, without giving precise examples of teacher strategies and the concomitant student behaviors. Therefore, we will demonstrate the meaning of inquiry teaching through examples as we describe the spectrum of options available for this strategy. Inquiry teaching requires a high degree of interaction among the learner, the teacher, the materials, the content, and the environment. Perhaps the most crucial aspect of the inquiry method is that it allows both student and teacher to become persistent askers, seekers, interrogators, questioners, and ponderers. The end result occurs when your students pose the question every Nobel Prize winner has asked: "I wonder what would happen if . . . ?"

Recall in Chapter 7 our plea to develop the question-asking skills of all students. In this chapter, we take questioning a step further, for it plays a crucial role in both the teaching and learning acts associated with the inquiry mode of learning. Questions lead to investigations as students attempt to understand the topic under study. The investigative processes of inquiry learning involve the student not only in formulating questions but also in limiting them, selecting the best means of answering them, and conducting the study.

As we mentioned, inquiry learning is an old technique. The distinguished trio of ancient Western culture—Socrates, Plato, and Aristotle—were all masters of inquiry processes. Their heritage has given us a mode of teaching in

Selected Views on Inquiry Teaching

- Inquiry methods require the learner to develop various processes associated with inquiry.

- Teachers and principals must support the concept of inquiry teaching and learn how to adapt their own teaching and administrative styles to the concept.

- Students at all ages and levels have a genuine interest in discovering something new or in providing solutions or alternatives to unsolved questions or problems.

- The solutions, alternatives, or responses provided by learners are not found in textbooks. Students use reference materials and textbooks during inquiry lessons just as scientists and professionals use books, articles, and references to conduct their work.

- The objective of inquiry teaching is often a *process*. In many instances the end product of an inquiry activity is relatively unimportant compared to the processes used to create it.

- All conclusions must be considered relative or tentative, not final. Students must learn to modify their conclusions as new data are discovered.

- Inquiry learning cannot be gauged by the clock. In the real world, when people think or create, it is not usually done in fifty-minute increments.

- Learners are responsible for planning, conducting, and evaluating their own efforts. It is essential that the teacher play only a *supportive* role, not an active one (that is, the teacher should not do the work for the students).

- Students have to be taught the processes associated with inquiry learning in a systematic manner. Every time a "teachable moment" arrives, the teacher should capitalize on it to further the building of inquiry processes.

- Inquiry learning complicates and expands the teacher's work, owing to the many interactions that may emanate from inquiry teaching and learning.

which students are vitally involved in the learning and creating processes. It is through inquiry that new knowledge is discovered. It is by becoming involved in the process that students become historians, scientists, economists, artists, businesspersons, poets, writers, or researchers—even if only for an hour or two, in your class.

Basic Inquiry Processes   The basic processes of inquiry learning are listed in the box on page 322 in order of complexity.

Reflect Reflect Reflect

■ Locate any book about the constructivist teaching philosophy. Compare the list in the box on selected views on inquiry methods to lists developed by constructivist writers. What do you find?

■ In what organizational contexts would it be easiest for you to apply inquiry teaching? What settings are antagonistic to the model?

Inquiry processes are all action oriented.

Inquiry Processes

1. *Observing.* Identifying objects, object properties, and changes in various systems; making controlled observations; ordering series of observations

2. *Classifying.* Making simple and complex classifications; tabulating and coding observations

3. *Inferring.* Drawing conclusions based on observations; constructing situations to test these conclusions

4. *Using numbers.* Identifying sets and their members and then progressing to higher mathematical processes

5. *Measuring.* Identifying and ordering lengths and then areas, volumes, weights, temperatures, and speeds

6. *Using space-time relationships.* Identifying movement and direction; learning rules governing changes in position

7. *Communicating.* Constructing graphs and diagrams to describe simple and then more complex phenomena; presenting written and oral reports

8. *Predicting.* Interpolating and extrapolating from data; formulating methods for testing predictions

9. *Making operational definitions.* Distinguishing between operational and nonoperational definitions; constructing operational definitions for new problems

10. *Formulating hypotheses.* Distinguishing hypotheses from inferences, observations, and predictions; constructing and testing hypotheses

11. *Interpreting data.* Describing data and inferences based on them; constructing equations to represent data; relating data to hypotheses; making generalizations supported by experimental findings

12. *Controlling variables.* Identifying independent and dependent variables; conducting experiments; describing how variables are controlled

13. *Experimenting.* Interpreting accounts of scientific experiments; stating problems; constructing hypotheses; conducting experimental procedures

> **Reflect Reflect** Reflect
>
> ■ Show the list of thirteen processes to peers who are studying art, history, or literature. Ask them to relate those processes to their respective disciplines.
>
> ■ What experiences has your teacher education program provided that will help you use the inquiry model of teaching?

Note that each process requires progressive intellectual development and that as this development takes place for one process, it spurs development on other processes. Development of observing, classifying, and measuring skills, for example, speeds development of inferring skills.

These processes are found in every learning episode that involves inquiry. Inquiry is not simply asking questions; it is a process for conducting a thorough investigation, and as such it applies to all domains of knowledge.

Each **inquiry process**—that is, the thirteen processes in the box on page 322—must be carefully developed and systematically practiced. This means that you must decide how much of *each lesson* will be devoted to building cognitive skills and how much to mastering processes—just as you did when you planned small-group discussions (see Chapter 8).

There is a link between the constructivist perspective and inquiry teaching.

Constructivism and Inquiry Teaching   In Chapter 2 we introduced the topic of constructivism. In our opinion there is nearly a perfect match between the notion of constructivism and the inquiry model of learning, as is implied by the following quote: "It is assumed that learners have to construct their own knowledge—individually and collectively. Each learner has a tool kit of conceptions and skills with which he or she must construct knowledge to solve problems presented by the environment. The role of the community—other learners and teacher—is to provide the setting, pose the challenges, and offer the support that will encourage . . . construction" (Davis, Maher, and Noddings 1990, p. 3).

The tool kit of inquiry consists of those thirteen process skills just presented. You, as the teacher, must make the invitation to students to learn through inquiry, and you must direct them to the proper tools. As you will shortly learn, you must have at your command several different techniques as an example of a simulation.

In Chapter 8 we referred to a cooperative lesson in world geography ("Comparing the United States and Europe"; see Richburg and Nelson 1991). Although the exercise was created for cooperative learning groups, it is precisely the kind of experience that can be adapted for inquiry and constructivist teaching. The exercise encourages active learning: students must synthesize data, classify information, make inferences, communicate individual findings to everyone else, and evaluate their ideas or conclusions.

An important tenet of the constructivist philosophy is that knowledge is constructed by different thought processes and patterns of thinking (Phillips and Soltis 1998). As we develop this chapter, you will discover the development

> ## Points of Agreement Between the Constructivist and Inquiry-Oriented Approaches
>
> - The focus is on the student.
> - The pace of instruction is flexible, not fixed.
> - Students are encouraged to search for implications.
> - Students are encouraged to generate multiple conclusions.
> - Students must justify their methods for problem solving.
> - Neither constructivism nor inquiry sees itself as the sole learning model for all content.
> - Nature provides the objects, and humans classify them.

of all inquiry-based learning, including problem solving, discovery, and critical thinking skills that require information to be processed and new patterns or ideas to emerge.

Another tenet of constructivism is that learners construct knowledge through active engagement or experiences. This does not preclude memorization of key facts or events; however, the learner needs to *do* something—read, study, observe, write, discuss, chart, graph, map, or communicate (Airasian and Walsh 1997). This kind of dynamic experimentation is also an essential part of the inquiry method.

Experiences are key to any active-learning model.

Finally, in a constructivist approach to education, the student assumes responsibility for acquiring knowledge. As you become experienced at conducting inquiry-oriented classes, you will allow more student-initiated learning; this is definitely an example of using a constructivist notion.

It is important to recognize that constructivism is not an instructional model, such as direct instruction; it is a theoretical model about how learners come to know (Airasian and Walsh 1997). We also caution that, unlike inquiry methods that have been used in the sciences for centuries, constructivism does not entail a set of procedural steps.

Inquiry teaching takes time and much teacher energy. In our experience we have never seen inquiry-oriented teachers sitting at their desks—they are on the go, and so are their students. Constructivist teachers behave the same way. We recognize that there are differences in social interpretations of the two approaches, but that is a topic for another book. Here, we close with a synthesized set of commonalities between constructivist and inquiry-oriented teachers, in the box above.

Inductive Instructional Models

Inductive inquiry may be performed using two techniques.

We have established the basics of inquiry as a teaching strategy. Now let's describe several different kinds of inquiry models that follow **empirical epistemology** (gaining knowledge through observation or experiment). Recall that in Chapter 5 we introduced inductive reasoning and gave models contrasting inductive and deductive teaching. In this section, we take inductive teaching a step further. **Induction,** or inductive logic, is a thought process wherein the individual observes a *selected number* of events, processes, or objects and then constructs a particular pattern of concepts or relationships based on these limited experiences. **Inductive inquiry,** then, is a method that teachers use when they ask students to infer a conclusion, generalization, or pattern of relationships from a set of data or facts. The student observes the specifics and then makes generalizations based on his or her observations.

Inductive inquiry may be approached in at least two different ways: guided and unguided. If you provide the specifics—that is, the data or facts—but want the students to make the generalizations, then you are conducting **guided inductive inquiry** (Tamir 1995). If you allow students to discover the specifics themselves before they make generalizations, the process is labeled **unguided inductive inquiry.** In most cases you will begin with guided experiences. This way you will know there is a fixed number of generalizations or conclusions that can be reasonably inferred, and you can then help students make them from the data provided. In our experiences with inductive inquiry, the guided method provides an easy transition from expository teaching to less expository teaching.

Inductive inquiry is appropriate at all levels of instruction, from preschool to university graduate schools. Obviously, the kinds and quality of induction will vary considerably. An important aspect of inductive inquiry is that the processes of observing, making inferences, classifying, formulating hypotheses, and predicting are all sharpened (or reinforced) by the experiences.

Guided Inductive Inquiry Pictures are usually the easiest way to introduce the concept of inductive inquiry. For young children, show different pictures of the same scene to the class. Ask the children to tell what they see in the pictures and to describe patterns they observe. Have them state these patterns as generalizations. Ask questions that require students to do some generalizing themselves, such as "What could cause this type of track in the snow?" or "Where have we seen this before?"

> Guided inductive inquiry is more "teacher initiated" than "student initiated."

Distinguish clearly between statements based on observations and those based on inferences. As the children respond, ask, "Is that an inference or an observation?" (Of course, you should begin the lesson by explaining and demonstrating the difference between observations and inferences.)

The process of inductive thinking is developed gradually. As the lesson progresses, prepare a simple chart or list on the blackboard of students' observations and inferences. Students' understanding of each process will gradually develop from studying these examples.

At all levels, ask students to write their observations and, beside them, their inferences. This method helps you determine what observations were the basis for any inferences or generalizations. The Instructional Strategies box on page 326 lists the steps to be used in arriving at generalizations through guided inductive inquiry.

> Inquiry learning cannot be rushed—flexible schedules are expected.

Time Requirements When you first use any type of inquiry activity in your classes, you must plan to spend at least twice as much class time on each lesson as you normally would. This time is spent on in-depth analyses of the content by the students. Furthermore, inquiry methods demand greater

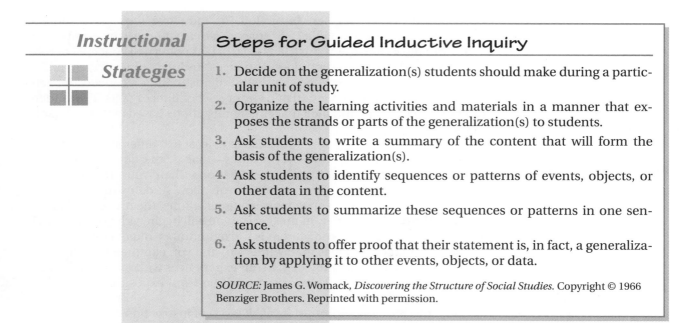

Instructional

Strategies

Steps for Guided Inductive Inquiry

1. Decide on the generalization(s) students should make during a particular unit of study.
2. Organize the learning activities and materials in a manner that exposes the strands or parts of the generalization(s) to students.
3. Ask students to write a summary of the content that will form the basis of the generalization(s).
4. Ask students to identify sequences or patterns of events, objects, or other data in the content.
5. Ask students to summarize these sequences or patterns in one sentence.
6. Ask students to offer proof that their statement is, in fact, a generalization by applying it to other events, objects, or data.

SOURCE: James G. Womack, *Discovering the Structure of Social Studies.* Copyright © 1966 Benziger Brothers. Reprinted with permission.

Reflect Reflect Reflect

- Search the literature or the Internet for two types of inductive inquiry experiences that you can use in your teaching.
- Examine a textbook published since 1999. What inquiry exercises or experiences do the authors provide?
- Explain this quote: "When you teach with the inquiry model, you teach less, but your students learn more."

interaction between the learner and the learning materials, as well as greater interaction between the teacher and the students (see Polman 2000).

Another caveat is required: when you use an inquiry method, the amount of material you can cover is reduced, because you will use more time developing process skills and less time covering facts. You cannot maximize thinking skills and simultaneously maximize content coverage. If you wish to build higher-order thinking skills, you must reduce some of the content and substitute processes instead (see Eylon and Linn 1988). By doing so, however, you will provide important instructional experiences that the student can apply across all disciplines.

Steps in Guided Inductive Inquiry   Figure 9.1 shows six major steps in the inquiry system it illustrates: (1) identifying the problem, (2) developing tentative research hypotheses or objectives, (3) collecting data and testing the tentative answers, (4) interpreting the data, (5) developing tentative conclusions or generalizations, and (6) testing, applying, and revising the conclusions. Im-

FIGURE 9.1

A General Model of Inquiry

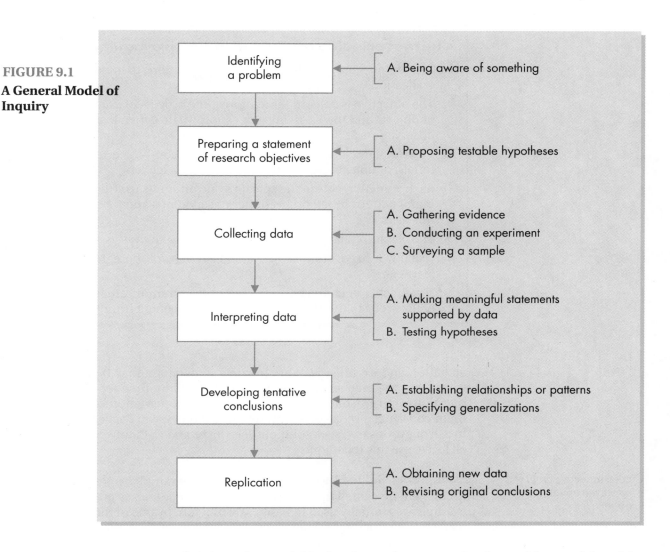

Identifying a problem	A. Being aware of something
Preparing a statement of research objectives	A. Proposing testable hypotheses
Collecting data	A. Gathering evidence B. Conducting an experiment C. Surveying a sample
Interpreting data	A. Making meaningful statements supported by data B. Testing hypotheses
Developing tentative conclusions	A. Establishing relationships or patterns B. Specifying generalizations
Replication	A. Obtaining new data B. Revising original conclusions

plicit in such a model is that the student recognize the problem and then follow the six steps to attempt to resolve it. Note how this model can be adapted to other inquiry models, such as problem solving (discussed later).

These steps usually are needed for introductory guided inductive lessons. Recall that the process objectives are to observe, to infer, and to communicate. The problem, if it can be called one, is to find a meaningful pattern in an array of events or objects. All inferences must be supported by some evidence—that is, observations or data. The latter may be obtained from some standard reference source such as the *Statistical Abstract of the United States*, almanacs, yearbooks, reports, or encyclopedias. The data become the focal point of the inquiry session and thus serve as a common experience for the entire class (see Orlich 1989; Holcomb 1999). Guided inductive inquiry includes the seven characteristics listed in the box on page 328.

At this point you may be thinking, "This certainly sounds like constructivism to me." For the most part, you would be correct. Constructivism is based on the idea that learners construct knowledge from their own thoughts,

Characteristics of Guided Inductive Inquiry Model

1. The learners progress from specific observations to inferences or generalizations.

2. The objective is to learn (or reinforce) the process of examining events or objects and then arriving at an appropriate generalization from the observations.

3. The teacher controls the specifics of the lesson—the events, data, materials, or objects—and thus acts as the class leader.

4. Each student reacts to the specifics and attempts to structure a meaningful pattern based on his or her observations and those of others in the class.

5. The classroom is to be considered a learning laboratory.

6. Usually, a fixed number of generalizations will be elicited from the learners.

7. The teacher encourages each student to communicate his or her generalizations to the class so that others may benefit from them.

activities, and experience. What learners understand may be quite different from what the teacher understands. By scheduling time for children to ask questions and to share their observations with one another, you will help them construct a sense of reality. By using inquiry, you challenge the student to ask questions and seek solutions (see Joyce and Calhoun 1998). Scholars at all levels use this technique.

Guided inductive inquiry is a good way to initiate active learning.

Examples of Guided Inductive Inquiry   Two examples of guided inductive inquiry are presented in the Instructional Strategies boxes on p. 329. The first example was initially used in Pasco, Washington, by one of the authors of this text while instructing teacher aides. The aides were given the challenge of determining the patterns observed when using a compound microscope so that they would be familiar with one of the most commonly used pieces of scientific equipment. This exercise has since been used widely at several grade levels. Note how simple such an exercise can be.

The second example, is a clever guided inquiry exercise that allows stu-

Reflect Reflect Reflect

- Think of a lesson with which you are familiar and create a guided inductive inquiry experience for use in teaching it.

- How can you restructure curriculum materials to make them more experiential for your students?

- How is thinking enhanced by guided inductive inquiry experiences?

Instructional Strategies

Guided Inductive Inquiry Using the Compound Microscope

- Provide observing experiences and have students describe what they observe in the microscope.
- List students' observations on the chalkboard. *Ask for generalizations about orientation of the viewed object.*
- Have students increase the power of magnification and make new observations. *Ask for generalizations about field size and magnification.*
- Focus the viewer so that different planes are seen on the slide. *Ask for generalizations about viewing.*
- Conduct task group discussions (Chapter 8) and compare various group reports.

Students will arrive at three generalizations:

1. Objects appear inverted and reversed left to right.
2. The field of observation is inversely related to the power of the lens being used. As the magnifying power of the lens increases, the area of the observed field decreases.
3. Materials can be viewed as three-dimensional objects and appear to be arranged on distinct planes.

Instructional Strategies

Adapting Guided Inductive Inquiry to the Fine Arts— Color Wheeling

- On an overhead transparency, lay sheets of colored overheads (blue, yellow, red) so students can observe color changes.
- Ask students how many different colors can be produced from these three primary colors.
- Have students work in cooperative small groups or task groups (refer to Chapter 8) to make observations and report results.

Students' findings will include the facts that green, purple, orange, and brown can be created and that the darkness of a color is a function of concentration or added thickness.

dents to learn about mixing colors from their own observations. This activity demonstrates how easy it is to adapt elements of guided inductive inquiry to the fine arts. Another aspect of Example 2 is that it readily lends itself to the use of the overhead projector. Later in this chapter we will discuss the use of transparencies in stimulating group instruction in an inquiry mode.

Inquiry techniques lead to student excitement when discovering concepts not found in a textbook. © Joel Gordon.

Questioning is a critical teacher competency.

The Role of Questioning within Guided Inductive Inquiry   We have noted that teacher questioning plays an important role in inquiry methods, because the purpose of inquiry is to pursue an investigation. The teacher thus becomes a question asker, not a question answerer. Teachers who are masters of guided induction inquiry state that they spend their time interacting with students but provide very few answers (see Bower and Lobdell 1998).

Question Stems: Dynamic Subjects

- What is happening?
- What has happened?
- What do you think will happen now?
- How did this happen?
- Why did this happen?
- What caused this to happen?
- What took place before this happened?
- Where have you seen something like this happen?
- When have you seen something like this happen?
- How could we make this happen?
- How does this compare with what we saw or did?
- How can we do this more easily?
- How can you do this more quickly?

Reprinted with permission from Orlich, D. C. and J. M. Migaki, "What is Your IQ-Individual Questioning Quotient?," NSTA Publications. Copyright © 1981 from *Science and Children*, National Science Teachers Association, 1840 Wilson Boulevard, Arlington, VA 22201-3000.

> ## Question Stems: Static Subjects
>
> - What kind of object is it?
> - What is it called?
> - Where is it found?
> - What does it look like?
> - Have you ever seen anything like it? Where? When?
> - How is it like other things?
> - How can you recognize or identify it?
> - How did it get its name?
> - What can you do with it?
> - What is it made of?
> - How was it made?
> - What is its purpose?
> - How does it work or operate?
> - What other names does it have?
> - How is it different from other things?

What kinds of questions should a teacher ask? The box on page 330 lists relevant question stems or lead-in questions for teachers who want to have a more inquiry-oriented class environment (Orlich and Migaki 1981). These question stems are suitable for use in social studies, literature, science, and mathematics—any class in which the teacher wants to stress the process of inquiry.

Note that this list is oriented to dynamic situations. These stems are probably best classified as prompting questions, similar to those described in Chapter 7. If you are examining more static living or nonliving objects, the stems shown in the box above will prove very useful. Again, note that these prompting questions help the student to examine all kinds of interrelationships—one of the desired goals of inquiry teaching and constructivism.

Table 9.1 provides examples of guided inductive inquiry in social studies at four different grade levels. The examples for grades 2, 7, and 10 are static, but think about how they could be connected to dynamic lessons. For grade 12 U.S. government classes, the examination of current events provides an easy application of dynamic inquiry teaching episodes. Be advised that several of the examples shown in Table 9.1 are very similar to actual test items used in the NAEP 1994 U.S. History Assessment (Beatty et al. 1996). The au-

Reflect Reflect Reflect

- Construct a set of guided inquiry experiences for one topic in your teaching specialty.

TABLE 9.1

Guided Inductive Inquiry: Social Studies Lessons

Grade Level	Materials	Questions	Goals
2	Magazine pictures of houses from around the world	What traits can you identify in these pictures?	Observing Inferring Communicating
7	Pamphlets and posters about World War II	What explicit and implicit messages are communicated by these materials?	Inferring Hypothesizing
10	Political cartoons	What are the key ideas and meanings conveyed by these cartoons? What is their context? What biases do they reveal?	Inferring Hypothesizing Making contextual references
12	A controversial court decision	What actions caused this case? What do you think will happen next? Have we studied any events similar to those in this case?	Analyzing Predicting Comparing

thors of that report also stated, "The NAEP 1994 U.S. History Assessment was rigorous; many tasks demanded knowledge of complex events and concepts and *abilities to analyze and interpret*" (p. 74, emphasis added by authors).

Unguided Inductive Inquiry As we have seen, during guided inductive inquiry, you, the teacher, play the key role in asking questions, prompting responses, and structuring the materials and situations. Again, using guided inductive inquiry is an excellent way to begin the shift from expository or deductive teaching to teaching that is less structured and more open to alternative solutions. Once the class has mastered the techniques of guided inductive inquiry, you can introduce or allow for student-initiated situations that enable the students to take more responsibility for examining data, objects, and events. Because the teacher's role is minimized, the students' activity increases. Let's briefly summarize the major elements of unguided inductive inquiry (see the box on page 333).

> Unguided inductive inquiry shifts some responsibilities from the teacher to the student.

When you begin to use unguided inductive inquiry, a new set of teacher behaviors must come into play. You must now begin to act as the **classroom clarifier,** guiding students to develop logical thinking skills. As students start to make their generalizations, gross errors in student logic are bound to appear: students will make generalizations that are too broad, infer single cause-and-effect relationships where there are several, and perceive cause-and-effect relationships where none exists. When such errors occur, you must patiently question the learner in a *nonthreatening* manner to verify the conclusion or generalizations. If errors exist in the student's logic or inferences, point them out. But you should *not* tell the student what the correct inference is, for this would defeat the purpose of any inquiry episode. These types of er-

Elements of Unguided Inductive Inquiry

1. Learners progress from making specific observations to making inferences or generalizations.

2. The objective is to learn (or reinforce) the processes of examining events, objects, and data and then to arrive at appropriate sets of generalizations.

3. The teacher may control only the materials provided or encourage student-initiated materials. He or she poses a question, such as, "What can you generalize from . . . ?" or "Tell me everything that you can about X after examining these. . . ."

4. The students, using the materials provided, ask all the questions that come to mind without further teacher guidance.

5. The materials are essential to making the classroom a laboratory.

6. Meaningful patterns are generated by students through individual observations and inferences and through interactions with other students.

7. The teacher does not limit the generalizations the students make.

8. The teacher encourages all students to communicate their generalizations so that all may benefit from each individual's unique inferences.

rors might appear in guided inquiry, but in that model the teacher is controlling the flow of information and can be more subtly directive through questioning. There is much less direct teacher probing in unguided inquiry.

We suggest that you have students work alone during initial unguided inductive experiences. When students work alone, they tend to do most of the work themselves. When they work in pairs or triads, one in the group usually takes the leadership role and dominates the group's thinking, so that there are really only one participant and two observers. When students demonstrate the necessary aptitude to use the inductive method successfully in an unguided fashion, you can assign small groups to work together.

Techniques for Unguided Inductive Inquiry   What are some tested ideas that can be used as prototypes for teachers wishing to incorporate appropriate inductive learning experiences into an ongoing lesson? Table 9.2 gives a few ideas that are expanded into a matrix of student tasks.

Reflect Reflect Reflect

- Examine both the guided and the unguided inductive instructional models. What areas are common to both? What areas are different?

- Use the Internet to conduct a search of the ERIC database for ideas on using newspapers as sources of material in inductive inquiry lessons.

- How can lessons and activities in art, physical education, social studies, and literature be made more inductive to learners?

TABLE 9.2

Unguided Inductive Inquiry: A Matrix of Tasks

Content Area	Lesson Goal	Material	Student Questions	Student Summaries, Patterns, Inferences	Student Generalizations
Social studies	To understand regional difference in the U.S. culture	Recycled telephone books	"How many different churches are there in Boston, Tulsa, Nashville, Salt Lake City?"	1. Lists from Yellow Pages 2. Lists of different denominations 3. Percentages computed 4. Inferences listed	1. Students list and discuss generalizations.
History, art	To interpret a classic artwork	Bayeux tapestry Encyclopedias	"What events are shown?" "What order is there to the tapestry layout?"	1. Events listed 2. Scenes counted and classified into categories 3. Types of persons identified 4. Chronology determined	1. Students interpret major themes. 2. Students draw conclusions. 3. Class discusses historical events. 4. Class compares means of communications.
Science	To learn about weather patterns	Recycled newspapers TV news	"How do weather systems usually hit the United States?" "What effect does the jet stream have on weather systems?"	1. Maps constructed showing major fronts 2. Patterns listed 3. Data collected north and south of jet stream paths	1. Students chart weather patterns. 2. Class analyzes patterns. 3. Students make conclusions and present them to class.

Section 3: Methods for Developing Higher-Level Thinking Skills

You should by now realize that as a classroom teacher, you can never be too aware of thinking skills. The encouragement of your students' active observation and exploration should be infused throughout your teaching so that you are not merely transmitting information but also enhancing thinking abilities. You have been introduced to the basic elements of inquiry teaching and can play a direct (guided inquiry) or indirect (unguided inquiry) role in classroom inquiry experiences. Within these overall contexts of teaching from an inquiry-based point of view, you also should know about several "variations on the theme"—that is, specific teaching approaches and techniques that are either directly related to or are themselves considered inquiry methods. The three approaches we focus on here have proven effective across many subject areas. They are problem solving, discovery learning, and techniques that emphasize higher-level critical thinking skills. We conclude by taking a brief look at assessment, which we cover in depth in the next chapter.

Problem Solving

John Dewey's ideas about problems are still relevant.

Problem-solving models of instruction are based on the ideas of John Dewey (1916, 1938). Among his major educational contributions was his advocacy of a curriculum *based on problems.* He defined a **problem** as anything that gives rise to doubt and uncertainty. Dewey held that a problem, to be an appropriate topic of study, had to meet two rigorous criteria: it had to be important to the culture, and it had to be important and relevant to the student.

Many curriculum projects developed between 1958 and 1970 in science, mathematics, and social studies were based on Dewey's problem-solving approach. In addition, most contemporary curricula and a large majority of textbooks suggest "problems" to be solved by students. Some of the curricula that you may encounter will stress elements of inquiry, discovery, or problem solving. Contemporary curricula, especially interdisciplinary ones such as environmental studies, rely heavily on the two criteria Dewey first suggested. If you assign research reports to your students, you are using elements of problem-solving instruction.

This technique, like any inquiry method, requires careful planning and systematic skill building. Implicit within the problem-solving framework is the concept of **experience,** or the idea that the totality of events and activities that students carry out under the school's direction as part of the planned learning processes will produce certain desirable traits or behaviors that will better enable them to function in our culture. Furthermore, the experiences provided by the schools should articulate the *content* and the *process* of knowing. Both knowing what is known and knowing how to know are important objectives for the learner (see Martinez 1998).

This description shows that problem solving contains many elements of the constructivist model. As we use it here, **problem solving** refers to an inquiry learning process in which students seek answers to a question relevant to themselves and their culture. The constructivist philosophy requires the learner to be actively engaged in the learning process. The model requires both content and process. Through the interaction of all those elements, the learner makes sense out of something. You, as the teacher, help by providing the environment that allows the student to participate and interact.

The Teacher's Role When using problem solving with learners, you must constantly play the role of clarifier or definer. Your role is to help the learners define precisely what is being studied or solved. Problem-solving methodologies focus on systematic investigation: students set up the problem, clarify the issues, propose ways to obtain needed information, and then test or evaluate their conclusions. In most cases, learners will establish written hypotheses for testing. We cannot overemphasize the fact that students need your continual monitoring. In a problem-solving model, you must continually receive progress reports from students engaged in the investigative process.

Students are not simply allowed to follow their whims. Problem solving requires building close relationships between students and teacher (see Verduin 1996; Delisle 1997). It also involves systematic investigation of the problem and the proposing of concrete solutions. Let us illustrate this with two case histories of real problems that took place in Washington, D.C., and Massachusetts elementary schools.

Problem solving requires a high degree of student responsibility.

Steps in Solving Problems Problem solving implies a degree of freedom (to explore a problem) and responsibility (to arrive at a possible solution). One tackles a problem to achieve objectives, not simply to use the process of inquiry per se. The steps listed in the box on page 337 are usually associated with the problem-solving technique, although students may not follow them in strict linear fashion. Further, refer to Figure 9.1, and compare the steps of each model.

If you decide to use a problem-solving episode in your classes, you must realize that it will usually last for days or even weeks. During that time, other learning may be accomplished as well—for example, using reference books, requesting information, interpreting data, presenting progress reports to the class, and taking responsibility for the conduct of a task.

Examples of Problem Solving Our first example is taken from one man's efforts to help break the poverty cycle and to instill an appreciation for basic school subjects that can ultimately improve students' economic well-being. Recall that in Chapter 8 we briefly discussed the national stock market simulation. Robert Radford (1991) of Washington, D.C., wanted to help children attending the Amidon Elementary School do the following:

- Gain insights into the American economic system
- Understand the concepts of compounding interest, increasing the value of money over time, and capital appreciation
- Practice the concept of delayed gratification (to break the poverty cycle)

In the Amidon project, intermediate-grade students were introduced to economics and business principles in practical ways. To demonstrate understanding, each student had to provide an example of the topics or concepts being discussed. Next, stock market activities were introduced. Students examined *Investor's Daily, Value Line Survey,* and *Barron's Financial Weekly.* The

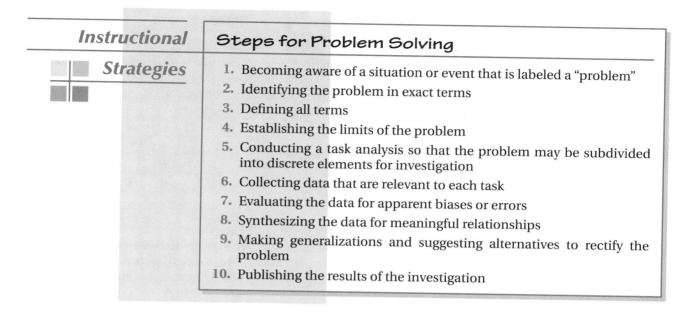

Instructional

Strategies

Steps for Problem Solving

1. Becoming aware of a situation or event that is labeled a "problem"
2. Identifying the problem in exact terms
3. Defining all terms
4. Establishing the limits of the problem
5. Conducting a task analysis so that the problem may be subdivided into discrete elements for investigation
6. Collecting data that are relevant to each task
7. Evaluating the data for apparent biases or errors
8. Synthesizing the data for meaningful relationships
9. Making generalizations and suggesting alternatives to rectify the problem
10. Publishing the results of the investigation

students read and reported on findings and even computed the Dow Jones Industrial Average.

Through hands-on experiences, they studied and discussed business cycles. They tracked selected stocks, graphed fluctuations in prices, and compared industrial stock profiles to that of the market as a whole. These real-life activities made a vivid impression on the children of their need to master arithmetic, reading, social studies, and language arts.

A decision was made by teachers and students to purchase Philadelphia Electric Company common stock (currently called Peco Energy). Money to purchase the shares came from gifts from seventy-five individuals who wanted to help in this project, plus the support of seventeen companies and corporations. Each graduating class purchased a number of shares of common stock of Peco Energy, which were then placed into trust accounts for each student.

To take the exercise a step further, several students attended the annual stockholders' meeting. With their peers' proxies in hand, the delegates cast their votes and presented issues to the stockholders at large.

Accompanying the real-life component of this project was a stock market simulation game. Each child received a hypothetical $50,000 portfolio containing ten different stocks. Students tracked their portfolios each week and thus acquired additional drill and practice in arithmetic and decision making.

Is this an example of real problem solving? John Dewey would applaud it. The project illustrates how students can be exposed to an *experientially* rich curriculum that helps them understand how to better themselves in *their own immediate future*. Having a trust fund will undoubtedly encourage these children to pursue socially valued occupations and professions.

Finally, the Amidon project illustrates how *affective* objectives may be integrated into the curriculum. Every kid feels like a winner, both intellectu-

The Amidon project let students engage in real-life problem solving.

> ## Reflect Reflect Reflect
>
> - What elements of problem solving can be applied to any school-taught topics?
> - To use problem solving most efficiently, sketch a task analysis chart (see Figure 5.4) showing the necessary student skills.
> - Prepare a lesson that incorporates some real problem solving for students.

ally and financially. And those feelings have a carryover effect on student behavior, ultimately sparking positive student actions.

In our second example, students in a Massachusetts elementary school collected data and presented it to their local school board to show that a major intersection was a grievous safety problem. The students then showed how a pedestrian overpass could be constructed; they even contacted architects to obtain cost estimates. The school board was impressed—and so was the city council, for the walk was constructed later just as the schoolchildren had proposed.

These are just two examples of how teachers and students can use problem solving in the real world. There are many others. For instance, a class might observe problems in the immediate school environment—parking shortages, long lunch lines, crowded locker rooms, noise—and investigate them with the goal of creating alternative situations. Or you could give students in high school English classes the problem of generating at least three criteria for determining which works of American literature should be added to or retained in the curriculum. Students will learn the difficulties associated with canon building, values, and curricular decision making.

Jennifer Nelson (1998) uses investigative techniques of problem solving by having her students study problems associated with the history of their own school. In a similar vein, Carol E. Murphy (1998) shows how the five themes of geography—location, movement, place, region, and human environment—are used to solve problems associated with the school site. Have you ever determined the "best" potato chip? Well, Juanita S. Sorenson and her colleagues (1996) illustrate how such a trivial problem can be used to develop real problem-solving skills. They also present scores of other high-interest problems for students in grades K–8. Our plea to you is to initiate problem-solving skills on day one. Doing so makes schooling an enjoyable and exciting experience—and worthwhile, too.

Pose thought-provoking problems by recasting familiar ideas in a new light.

Discovery Learning

Who really discovered America? Native American people have been here for upwards of thirteen thousand years, and although Leif Ericson seems to have been the first European to visit our shores, Christopher Columbus gets the credit for the discovery simply because he announced it first. But the territory is named for the map-maker Amerigo Vespucci because he knew Columbus had landed on a brand-new continent rather than in India. Thus defining what we mean by a *discovery* is difficult.*

In this vein, Kenneth A. Strike's comprehensive analysis (1975) of methods associated with **discovery learning**—an inquiry process in which learners pose questions and seek answers—may be of use. Strike establishes two categories of discovery: *absolute* discovery and *relative* discovery. Absolute discovery is that attributed to those classic "firsts"—the discovery of the DNA molecule's reproduction mechanism; the discovery of America; the discovery of new planets, theories, or synthetic materials. Relative discovery means that an individual has learned or found out something for the first time.

Strike also presents four model of discovery:

1. Knowing that
2. Knowing how
3. Discovering that
4. Discovering how

Finally, he provides a basic criterion that is essential for any act to be labeled a discovery. The discoverer must communicate both the *what* and the *how* to others. Thus if you discover the Lost Dutchman Mine in Arizona but do not tell a single individual, you have not made a discovery.

Strike's four modes of discovery are consistent with the thirteen major inquiry processes described earlier in this chapter. For example, communicating is a major inquiry process and is very much a part of discovery. Also, the model that Strike describes implies that learners must "know" something before they can "discover" something. Content, knowledge, fact, and processes are all very much a part of the discovery strategy.

Although there is much luck involved in discovery, Louis Pasteur's statement that "chance favors the prepared mind" is still valid. The most important discoveries made by scientists—including social and behavioral scientists—are the result of careful observation and systematic research. Discovery makes use of the same processes and skills we described as being part of inductive inquiry and problem solving. This should come as no surprise, because inquiry requires systematic conduct, not haphazard bungling.

Environmental education is a rich arena for discovery learning and problem solving. Students can collect water-quality data using standard, scientifically accepted practices and collect data to be analyzed and discussed. They *construct* meaning from data (Orlich et al. 1999).

Judith Miles, a student in Lexington, Massachusetts, wondered how spiders would spin webs in a weightless environment. The subject of her curiosity became one of nineteen student projects conducted on board the earth-orbiting space station Skylab in 1973. Judith's experiment demonstrated that a black widow spider was initially "confused" by a lack of gravity and did not spin the appropriate web pattern. But within a relatively short time, the spider did, in fact, spin the appropriate web!

Discovery learning has four different dimensions.

Student curiosity led to major scientific discoveries in space science.

*We thank Kenneth A. Strike (1975) for the idea about Christopher Columbus.

Is this an example of problem solving or discovery? We think that it fits in the category of *absolute* discovery, because it was the first time that anyone had communicated the problem and completed the research. Her science teacher, J. Michael Conley, encouraged Judith to submit her idea in a contest sponsored by the National Science Teachers Association in conjunction with the National Aeronautics and Space Administration (NASA). This demonstrates the partnership that develops when learners and teachers share in the excitement of inquiry.

Similarly, Todd Nelson, a student from Adams, Minnesota, designed an experiment for the third mission of the space shuttle *Columbia* (in March 1982). Nelson suggested that *Columbia*'s crew videotape the behavior of selected flying insects—velvet bean caterpillar moths, honey bees, and common houseflies—to determine the effects of a gravity-free environment on their flight patterns. Todd's experiment was selected along with those of Ph.D. research botanists to determine the same effect on pine tree, oat, and Chinese bean sprouts. Again, this experiment demonstrates absolute discovery—and by high school students, too.

Media can be effective tools to excite student discovery.

Not all discovery learning needs to be as dramatic as the NASA experiments. One common way to generate the fun and discipline of discovery is to use an overhead projector to present an event that requires student analysis. In the Mystery Island activity, the teacher makes a set of overlays that depict an unnamed island (Zevin 1969). The initial transparency shows the outline of the island. The map contains some standard clues to the island's general location, such as topographical symbols, rivers, and latitude and longitude symbols. This device is used primarily to focus the learner's attention on the event or to motivate inquiry.

The teacher usually begins the activity by telling the class that the island

---

Instructional Strategies

Computer Applications to Enhance the Development of Thinking Skills

Nancy Ridenour, who teaches at the Bridgeport, Washington, Middle School, uses the inquiry model for student small-group research projects. Students visit local Marina Park, located on the Columbia River. They decide on the topic for their research question and the method of data collection. The students prepare a written plan, which Nancy evaluates. Obviously, safety and appropriate science techniques are double-checked. The student teams collect data during the semester and make Powerpoint presentations. The students integrate photographs into the system by using a digital camera. By placing the projects on-line, the students share their data and presentations with other students and community members. They are also available for examination anywhere in the world. This application of inquiry and computer technology is only one of many possibilities. We suggest reviewing Mark and Cindy Grabe's excellent resource, *Integrating Technology for Meaningful Learning* (3rd edition) (2001) for a wealth of ideas associated with computers and inquiry.

Reflect Reflect Reflect

> **Reflect Reflect** Reflect
>
> ■ Compare and contrast discovery learning and problem solving.
> ■ Prepare a lesson that incorporates discovery learning.

is uninhabited and that they are going to be the first persons to land on it. The students' first task is to choose where they will settle and to justify their choice. Ultimately they are given other tasks, such as to find the places that may be the best for farming, industries, railroads, harbors, airports, resorts, and the like. The students must make inferences concerning rainfall, winds, deserts, and other natural phenomena. Following Strike's four elements, the activity requires students both to *know* and to *discover* "that" and "how." The opportunities for inquiry are limitless.

The entire arena of inquiry and thinking, including problem solving and discovery approaches, naturally lend themselves to high-tech applications. We present one interesting example in the Instructional Strategies box on page 340.

Techniques That Focus on Critical Thinking Skills

Implicit in the techniques we present in this section is the assumption that information-processing psychology and schema theory are the most useful explanations of how students learn. **Information-processing psychology** asserts that learning is an interactive process between the learner and the environment, a process to which both contribute; that is, the learner is not just a passive receiver of stimuli (see Wakefield 1996 for discussion). **Schema theory** asserts that we organize what we learn according to patterns, or *schemas,* that help us make sense of the multiple stimuli we constantly receive. Learning becomes an *individual meaning-building process* in which the student either relates new data to existing patterns or creates new schemas to understand (see Marzano 1998). These are also basic assumptions of the constructivist approach.

Starting from this base of instructional assumptions, the teacher behaviors in the Instructional Strategies box on page 342 can help students improve their thinking processes. These techniques have proven useful across a broad range of subjects, from primary grades to graduate school.

The first behavior, which is of primary importance, is to plan your instruction to emphasize thought processes. The resulting plan may bear little relationship to a standard content outline. Most history texts, for instance, organize facts chronologically; however, such a structure does not resemble the way people think critically about history. A more *effective* organizer is to arrange historical facts around selected basic concepts and generalizations. Facts must be related to broader concepts or generalization before they have significance. Thus effective instructional planning first determines the primary concepts and generalizations relevant to a unit or a course. These become the subjects of discrete lessons, which are planned around the facts needed to understand each concept. If you do use the instructional strategies

Try to draw examples for critical thinking when possible.

Thinking behaviors can be taught.

Instructional

Strategies

Ten Teacher Behaviors That Encourage Thinking Skills

1. *Plan for thinking.* Develop units and lessons based on concepts and generalizations.
2. *Teach for meaning.* Connect each lesson to students' experience.
3. *Ask thought-provoking questions.* "How do you know?" "What is the main idea?" "What alternatives can we think of?"
4. *Make students aware of their mental processes.* "From your observations about prices in this chart, what might we infer about supply and demand?"
5. *Explain your thought processes frequently.* "On this tape, I recorded my thoughts as I planned today's lesson. As you listen to it, identify examples of the following thinking skills."
6. *Keep data before students.* Summarize and record student answers on the board or a transparency.
7. *Call on students to explain.* Give students frequent opportunities to explain what they do or don't understand.
8. *Encourage credibility as a criterion.* "Does this make sense?" "Why not?"
9. *Be consistent.* Thinking instruction should be part of each lesson, each day.
10. *Be patient.* Significant change requires at least a semester.

carefully and consistently, with an emphasis on students' understanding rather than rote memorization, you will develop their thinking skills effectively, and your content coverage will have a meaningful pattern for students.

Strategic Learning Skills   Critical thinking skills are also labeled **strategic learning,** meaning that students develop a capacity to accelerate learning (see Gettinger and Callan Stoiber 1999, p. 952). In the box below, these re-

Assumptions About Learners and Learning

- New skills, knowledge, competencies, and interests are built on previous ones.
- Information is remembered when it is meaningful and gained through active and enjoyable learning.
- Motivation is reinforced when learners feel competent.
- Opportunities must be provided to practice critical thinking and problem solving in various formats.

searchers provide four major assumptions under which we operate when developing student strategic learning skills.

We now present three specific techniques that you can use to help your students build their critical thinking and strategic learning skills.

Integrated Approach   Consider a high school unit in U.S. history that focuses on the Colonial period. One way to combine content and thinking skills coverage is to have students prepare a large wall chart listing specific characteristics of several colonies. These might be geographic features, economic characteristics, or social backgrounds and attitudes. From these data, students could infer and hypothesize about colonists' possible attitudes toward future events, such as declaring independence, providing free public education, or abolishing slavery. Similarly, science teachers could help students create a periodic table of the elements through observing, inferring, and generalizing rather than simply by studying a given example.

Note that these activities tend to reinforce many of the thinking skills listed earlier in the chapter. Depending on the instructional emphasis, students could be involved in virtually all thinking processes, from low-order skills (observing and classifying) to high-level skills (distinguishing relevant from irrelevant statements). Proponents of this integrated approach (Beyer 1998; see also Zemelman, Daniels, and Hyde 1998) assert that such flexibility—the applicability of virtually any subject matter to teach a full range of thought processes—is its primary strength.

Think-Aloud Modeling   Another method is to use your thought processes as examples. This will help make students aware of their own thought processes (see the fourth and fifth teacher behaviors in the Instructional Strategies box on page 342 and the related discussion of metacognition on page 344). Share with students the thinking steps you follow in planning a lesson, making a conclusion, or performing any relevant activity. Have your students identify the particular skills you use and suggest other strategies you might follow. Such demonstrations can take the forms of printed handouts, audiotapes, or even an unrehearsed problem-solving exploration of a student's question.

Lest you think this idea is simply a theory, we offer Professor Glenn Crosby, who teaches graduate-level physical chemistry classes by narrating his thought processes as he works out problems on the chalkboard. You can use this method to interpret O'Henry, Richard Nixon, or Langston Hughes, as well as chemistry.

Once students understand the think-aloud process, they can pair up and practice it, using selected topics related to classroom issues and the subject matter being studied. A useful exercise is for pairs of students to explain to each other their understanding of an assignment and the steps they will follow in completing it. This exercise uncovers ambiguities in assignments and helps students identify productive thinking and study strategies. Two considerations, though, are paramount in all thinking-aloud exercises: each student must have as much practice as possible, and the *process* of thinking is more important than the *product* of thinking—the objective is to identify effective thinking steps, not necessarily to find a particular solution. This technique is ideal for open-ended activities.

Rules for Summarizing

- To stimulate understanding of the material summarized, insist that students use their own words, not quotations.
- Limit the length of the summary, whether written or oral, to ensure that students have judged the relative importance of ideas.
- Have students discuss their summaries, especially the criteria they used for including and excluding information.
- Have students discuss the summarizing process: What steps did they follow? What dead ends did they come to? What problems developed?

Reflect Reflect Reflect

- How could you organize your classes to use the think-aloud technique?
- How could student journals be used to encourage thinking, reflecting, and summarizing?

Summarizing   Another technique that has been found generally useful for encouraging thinking behaviors is to have students summarize. Ask students to outline the steps in a math solution, list the causes of a social condition, give reactions to an assembly speaker, and so on. Your imagination is the only limit to the choices. The summary can be made in writing or presented orally. Considerable evidence (see Hayes 1990; Manning, Manning, and Long 1997) suggests that the act of writing is itself both an exercise of thinking skills and a generator of those skills. We must think to write—but in addition, when writing, we frequently come up with new statements and ideas we did not think up beforehand. Thus any writing is probably useful in learning. Writing summaries is particularly effective, however, since it forces the student to develop **criteria**—characteristics used to organize or rate ideas or products—for identifying some ideas as more important than others. This activity stimulates and reinforces the highest-level thinking skills (Gourgey 1998).

Oral summaries are also effective in helping students develop speaking skills that will readily transfer beyond school. Moreover, oral summaries can be part of class discussions that are also essential activities for developing critical reasoning (see Manning and Payne 1996). As you incorporate student oral summaries in your teaching style, remember to subtly shift your efforts to an inactive instructional role while the class members assume an active one. Only you will know the difference.

When you assign a summarizing activity to a student, observe the four rules listed in the box above.

Summarizing is one easy way to get students to synthesize information.

Metacognitive Skills   **Metacognition** means being aware of your thought processes while you are thinking (see Paris and Winograd 1990 for an extended treatment). Thinking aloud is one example. Research indicates that effective problem solvers subvocalize; that is, they talk to themselves (see Simons 1995; Resnick and Klopfer 1989), constantly restating the situation, rechecking their progress, and evaluating whether their thinking is moving in an appropriate direction.

The following are several techniques that have been found useful for helping students become accustomed to thinking about and stating their thoughts.

Describing Self-Thought   Perhaps the most effective technique is simply to have students describe what is going on in their minds while they are thinking. Have students practice this technique in pairs for three to five minutes several times a week to overcome awkwardness with the method (and even to practice cooperative learning). Once they are accustomed to the process, students can recall their thinking processes in larger groups or before the entire class to maintain the skill. You should also model this behavior as often as possible, of course.

Students should be encouraged to use metacognition during recitation.

Identifying What Is Known and Not Known   Another approach to metacognitive instruction is to have students identify what is known about a situation or problem, suggest what needs to be learned, and list steps required to obtain the information. For example, this question might be asked in a science class: "Is Pluto accurately classified as a *planet* in the solar system?" Students' initial responses (which the teacher lists on the board) constitute what is known about this question. In small groups, students then generate lists of what else they need to learn about it and how to obtain the information. Such exercises, done frequently and with attention to identifying relevant processes, will help students use similar steps in their own thinking.

Reciprocal Teaching   One more technique helpful to the metacognition "package" is known as **reciprocal teaching,** where students and teachers switch roles in a lesson. This model was designed by Annmarie Sullivan Palincsar (in Gettinger and Callan Stoiber 1999). Her approach has been used successfully with middle-level students and improves reading comprehension. (Recall our plea to teach for understanding in Chapter 3.) The four basic steps in reciprocal teaching are listed in the box below. Note how this strategy synthesizes several aspects of discussions, inquiry, thinking, and metacognition.

When using *reciprocal teaching,* the teacher leads the discussion or recitation period on the material the students have read. At that point, the stu-

---

Elements of Reciprocal Teaching

1. *Summarizing.* Identify or paraphrase the main ideas.
2. *Questioning.* Ask oneself questions about the information.
3. *Clarifying.* Determine whether ideas are understood.
4. *Predicting.* Speculate on what comes next.

dents are given four tasks: (1) predict what comes next in text, (2) generate self-testing questions, (3) summarize the information read, and (4) clarify any misunderstandings or unclear points. Following these steps, the teacher becomes a class participant and students assume the role of "teacher." Did we mention that this is a great technique for generating personal interaction? It does (see Burns, Roe, and Ross 1999).

Analyzing Others' Thinking   You can also encourage metacognition by having students study how others think, particularly persons who are famous for their thinking. Students may be surprised to discover that high I.Q. is not necessarily associated with achievement; the *application* of intellect is what matters. They could explore and discuss how Einstein or Mozart worked, what steps they took, and what things were important to them in achieving. Students can interview accomplished people from their own community, or such individuals can visit the class to discuss what thoughts go through their head while they paint a picture, run a race, or write a newspaper article.

Metacognition is widely used by scientists who must solve problems.

Monitoring Academic Behavior   Teaching metacognition can also include having students monitor their own academic behavior. Do they have test-taking strategies? Are the strategies effective? Might they be improved? What about learning strategies? Do they know whether they learn better from visual, auditory, or kinesthetic stimuli? Do they have strategies to help in each area? All of these questions are relevant to students' school experience. All are areas that you can explore with students as you help them share with one another and provide useful information (see Gallagher 1998; Tanner and Casados 1998). The result will be improved metacognition and application of selected thinking processes.

Assessing Higher-Level Thinking Activities

We saved the toughest part until last, but in keeping with our lesson-planning model, assessment must be considered. The challenge encountered when using any higher-level strategy—inquiry, problem solving, critical thinking—is that in most learning episodes, there is no one right answer. Thus you assess the processes.

In Chapter 10, we will introduce the technique of using rubrics to evaluate student work. In using rubrics, you establish a set of criteria by which to assess a product, paper, argument, conclusion, or methodology (see Busching 1998; Taggart et al. 1998). The overarching method of inquiry is interaction. In Chapter 8, we illustrated two forms (Figures 8.2 and 8.3) that you can adapt to fit higher-level thinking lessons. Perhaps the most critical aspect of assessment is simply to provide feedback to all students so they continually improve their use of logic and become more systematic in solving any problem.

In closing this chapter, we want to acknowledge the lamentable reality that few schools really teach thinking as an integral part of the curriculum. Our plea is for all educators to integrate the best teaching and thinking strategies into the curriculum systematically and diligently. Obviously, you must

A Closing Reflection Reflection Reflection

- How can you integrate the different types of inquiry and the host of skills associated with thinking into your classroom instruction?
- In what ways can metacognition techniques help student thinking?
- Review the list of ten teacher behaviors that encourage thinking skills. How can you incorporate those steps into an already crowded curriculum?
- If you want to stress the messages of this chapter in your teaching, who else in your school must you involve?

begin slowly and thoughtfully. The challenge is yours. We have confidence that you will address the challenge as one that is intentionally inviting.

Summary

1. The goal of inquiry methods is to encourage students to ask questions, seek information, and become better thinkers.
2. The basic processes of inquiry learning include observing, classifying, inferring, measuring, communicating, predicting, formulating hypotheses, interpreting, and experimenting.
3. Inquiry teaching shares many characteristics with constructivism; these include a focus on the student, flexibly paced instruction, encouragement of multiple conclusions, and an emphasis on process.
4. Two models for inquiry teaching are guided inductive inquiry and unguided inductive inquiry. Both are based on inductive reasoning, a method of thinking that moves from the specific to the general.
5. Three other methods of inquiry learning instruction are the problem-solving method, discovery learning, and the use of specific critical thinking techniques. All these methods may be used to infuse critical thinking skills into the curriculum.
6. Classroom use of any inquiry model or method increases the amount of student-engaged time needed to complete a lesson and adds complexity to unit or lesson planning.
7. Using the integrated approach, think-aloud modeling, and summarizing helps students build their critical thinking and strategic learning skills.
8. Describing self-thought, identifying what is and is not known, reciprocal teaching, analyzing others' thinking, and monitoring academic behavior help students become accustomed to thinking about and stating their thoughts.

Key Terms

classroom clarifier (p. 332)	**inquiry process** (p. 323)
criteria (p. 344)	**inquiry teaching** (p. 314)
discovery learning (p. 339)	**metacognition** (p. 344)
empirical epistemology (p.324)	**problem** (p. 335)
experience (p. 335)	**problem solving** (p. 335)
guided inductive inquiry (p. 325)	**reciprocal teaching** (p.345)
induction (p. 325)	**schema theory** (p. 341)
inductive inquiry (p. 325)	**strategic learning** (p. 342)
information-processing psychology (p. 344)	**unguided inductive inquiry** (p. 325)

Helpful Resources

We found it very difficult to designate only a few references as must reading on this topic. You may want to review these before you begin using inquiry or thinking strategies.

Eylon, B., and M. C. Linn. "Learning and Instruction: An Examination of Four Research Perspectives in Science Education." *Review of Educational Research* 58 (1988): 251–301.

Don't be alarmed at the title of the journal. We view this paper as the seminal work advocating the concept that "teaching less is teaching more." The authors illustrate the power of using an inquiry-based instructional system.

Sternberg, R. J., and L. Spear-Swerling. *Teaching for Thinking.* Washington, DC: American Psychology Association, 1996, 163 pp.

This short book is a mind stretcher for the novice, but the authors critically examine thinking and creativity.

Sorenson, J. S., L. R. Buckmaster, M. K. Francis, and K. M. Knauf. *The Power of Problem Solving: Practical Ideas and Teaching Strategies for Any K–8 Subject Area.* Boston: Allyn & Bacon, 1996, 281 pp.

The authors provide a plethora of "hands-on, minds-on" projects to be solved using a variety of inquiry techniques.

Campbell, J. R., K. E. Voelkl, and P. L. Donahue. *Report in Brief: NAEP 1996 Trends in Academic Progress.* Washington, DC: National Center for Educational Statistics, revised August 1998, 29 pp. NCES 98-530.

The National Assessment of Educational Progress (NAEP) is the sponsor of a series of tests in English, mathematics, science, art, writing, civics, and history that are administered to samples of fourth-, eighth-, eleventh- and twelfth-graders and students aged nine, thirteen, and seventeen. We consider these tests to be the best indicators of the levels of thinking at which students achieve and teachers teach. Examine the most current reports to understand our plea for higher-level teaching and for ideas on how to reach those levels.

Internet Resources

❖ The Chemical Engineering Department at Washington State University has a Web site featuring several teacher-designed modules that illustrate inductive, problem-solving, and discovery models for grades 7–12.

http://www.che.wsu.edu/modules/

❖ The Mid-Continent Regional Educational Laboratory (McREL) maintains a site covering topics from constructivist teaching to technology integration. Their index is a useful search tool.

http://www.mcrel.org/search/

❖ The Longview Community College, Lee's Summit, Missouri, offers an interesting Web site that explores the "core concepts" of critical thinking.

http://www.kcmetro.cc.mo.us/longview/ctac/corenotes.htm

❖ The University of Toronto offers a "free" short course relating to metacognitive techniques.

http://snow.utoronto.ca/Learn2/introll.html

References

Adey, P., and M. Shayer. *Really Raising Standards: Cognitive Interventions and Academic Achievement.* New York: Routledge, 1994.

Airasian, P. W., and M. E. Walsh. "Constructivist Cautions." *Phi Delta Kappan* 78(6) (1997): 444–449.

Banks, J. A. *Teaching Strategies for Ethnic Studies* (6th edition). Boston: Allyn & Bacon, 1997.

Beatty, A. S., C. M. Reese, H. R. Persky, and P. Carr. *NAEP 1994 U.S. History Report Card: Findings from the National Assessment of Educational Progress.* National Center for Education Statistics. Washington, DC: U.S. Government Printing Office, 1996, NCES 96-085.

Beyer, B. K. "Teaching Thinking: An Integrated Approach." In *Teaching for Thinking.* W. Keefe and H. J. Walberg, editors. Reston, VA: National Association of Secondary School Principals, 1992.

Beyer, B. K. *Improving Student Thinking: A Comprehensive Approach.* Boston: Allyn & Bacon, 1997.

Beyer, B. K. "Improving Student Thinking." *Clearing House* 71(5) (1998): 262–267.

Bigge, M. L., and S. S. Shermis. *Learning Theories for Teacher* (6th edition). New York: Longman, 1999.

Bower, B., and J. Lobdell. "History Alive! Six Powerful Constructivist Strategies." *Social Education* 62(1) (1998): 50–53.

Burns, P. C., B. D. Roe, and E. P. Ross. *Teaching Reading in Today's Elementary Schools* (7th edition). Boston: Houghton Mifflin, 1999.

Busching, B. "Grading Inquiry Projects." *New Directions for Teaching and Learning* 74 (1998): 89–96.

Campbell, J. R., K. E. Voelkl, and P. L. Donahue. *Report in Brief: NAEP 1996 Trends in Academic Progress.* NCES 98-530. Washington, DC: National Center for Educational Statistics, revised August 1998.

Davis, R., C. A. Maher, and N. Noddings, editors. *Constructivist Views on the Teaching and Learning of Mathematics.* Reston, VA: National Council of Teachers of Mathematics, 1990.

Delisle, R. *How to Use Problem-Based Learning in the Classroom.* Alexandria, VA: Association for Supervision and Curriculum Development, 1997.

Dewey, J. *Democracy and Education.* New York: Macmillan, 1916.

Dewey, J. *Experience and Education.* New York: Macmillan, 1938.

Ennis, R. H. "Critical Thinking and the Curriculum." *National Forum* 65(1) (1985): 28–31.

Eylon, B., and M. C. Linn. "Learning and Instruction: An Examination of Four Research Perspectives in Science Education." *Review of Educational Research* 58 (1988): 251–301.

Gallagher, S. A. "The Road to Critical Thinking: The Perry Scheme and Meaningful Differentiation." *NASSP Bulletin* 82(595) (1998): 12–20.

Gettinger, M., and K. Callan Stoiber. "Excellence in Teaching: Review of Instructional and Environmental Variables." In *The Handbook of School Psychology* (3rd edition). C. R. Reynolds and T. B. Gutkin, editors. New York: John Wiley, 1999, 933–958.

Gourgey, A. F. "Metacognition in Basic Skills Instruction." *Instructional Science* 26(1-2) (1998): 81–96.

Hahn, C. L. "Investigating Controversial Issues at Election Time: Political Socialization Research." *Social Education* 60(6) (1996): 348–350.

Hayes, J. R. "Individuals and Environments in Writing Instruction." In *Dimensions of Thinking and Cognitive Instruction.* F. Jones and L. Idol, editors. Hillsdale, NJ: Lawrence Erlbaum Associates, 1990.

Holcomb, E. L. *Getting Excited About Data: How to Combine People, Passion and Proof.* Thousand Oaks, CA: Corwin Press, 1999.

Imel, S. *Work Force Education: Beyond Technical Skills. Trends and Issues Alert No. 1.* Columbus, OH: ERIC Clearinghouse on Adult, Career and Vocational Education, 1999.

Joyce, B. R., and E. F. Calhoun. *Learning to Teach Inductively.* Boston: Allyn & Bacon, 1998.

Manning, M. M., G. Manning, and R. Long. *The Theme Immersion Compendium for Social Studies Teaching.* Portsmouth, NH: Heinemann, 1997.

Manning, B. H., and B. D. Payne. *Self-Talk for Teachers and Students: Metacognitive Strategies for Personal and Classroom Use.* Boston: Allyn & Bacon, 1996.

Martinez, M. E. "What Is Problem Solving?" *Phi Delta Kappan* 79(8) (1998): 606–609.

Marzano, R. J. "What Are the General Skills of Thinking and Reasoning and How Do You Teach Them?" *Clearing House* 71(5) (1998): 268–273.

Murphy, C. E. "Using the Five Themes of Geography to Explore a School Site." *Social Studies Review* 37(2) (1998): 49–52.

Nelson, J. "Get to Know Your School: Involving Students in the Historical Process." *Southern Social Studies Journal* 23(2) (1998): 37–42.

Orlich, D. C. "Science Inquiry and the Commonplace." *Science and Children* 26 (1989): 22–24.

Orlich, D. C. "Education Reform and Limits to Student Achievement." *Phi Delta Kappan* 81(6) (2000): 468–472.

Orlich, D. C., J. C. Horne, C. Carpenter, and J. Brantner. "Water Plus Science Equals Active Student Learners (W + S = ASL)." Presentation at the National Science Teachers Association National Convention, Boston, March 27, 1999.

Orlich, D. C., and J. M. Migaki. "What Is Your IQQ—Individual Questioning Quotient?" *Science and Children* 18 (1981): 20–21.

Paris, S. G., and P. Winograd. "How Metacognition Can Promote Academic Learning and Instruction." In *Dimensions of Thinking and Cognitive Instruction.* B. F. Jones and L. Idol, editors. Hillsdale, NJ: Lawrence Erlbaum Associates, 1990.

Parker, W., and J. Jarolimek. *Social Studies in Elementary Education* (10th edition). Upper Saddle River, NJ: Merrill, an Imprint of Prentice Hall, 1997.

Phillips, D. C., and J. F. Soltis. *Perspectives on Learning.* New York: Teachers College Press, 1998.

Polman, J. L. *Designing Project-Based Science: Connecting Learners Through Guided Inquiry.* New York: Teachers College Press, 2000.

Radford, R. "Young Investors Forum: A Tutorial for Children and Parents." *Washington Parent* (September/October 1991): 11.

Resnick, L. B., and L. E. Klopfer, editors. *Toward the Thinking Curriculum: Current Cognitive Research.* Arlington, VA: Association for Supervision and Curriculum Development, 1989.

Richburg, R. W., and B. J. Nelson. "Where in Western Europe Would You Like to Live?" *The Social Studies* 82(3) (1991): 97–106.

Richburg, R. W., and B. J. Nelson. "Integrating Content Standards and Higher-Order Thinking: A Geography Lesson Plan." *Social Studies* 89(2) (1998): 85–90.

Ridenour, N. *Private communication with authors.* November, 15, 1999.

Simons, P. R.-J. "Metacognitive Strategies: Teaching and Assessing." In *International Encyclopedia of Teaching and Teacher Education* (2nd edition). L. W. Anderson, editor. Tarrytown, NY: Elsevier Science, 1995, pp. 481–485.

Snowman, J., R. Biehler, and C. J. Bonk. *Psychology Applied to Teaching* (9th edition). Boston: Houghton Mifflin, 2000.

Sorenson, J. S., L. R. Buckmaster, M. K. Francis, and K. M. Knauf. *The Power of Problem Solving: Practical Ideas and Teaching Strategies for Any K–8 Subject Area.* Boston: Allyn & Bacon, 1996.

Sternberg, R. J., editor. *Thinking and Problem Solving.* San Diego, CA: Academic Press, 1994.

Sternberg, R. J., and L. Spear-Swerling. *Teaching for Thinking.* Washington, DC: American Psychological Association, 1996.

Strike, K. A. "The Logic of Learning by Discovery." *Review of Educational Research* 45 (1975): 461–483.

Taggart, G. L., S. J. Phifer, J. A. Nixon, and M. Woods. *Rubrics: A Handbook for Construction and Use.* Lancaster, PA: Technomic Publishing Co., 1998.

Tamir, P. "Discovery Learning and Teaching." In *International Encyclopedia of Teaching and Teacher Education* (2nd edition). L. A. Anderson, editor. Tarrytown, NY: Elsevier Science, 1995, pp. 149–155.

Tanner, M. L., and L. Casados. "Promoting and Studying Discussions in Math Classes." *Journal of Adolescent and Adult Literacy* 41(5) (1998): 342–350.

U.S. Department of Education. National Center for Educational Statistics. *The Condition of Education 1999.* NCES 1999-022. Washington, DC: 1999.

U.S. Department of Education. National Center for Educational Statistics. *NAEP 1998 CIVICS Report Card Highlights.* NCES 2000-460. Washington, DC: 1999.

U.S. Department of Labor. *Learning a Living: A Blueprint for High Performance.* A SCANS Report for America 2000. Washington, DC: U.S. Government Printing Office, 1992.

Verduin, J. R. Jr. *Helping Students Develop Investigative, Problem Solving and Thinking Skills in a Cooperative Setting.* Springfield, IL: Charles C. Thomas, 1996.

Wakefield, J. F. *Educational Psychology: Learning to Be a Problem Solver.* Boston: Houghton Mifflin, 1996.

Walberg, H. J. "Productive Teaching and Instruction: Assessing the Knowledge Base." In *Effective Teaching: Current Research.* H. C. Waxman and H. J. Walberg, editors. Berkeley, CA: McCutchan Publishing, for the National Society for the Study of Education, 1991.

Whimbey, A. "Teaching Sequential Thought: The Cognitive-Skills Approach." *Phi Delta Kappan* 58 (1977): 255–259.

Winne, P. H. "Information Processing Theories of Teaching." In *International Encyclopedia of Teaching and Teacher Education* (2nd edition). L. W. Anderson, editor. Tarrytown, NY: Elsevier Science, 1995, pp. 107–112.

Womack, J. G. *Discovering the Structure of the Social Studies.* New York: Benziger Brothers, 1966.

Wright, J. "Using the Social Studies Textbook to Teach Critical Thinking." *Canadian Social Studies* 30(2) (1996): 68–71, 82.

Zemelman, S., H. Daniels, and A. Hyde. *Best Practice: New Standards for Teaching and Learning in America's Schools* (2nd edition). Portsmouth, NH: Heinemann, 1998.

Zevin, J. "Mystery Island: A Lesson in Inquiry." *Today's Education* 58 (1969): 42–43.

10

Monitoring Student Successes

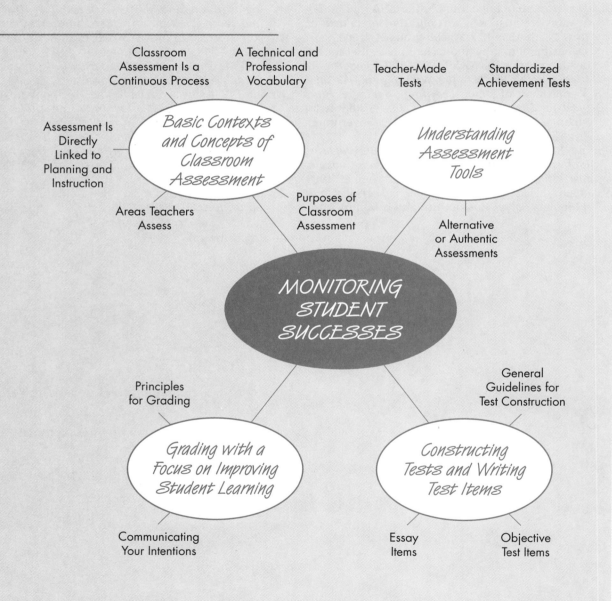

Classroom Assessment Is a Continuous Process

A Technical and Professional Vocabulary

Teacher-Made Tests

Standardized Achievement Tests

Assessment Is Directly Linked to Planning and Instruction

Basic Contexts and Concepts of Classroom Assessment

Understanding Assessment Tools

Areas Teachers Assess

Purposes of Classroom Assessment

Alternative or Authentic Assessments

MONITORING STUDENT SUCCESSES

Principles for Grading

General Guidelines for Test Construction

Grading with a Focus on Improving Student Learning

Constructing Tests and Writing Test Items

Communicating Your Intentions

Essay Items

Objective Test Items

Truc Than, a new teacher at Emerson Middle School, has been reviewing the school board's policy on assessment and testing: "Teachers are expected to provide an objective evaluation of all students enrolled in their classes. Although some testing will be norm-referenced and objective in format, we encourage the use of essay and criterion-referenced tests as well. Further, we encourage all teachers to use, as appropriate, portfolios, authentic measures, and performance assessments. This policy does not preclude the use of other indicators in the evaluation process." Truc silently muses on how he'll plan this process for his social studies and English classes.

No doubt you have already had considerable experience with assessment: you were tested in most classes in elementary and secondary school; you probably took the Scholastic Aptitude Test or other entrance exams before college; and you are likely being tested in your present classes. But now it's time for you, like Truc Than, to start thinking of assessment from the teacher's point of view. This chapter will help you answer these questions:

- How do I coordinate planning, instruction, and assessment?
- What kinds of assessment tools are available to classroom teachers, and when is it appropriate to use each one?
- What impact has educational reform had on classroom assessment?
- How can I use performance assessments in my classroom?
- How can I communicate the results of my assessments to students, parents, and appropriate administrators?

Section 1: Basic Contexts and Concepts of Classroom Assessment

Classroom Assessment Is a Continuous Process

Which of the classroom activities listed below do you consider to be assessment issues?

Observing which students work best together when they sit near each other in the classroom

Asking students a question to check understanding

Noticing a student who seems not to hear well

Giving a quiz on recent instruction

Noticing that students seem bored and restless during a lesson

Giving a final test covering a unit

Assigning grades to students

Reviewing yesterday's lesson

All of the activities are examples of what teachers do—formally and informally—to monitor and guide student learning. They gather information,

> ### Reasons for Classroom Assessment
>
> 1. Provide feedback to students
> 2. Make informed decisions about students
> 3. Monitor, make judgments about, and document students' academic performance
> 4. Aid student motivation by establishing short-term goals and feedback
> 5. Increase retention and transfer of learning by focusing learning
> 6. Evaluate instructional effectiveness
> 7. Establish and maintain a supportive classroom learning atmosphere

Assessment relates to many classroom elements.

interpret it, and then make decisions of whether and how to respond. Thus assessment is a continuous process whose primary purpose is to improve student learning (Gronlund, 1998, p. ix). This chapter is offered to help you plan, organize, implement, and interpret classroom assessments to become a more effective teacher. Why is it important for you to know about assessment to be an effective teacher? Several key reasons are noted in the box above.

A Technical and Professional Vocabulary

Before proceeding, let's clarify several terms. It is customary to distinguish among the terms *assessment, test,* and *measurement* in the following ways (Linn and Gronlund, 1995, pp. 3–6): **Assessment,** the most general term, includes a broad range of processes by which teachers gather information about student learning. These processes include paper-and-pencil tests, performance and project ratings, and observations. Assessment is in part a qualitative description—making a value judgment in response to the question "How well does the student perform?"

A **test** is simply a particular type of assessment, usually a set of questions that all students must answer in a fixed period of time and under similar conditions to demonstrate learning. Teachers use tests to determine how well students perform on a specific set of tasks and to obtain comparative measurements of students' performance.

Measurement is a process that assigns numbers to assessment results, such as the number of correct answers or points on a project. It is a quantitative description and makes no statement about the quality of a student's performance.

A **standardized test,** such as the *Scholastic Aptitude Test* or the *Iowa Test of Basic Skills,* is usually a paper-and-pencil test that has been developed by a major test publisher, standardized for a large population (called a norming group), and administered under the same conditions and time limits to all takers. The purpose of a standardized test is to rank each individual's score by comparing it to the scores of the entire norming group. Both the norming process and the fact that the same test is given to all takers under identical conditions make the test "standardized." Such tests have been part of American education for most of the twentieth century.

Several other terms—validity and reliability—need clarification (see Nitko 1996, pp. 36–77 for a full discussion). These characteristics are of the utmost importance in all assessments. **Validity** refers to the degree to which a test measures what it is intended to measure. A ruler, for instance, is a valid tool to measure the dimensions of a table. The measurements it provides can be trusted in making decisions about where the table will or won't fit, for example. However, a ruler would be useless for measuring the weight of the table; for this task it is an invalid tool.

Now consider a math test that includes verbal problems. To what extent do the measurements that such problems provide reflect students' reading abilities as well as their math knowledge? To that extent the test is invalid as a test purely of math skills. Is there an easy solution to this dilemma? None that we know of—you simply must keep the idea of validity in mind at all times. The fundamental question to ask is, "What evidence do I have that the test I'm giving, whether I made it or not, is measuring what I intend it to measure?" Notice also that validity is relative to purpose—a test may be valid for one purpose but not for another.

Reliability refers to the consistency of test results. If the same group of students could be retested several times and get about the same scores, then the test can be considered reliable. Obviously, you can't use this method to determine a test's reliability, since students would learn from each retaking. However, several methods are available to teachers for estimating test reliability (see the Helpful Resources section at the end of this chapter). One general rule for you to remember is that reliability increases with test length. The box below lists questions you should ask in determining an assessment instrument's validity and reliability.

Finally, in this "minilexicon" of important assessment terms, we want to call your attention to the term *rubric,* a word that has become increasingly significant in the world of classroom assessment. A **rubric** offers a means of evaluating a student's work by comparing that student's efforts with an appropriate model of excellence. Rubrics are most typically used within the context of alternative or authentic assessment, a context we will explore in detail later in this chapter. Rubrics usually illustrate superior, average, and unacceptable models of performance. The student examines these models and then monitors and evaluates both his or her own work and that of classmates.

Validity and Reliability

Validity

- Does this test measure what it is intended to measure?
- Can I make sound decisions about achievement on the basis of these test scores?
- Does this test sample a representative portion of the content being assessed?

Reliability

- Does this test give similar results with each use?
- Are the results of this test consistent with those of other measures?

Reflect Reflect Reflect

■ Consider a test you took recently to determine its validity and reliability. Did the test measure what it claimed to measure? Did it assess a reasonable portion of the content? If you repeated the test, with no learning gain, would the results be similar?

Purposes of Classroom Assessment

As a skilled teacher, you will use classroom assessment in four major ways to accomplish four different, important purposes. The list in the box below (adapted from Linn and Gronlund 1995, p. 18) describes these four purposes, and we provide further detail below.

Placement   Recall Benjamin Bloom's estimate in Chapter 4 that 50 percent of the variance in student achievement resulted from lack of sufficient knowledge or skill to begin new instruction. Therefore, before beginning instruction, many effective teachers use a **pretest** to assess their students' current knowledge. There are at least three reasons for doing so. First, such a test will identify any students who do not know enough to begin the new material; the teacher can then provide these students with prerequisite work. Second, assessing the general level of students' prior knowledge helps determine where to begin instruction and what to present. Finally, scores on a valid and reliable pretest can serve as a baseline from which to measure progress. Depending on the material and the objectives, both multiple-choice and performance measures can be useful as pretests. Placement tests are generally produced by test manufacturers, although they can also be made by teachers.

Diagnosis   Another purpose of assessment is to determine specific areas of learning difficulty. The tool used, a **diagnostic test,** is most often a commercial product, although teachers may sometimes make it. Its purpose is to identify students' strengths and weaknesses, specifically what students need to learn in designated fields. Typically, diagnostic tests are used in

---

Purposes of Classroom Assessment

■ For *placement*. To determine if student has prerequisite skills to begin instruction

■ For *diagnosis*. To determine causes (physical, intellectual) of persistent learning problems

■ For *formative evaluations*. To monitor learning progress, provide feedback to reinforce learning, correct learning errors

■ For *summative evaluations*. To determine final achievement for assigning grades or certifying mastery

conjunction with specialists—teachers of reading, foreign languages, or in special education, or counselors and psychologists—to identify problems or to screen for programs.

Formative Evaluations   At the heart of your job as a teacher is your students' growing competence and their successes in learning. Therefore, arguably the most important kind of classroom assessment you will engage in is that of *formative* education—that is, ongoing assessments to monitor your students' progress. The purposes here are to verify that learning is occurring and that the curriculum is appropriate. In this instance, the primary user of the information is the teacher. Evaluation need not be a formal assessment. Systematic, recorded observations of each student by the teacher (called anecdotal records and discussed later in this chapter) are often used.

Formative assessment is also used to provide feedback to students, to answer their need to know "How am I doing?" The form of the assessment will be whatever can most reasonably answer this question for the student and provide the quickest possible feedback. Usually formative assessments consist of daily quizzes, homework, and short tests.

Summative Evaluations   Finally, summative assessment is used to make evaluative judgments and to certify completion of projects, classes, and programs. The users of summative evaluation (which often consist of a letter grade) include not only students but also their parents and perhaps future schools and employers. We devote the final section of this chapter to the process of grading, because it is perceived by all those people to be a major part of schooling. Formative and summative tests are usually made by teachers, although they may be included in the supplementary materials that accompany textbooks.

Areas Teachers Assess

Now that you are familiar with a teacher's primary *purposes* for assessment, it will be helpful for you to know about the *kinds* of behaviors, activities, and knowledges you will be evaluating. (As you read this section, you might ask yourself which areas would be most suited to one or more of the purposes of assessment.)

Recall that in Chapter 3, you studied three domains of learning—cognitive,

---

Areas Teachers Assess

- Classroom behavior
- Skills
- Knowledge and conceptual understanding
- Thinking
- Attitudes

Effective teachers make assessments in all three domains—cognitive, affective, and psychomotor.

affective, and psychomotor. Effective teachers make assessments in each domain. However, as you probably noticed in reading that chapter, many activities involve more than one domain. Making a wall poster, for instance, is in part a psychomotor activity, but the poster's quality depends in part upon the students' knowledge of what to include and on their feelings about or motivation for making it. The discussion below, then, uses the term *areas* to identify what you assess (see the box on page 357), and each area involves one or more of the domains. The areas and techniques are suggestive but not comprehensive. The techniques mentioned in each category will be explained later in the chapter.

Classroom Behavior   Not all teachers agree that students' classroom behavior or deportment should be assessed, but all teachers from kindergarten through high school are concerned with it. Particularly if you wish to alter students' behavior, you need some techniques for monitoring it and assessing your attempts at change. Anecdotal records are useful here, as are checklists, which both teachers and students can use to assess themselves and others. Group work requires specific student behaviors for it to be an effective instructional method (see Chapters 8 and 9). Checklists and anecdotal records are practical monitoring devices for these activities.

Skills are one of the things you most need to assess.

Skills   There are many types of skills—physical, learning, social, thinking, math, problem solving—and a wide variety of tools can be used to assess them. Various kinds of paper-and-pencil tests may be appropriate for math or problem solving, while a demonstration is a reasonable way to display physical education skills. Portfolios may well be the assessment tool of choice for art, composition, or drafting classes, while performance may be the first choice for a music class. The point is to consider all the areas in your curriculum that involve any kind of skill, and then ask yourself, "What can each student do to indicate progress?"

Knowledge and Conceptual Understanding   This, of course, is the usual area we associate with testing. It is, however, a very broad area, and you will use different assessment methods for different types of knowledge. It is particularly important to identify objectives here before considering assessment methods (see Chapter 3). If, for instance, the objective was memory work—math facts, perhaps—then you should test students' recall of information, either orally or in writing. However, if conceptual understanding was the objective (of a concept such as photosynthesis, for instance) such understanding is best evaluated by having students explain the concept in their own words, either orally or written; by having them identify examples of the concept; or by having them create new examples of it. Again, ask yourself, "How can each student demonstrate understanding?"

Thinking   We place this domain in a separate category, although some teachers refer to thinking as a skill. In the sense that one can improve one's performance at it, thinking *is* a skill. However, thinking seems to be much more than just a skill, and assessment can involve multiple-choice tests, problem-solving exercises, and oral or written explanations.

Attitudes   Especially in relation to building a group spirit and sense of inter-dependence in a class (see Chapter 8), it is useful to inquire about students' feelings toward one another and about school in general. Sociograms, attitude inventories, anecdotal records, and checklists can provide considerable data without compromising confidentiality or privacy rights.

Assessment Is Directly Linked to Planning and Instruction

Now that you understand several core concepts about classroom assessment and the primary contexts for your decisions about that assessment, we want to take another brief look at planning and how it relates to assessment.

Assessment planning should be part of all instructional planning.

Ideally, assessment planning should be an integral part of your instructional planning, not a process added on at the conclusion of instruction. Done carefully, such "whole package" planning will ensure that instructional outcomes are clear to both you and your students; that instruction is sequenced rationally; that instruction and assessment are congruent; and that your assessment measures all the outcomes you intended. Recall from Chapter 3 that this process is called curriculum alignment. As we explained there, in its simplest form, a curriculum is composed of objectives, instruction, and assessment. When all three elements match—that is, when instruction and assessment focus on stated objectives—alignment exists.

The other point that is critical for you to remember is that all three instructional processes inform one another. That is, your planning decisions will undoubtedly require adjustment once you actually teach from them and reflect on the day's instruction. Likewise, your ongoing observing and monitoring of your students' learning—your daily classroom assessment—should directly affect instructional decisions. Have students learned the intended concepts well? If not, where does the problem lie—in the instructional methods, in students' background preparation, or perhaps elsewhere? Which of the methods you have selected seems to generate the most motivation and interest among students? What are an individual student's strengths and weaknesses in a specific area? The answers to all of these questions, gleaned through assessment on a continuous basis, will affect both the next lesson's planning and its instruction.

A few other comments about assessment and the planning process are in order. Some teachers find it useful, once they have written their objectives, to begin their planning with the assessment phase. They specify how students will demonstrate achievement of the objectives and then work back and forth between the instructional plan and the assessment plan to determine what must be included in the teaching (see Wiggins and McTighe 1998).

Sometimes teachers enter the instructional planning cycle at the learning activity phase. Having found an activity that stimulates student interest and enthusiasm, the teacher specifies which objectives the activity will attain and develops assessments to monitor and measure achievement.

Keeping in mind that planning the assessment while you are planning a unit's instruction and activities is the best way to be sure that all the parts fit together and support one another, study the following two general pointers about assessment and planning.

Begin with Report Cards   One practical way to plan assessments is to begin with the report cards that you will eventually be expected to prepare. What information is expected there? How often? Are letter grades used? Do you need to prepare comments? Are there check-off items? What sorts of data will you need to prepare report cards? How might you obtain all the required information?

These questions may sound simplistic and obvious, but your authors have seen many instances in which beginning teachers didn't ask about report cards until a few days before they had to prepare them—which is too late! Since you will be expected to document student progress at least four times a year, both practicality and professional responsibility require that you make adequate preparation to do so.

Teachers at different grade levels tend to use different types of assessments (Daniel and King 1998). Elementary teachers depend much on observations of students, periodic quizzes, and worksheets, supplementing sometimes with standardized tests of basic skills. A glance at the report card explains why. Elementary curriculum involves many skills and behaviors, which are quite standard across districts (basic reading, writing, spelling, math). A checklist approach is an effective method of providing feedback.

Through the middle school and secondary years, the curriculum becomes much more content oriented and less basic skill oriented than in the elementary programs. Checklists seem less useful, and the traditional response has been a letter grade to indicate achievement. Grading will be discussed at the end of the chapter, but the point here is that examining report cards is an efficient way to determine at least part of what you need to assess, in what form, and how often.

Timing when you assess is important.   **Consider the Timing of Assessments**   Timing of assessments is a next step in preliminary planning. The box below shows some important considerations for testing to make maximum contribution to learning (Dempster and Perkins 1993).

The effective teacher, then, will build a preliminary calendar around required assessments for administrative purposes and necessary assessments for maximum learning gains.

Timing of Assessments

1. Newly introduced material should be tested relatively soon.
2. Frequent testing encourages continuous study and reduces test anxiety.
3. Tests should be cumulative—including some material from earlier assignments.
4. Testing helps in aiding retention.

Reflect Reflect Reflect

- The four statements below address important issues in classroom assessment. In small groups, reflect on each other's experiences and then make a short class presentation of your conclusions.
  - a. Teachers should assess continuously.
  - b. Classroom testing is frequently weak in both validity and reliability.
  - c. In your experiences, list the purposes that classroom assessment serves and compare them to the purposes they should serve.
  - d. List the ways that assessment methods might differ in the cognitive, affective, and psychomotor domains.

Section 2: Understanding Assessment Tools

Classifying assessment tools is similar to classifying animals or plants—there are many ways you might proceed. A dog, for instance, might be placed in any of the following categories—animal, mammal, four-legged creature, canine animal. The same is true of assessment tools—there are many categories, and most instruments or techniques can be placed in several of them. We saw in the preceding section how assessment can be organized and categorized according to the purposes a classroom teacher needs to consider. Here we lay out a different kind of grouping of assessment tools, organized according to the nature and characteristics of the tools.

First we examine a category undoubtedly familiar to all of us as students—informal, teacher-made tests. Next we delve further into the components and strengths and weaknesses of formal, standardized tests. Finally, we look at a kind of assessing that has developed recently, partially in reaction to the overuse or misuse of standardized testing: alternative or authentic assessment. Our view is that there is a place within your overall classroom assessment for all three kinds of tools. How and when you decide to use a specific tool always depends on your purposes and your students' needs.

Teacher-Made Tests

As your experience will no doubt verify, most classroom assessments involve teacher-made tests. There are good reasons for this. First, the teacher has monitored the learning experiences in the class and so has a much better idea than anyone else what needs to be assessed. Remember that to keep curriculum and assessment aligned, "We teach what we test and test what we teach." Second, we assess the learning form that we taught. If we taught for memory of facts, that's what we assess. If we taught for application, we assess for that. (As we've noted before, the techniques are quite different.) Again, the teacher is the best person to make these decisions. A third reason is that the teacher is familiar with the students as well as the instruction, which may affect the what and how of assessment.

How exactly *do* teachers make tests? A major section of this chapter (Section 3, "Constructing Tests and Writing Test Items") details that process, but here we offer some overall guidelines to help you produce valid, reliable measures of your students' achievement.

First, as we've mentioned, plan the test as you plan instruction rather than waiting until the instruction is over. Knowing in advance how and what to assess can be an important aid in instruction, especially in keeping it focused and not dwelling too long in some areas and omitting others.

Second, remember that the overall context for classroom testing involves a variety of assessment methods. You will also be letting students demonstrate their skills and understandings in a variety of valid ways—reports (oral and written), posters, videos, music, plays, stories, models, performances. Sometimes, however, a paper-and-pencil test created by the teacher *will* be the most appropriate assessment choice.

Finally, weave assessment, including testing, throughout the instruction; don't tack it on at the end. If students are assessed throughout the duration of a unit, you and they will have a much more realistic picture of their understanding than a single test at the end of the unit will provide.

Standardized Achievement Tests

Standardized testing is a large topic; there are many books devoted to it. Excellent coverage of the technical aspects of these tests and interpretation of

Assessment provides relevant feedback to students and teachers.
© Joel Gordon.

the several kinds of scores they generate can be found in Salvia and Ysseldyke's *Assessment* (1998), cited in Helpful Resources at the end of the chapter. The focus in the following section is on several strengths of these tests and how you might use their results in your instructional decision making. Then we treat some of the questions, concerns, and reforms related to standardized tests.

Strengths and Potential Uses   Schools use standardized tests mainly for districtwide and statewide achievement testing and for aptitude assessments prior to high school graduation. The primary consideration in using these tests is to be sure that there is congruity between what is taught (the curriculum) and what the test measures. A close study of the test itself and its supplementary manuals will reveal this.

As you teach, always remember that no single test gives (or even claims to give) a complete picture of a student's achievement. Test scores must be supplemented with samples of student work, observation of students, and the quizzes, tests, and assignments that you create for your students. Only then can a professional evaluation of achievement be made.

No single test gives a complete picture of a student's achievement.

The following list identifies the strengths of standardized achievement tests (adapted from Linn and Gronlund 1995, pp. 336–368; Herman, Aschbacher, and Winters 1992; Madaus and Kellaghan 1993; Worthen 1993).

1. *Technical excellence in questions.* The questions on standardized tests are written by specialists, reviewed by experts on the subject matter being tested, reviewed for bias, and field-tested for flaws.

2. *Extensive technical data.* Standardized tests are accompanied by extensive helpful data on norming, validity, and reliability.

3. *Cost-efficiency.* The development costs of most standardized tests have long since been recovered, which means they can deliver the highest technical proficiency at the least cost per pupil. By contrast, most alternative assessments are not cost efficient.

4. *Easy-to-use data.* Standardized tests provide separate printouts for class records, individual student reports, reports to parents, and many other uses. They provide a variety of scores—percentiles, grade equivalencies, stanines—for use in comparing each student's score to the norming group's scores. In addition, scores are available to show mastery or nonmastery of specific skills and objectives.

5. *Ease of administration and scoring.* Unlike alternative and most teacher-made tests, standardized tests are extremely easy to administer and score.

6. *Customization.* Standardized tests can be custom-crafted to fit a district's specified objectives.

Questions, Concerns, and Reform   In the 1980s and 1990s, there was a great deal of dissatisfaction with standardized testing. In essence, this dissatisfaction stemmed from the inappropriate use of such testing—using test results to drive the curriculum, using test scores as the *only* indicator for high-stakes decisions, and overemphasizing basic skills in instruction as a result of standardized test results.

Another core problem was that many of the higher-level thinking processes are difficult to assess using a multiple-choice test. For instance, a math test might ask the student to select the correct response from four choices. Does doing so demonstrate the use of the same mental processes as calculating the answer? Many argued that it did not and that the only realistic way to assess such skill is by demonstration. The same arguments were made in many areas, including composition, speaking, foreign language, and music.

As a result of these and related concerns, reformers began demanding increased attention to many issues left out or ignored by the standardized testing movement—instructional emphasis on thinking and problem solving, local determination of learning outcomes, alignment of what is tested with what is taught, and making students lifelong learners rather than stressing rote memorization of content. The result of teachers' continued dissatisfaction with testing, coupled with school reform efforts of the early 1990s, was a significant change in goals, processes, governance, curriculum, and assessment in the schools (see Linn 1998; Popham 1999).

The primary change, in both assessment and curricula (the two cannot logically be separated), was a shift in focus. For many decades, schools had concentrated on classifying and sorting students—ranking them and placing them in various groups. Standardized achievement tests, normed on a national sample, effectively accomplished this. The process was reinforced by a grading system in which the final result was a grade point average and a ranked class standing.

Reform efforts turned away from using numerical scores and averages as indicators of success and toward a focus on each student's competency in the skills that will be most useful in life—being a critical thinker, knowing how to analyze and solve problems, working productively in groups, monitoring one's own learning, and evaluating one's own efforts (see Stiggins 1994, pp. 20–37, for a detailed account).

This shift in focus is perhaps best identified in a movement that began in the late 1980s—that of alternative assessment, sometimes also called authentic or performance-based assessment. **Alternative** or **authentic assessment** is a way to evaluate student performance other than by traditional testing (observation and conferences). It does not lend itself to comparing or ranking students the way standardized testing does (Stiggins 1997, pp. 29–35). Instead, alternative assessment seeks to determine not only what students know but also what they can do. Proponents argue that such assessment is more aligned with "real-life" practice, reduces competition for grades, and helps students become proficient judges of their own efforts (Herman, Aschbacher, and Winters 1992).

Because the alternative assessment movement has proved to be a lasting and significant one, bringing many worthwhile forms of informal classroom assessment to the fore, we investigate it in more detail in the next section. Before we do, we call to your attention some recent developments pertaining to standardized testing.

Recall our earlier discussions of standards in Chapters 1, 2, and 3. During the last half of the 1990s, critics of state mandated and sponsored tests are questioning whether these tests are reliable indicators of student achievement. Reporting on an analysis on the "Washington Assessment of Student Learning," Linda Shaw (1999) reported that nearly two-thirds of the fourth-grade mathematics tests were developmentally inappropriate (based on

Piagetian levels) for children of this age. Further, the bulk of questions were at the higher stages of Bloom's Taxonomy.

It is becoming obvious that imposed state government testing policies are being applied uniformly to *all* children. Such practice may violate the civil rights of the disabled, be inherently unfair to non-English-speaking children, and may even be an unreliable measure of student achievement. (See Orlich 2000 for a more detailed analysis.)

Alternative or Authentic Assessments

We pointed out in the previous section that alternative or authentic assessments have gained much popularity and earned much attention in recent years, partially as a reaction to the misuse and overuse of standardized testing. Although this is certainly true, we want to rephrase another important point before presenting some specific alternative tools.

Alternative assessment focuses on understanding, application, and problem solving.

Teachers have *always* had, and used, alternatives to standardized tests, and they have always assigned students authentic, or realistic, tasks in which to demonstrate mastery of subject matter. We argue that effective assessment measures achievement with the most appropriate tool. Another way to state this is that there is not necessarily a conflict between standardized and alternative assessment; it should not be regarded as an either-or choice. You simply need to be sure what is to be assessed and then select the most appropriate method.

Performances and Products   There are many areas of student achievement that are more effectively assessed with a performance-based assignment than with a test question. "Knowing *how*" is often as important as "knowing *that*." Language arts teaches speech and listening as well as reading and writing. Both are assessed most directly by observing students' performances. The same is true of science lab procedures, social studies community projects, and reports of observations in health or earth science class. Physical education, music, art, home economics, and the industrial arts are all based on knowing *how*.

Performance items show what students can do as well as what they know.

Performance-based items do not have a single best response. Instead, students are required to organize and present the material in their own way within the stated bounds of the task. In essence, performance-based assessments ask the student to do whatever will reasonably demonstrate competence. These assessments do, however, involve expert judgment in what constitutes competence and to what degree, and are time consuming.

Performance-based assessment can involve the evaluation of either actual student performances (demonstrations) of a task or authentic student products (original creations).

Performances   **Performances** are active demonstrations that assess student learning, such as oral presentations, musical and dramatic performances, and kinesthetic activities. Students can demonstrate mastery of objectives in numerous ways. Oral explanations, for instance, are a key way to improve students' learning and understanding. The more time students spend explaining what they have learned to the teacher or other students, the more effective their learning will be. A mix of formal and informal presentations will provide many opportunities for students. Music, drama, and physical education teachers have long used many types of performance measures; they can give you some excellent suggestions and models.

Products   This large area is often underutilized by teachers. At all grade levels, students produce products—book reviews, term papers, homework assignments, display boards, murals, and posters. The key to assessment is to specifically inform students of what will be assessed—form, content, spelling, design, whatever. Then provide models, or rubrics (defined earlier) so students will know what an acceptable or superior product looks like.

The following tools are basic to performance and product assessment: rating scales, checklists, observations, anecdotal records, portfolios, and the rubrics that guided the project. We will discuss and provide examples of each of these.

Rating Scales and Checklists   In general, rating scales provide a list of characteristics to be observed and a scale showing the degree to which they are

FIGURE 10.1

Examples of a Rating Scale

Instructions: Rate the presenter on the following characteristics by placing an "X" anywhere on the line under each item. In the comment space, add any thoughts that will clarify your rating.

1. Presenter spoke loudly and clearly so all could understand.

1	2	3	4	5
Difficult to understand		Understood most of presentation		Clearly understood entire presentation

Comments:

2. Presenter maintained eye contact with class.

1	2	3	4	5
Read notes instead of looking at class		Made eye contact about half the time		Maintained eye contact through most of presentation

Comments:

3. Presenter made biography interesting.

1	2	3	4	5
Very few "humanizing" details		Quite a few interesting details		Made subject come to life. We learned what this person was like

Comments:

FIGURE 10.2

Example of a Checklist

Homework Grading Guide

	Yes	No
1. Is the handwriting legible?	_____	_____
2. Is the response correct?	_____	_____
3. Are the statements clear?	_____	_____
4. Were all necessary data included?	_____	_____

present. To the extent that it is keyed to learning outcomes that can be observed and is used appropriately to evaluate processes or products, a rating scale is a useful assessment tool. See Figure 10.1 for examples.

Checklists, or "yes-no" rating scales, are useful when a process can be divided into steps and each one checked for its presence. Figure 10.2 illustrates an example.

The use of checklists and rating scales promotes learning by providing specific feedback to students.

Rating scales and checklists have widespread utility in the classroom. Although it is neither necessary nor desirable to grade everything students do, providing feedback to students promotes and strengthens learning. (See Sadler 1998 and Black and Wiliam 1998a and 1998b for a thorough discussion of using feedback to improve learning.) Feedback in the form of rating scales and checklists identifies specific tasks and portions of tasks and points out strong and weak areas, giving students the information they need to improve their learning. Indeed, one of the primary strengths of these assessment tools is that, if used carefully, they provide the student with a model or rubric that specifies what an acceptable performance looks like and what its important parts are. Note how the checklist in Figure 10.2 does just that.

A second value of these performance assessments is their utility in grading. Again, you don't formally "grade" everything students do—learning must include the freedom to experiment and make mistakes—but you must grade enough of their work to monitor and sustain progress. Also, when it is time to make a summative judgment of a student's achievement, you will use every indicator available so as to make the most accurate assessment possible. Conscientious and professional assessments of achievement should recognize and record that the student did outstanding work on a project, made acceptable scores on three speeches, is improving in penmanship, contributes readily and usefully to class discussions, functions well in all roles as

Reflect Reflect Reflect

- Develop a rating scale or checklist for one of the following performances: a class presentation, a student drawing, an essay, or courteous behaviors in the classroom.

a work-group member, and so on. Such data can help the student to learn and the teacher to accurately record and report student progress.

Like all the other forms of assessment, however, checklists and rating scales have limitations. They can be unreliable—giving varying results when used by different teachers or at different times by the same teacher. A clear statement of the objective to be assessed and the criteria to judge by can alleviate this problem.

Observations and Anecdotal Records   Anecdotal records are recorded observations of student behaviors made during routine class work and perhaps in the halls or on the playground. What do you observe? Primarily, you observe those behaviors that you can't assess any other way—John seems slow in responding to requests; Cheryl is never asked into groups; Archie doesn't seem well much of the time. A single notice of any of these, and similar behaviors, probably means little, but repeated and recorded over time, these observations can provide insights that will allow you to help students in areas you might otherwise overlook.

There are four keys to the effective use of anecdotal records (summarized in the Instructional Strategies box below). First, don't try to record everything about everybody. Record the unusual, but do it systematically, briefly, and nonjudgmentally; this is simply a record of what, where, and when (and your response, if appropriate). The note is quickly made, taking only a couple of minutes during lunch or after school: "Date of 4/3/01. Jack hit Sam in the face during recess. This is the 2nd fight between them in 3 days. Each accuses the other of initiating it. I have sent both boys to the vice principal, as per school policy for fighting."

Second, be consistent, both in watching and recording. You should make a few observations each day, recording them on index cards or note paper and keeping the notes in your files or some other private place. Although the practice may seem tedious at first, it soon becomes a habit and is quickly done. The first time you alert a parent to a possible medical problem on the basis of anecdotal records, you'll become an enthusiastic recorder.

Anecdotal records can help you ensure that students receive needed assistance.

In situations where you have discipline difficulties with a student—defiance, abusive language, fighting in class—such records can become very important. Obtaining help for the student (and you) generally depends on following due process for student rights. This is greatly facilitated by dated records of all incidents relevant to the problem. If you have kept these as described, particularly in nonjudgmental language, help can be arranged and problems resolved much more quickly.

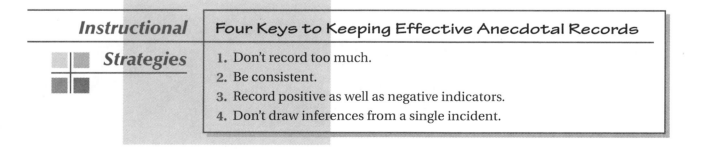

Instructional

Strategies

Four Keys to Keeping Effective Anecdotal Records

1. Don't record too much.
2. Be consistent.
3. Record positive as well as negative indicators.
4. Don't draw inferences from a single incident.

Third, record positive indicators of growth, not just evidence of problems. A surly student's voluntary class contribution, the class bully's politeness to a substitute teacher—these and more can be indicators of growth and should be part of your assessments.

Fourth, don't draw inferences about student behavior from a single incident. The unusual may be simply that—unusual. Patterns, observed over time, are necessary for drawing inferences about health or behavioral problems (Mamchak and Mamchak 1993).

The purpose of a portfolio is to demonstrate a student's progress toward achieving particular learning objectives.

Portfolios   Portfolios are collections of student work. The concept of teachers' assembling such collections to monitor student progress and to share with parents and administrators is not new. Many elementary school teachers, as well as fewer numbers of middle school and high school teachers, have routinely done so for many years.

What is new, within the last few years, is the idea that much student achievement can be more effectively demonstrated by a product than by scores on a paper-and-pencil test alone. The portfolio is the container of these products, and if carefully and purposefully assembled, it can be a valuable assessment tool.

Purposeful, of course, is the key word. For assessment use, a portfolio cannot be just a collection of student papers. Instead, it must be a collection intended to demonstrate student effort and progress toward achieving particular learning objectives. (The Instructional Strategies box below lists the characteristics of a carefully planned portfolio.) Many classes or particular units within a class contain objectives that are readily and effectively assessed with work samples. In social studies and history—whether in third grade or high school—maps and charts are basic tools. Students produce these as aids to understanding, and portfolios that include them provide a practical record of student progress. Oral presentations are (or should be) part of most classes, and a portfolio can contain rating sheets from these, documenting student improvement. The more you think of objectives, the more ways you will find to use a portfolio to document progress.

Instructional *Strategies*

Characteristics of a Carefully Planned Portfolio

1. Objectives are determined jointly by the student and the teacher.
2. The focus is on student products as evidence of progress.
3. Student strengths are emphasized rather than student mistakes.
4. Students help decide what will be included and help determine evaluative criteria.
5. Students have access to their portfolios.
6. Portfolios contain a definition of unit goals, student explanations of the goals, and evaluative comments by both the student and the teacher.

SOURCE: Adapted from Oosterhof 1996, pp. 176–177.

Portfolios are a useful assessment tool if you use them to focus on specific objectives.

Grading a portfolio is a matter of assessing the student's entries in relation to the objectives specified. The tools you have already studied—rating scales and checklists—are useful, particularly when the student has them as guides while constructing the entries. Sharing portfolios with parents on special occasions can reinforce a positive link between home and school.

Portfolios are broadly used in English classes and are becoming increasingly used in mathematics classes, partly as a result of the standards adopted by the National Council of Teachers of Mathematics in 1989. Most of the other content areas have adopted national standards within the last several years (see Chapter 3). All of the new standards emphasize problem solving and thinking skills, which are more accurately reflected by portfolios than by standardized achievement tests (Far West Laboratory 1992; Abruscato 1993). Indeed, in 1990, Lewis and Clark College of Portland, Oregon, initiated an admission policy for academically talented students that allowed them to submit portfolios of their work in place of the usual SAT scores and admission essay (Stiggins 1994, pp. 421–422).

Additional perspectives on performance and alternative assessments can be found in the following: Herman et al. 1997; Eisner 1999; Haertel 1999; and Madaus and O'Dwyer 1999.

Rubrics   Rubrics provide you another means of evaluating student achievement. Especially when students themselves are involved in the construction of the rubrics, this assessment tool can provide readily comprehensible feedback to students. Rubrics (defined earlier) contain two primary components— *criteria,* which are really categories that describe *what* is being evaluated, and *standards,* which describe the level of achievement and tasks involved in reaching that level.

Some guidelines for writing rubrics are listed below, and Table 10.1 demonstrates what one kind of rubric might look like (both from Burns, Roe, and Ross 1999):

Base standards on samples of student work that represent each level of proficiency.

Use precise wording that describes observable behaviors in terms that students can understand.

Reflect Reflect Reflect

- Ask a teacher to share some anecdotal records and portfolios that might be available without invading anyone's privacy. Examine them for objectivity.
- Create a portfolio rating scale for some class attribute, such as completion of seat-work. Then surf the Net to locate any information about Likert scales.
- Locate two books or articles on portfolio assessment and examine the pros and cons of this technique.

TABLE 10.1

Rubric for Evaluating Research Reports

Criteria	Standards		
	3	2	1
Content	This report covers all major aspects of the topic and is focused. It shows evidence of higher-order thinking and is based on three or more references.	This report covers several aspects of the topic but omits some important information. It makes use of two or more references.	This paper is limited to one or two aspects of the topic. Only one source (or no source) of information is given.
Organization	This report is logically organized and easy to follow. The introduction presents the topic, the content follows in reasonable order, and the conclusion pulls information together.	This report shows some evidence of organization, but it lacks a clearly constructed beginning, middle, and end. Connections among subtopics are sometimes unclear.	This report is difficult to follow because it lacks a logical organizational plan. It shifts from one idea to another without making logical connections.
Use of conventions	This paper shows consistent use of standard English and correct spelling, punctuation, capitalization, and paragraphing. It is neat and legible.	This paper indicates a general observance of conventions, but several errors exist in spelling, mechanics, and form.	This paper shows little awareness of writing conventions. Neatness and legibility are minimal.

SOURCE: Burns, Roe, and Ross, *Teaching Reading in Today's Elementary Schools*, 7/e. Houghton Mifflin Co., 1999.

Avoid negative statements, such as "cannot make predictions."

Construct rubrics with 3-, 4-, or 5-point scales, with the highest number representing the most desirable level.

Limit criteria to a reasonable number.

Section 3: Constructing Tests and Writing Test Items

Having considered why and what to assess, as well as the steps in test planning, we now have a foundation for writing specific test items. Such writing is, in part, an art; but with some basic techniques, persistence, and practice, the skill develops rapidly. This chapter can include only a small portion of available information, however, so you are once again urged to supplement your learning with suggestions from the Helpful Resources section.

We begin with some general guidelines to help you as you map out and structure your test. Then we take a finer, more detailed look at writing actual test items. We divide item types into the following categories and discuss them in that order:

1. Short-answer, matching, and true-false items for measuring knowledge-level outcomes
2. Multiple-choice items for measuring both knowledge-level and more complex learning outcomes
3. Interpretive items for assessing complex, higher-level objectives
4. Essay items for assessing higher-level outcomes

General Guidelines for Test Construction

Your work in writing a specific test will be greatly facilitated if you follow the six rather simple steps we outline below:

1. Determine how much importance and instructional time you will give to the major topics to be tested and then make the number of test items for each topic proportionate. For example, if you plan to teach four main ideas and devote equal time to teach, 25 percent of the questions on your test should relate to each topic. However, if time constraints caused two of the topics to receive less attention, their coverage on the test should decrease. Yes, test on what you taught, even if it differs from what you planned.

2. Decide on the format and item type you will use. Remember: test the format that you taught. If you teach for concept understanding, don't test for factual recall. Doing this is more difficult to do than it appears. Fact and recall questions are much easier to write and score than understanding questions—and far more common on tests. Up to 90 percent of secondary school test questions are at the lowest level (knowledge) of Bloom's cognitive taxonomy (Daniel and King 1998).

3. Determine a balance between the available testing time and the number of questions to include. How many questions a student can reasonably answer in a given time is a variable that you will understand with experience. The average high school student can complete two true-false items, one multiple-choice item, or one short-answer item per minute of testing time. Essay items require more time, especially to elementary students (Linn and Gronlund 1995, p. 307).

   However, remember that some students work more slowly than others, and time is needed to both begin and end the test. You will get a more valid picture of achievement if you allow plenty of time—even if it means dividing the assessment over several days—another reason for more frequent testing. You must also remember the special needs of your students with disabilities and your non-English-speaking students.

4. You will find it useful to use a matrix, such as the Kaplan's Matrix that we illustrate in Tables 4.1 and 4.2, to help organize your planning. One method is to list main ideas on the left, with headings that indicate the anticipated cognitive level across the top. The Instructional Strategies box on page 373

Allow your students enough time.

A matrix is a handy planning tool.

Instructional

Strategies

Example of Planning Matrix			
Unit Test, Causes of Civil War			
Major Ideas	Number of Knowledge Level Questions	Number of Understanding Level Questions	Total Number Of Questions
Political factors	3	4	7
Economic factors	2	3	5
Geographic factors	2	3	5
Social factors	3	3	6
Total items	10	13	23

illustrates the concept with a unit on the U.S. Civil War. The example refers only to objective questions such as multiple choice or matching. Certainly essay items would be relevant, but we've omitted them for clarity.

Notice the strengths of the format in the matrix. Main ideas are identified and can be emphasized in instruction and reviewed before the test. Cognitive levels are noted so you don't unintentionally use too many recall items. The time necessary to take the test can then be estimated.

5. Plan an activity for those students who finish early. Don't wait for this; it always happens.
6. Develop the test items, which we discuss next.

Objective Test Items

Objective test questions have a single best answer.

Objective items are so-called because they have a single best or correct answer. There is no (or very little) dispute about the correct responses to objective items. No professional judgment is required to score them; the real skill involved here is at the other end—in their careful, fair, systematic construction. Objective items are of two types: *selection type,* in which a response is chosen from among alternatives given, or *supply type,* in which the student supplies a brief response. If no clear choice between supply or selection items is specified by the learning outcome, use the selection type. It provides greater control of the response and more objective scoring. But remember to test the format you taught.

True-False Items   True-false, matching, and short-answer items are often grouped together as comparatively simple items useful mostly for measuring knowledge-level achievement. Of the three, the **true-false** (or alternate choice) **question** is perhaps the least useful. Because these items have only two possible options, students who guess have a 50 percent chance of getting a correct response. The examples in Figure 10.3 illustrate possible formats and uses for these items. Note especially the specificity of the directions.

FIGURE 10.3

Sample True-False Format Questions

Directions: Read each statement. If the statement is always true, circle the T. If it is always false, sometimes false, or partially false, circle the F.

T   F   **1.** Water always boils at 100 degrees centigrade.
T   F   **2.** 51% of 40 is more than 20.

Directions: Read each statement. If the statement is a fact, circle the F. If the statement is an opinion, circle the O.

F   O   **1.** Other countries should have a Bill of Rights like ours.
F   O   **2.** A red light requires a motorist to stop.

Directions: Circle the correct choice inside each pair of parentheses.

1. Give it to (whoever, whomever) you please.
2. Submit the papers to either the principal or (me, myself).

Matching exercises should contain homogeneous material.

The Matching Exercise **Matching exercises** are a variation on the true-false format. They too assess mostly recall. Their best use is in identifying relationships within homogeneous material. The same cautions and shortcomings apply to matching exercises as to true-false ones. The example in Figure 10.4 illustrates a matching test. Again, note the instructions.

Several cautions apply to the writing of matching questions. First, use only homogeneous material—don't mingle people, events, book titles, and geographic regions in the same lists. This is confusing to the student and tends to provide clues to the test-wise. Keep your lists to about eight items, and use more options than there are items to be matched. Finally, be sure there is one best option for each item.

Short Answer and Completion Items **Short-answer** and **completion items** are supply-type rather than selection-type items. They typically require the

FIGURE 10.4

Sample Matching Questions

Directions: On the line to the left of each name in Column A, write the letter of the statement in Column B that best identifies that person. Statements in Column B may be used once, more than once, or not at all.

Column A

_____ **1.** Cook
_____ **2.** Columbus
_____ **3.** Da Gama
_____ **4.** Hudson
_____ **5.** Magellan

Column B

A. The first European to navigate a southern route around South America.
B. He made four voyages to the New World.
C. The first European to sail the length of Africa's west coast.
D. His major discoveries were in eastern North America.
E. He located and conquered the Aztecs.
F. The first European to locate Australia.
G. The first European to navigate the Northwest Passage.

FIGURE 10.5

Sample Short-Answer and Completion Questions

Directions: For each statement, write the correct word or numbers in the blank. If computations are needed, show your work on this paper, numbered appropriately. Spelling will not be counted in your score.

1. A ship is sailing on a compass heading of southwest. If it makes a ninety-degree turn to the left, in what direction will it now be sailing? _____

2. Walnut furniture wood sells for $4.12 per board foot. You need 31 board feet to complete a project. What will the wood cost? _____

3. Write the formula that describes the relationship among current, resistance, and energy in electrical problems. _____

4. What device is used to measure current? _____

5. In the statement $2x + 3 = 6 - 4x$, what number does x represent? _____

Completion items can measure at the comprehension level.

student to provide a word, phrase, or symbol. Students are asked not to simply identify a correct choice but to retrieve it from memory—a different, perhaps intellectually more complex process. Science and math teachers are particularly fond of this format since it seems to directly measure computational and problem-solving skills and can conveniently allow students a place to display their work. Figure 10.5 illustrates various formats.

Multiple-Choice Items   The **multiple-choice item** is generally considered the most useful objective test item. It can measure both knowledge and higher-level learning outcomes.

FIGURE 10.6

Sample Multiple-Choice Questions

Directions: Circle the best choice for each question.

1. **Who was the second president of the United States?**
   A. James Buchanan
   B. Thomas Jefferson
   C. James Madison
   D. John Adams

2. **Boyle's Law shows a relationship between**
   A. Density and pressure of gases
   B. Pressure and volume of a gas
   C. Density and molecular weight of a gas
   D. Pressure and temperature of liquids

3. **What should you do if the car you are driving starts to skid on a rain-slicked highway?**
   A. Steer into the direction of the skid
   B. Apply the hand brake to slow down gradually
   C. Turn the wheels in the opposite direction of the skid
   D. Quickly apply the foot brake

Multiple-choice questions can measure more cognitive levels than other objective types of questions.

Multiple-choice items consist of two parts: a question or problem and a list of possible solutions. The problem, called the **stem,** may be phrased as either an incomplete statement or a question. The possible responses to the stem are called the **alternatives.** The correct alternative is the answer; the remaining ones are called **distractors.** Their function is literally to distract the unknowing student from the answer while not confusing the knowing student. Creating effective distractors is one of the most difficult parts of writing multiple-choice items.

There are many ways of effectively using multiple-choice questions to assess almost any level of achievement (Bloom 1971). The examples in Figure 10.6 illustrate multiple-choice questions at several cognitive levels. The first question tests factual recall. The second question tests knowledge of a principle. The third question tests application of a principle.

Interpretive exercises are useful for assessing critical thinking and interpretation skills.

Interpretive Exercises   A specialized form of objective test is called the **interpretive exercise.** It is the form of choice for objective assessment of such complex processes as critical thinking; recognition of underlying assumptions, inferences, hypotheses, and limitations of data; and the ability to interpret such data. (Obviously, in some instances, performance assessments may be more useful. Which to use is determined by the objectives being assessed.) You have seen these before—they consist of a map, chart, diagram, or text passage followed by a series of multiple-choice or alternate-choice questions or statements that ask the student to interpret the information given in the ways listed above.

Figure 10.7 illustrates the format.

Reflect Reflect Reflect

- What complex processes are assessed by the example interpretive question given in Figure 10.7?
- With a few of your peers, list some appropriate objectives for each of the test types discussed in this chapter.
- What commonalities did you find among the item types?
- Examine reports such as the National Assessment of Educational Progress. What types of tests do they use to determine the achievement of our nation's youth?

Essay Items

Essay questions are best used to measure complex, rather than knowledge-level, outcomes.

The essay item is an excellent way to assess students' higher thinking processes—comprehending and analyzing—as well as skills in organizing and presenting one's ideas. Below we describe the primary kinds of essay items, and then we discuss scoring essay question responses.

Types of Essay Items   In general, there are two types of essay items: restricted response and extended response.

FIGURE 10.7

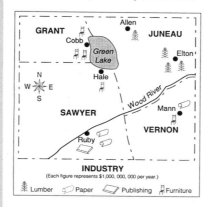

Directions: This is a map of a make-believe country of four states. Use this map to answer questions 1 and 2.

INDUSTRY
(Each figure represents $1,000, 000, 000 per year.)

🌲 Lumber   Paper   Publishing   Furniture

Directions: Use the table below to answer questions 3 and 4.

A Comparison of Some Running Shoes

Brand	Cost	Weight	Sizes	Comments
A men's	$55	12 oz.	6-12, 13 Med. 8-12 Wide	Adequate cushioning & durability
A women's		9.3 oz.	5-10, 11	
B men's	$125	11.7 oz.	6-12, 13	Excellent cushioning & stability
C women's	$105	9.1 oz.	5-11, 12	Excellent support, durability, cushioning & fit
D men's	$40	11.6 oz.	7-12, 13	Not meant for competitive runners
D women's		8.4 oz.	5-10	
E men's	$60	11.2 oz.	7-12, 13	Wide in forefoot and narrow in heel
E women's		9.2 oz.	5-11	

1 Which state is the major lumber producer in this country?

  A Grant
  B Juneau
  C Sawyer
  D Vernon

2 What is the value of the furniture manufactured in Grant in a year?

  J $1,000,000,000
  K $2,000,000,000
  L $3,000,000,000
  M $5,000,000,000

3 Who would be most likely to buy a pair of brand D running shoes?

  A A girl on a track team
  B A student on a cross-country team
  C A student who needs shoes for gym
  D A boy who needs a size-ll wide shoe

4 Which two brands have shoes to fit a boy with a size-6 foot?

  J Brands A and B
  K Brands A and C
  L Brands A and D
  M Brands A and E

1. **Restricted Response.** This is the item of choice when your objective is to assess students' abilities to explain, interpret, and apply information. It focuses on specifics, and the question must be phrased to restrict the response in that way. Note the examples in Figure 10.8. (See Verma and Chhatwal 1997 for an extension of this concept.)

2. **Extended Response.** When you wish to sample your students' abilities to select, organize, and evaluate ideas, this is an appropriate format. As the examples in Figure 10.8 show, the student has great latitude in all of these areas. However, this makes it an inefficient way to measure factual knowledge.

Scoring Responses to Essay Questions   After reading the examples in Figure 10.8 (both the restricted- and the extended-response questions), consider

FIGURE 10.8

Sample Essay Items

Examples of Restricted-Response Essay Questions

1. Explain two reasons leading to the conflict in which Magellan was killed.
2. In one paragraph, explain how sailing vessels proceeded when the wind failed.
3. In no more than one page, explain in detail why Cook and other early explorers had great trouble finding again the islands they had "discovered" in the Pacific Ocean.

Examples of Extended-Response Essay Questions

1. A paved, four-lane highway of about thirty miles is to be built across Washington's temperate rain forest. Discuss the possible ecological consequences.
2. Compare England's experience during the American Revolution to the U.S. experience in Vietnam. Note specifically the concluding phases of both wars.

how you would assess them if you were the teacher. Your assessment might well differ from that of your colleagues. Reliability of grading (different graders giving the same grade, or the same grader giving the same grade over several readings) is a major concern with essay items. Extensive experience has shown that consistency of grading (reliability) is not easy to achieve with essay questions, but with careful planning and much experience, a reasonable level of reliability can be attained.

Before writing the questions, decide what learning outcomes are to be assessed (organizing ability, selection of relevant data, comprehension). Then be sure the question is phrased to elicit this objective.

Preparing a sample response increases reliability in scoring essay items.

Prepare a sample response, which should include the major points you expect to see, the appropriate format or organization, and the amount of credit to be given for each part or question. Many teachers also extend the sample into a rubric that shows what superior, adequate, and inadequate responses will contain.

Holistic scoring is assessing a student's work on its entirety rather than judging specific parts.

Use **holistic scoring** for extended-response items. The outcomes being assessed here are global ones, such as organization and selection of relevant material. Since each paper will demonstrate these in different ways, it is necessary to judge each response on its overall quality. Arranging the students' papers into perhaps five categories of acceptability for each question provides as much precision and reliability as you are apt to get. You then total the scores on the separate questions to determine an overall grade. When the categories are carefully defined, and raters understand the categories, considerable reliability is achieved (see Herman, Aschbacher, and Winters 1992, Chapters 5 and 6, for a thorough discussion and numerous examples of rubrics and ways to ensure reliable scoring).

Analytic scoring assesses student performance using a rating system.

Use **analytic scoring** for restricted-response items. Because of the restrictions, you can directly compare responses to the scoring rubric and assign points. As a general rule of grading, it is useful to use quantitative scores (5 points, 4 points) rather than descriptive words (excellent, needs improvement) or symbols (+, –, smiley face). You will eventually have to combine your judgments about individual tests and projects into an overall assessment of achievement—a grade. You can do this more fairly, we believe, through a consistent use of numbers.

Develop a coding system that conceals the students' names. This reduces the tendency to evaluate on personal qualities or other work the student has done. Some teachers assign students an arbitrary identification number to use for essay responses. Whatever system you use, you will likely soon recognize particular students' papers. Try not to let that influence your evaluation.

If there is more than one essay question, read all student answers to question 1 before going on to question 2, and so forth. This reduces the **halo effect**—the teacher's tendency to assess a student's performance based on the quality of earlier performance rather than an objective assessment. Also, reading all responses to one question first gives you an overall impression of misconceptions, well-learned areas, and areas needing further instruction.

A final issue related to essay tests is the practice of giving students a choice of items (such as having them write on any three of four questions) or, similarly, handing out a list of topics a few days before the test, with instructions to be prepared to write on the questions. In general, such practices should be avoided. Particularly when you use restricted-response questions, giving students a choice means you will not be assessing all students on the same objectives and will thus lose comparability of scores as well as some validity (see Weber and Frary 1995).

Reflect Reflect Reflect

- To what extent is matching each assessment item to a specific objective essential?
- What techniques can you use to ensure greater fairness in the scoring of essay tests?
- To what extent are objective and essay test questions subjective?

Section 4: Grading with a Focus on Improving Student Learning

We end this chapter by considering the summative judgments you make about student achievement (that is, grades) and how you report those judgments to students, parents, administrators, and others.

Assessment, including grading, should focus on improving student learning.

As an instructional tool, grading and reporting should focus on improving student learning and development by clarifying instructional objectives, indicating students' learning strengths and weaknesses, showing students' personal and social development, and adding to students' motivation (Linn and Gronlund 1995, p. 334). This is certainly more than can be included in the traditional letter grade, but supplementing the nine-week or semester grade

> **Reflect Reflect Reflect**
>
> ■ Devise a format for communicating to parents that will help them keep aware of class efforts and activities.

with other periodic reports can help achieve these goals. Periodic reports can also establish a positive climate of communication between you and parents, further reinforcing learning and adding to your students' motivation.

One of the authors of this text is acquainted with several teachers, at both the elementary and middle school levels, who send weekly class newsletters to parents. Groups of three or four students prepare them, on a rotating schedule, and the newsletters highlight learning objectives and their accompanying activities. The teachers report that most students enjoy working on the newsletters, and parents appreciate the communication.

Some elementary and middle schools use checklists containing descriptive statements about students' academic skills, behavior, and attitudes in place of or as a supplement to letter grades, and others use narrative descriptions as a supplement (Oosterhof 1996, p. 206). Also, generally below grade 4, it is unlikely that children understand what an abstract letter grade means (Newman and Spitzer 1998). In addition, some schools hold "portfolio nights" routinely, allowing students to share their efforts with their parents. This adds more reinforcement to students' learning and motivation.

All of the above ideas are attempts to provide more and better information about student achievement than a letter grade communicates. Even so, it seems unlikely that letter grades will be replaced very soon. Besides being traditional, they are a convenient administrative tool—for determining honors, promotion, and athletic eligibility and for reporting to other schools—that is not readily duplicated by other means. Since most of you will be required to determine letter grades, we offer some help with that process in this section.

Principles for Grading

The Inclusion Principle   One of the first principles of grading is that you can't have too much data. No matter how many test scores, homework exercises, and class activities you have assessed, you will likely feel that you need more information to make summative evaluations. By giving your students many opportunities to show achievement, you provide yourself with more data for a fair, professional judgment, and you also provide each student with every possible chance to succeed.

The first principle of grading is that you can't have too much data.

The range of activities you can include in grading is limited only by your imagination. Most teachers include at least the following (not listed in order of importance):

- Unit tests
- Periodic quizzes

- Assigned work done in class
- Homework
- Projects—both group and individual
- Papers and reports

The goal is to use a large enough variety that every student finds several areas in which to operate at his or her preferred learning mode and to achieve success.

Some teachers also include conduct and participation in grading, while others argue that a grade should represent achievement only. Those who include participation and conduct argue that, especially in elementary and middle school, these are important learning areas—we expect students to learn how to behave and participate in social situations, so we should evaluate students on their progress in these areas. The choice is yours (depending, of course, on your school's policy), but if you intend to include these areas in grading, you should keep systematic data on them. This can be done quite easily, by the way, with checklists, rating scales, and anecdotal records.

Which Assessment Tools?   Having decided on areas and activities to base grades upon, your next step is to determine what instruments—portfolios, objective tests, attitude inventories, checklists—will best provide valid, reliable data. Information from this chapter and study of several sources in the references—plus experience—will help. Whatever instruments you choose, we repeat our previous suggestion that you use a number system to record data. (Many teachers assign point values to every piece of student work.) This will greatly simplify your efforts to convert all your data to a letter grade.

Where to record your data may puzzle beginning teachers. School districts usually provide a grade book, but the books don't typically provide enough space to include everything. Many teachers make grade sheets on large sheets of paper, with sections labeled for each type of data, such as Unit Tests, Quizzes, Projects, and Homework. That way, all scores are recorded as you collect them. This too is a convenience when you assign term grades. Many teachers also use (and some districts require) a computer grading program, which records whatever you enter, does calculations, and prints out results. With this system, you can tell a student at any time what his or her grade is, at least that portion represented by numbers. Teachers who use a computer grade book often keep a backup, either on another disc, on paper, or both. Losing records of student achievement is both inconvenient and unprofessional.

Devising a Grading System   Deciding what to record and how to record it are your first steps. Next is adopting a system for assigning grades. Several systems are used, but the *percent* or *absolute* system seems to dominate (Kim and Kellough 1991, pp. 396–397; Ornstein 1989, pp. 365–366). You are likely familiar with this method from experience. It works like this: as we described above, each graded activity is assigned a total numerical or point value. Student points are recorded for each activity, and at the end of the grading period the student's grade is based on the percentage of the possible points he or she obtained. A typical example of grades and percentages follows.

A = 90% or higher

B = 80–89%

C = 70–79%

D = 60–69%

F = below 60%

Having decided what to grade, the next step is to determine the proportion each activity will contribute to the total grade. That is, do you want homework to count 90 percent or 15 percent or some other portion of the grade? (Authorities differ, by the way, on whether homework should be included in a grade or not. See Cooper 1989 and Nottingham 1988 for a discussion.) Teachers commonly use approximations of the following weightings:

Tests and quizzes: 50–60%

Classwork: 15–30%

Projects and papers: 10–15%

Homework: 10–15%

If you include participation and conduct, these too must be assigned a weight. Conduct in a shop class, for instance, where dangerous machinery is used, would reasonably be an important part of achievement.

Watch for grading errors.

Avoiding Grading Errors   There are five errors you should try to avoid in testing and grading (Daniel and King 1998):

1. *Using pretest scores in determining grades.* Such scores should indicate only where to begin instruction.

2. *Not adequately informing students of what to expect on a test.* This leaves students trying to decide what's important, which is the teacher's responsibility.

3. *Assigning a zero for missing or incomplete work.* A zero misrepresents achievement and has a profound effect on an average. One alternative is to use the median (middle-ranking) score as an indicator rather than using the average.

4. *Using grades for rewards or punishment.* Achievement of learning objectives should be the only consideration in assigning grades (Gronlund 1998, p. 174).

5. *Assigning grades contingent on improvement.*

You might determine other errors after a few years of teaching.

Communicating Your Intentions

A final major principle of effective grading is communication. Whatever your system, you must explain it clearly—with appropriate handouts and examples—to your students during the first days of class. Students can and should be taught to keep track of their own grades, and a few minutes can be spent one day a week to be sure each student has recorded his or her current scores. At this time, students can discuss questions and difficulties and calculate

Instructional	## Steps in the Assessment Process
Strategies	1. Align your assessment technique with your instructional strategies and objectives.
	2. Learn how to interpret the results of your tests and your other assessments and those of standardized tests.
	3. Use the assessment results to evaluate and change your curriculum.
	4. Develop appropriate grading practices based on your assessment model.
	5. Communicate your assessment results to your students and their parents.

SOURCE: Nitko 1996, pp. 429–431.

their grades. Students will know at all times what their progress is, where their achievement is strong, and what areas need attention. There should be no surprises at report card time. Many secondary and middle school teachers distribute a course outline or syllabus that includes a description of the grading system for the class and then have each student and parent or guardian sign it to indicate that they received, read, and understood the contents. This type of communication prevents unnecessary confusion and disagreement and meets our intended goal of making grading more objective in a very subjective business.

Earlier in this chapter, we briefly mentioned report cards. With the advent of school reform, these communication devices have evolved into monumental checklists that parallel various state or local standards. We examined one school district's newly distributed fourth grade "Student Progress Report." It has eleven different categories with a total of ninety items to be evaluated on

A Closing Reflection Reflection Reflection

- Examine a sample of the *Iowa Test of Basic Skills.* How do the various questions align with various curricula you have studied for K–12? (Be sure to select the appropriate version of the test.)
- Examine the fall issues of *Phi Delta Kappan.* Each fall this journal publishes the annual PDK/Gallup poll about what people think about America's schools. What trends do you observe relating to achievement or assessment?
- Select any school district's policy handbook and then examine the section on testing and grading. How do the policies compare to what we have discussed?

a five-point scale. *Thus a teacher will make a minimum of 450 decisions for each student.* We leave any reflections on this to you. However, in closing, one school district is field-testing an eleven-page report card. We'd simply call that *reductio ad absurdum!*

The sequence of steps we've outlined in this chapter and that we recommend you use as you develop your own classroom assessment approach is outlined in the Instructional Strategies box on p. 383.

Summary

1. Assessment is a continuous process whose primary purpose is to improve student learning.

2. Classroom assessments are used for four primary purposes: to determine placement; to diagnose persistent problems; to monitor progress, provide feedback, and correct errors; and to assign grades.

3. Using various methods, you can assess students' behaviors, skills, knowledge, thinking, and attitudes.

4. Curricular alignment can best be obtained if you plan assessment at the same time you plan instruction.

5. Educational reform has pointed to the need for alternative assessment methods, such as portfolios. Teachers have many choices of assessment methods and should select the one that best matches their particular goals of instruction.

6. Standardized tests provide comparative data on a broad scale.

7. Alternative or authentic assessments focus on student performances and student products.

8. Performance assessment tools include rating scales, checklists, observations and anecdotal records, portfolios, and rubrics.

9. Objective test items include true-false, matching, short-answer and completion, and multiple-choice questions.

10. Essay items are an excellent means of assessing students' higher-level thinking processes.

11. The purpose of grading is to improve student learning by clarifying learning objectives, indicating each student's strengths and weaknesses, evaluating the student's personal and social development, and motivating the student.

12. Fairness and objectivity are two grading criteria that teachers and students typically infer.

13. Assessing instructional outcomes is a very complex craft and scientific skill that requires a high degree of technical proficiency.

Key Terms

alternative assessment (p. 364)

alternatives (p. 376)

analytic scoring (p. 378)

anecdotal records (p. 368)

assessment (p. 354)

authentic assessment (p. 364)

checklists (p. 367)

completion items (p. 374)

diagnostic test (p. 356)

distractors (p. 376)

halo effect (p. 378)

holistic scoring (p. 378)

interpretive exercise (p. 376)

matching exercises (p. 374)

measurement (p. 354)

multiple-choice item (p. 375)

objective items (p. 373)

performances (p. 365)

pretest (p. 356)

reliability (p. 355)

rubric (p. 355)

short-answer items (p. 374)

standardized test (p. 354)

stem (p. 376)

test (p. 354)

true-false question (p. 373)

validity (p. 355)

Helpful Resources

The field of student assessment has a plethora of publications to aid the novice in learning more about the process. However, we attempted to identify four that would be of immediate and practical use.

Marzano, R. J. "An Array of Strategies for Classroom Teachers." *Momentum* 28(2) (1997): 6–10.

This journal article provides a quick summary of five assessment methods with examples to aid the teacher.

Salvia, J., and J. E. Ysseldyke. *Assessment* (7th edition). Boston: Houghton Mifflin, 1998, 816 pp.

We suggest this textbook as a handbook on the topic. The authors wrote the book with novices in mind. Everything you want to know about assessment is here in one source.

Association for Supervision and Curriculum Development. *A Teacher's Guide to Performance-Based Learning and Assessment.* Alexandria, VA: Association for Supervision and Curriculum Development, 1996, 294 pp.

This guide, written by a group of Connecticut educators, provides you with portfolios, exhibitions, lists, rubrics, and other techniques that will expand your knowledge base for using performance-oriented assessments.

Taggart, G. L., S. J. Phifer, J. A. Nixon, and M. Woods. *Rubrics: A Handbook for Construction and Use.* Lancaster, PA: Technomic Publishing Co., 1998, 152 pp.

The authors provide a detailed compilation of rubrics examples, models, designs, and scoring techniques.

Internet Resources

✤ On-line resources to help you obtain the information you need to evaluate standardized tests can be found in the ERIC Clearing House on Assessment and Evaluation Test Locator:

http://www.ericae.net/testcol.htm

✤ Information about standardized tests and other related products developed by the Educational Testing Service may be found at:

http://www.ets.org/

References

Airasian, P. W. *Classroom Assessment* (3rd edition). New York: McGraw-Hill, 1997.

Black, P., and D. Wiliam. "Assessment and Classroom Learning." *Assessment in Education: Principles, Policy and Practice* 5(1) (1998a): 7.

Black, P., and D. Wiliam. "Inside the Black Box." *Phi Delta Kappan* 80(2) (1998b): 139.

Bloom, B. S., et al. *Taxonomy of Educational Objectives: Handbook I, Cognitive Domain.* New York: D. McKay, 1956.

Bloom, B. S. "Learning for Mastery." *Evaluation Comment* 1(2) (1968): 2.

Bloom, B. S., et al., editors. *Handbook on Formative and Summative Evaluation of Student Learning.* New York; McGraw-Hill Book Company, 1971.

Brown, W. R. "Test Mapping: Planning the Classroom Test." *Clearing House* 71(3) (1998): 153.

Burns, P. C., B. D. Roe, and E. P. Ross. *Teaching Reading in Today's Elementary Schools* (7th edition). Boston: Houghton Mifflin, 1999.

Carey, L. M. *Measuring and Evaluating School Learning* (2nd edition). Needham Heights, MA: Allyn & Bacon, 1994.

"Class Management Guide." *Comprehensive Tests of Basic Skills* (4th Edition). Monterey, CA: CTB, a Macmillan/McGraw-Hill Company, 1990.

Cooper, H. "Synthesis of Research on Homework." *Educational Leadership* 47(3) (1989): 85–91.

Daniel, L. G., and D. A. King. "Knowledge and Use of Testing and Measurement Literacy of Elementary and Secondary Teachers." *Journal of Educational Research* 91(6) (1998): 331.

Dempster, F. N., and P. G. Perkins. "Revitalizing Classroom Assessment: Using Tests to Promote Learning." *Journal of Instructional Psychology* 20(3) (1993): 197.

Eisner, E. W. "The Uses and Limits of Performance Assessment." *Phi Delta Kappan* 80(9) (1999): 658.

Far West Laboratory. "Using Portfolios to Assess Student Performance." *Knowledge Brief.* San Francisco, CA: Number Nine, 1992.

Gathercoal, P. "Principles of Assessment." *Clearing House* 69(1) (1995): 59.

Graham, N., and J. Gearge. *Marking Success: A Guide to Evaluation for Teachers of English.* Markham, Ontario, Canada: Pembroke Publisher, 1992.

Gronlund, N. E. *Assessment of Student Achievement* (6th edition). Boston: Allyn & Bacon, 1998.

Haertel, E. H. "Performance Assessment and Education Reform." *Phi Delta Kappan* 80(9) (1999): 662.

Hattie, J., and R. Jaeger. "Assessment and Classroom Learning: A Deductive Approach." *Assessment in Education: Principles, Policy and Practice* 5(1) (1998): 111.

Herman, J. L., P. Aschbacher, and L. Winters. *A Practical Guide to Alternative Assessment.* Alexandria, VA: Association for Supervision and Curriculum Development, 1992.

Herman, J. L., et al. "American Students' Perspectives on Alternative Assessment: Do They Know It's Different?" *Assessment in Education: Principles, Policy and Practice* 4(3) (1997): 339.

Kim, E. C., and R. D. Kellough. *A Resource Guide for Secondary School Teaching* (5th edition). New York: Macmillan Publishing Company, 1991.

Lemann, N. "The Structure of Success in America." *Atlantic Monthly* 276(2) (1995a): 41–60.

Lemann, N. "The Great Sorting." *Atlantic Monthly* 276(3) (1995b): 84–100.

Linn, R. L. *Assessments and Accountability. CSE Technical Report 490.* University of California, Los Angeles: Center for the Study of Evaluation, November 1998.

Linn, R. L., and N. E. Gronlund. *Measurement and Assessment in Teaching* (7th edition). Englewood Cliffs, NJ: Merrill, an Imprint of Prentice Hall, 1995.

McDaniel, E. *Understanding Educational Measurement.* Madison, WI: Brown and Benchmark, 1994.

Madaus, G. F., and T. Kellaghan. "The British Experience with Authentic Testing." *Phi Delta Kappan* 74(6) (1993): 458–469.

Madaus, G., and L. M. O'Dwyer. "A Short History of Performance Assessment." *Phi Delta Kappan* 80(9) (1999): 688.

Madgic, R. F. "The Point System of Grading: A Critical Appraisal." *NASSP Bulletin* 72(507) (1988): 29–34.

Mamchak, S., and S. R. Mamchak. *Teacher's Time Management Survival Kit.* Englewood Cliffs, NJ: Prentice Hall, 1993.

Marzano, R. J., D. Pickering, and J. McTighe. *Assessment Student Outcomes: Performance Assessment Using the Dimensions of Learning Model.* Alexandria, VA: Association for Supervision and Curriculum Development, 1993.

Newman, R. S., and S. Spitzer. "How Children Reason About Ability from Report Card Grades: A Developmental Study." *Journal of Genetic Psychology* 159(2) (1998): 133.

Nitko, A. J. *Educational Assessment of Students* (2nd edition). Englewood Cliffs, NJ: Merrill, an Imprint of Prentice Hall, 1996.

Nottingham, M. "Grading Practices: Watching Out for Landmines." *NASSP Bulletin* 72(507) (1988): 24–28.

Oosterhof, A. *Developing and Using Classroom Assessments.* Englewood Cliffs, NJ: Prentice Hall, 1996.

Orlich, D. C. "Education Reform and Limits to Student Achievement." *Phi Delta Kappan* 81(6) (2000): 468–472.

Ornstein, A. C. "The Nature of Grading." *Clearing House* 62(8) (1989): 365–369.

Ornstein, A. C. "Essay Tests: Use, Development and Grading." *The Clearing House* 65(3) (1992): 175–177.

Ornstein, A. C. "Grading Practices and Policies: An Overview and Some Suggestions." *NASSP Bulletin* 78(561) (1994): 55–64.

Palardy, J. M. "Another Look at Homework." *Principal* 75(5) (1995): 32–33.

Popham, W. J. *Educational Evaluation* (3rd edition). Needham Heights, MA: Allyn & Bacon, 1993.

Popham, W. J. "Why Standardized Tests Don't Measure Educational Quality." *Educational Leadership* 56(6) (1999): 8.

Sadler, D. R. "Formative Assessment: Revisiting the Territory." *Assessment in Education: Principles, Policy and Practice* 5(1) (1998): 77.

Salvia, J., and J. E. Ysseldyke. *Assessment* (7th edition). Boston: Houghton Mifflin, 1998.

Sax, G. *Principles of Educational and Psychological Measurement and Evaluation* (3rd edition). Belmont, CA: Wadsworth, 1989.

Schmuck, R. A., and P. A. Schmuck. *Group Processes in the Classroom* (6th edition). Dubuque, IA: Wm. C. Brown, Publishers, 1992.

Shaw, L. "State's Fourth-Grade Math Test Too Difficult for Students' Developmental Level, Critics Say." *The Seattle Times,* October 10, 1999, pp. 1 & 14.

Stiggins, R. J. *Student-Centered Classroom Assessment.* New York: Macmillan, 1994.

Stiggins, R. J. *Student-Centered Classroom Assessment* (2nd edition). Upper Saddle River, NJ: Merrill, an Imprint of Prentice Hall, 1997.

"Test Coordinator's Handbook." *Comprehensive Test of Basic Skills* (4th edition). Monterey, CA: CTB, a Macmillan/McGraw-Hill Company, 1990.

Verma, M., and J. Chhatwal. "Reliability of Essay Type Questions—Effect of Structuring." *Assessment in Education: Principles, Policy and Practice* 4(2) (1997): 265.

Weber, L. J., and R. B. Frary. "Allowing Students a Choice of Items on Objective Examinations." *Assessment and Evaluation in Higher Education* 20(3) (1995): 301.

Wiggins, G., and J. McTighe. *Understanding by Design.* Alexandria, VA: Association for Supervision and Curriculum Development, 1998.

Worthen, B. R. "Critical Issues That Will Determine the Future of Alternative Assessment." *Phi Delta Kappan* 74(6) (1993): 444–454.

Wright, R. G. "Success for All: The Median Is the Key." *Phi Delta Kappan* 75(9) (1994): 723–725.

A Final Word

As the twenty-first century unfolds, schools and teachers are being subjected to increased public scrutiny and criticism. One point that you will undoubtedly hear is "teachers are not prepared to teach." Usually uninformed persons, many with hidden political agendas or advocates of some "magic educational elixir," express this opinion. At this point in your educational career, however, you have a very firm knowledge base that has been soundly validated through empirical studies. The ten chapters of this book have given you the prerequisite knowledge about instructional techniques and issues from which you can make reasoned and reflective choices. Additionally, you now have the background to expand your basic understandings by enrolling in graduate courses that are curriculum or instruction related.

We bring these points up because successful practitioners tend to forget that through years of experiences, they have accumulated a vast reservoir of knowledge, techniques, solutions to specific problems, and a general understanding of the respective age groups with which they interact. As you gain teaching experience, you too will have a much wider repertoire of teaching techniques, skills, and understandings. That is the essence of being a lifelong learner.

We hinted above that the instructional techniques espoused in this book have been empirically validated. As you reflect on the key elements of instruction that you have mastered through experiencing your current expedition into instruction, you might be surprised to realize that the techniques are indeed research based. For example, virtually every technique presented from Chapters 3 through 9 has an undeniable research basis. The most reputable educational journals have long published papers that support the treatments discussed for planning, instructional design, models of instruction, classroom management, questioning, discussion leading, inquiry, and thinking. While not based on research evidence, Chapter 10 illustrates the basic components of classroom assessment. Thus we might add that "best practices" are reflected in our treatments.

As an author team, we advocate the concept of *instructional equity*. That term implies that every child who shows up at school is treated with dignity and respect. The term further implies that as a teacher, you try to be fair to every child when conducting recitations, discussions, classroom activities, computer sessions, or any allocation of intellectual or material resources. We know that it is a challenge to practice instructional equity, but you are now sensitized to this concept.

As you studied the various topics presented in this text, you had to be aware of increasing your *craft knowledge*. Developing into a *master teacher* will require even greater skills and knowledge. It is to that end that you become proactive and seek new tools of the trade.

Congratulations on your decision to become a teacher. Now all you need is a class, a mirror, and feedback. Good luck.

Glossary

adult model of learning A reflective learning process, used by older learners and practitioners, that combines theoretical and classroom learning with insights gained from real-world experience.

advance organizer A frame of reference for a lesson that presents the main facts, concepts, or generalizations to be learned. An advance organizer may be a chart, study guide, illustration, list, or graph; students add information to it during the lesson.

affective domain The area of learning that encompasses ethical, emotional, attitudinal, and social knowledge.

Afrocentric Focusing on African or African American history and culture.

alternative assessment A means of evaluating student performance other than by traditional testing (observations, conferences, performance ratings, portfolios, and so on).

alternatives The different possible responses to a multiple-choice test question.

analysis The process of discovering relationships, interactions, and causality among ideas, concepts, and situations.

analytic scoring The assessment of student performance by means of a rating system.

anecdotal records Notes written objectively on a periodic basis to track student performance; may include checklists, student self-reports, and teacher observations.

application The process of employing abstract ideas and concepts in real-world situations; hands-on learning and problem solving.

assessment The process of evaluating student performance, using a variety of measurements (tests, observations, ratings, portfolios).

awareness The ability of a teacher to recognize student needs and demands and adjust the classroom environment to meet them.

behavior modification The process of changing behavior by rewarding desired actions and ignoring or punishing undesired actions.

behavioral perspective An educational approach that stresses changing student actions by rewarding and reinforcing desired actions and outcomes.

bilingual education The teaching of students in both their first and second language (often Spanish and English) simultaneously.

brainstorming A discussion process in which the leader presents a topic or problem and solicits open-ended ideas about it from all group members.

categorical school aid Federal funds paid to schools for specific programs, such as vocational or special education.

checklists An assessment tool used by a teacher or student to document work completed or skills learned.

classroom clarifier The role the teacher takes during inquiry learning to guide students toward developing logical thinking skills.

classroom management The methods of organization, disciplinary procedures, and routines established by the teacher to ensure positive student behaviors that are conducive to learning and social interaction.

cocurricular activities Supplemental programs, such as sports or clubs, that offer social and learning opportunities.

cognitive domain The area of learning encompassing intellectual aspects, such as information processing, memorization, and thinking skills.

cognitive psychology An area of psychology that focuses on inner mental processes rather than behavior.

cohesion The tendency of a group to stick together and support all members.

completion items Test items that contain an incomplete statement and require the student to fill in a missing word, phrase, or symbol.

concept An expression or abstraction based on observations of a group of stimuli, facts, or objects having common characteristics; for example, the concept "animal" encompasses and describes dogs, cats, and elephants.

concept analysis The process of identifying the components of a concept to be taught and deciding whether to teach it inductively (from underlying specific examples to broader generalizations) or deductively (from broader generalizations to underlying specific examples).

concept review questioning technique   The inserting of review questions throughout the recitation period.

concrete operational stage   A stage of cognitive development (ages 8–11) in which children learn best through visual and hands-on activities.

content   The subject matter, substance, or materials of a lesson, consisting of facts, concepts, and generalizations.

content-specific   Based on the scope and sequence of topic or concepts to be taught.

convergent questions   Questions that require students to give factual or specific answers.

cooperative learning   Learning based on a small-group approach to teaching in which students are held accountable for both individual and group achievement.

correlation   A relationship between two factors, but not necessarily one of cause and effect.

criteria   Characteristics used to categorize or rate ideas or products.

cultural pluralism   The practice of honoring diverse cultures within a given society.

curriculum guides   A set of goals and objectives published by a school district to guide teachers in developing instruction by stating what students should learn at each grade level and in each content area.

deductive reasoning   The process of discovering specific examples or facts from a generalizing framework; a thinking process that moves from the general to the specific.

defect approach   An outlook on staff development that views teachers as inept, lacking needed skills, and in need of a quick fix.

democratic discipline   A classroom management approach that treats diverse students equally and expects them to take responsibility for their own behavior.

dependent skills   Those items of information that are typically taught in a carefully structured or linear manner. For example, one teaches decimals before introducing percents.

desist strategies   Discipline techniques in which the teacher systematically communicates his or her desire for a student to stop a particular behavior, using either private or public communication.

diagnostic tests   Assessment tools that pinpoint students' strengths and weaknesses, specifically what students need to learn in designated fields.

direct instruction   Teacher-initiated whole-class learning.

discipline   The setting of behavioral parameters for the classroom, both by the teacher alone and in response to teacher-student interactions and situational factors.

discovery learning   An inquiry process in which learners pose questions and seek explanations.

discussions   An interactive learning process involving the exchange of information, perceptions, and ideas in a small group.

distractors   The incorrect alternative answers on a multiple-choice test.

divergent questions   Questions that encourage students to give complex, creative, longer answers.

eclectic   Made up of a mix of varied approaches or teaching models.

efficacy   Effectiveness; the ability to reach a goal or complete a task.

empirical epistemology   The process of knowing or learning through observation or experimentation.

empirically   Based on practical, real-life experience.

enabling skills   Facts, concepts, and processes students must be taught before they can learn more complex facts, concepts, and processes.

entry skills   The knowledge and perceptions students possess at the beginning of a given lesson.

evaluation   The process of making judgments and supporting one's viewpoints with specific criteria, facts, and values; also, determining the effectiveness of a lesson or unit in terms of student outcomes.

evaluative criteria   Parameters for questioning that ask students to make a choice about where they stand on a given issue or question.

evaluative questions   Questions that ask students to make a personal judgment and then defend their position with criteria that support the position taken.

example   A concrete or specific form of a more abstract concept; for example, "England" is an example of "a constitutional monarchy."

exceptionality   Departure from the norm; a condition in which a student qualifies for special services by virtue of his or her physical, cognitive, or emotional characteristics and abilities.

experience   The totality of the events and activities a student has participated in as part of planned learning processes.

expert training   Education that provides skills and proficiency in a given area and creates a very proficient person.

facilitating   The supportive role a teacher takes by giving students the skills, materials, and opportunities they need to direct their own learning experiences.

formal operations stage   A stage of cognitive development (ages 11–15 and above) in which adolescents develop knowledge through systematic reasoning.

framing   The technique of asking a question very precisely, pausing, then calling on a student.

generalization   An inferential statement that expresses relationships between concepts and has predictive value.

generational disaffiliation An emotional state wherein young people disengage from the values and practices of their parents and the wider culture they represent.

goals The broad, general outcomes students should reach as the result of a learning experience, lesson, or unit of study; for example, "students will learn to appreciate and interpret drama."

graphic organizers are pictures, outlines, sketches, or some pictorial display that helps the learner to obtain a quick mental perception or image of the topic.

growth approach A process of staff development that assumes teachers are competent and want to engage in a continuous process of learning that enhances their skills.

guided inductive inquiry A learning process in which the teacher provides specific facts or ideas, from which students make their own generalizations.

halo effect The tendency of a teacher to assess a student's later performance based on the quality of earlier performance rather than being totally objective.

holistic scoring The assessing of a student's work in its entirety rather than judging specific parts.

humanistic orientation An outlook that views all students as unique individuals deserving acceptance and respect.

idiosyncrasies Teacher behaviors and habits that interfere with effective classroom interaction.

imposed-discipline systems An approach to discipline in which the teacher dictates appropriate classroom behaviors and consequences for misbehavior.

inclusion Placing and serving all children, including those with special cognitive, affective, or psychomotor needs, in regular classrooms. See also **mainstreaming.**

individualized education program (IEP) An agreement between a student with special learning needs and his or her classroom teachers, special education staff, and parents that outlines educational goals, procedures, and expected outcomes.

induction The process of analyzing specific ideas to form more general concepts.

inductive inquiry The process of inferring generalizations from a set of specific ideas or facts.

inductive reasoning The process of studying examples or facts in order to develop generalizations or concepts; a thinking process that moves from the specific to the general.

information-processing psychology A branch of psychology that holds that learning is an interactive process between learners and their environment.

inquiry discussion group A specific kind of small group in which students develop questioning and problem-solving skills through a process of discovery and analysis.

inquiry process An investigative learning process, such as classifying, predicting, and experimenting.

inquiry teaching An investigative process of learning in which students are asked to pose questions, analyze data, and develop conclusions or generalizations.

instructional equity The provision of equal learning opportunities to students of both genders and diverse backgrounds and cultures.

integrative reconciliation The third step in the advance organizer model; the process of teaching students how main concepts and underlying facts are related (vertical reconciliation) or how underlying facts are similar or different (horizontal reconciliation).

interdisciplinary thematic unit A unit of instruction that incorporates various content areas while covering an over-all topic or theme; for example, "Dinosaurs" or "Seeds."

internalize To make something part of one's unconscious, automatic learning processes.

interpersonal Occuring between people.

interpretation Giving meaning to a new concept by relating it to another, known concept.

interpretive exercise A means of assessment in which students analyze data, charts, maps, or written passages, using higher-level thinking skills.

intrapersonal Occurring within an individual.

intrinsic motivators Incentives, such as pride, self-esteem, and the desire to learn, that come from within the student.

job satisfiers Incentives or rewards for doing a particular job well.

Kaplan matrix A curriculum planning chart that includes the different levels of thinking in Bloom's taxonomy.

knowledge Recognition and recall of facts and explicitly stated concepts.

learned helplessness A state of being in which students quit trying because they have repeatedly had their efforts neglected.

learning activities Hands-on, interactive classroom experiences.

learning modality Ways of gaining knowledge or expression by various senses, e.g., auditory, tactile, visual, kinesthetic.

least restrictive environment The classroom setting that is as close to the "regular" classroom as possible and still provides the learning opportunities needed to address a student's special needs.

lesson A piece of a unit, in which a given set of objectives or concepts are taught.

liaison A person who acts as a communications link and information disseminator between different agencies or institutions.

mainstreaming Placing and serving children with special cognitive, behavioral, or psychomotor needs in regular classrooms. See also **inclusion.**

master teacher   A teacher who possesses much experience and expertise and may serve as a role model or mentor for other teachers.

matching exercises   Test items that require students to match words or concepts in one column to statements listed in another column; for example, identifying a word with its definition.

measurement   The process of assigning numerical achievement indicators to student performance.

mentor   An experienced teacher who provides professional support to a beginning teacher.

metacognition   Conscious awareness of one's own thinking and learning process.

metaphor   A figure of speech describing something with implied terms.

mnemonics   A strategy for remembering facts by using the first letter of each fact to make up a sentence.

motivation   The desire or incentive to learn something or to behave in a given way.

multiculturalism   The practice of including and honoring diverse cultures within school curricula and instruction.

multimethodology   The teaching practice of using a wide variety of techniques during lessons so that every student will enjoy at least one mode of every presentation. For example, you might open with a video film clip, followed by a reflective question. From that the class progresses into small discussion groups. Short reports would be prepared by the students and presented to the entire class. In short, you are not captured by just one teaching technique and your classes are more exciting.

multiple-choice items   Test items that contain a question and asks students to choose an answer from a list of provided alternatives.

multiple-response questions   An instructional technique in which the teacher asks multiple students to respond to a single question, thus encouraging divergent thinking.

negative interdependence   A management system that encourages students to work against one another in competition for academic resources and recognition.

norm   An unwritten behavioral rule, pattern, or habit accepted by a particular group of people or culture.

objective items   Test items that have a single best or right answer.

objectives   The specific steps that must be achieved to realize a broader goal.

operant conditioning   The process of reinforcing desired responses by giving positive stimuli.

oral tradition   The practice among education professionals of communicating and networking to gain technical knowledge and support.

organizational ethos   The set of basic values and characteristics of an institution.

organizational health   The degree to which an institution, such as a school, functions effectively in meeting staff and student needs.

performance objectives   Specific observable outcomes students should reach as the result of a learning experience or lesson; for example, "after reading the play, students will write an essay naming and describing five characters."

performances   Active demonstrations used to assess student learning, such as oral presentations, musical and dramatic performances, and kinesthetic activities.

planning   The process of choosing instrctional goals, content, materials, and activities before teaching.

pluralism   The idea that a society should reflect the diverse mix of racial and other groups of which it is composed.

positive interdependence   A management system that encourages students to work together, with the assumption that the success of each student enhances the quality of learning for all students.

power   The influence teachers have over students by virtue of their age, authority, role, or physical strength.

preoperational stage   A early stage of cognitive development (ages 2–8) in which children learn through intuition, experience, and concepts.

prerequisite skills   The skills or knowledge students must have before they begin a new learning experience.

pretest   An assessment given before instruction begins to determine students' entry skills.

problem   A question that has relevance to a student and his or her culture.

problem solving   An inquiry learning process in which students seek answers to a question that is relevant to themselves and their culture.

processing information   A means used to learn and remember knowledge.

process objectives   Statements that focus on the way students learn (how) rather than the specific outcomes of learning (what).

programmed instruction   A teaching method in which skills are presented in small segments, with immediate feedback and continual practice.

progressive differentiation   The second step in the advance organizer model, in which the basic facts, details, and concepts underlying a main concept or generalization are identified.

psychomotor domain   The area of learning encompassing physical movement, including gross and fine motor skills and coordination.

rationale   A reason or purpose.

readiness   The willingness and ability of a student to begin learning.

recitation   A learning technique in which the teacher calls on a different student to answer each factual or knowledge-based question, thus limiting students to one "correct" response.

reflective questions   Questions requiring students to develop higher-order thinking. A reflective question attempts to elicit motives, inferences, speculations, impact, and contemplation.

regional diversity   The differences in beliefs, values, and practices among people living in different parts of the same country.

regulatory agency   An office or board that sets standards, rules, and regulations.

reinforcers   Rewards that encourage students to repeat positive behaviors.

reliability   The degree to which a test consistently measures a given attribute.

ripple effect   The negative effects felt by all class members when a teacher responds negatively to a student.

role   An assigned set of responsibilities given to a student as a member of a group; for example, group leader, group recorder, group timekeeper, group evaluator.

role playing   A learning process in which students act out or simulate a real-life situation.

routines   Daily organizational tasks, such as taking attendance and checking papers, that must be part of a classroom time management plan.

rubrics   Examples of different types, models, illustrations, or levels of possible responses that are used as guidelines for assessing student work.

schema   A mental scaffold for learning, made up of previously learned concepts to which new concepts are attached.

schema theory   An assumption that learners have internal, cognitive frameworks into which they fit new knowledge, concepts, and experiences.

school culture   The environment of a school, including its values, management systems, communication styles, and interpersonal relationships.

school ethos   The tone of the interactions within a school's environment.

sensorimotor stage   A period of cognitive development (ages 0–2) during which children learn through sensations and movement.

sequencing   The process of placing curricula or learning tasks in order; the process of organizing instruction.

sex-role stereotyping   Making assumptions about students' abilities based on their gender.

short-answer items   Test items that pose a question and require students to give a brief, two- to three-sentence response.

simulation   A pretend setting or situation that parallels a real-world setting or situation and allows students to practice problem-solving skills.

small-group discussions   Verbal exchanges of ideas and information in groups of four to eight students.

small groups   Purposefully constructed sets of four to eight students who work together to learn.

standardized test   A nationally normed test that compares a student's performance to that of other students across the nation (if norm referenced) or to expected levels of achievement (if criterion referenced).

standards   Criteria for determining what knowledge and learning processes students should be taught in a given subject area.

stem   The part of a multiple-choice test item that poses the question or problem.

student-initiated learning   An instructional technique in which students decide the content, means, and pace of the learning process.

synergism   The increased energy created when individual elements work together as a whole, smooth-functioning, creative system.

synthesis   A process of creatively combining facts, concepts, and learning processes into new knowledge.

task analysis model   The process of subdividing the content, concepts, or processes of a lesson into smaller, sequential steps that begin with the least complex and progress to the most complex.

task group   A small group of students who work together to complete a particular assignment or job.

taxonomy   A set of standards for classifying ideas or objects into hierarchical categories; for example, Bloom's taxonomy of cognitive skills.

test   An assessment instrument that requires students to answer questions to demonstrate learning.

topics   Various subjects used by teachers to help organize their lesson plans.

transfer of learning   The application of knowledge or behaviors learned in one setting to a new situation.

translation   A thinking skill in which one form of expression is changed into another form.

true-false question   A test item that requires students to determine whether a given statement is correct or not.

two-way interactive television   Broadcast between distant sites, in which a teacher in one location interacts visually and orally on television with students in another location.

unguided inductive inquiry   A learning process in which students discover specific facts or ideas themselves and then make their own generalizations based on them.

units   Blocks of lessons grouped together based on related skills, concepts, or themes.

validity The degree to which a test measures what it is intended to measure.

wait time 1 The time between when a teacher poses a question and then calls on a student to answer it.

wait time 2 A silent period that occurs after a student responds to a teacher's question.

zone of proximal development The difference between the intellectual level a child can reach on his or her own and the level that can be reached with expert assistance.

Index

✔ **Instructional Strategies** provides up-to-date ideas and techniques for direct application in the classroom.

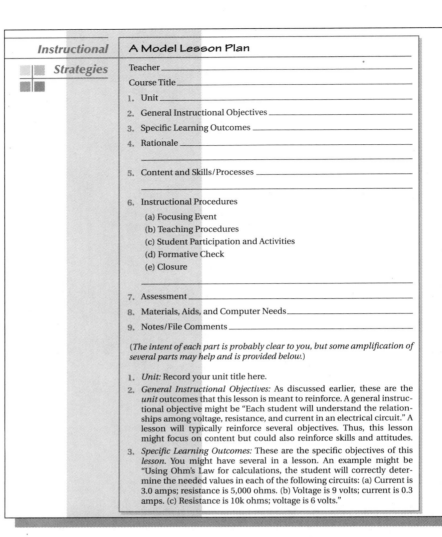

Instructional
    Strategies

A Model Lesson Plan

Teacher _____
Course Title _____
1. Unit _____
2. General Instructional Objectives _____
3. Specific Learning Outcomes _____
4. Rationale _____
   _____
5. Content and Skills/Processes _____
   _____
6. Instructional Procedures
      (a) Focusing Event
      (b) Teaching Procedures
      (c) Student Participation and Activities
      (d) Formative Check
      (e) Closure
   _____
7. Assessment _____
8. Materials, Aids, and Computer Needs _____
9. Notes/File Comments _____

(*The intent of each part is probably clear to you, but some amplification of several parts may help and is provided below.*)

1. *Unit:* Record your unit title here.
2. *General Instructional Objectives:* As discussed earlier, these are the *unit* outcomes that this lesson is meant to reinforce. A general instructional objective might be "Each student will understand the relationships among voltage, resistance, and current in an electrical circuit." A lesson will typically reinforce several objectives. Thus, this lesson might focus on content but could also reinforce skills and attitudes.
3. *Specific Learning Outcomes:* These are the specific objectives of this *lesson.* You might have several in a lesson. An example might be "Using Ohm's Law for calculations, the student will correctly determine the needed values in each of the following circuits: (a) Current is 3.0 amps; resistance is 5,000 ohms. (b) Voltage is 9 volts; current is 0.3 amps. (c) Resistance is 10k ohms; voltage is 6 volts."

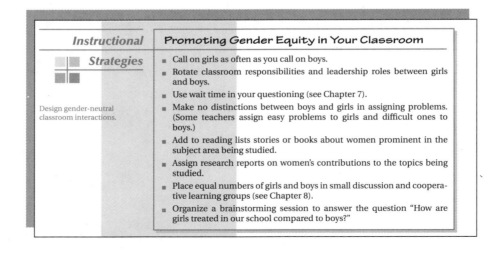

Instructional
    Strategies

Design gender-neutral classroom interactions.

Promoting Gender Equity in Your Classroom

- Call on girls as often as you call on boys.
- Rotate classroom responsibilities and leadership roles between girls and boys.
- Use wait time in your questioning (see Chapter 7).
- Make no distinctions between boys and girls in assigning problems. (Some teachers assign easy problems to girls and difficult ones to boys.)
- Add to reading lists stories or books about women prominent in the subject area being studied.
- Assign research reports on women's contributions to the topics being studied.
- Place equal numbers of girls and boys in small discussion and cooperative learning groups (see Chapter 8).
- Organize a brainstorming session to answer the question "How are girls treated in our school compared to boys?"